THE OFFICIAL®
1993
BLACKBOOK
PRICE GUIDE OF
UNITED STATES
POSTAGE
STAMPS
FIFTEENTH EDITION

BY MARC HUDGEONS, N.L.G.

W9-APF-470

HOUSE OF COLLECTIBLES • NEW YORK

𝕳𝕮 This is a registered trademark of Random House, Inc.

©1992 by Random House, Inc.

Pictured on front cover: Left to right. Fifty-cent stamp—design of a western mining prospector; one-dollar stamp—design of western cattle in a storm; two-dollar stamp—design of the Mississippi River Bridge, St. Louis. All stamps were issued in 1898 for the Trans-Mississippi Exposition held in Omaha, Nebraska, June 1 through November 1. *Stamps courtesy of Ivy, Shreve & Mader, Dallas, NYC. Photo by George Kerrigan.*

All rights reserved under International and Pan-American Copyright Conventions.

Published by: House of Collectibles
            201 East 50th Street
            New York, New York 10022

Distributed by Ballantine Books, a division of Random House, Inc., New York, and simultaneously in Canada by Random House of Canada Limited, Toronto.

Manufactured in the United States of America

Library of Congress Catalog Card Number: 80-644087

ISBN: 0-876-37839-4

Fifteenth Edition: July 1992

10 9 8 7 6 5 4 3 2 1

TABLE OF CONTENTS

The publisher also wishes to express special thanks to Mr. Armin R. Crowe at the Collectors Institute, Ltd., Omaha, Nebraska 68144, the United States Postal System for photographs and illustrations, and for the special help provided by *Linn's Stamp News*.

MARKET REVIEW

The past year in the philatelic collector marketplace has been fairly quiet, with the most attention being focused on the new releases issued by the U.S. Postal Service.

As far as the pricing trends for the most popularly traded and collected stamps are concerned, the market seems to be even with last year's average prices, with the most activity reflected by the better condition and hard-to-get specimens. The lack of disposable income for most collectors is making it very difficult for them to make the purchases that they would not have given a second thought to making a couple of years ago. As the end of 1992 approaches and the recession starts to lift, collector activity should increase as well. Most dealers are viewing the coming year very optimistically.

The time is "NOW" for the stamp collector. The American Stamp Dealers' Association's National 1991 Stamp Show, which has long been regarded as the nation's forecaster of the general health of the stamp market, reported a dramatic increase in attendance of young collectors. This trend is being perceived as indicating a significant increase in activity in the stamp marketplace. Bargains galore are very prevalent. If, as a collector, you do your homework and search for bargains, your efforts will be rewarded.

Of the stamps released in the past year, the "Olympic—Barcelona" series and the "Space Exploration" series were the most popular. The U.S. Postal Service has planned to release thirty-three issues and 120 new designs. In the coming year, we expect the most interest to be with the "Winter Olympics," the extensive "Wildflower" series (fifty stamps in one single pane), and the "Space" series stamps.

We look forward to a brighter year and hope that the hobby continues to maintain the same level of enthusiasm that has been evident during the past decade. We also look for the dealers to remain active in promoting the hobby and sharing their knowledge with the young and old that are starving for accurate information. This will help keep the stamp market strong and the object of interest for many new collectors.

THE STORY OF U.S. STAMPS

The world's first postage stamps were issued by Great Britain in 1840 and pictured its new queen, Victoria, then 21 years old. It was not until 1847 that the U.S. released postage stamps, but prior to that time some city postmasters issued stamps of their own. These very valuable stamps, known as "postmaster provisionals," were used in St. Louis, New York, Annapolis and a number of other cities.

The first federally released postage stamps comprised a 5¢ denomination picturing Benjamin Franklin and a 10¢ showing George Washington. Their size was very similar to that of modern non-commemoratives and they had gummed backs, just like our stamps. The chief difference was that they carried no little holes or perforations between each specimen on a sheet, to aid in separation. Instead they had to be cut apart with scissors or creased and torn by hand. These stamps are called "imperforates," or "without perforations." All stamps in those days, including Europe's, were made in this way. The U.S. did not start perforating its stamps until 1857, ten years later.

Imperforates rank today as the hobby's aristocrats, its elder statesmen and foremost classics. They have long been dear to the hearts of collectors, and not merely on grounds of their antiquity. Some specialists maintain that these issues, every one of them bearing a statesman's portrait, are more elegantly engraved than any of their descendants. In addition, they can be found (with luck and the necessary cash) in super specimens that put ordinary perforated stamps to shame. When a stamp is perforated, every one on the sheet is of identical size. Some sheets may be better centered than others, depending on how the paper is fed, but no specimens will be physically larger than any others. With imperforates, it's quite another matter. The cutting was never done very evenly. Some specimens were cropped or cut into by scissor wielders and left with margins so immense that portions of all the surrounding stamps are visible. These are called jumbo margin copies and the prices collectors will give for them are often astronomic, provided the condition is otherwise good. It is not at all unusual for one of these oversized beauties to command three or four times the normal sum. Collectors must take care though, because in philately, as in most other things, all that sparkles is not necessarily diamonds. Larcenous persons have been known to take very ordinary average stamps and add fake margins.

Not all imperforates are equally easy (or hard) to get with four full margins. This is all a matter of how closely together they were printed on the sheet. The cutter is less apt to make a mistake if the stamps are further apart on the sheet. Scott's #11, the 3¢ 1851, is by far the most difficult to find with full margins. It also happens to be the least expensive imperforate, thanks to the enormous quantities printed. While the usual specimen will fetch only $8–$10 used, a jumbo margin #11 has no trouble selling for $20, $30 or more.

The second series of imperforates, issued from 1851 to 1856, comprised values from 1¢ to 12¢. There were five stamps, with Washington appearing on three of them; the other two used portraits of Franklin and Jefferson. In 1857 the same group of stamps was released again, this time with perforations and three high values: a 24¢ and 90¢ pictured Washington, and a 30¢ portrayed Franklin. The 90¢ stamp was not exceeded in face value until the Columbian Exposition series in 1893. Because very little mail required the paying of so much postage, most specimens of the 90¢ 1857–1861 that went to private hands never got on letters. Consequently, this stamp is much more difficult to find used than unused, a rare circumstance for a U.S. issue. Needless to say, counterfeit cancels exist.

There was no question that by this time postage stamps had scored a big success. Any doubts or complaints that some users may have had about them at the beginning had long since vanished. Certain persons became so fond of stamps that they began saving them, used as well as unused, and thus the hobby of philately was born. For the government, stamps brought greater economy to the postal service than anticipated. They also allowed mail to travel faster. There was just one problem: some people were abusing the system. During the Civil War, and shortly thereafter, it became apparent that many stamps were going through the mails twice or more. People were cleaning off the cancels and using them again. This may have been done by individuals but, more likely, it was a large-scale operation in which used stamps were cleaned in wholesale quantities and sold to business houses and other volume mailers at a discount. The government was being bilked out of thousands of dollars, but there seemed no solution until a plan was devised to use "grills" on the faces of stamps in 1867. These were networks of tiny embossed dots which weakened the paper and would, presumably, cause it to break apart if any attempt was made at erasing the cancel. After just two years the grill was dropped, but it had appeared on enough stamps in that short time to provide philatelists with an intriguing subspecialty. Not all the grills were alike. They differed in size and style and collecting them is quite a sport.

The year 1869 marked the first year of U.S. pictorial stamps that portrayed things or events rather than portraits. They cannot really be termed commemoratives in the modern sense, but they were extremely pictorial. Subjects included a pony express rider, a rail locomotive, panoramas of the landing of Columbus, the signing of the Declaration of Independence, and others. This series also presented the first stamps to be printed in more than one color. Multicolor printing was no small operation in those days. It required two separate plates; one consisting of frames to be printed in one color, and the other central designs to be printed in a different color. The sheets were fed through one press, allowed to dry, then fed into the next to receive the final printing. As the feeding was done by hand, human error occasionally occurred. A few sheets were fed upside down the second time around, resulting in the first, but not the most famous, U.S. inverts, or stamps with upside down centers. These are very valuable and seldom offered on the market. The king of all United States inverts is a twentieth century stamp, the 24¢ airmail of 1918. This small stamp has a central design of a Curtiss Jenny single engine plane. It was printed 100 to a sheet. On the day it was issued, a Washington, D.C. collector, William T. Robey, took a few minutes from his lunch hour to go into the local post office and buy a sheet. He had no intention of using the stamps but merely wanted them for his collection. After putting down his $24 he received what appeared to be a normal sheet, but after looking closer, Mr. Robey found that on every stamp the airplane was upside down. This incident stirred a furor of considerable proportion. The government was embarrassed since it had claimed that the old 1869 inverts could not happen again with its new machinery and rigid controls. It tried, without success, to buy the sheet back from Robey. Meanwhile it notified postmasters around the country to check their stocks for further error sheets. No more were found, and when it became evident that Robey's sheet was the only one in existence he began receiving substantial offers from collectors and dealers. The offers seemed tempting and he finally sold his treasure for $15,000 to Eugene Klein of Philadelphia, a prominent dealer. Klein immediately resold the sheet to Col. Edward H. R. Green of New York, the legendary collector who also owned the only five known specimens of the 1913 Liberty nickel. It is believed Green paid at least $17,500 for this philatelic morsel, a huge sum in those days but only about one third as much as each of the 100 stamps are now individually worth. Green broke up the sheet into blocks, selling most of them and recovering his entire cost. Several single specimens were subsequently lost; one was supposed to have disappeared into a vacuum cleaner while Green's housekeeper was tidying up.

FACTORS BEHIND STAMP PRICES

The collector value (or "market value") of any stamp rests with a variety of factors. Philately becomes a bit less mysterious when one understands the forces at work in the stamp marketplace.

A beginner will normally presume that expensive stamps are expensive because of rarity. Certainly there is a great deal of talk about stamp rarities within the hobby, and so it is natural enough to ascribe high prices to the phenomenon of rarity. In fact, rarity is only one of several factors that influence stamp prices, and the influence it carries is not particularly clear-cut.

In this book you will note some stamps (mostly among the early regular issues) with values of $1,000, $2,000, and even higher. Obviously these stamps are rarer than those selling for $10 or $15. But once having said that, we have virtually summed up our useful knowledge of rarity and its effect on prices. A comparison of prices, between stamps in roughly similar ranges of value, does not indicate which is the rarer. A stamp selling for $1,000 is not necessarily rarer than one selling for $500. A $10,000 stamp may actually be more abundant than one which commands $5,000. This hard-to-comprehend fact of philatelic life prevails because of the other factors involved in determining a stamp's price. If rarity were the only factor, one could, of course, easily see which stamps are the rarest by the prices they fetch.

The word "rare" is an elixir to many collectors, not only of stamps but other collectors' items. Sellers are well aware of this, and seldom fail to sprinkle the word liberally in their sales literature. There is no law against calling a stamp rare, as this represents a personal opinion more than anything else and opinions are allowable in advertising. Unfortunately, there is no standard definition for rarity. Does "rare" mean just a handful of specimens in existence, with one reaching the sales portals once in five years? Does it mean 100 in existence, or 1,000, or some other number? Since stamps are—today, at any rate—printed in the multimillions, a thousand surviving specimens might seem a very tiny total to some people. Further complicating this situation is the fact that the specific rarity of most stamps cannot be determined, or even estimated, with any hope of accuracy. The quantities printed are recorded for most of our stamps, going back even into the nineteenth century, but the quantity *surviving* of any particular stamp is anyone's guess. It is obvious that a stamp that goes through the auction rooms once a year is fairly rare, but this provides no sound basis for guessing the number of specimens in existence. That could only be accomplished if some sort of grand census could be taken, and all specimens tallied. This, of course, is nothing but a pipe dream. Some collectors would not participate in such a census; some might be unaware that it was being conducted. Then, too, there are many scarce or rare stamps in hands other than those of collectors, such as dealers and museums. Additionally, there could be (and probably are) existing specimens of rare stamps yet to be discovered, as fresh discoveries are made periodically in the hobby through attic cleaning and the like.

In terms of influence on price, rarity is outdistanced somewhat by *popularity.* Some stamps, for one reason or other, are simply more popular than others. They have a sort of innate appeal for hobbyists, either through reputation, exquisite designing, circumstances of issue, oddity, or various other potential reasons. These stamps sell out rapidly from the stocks of dealers, while some stamps that are supposedly scarcer will linger in stock albums for ages and ages waiting to tempt a customer. It is no wonder, then, that the prices of popular stamps rise more quickly than those that are scarce but not in brisk demand. The Columbian series typifies the effect of popularity on stamp values. If stamp prices were fixed by scarcity alone, none of the Columbians would be selling for nearly as much. Much of their value derives from their overwhelming popularity with collectors of U.S. stamps. It would be safe to say, in fact, that *all* of the Columbians, from the lowest face value to the $5, are more plentiful than other U.S. stamps selling for precisely the same sums. Every dealer has Columbians in stock, and quite a few dealers have the high values of the set, too. They are not "hard to get." But they *are* very costly.

Popularity, of course, does not remain constant forever. There are shifts in philatelic popularity, usually slight but occasionally extreme. The popularity of commemoratives as a whole versus regular issues as a whole can change from time to time. Then, too, there are swings of popularity for airmails, first day covers, blocks, coil pairs, mint sheets, and all other philatelic material. A climb or decline in the price of any philatelic item is often an indication of the forces of popularity at work. Then there are activities of investors to consider, whose buying habits seldom reflect those of the pure collector. A great deal of buying by investors in any short period of time (such as occurred during 1979 and 1980, and to less extent in 1981) can make prices seem well out of balance.

Also on the subject of prices, it is important for the beginner to realize that arithmetic is usually futile when dealing with stamp values. You cannot determine the price of one philatelic item by knowing the value of a similar one. This can best be shown by the relative values of singles and blocks of four. A block of four is, as one would expect, worth *more* than four times as much as single specimens of that stamp. It is not just four specimens of the stamp, but four of them *attached,* which lends added scarcity and appeal. The difficulty lies in trying to use mathematics to determine a block's value. Some blocks are worth five times as much as the single stamp; some six times; some ten times or even more. Almost all blocks—except very common ones—will vary somewhat in value, in relation to the value of the individual stamp. There is no satisfactory explanation for this, other than the presumption that some blocks are scarcer than others or just in greater demand than others.

In the case of common philatelic items, the value hinges greatly on the method of sale. If you want to buy one specimen of a common cover, you may have to pay $1.50. But if you were willing to buy a hundred common first day covers *of the dealer's choice,* you could very likely get them for $75 or 75¢ each. Buying in quantity, and allowing the dealer to make the selections, can save a great deal of money. Of course one may then ask: What is the real value of those covers? Is it $1.50 or 75¢? The only answer is that it depends on how you buy!

If this article seems to raise a great many questions without supplying many answers, it will, hopefully, serve to show that stamp collecting is not bound to rigid formulas. What happens in the stamp market is largely beyond prediction, or precise explanation. This, indeed, is one of the exciting aspects of the hobby.

STAMP COLLECTORS' TERMINOLOGY

Adhesives—A term given to stamps that have gummed backs and are intended to be pasted on articles and items that are to be mailed.

Aerophilately—The collecting of airmail or any form of stamps related to mail carried by air.

Airmail—Any mail carried by air.

Albino—An uncolored embossed impression of a stamp generally found on envelopes.

Approvals—Stamps sent to collectors. They are examined by the collector, who selects stamps to purchase and returns balance with payment for the stamps he retained.

Arrow Block—An arrow-like mark found on blocks of stamps in the selvage. This mark is used as a guide for cutting or perforating stamps.

As-Is—A term used when selling a stamp. It means no representation is given as to its condition or authenticity. Buyers should beware.

Backprint—Any printing that may appear on reverse of stamp.

Backstamp—The postmark on the back of a letter indicating what time or date the letter arrived at the post office.

Bantams—A miniature stamp given to a war economy issue of stamps from South Africa.

Batonne—Watermarked paper used in printing stamps.

Bicolored—A two-color printed stamp.

Bisect—A stamp that could be used by cutting in half and at half the face value.

Block—A term used for a series of four or more stamps attached at least two high and two across.

Bourse—A meeting or convention of stamp collectors and dealers where stamps are bought, sold, and traded.

Cachet—A design printed on the face of an envelope, generally celebrating the commemoration of a new postage stamp issue. Generally called a first day cover.

Cancellation—A marking placed on the face of a stamp to show that it has been used.

Cancelled to Order—A stamp cancelled by the government without being used. Generally remainder stamps or special issues. Common practice of Russian nations.

Centering—The manner in which the design of a stamp is printed and centered upon the stamp blank. A perfectly centered stamp would have equal margins on all sides.

Classic—A popular, unique, highly desired or very artistic stamp. Not necessarily a rare stamp, but one sought after by the collector. Generally used only for nineteenth-century issues.

Coils—Stamps sold in rolls for use in vending machines.

Commemorative—A stamp issued to commemorate or celebrate a special event.

Crease—A fold or wrinkle in a stamp.

Cut square—An embossed staple removed from the envelope by cutting.

Dead Country—A country no longer issuing stamps.

Demonetized—A stamp no longer valid for use.

Error—A stamp printed or produced with a major design or color defect.

Essay—Preliminary design for a postage stamp.

Face Value—The value of a stamp indicated on the face or surface of the stamp.

Frank—A marking on the face of an envelope indicating the free and legal use of postage. Generally for government use.

Fugitive Inks—A special ink used to print stamps, which can be rubbed or washed off easily, to eliminate erasures and forgeries.

General Collector—One who collects all kinds of issues and all types of stamps from different countries.

Granite Paper—A type of paper containing colored fibers to prevent forgery.

Gum—The adhesive coating on the back of a stamp.

Handstamped—A stamp that has been handcancelled.

Hinge—A specially gummed piece of glassine paper used to attach a stamp to the album page.

Imperforate—A stamp without perforations.

Inverted—Where one portion of a stamp's design is inverted or upside down from the remainder of the design.

Local Stamps—Stamps that are only valid in a limited area.

Margin—The unprinted area around a stamp.

Miniature Sheet—A smaller than usual sheet of stamps.

Mint Condition—A stamp in original condition as it left the postal printing office.

Mirror Print—A stamp error printed in reverse as though looking at a regular stamp reflected in a mirror.

Multicolored—A stamp printed in three or more colors.

Never Hinged—A stamp in original mint condition never hinged in an album.

Off Paper—A used stamp that has been removed from the envelope to which it was attached.

On Paper—A used stamp still attached to the envelope.

Original Gum—A stamp with the same or original adhesive that was applied in the manufacturing process.

Pair—Two stamps unseparated.

Pen Cancellation—A stamp cancelled by pen or pencil.

Perforation Gauge—A printed chart containing various sizes of perforation holes used in determining the type or size of perforation of a stamp.

Perforations—Holes punched along stamp designs allowing stamps to be easily separated.

Philatelist—One who collects stamps.

Pictorial Stamps—Stamps that bear large pictures of animals, birds, flowers, etc.

Plate Block Number—The printing plate number used to identify a block of four or more stamps taken from a sheet of stamps.

Postally Used—A stamp that has been properly used and cancelled.

Precancels—A stamp that has been cancelled in advance. Generally used on bulk mail.

Reissue—A new printing of an old stamp that has been out of circulation.

Revenue Stamp—A label or stamp affixed to an item as evidence of tax payment.

Seals—An adhesive label that looks like a stamp, used for various fund raising campaigns.

Se-tenant—Two or more stamps joined together, each having a different design or value.

Sheet—A page of stamps as they are printed, usually separated before distribution to post offices.

Soaking—Removing used stamps from paper to which they are attached by soaking in water. *(NOTE: Colored cancels may cause staining to other stamps.)*

Souvenir Sheet—One or more specially designed stamps printed by the government in celebration of a special stamp.

Splice—The splice made between rolls of paper in the printing operation. Stamps printed on this splice are generally discarded.

Tete-Bechs—A pair of stamps printed together so that the images point in opposite vertical directions.

Transit Mark—A mark made by an intermediate post office between the originating and final destination post office.

Typeset Stamp—A stamp printed with regular printer's type, as opposed to engraved, lithographed, etc.

Ungummed—Stamps printed without an adhesive back.

Unhinged—A stamp that has never been mounted with the use of a hinge.

Unperforated—A stamp produced without perforations.

Vignette—The central design portion of a stamp.

Want List—A list of stamps a collector needs to fill gaps in his collection.

Watermark—A mark put into paper by the manufacturer, not readily seen by the naked eye.

Wrapper—A strip of paper with adhesive on one end, used for wrapping bundles of mail. Especially in Britain, it refers to any bit of paper to which a used stamp is still attached.

HOW TO GRADE STAMPS

A person need not be an expert to judge the quality or grade of a stamp. All he needs is a discerning eye, possibly a small linear measuring device, and the grading instructions listed below.

The major catalogs traditionally list stamps simply as "Unused" or "Used." Auction houses, however, will describe the stamps for sale in a more informative manner. The greater the value of the stamp, the more thoroughly it is described.

There is no officially accepted system of grading stamps. What we have done in this book is essentially to set up a system of grading stamps using the suggestions and practices of stamp dealers from all over the country. Total agreement was made to the following categories and grades of stamps that are most frequently traded.

CATEGORIES

Mint—The perfect stamp with superb centering, no faults and usually with original gum (if issued with gum).

Unused—Although unused this stamp may have a hinge mark or may have suffered some change in its gum since it was issued.

Used—Basically this will be the normal stamp that passed through the government postal system and will bear an appropriate cancellation.

Cancelled to Order—These are stamps that have not passed through the postal system but have been carefully cancelled by the government usually for a commemoration. These are generally considered undesirable by collectors.

GRADE—STAMP CENTERING

Average—The perforations cut slightly into the design.

Fine—The perforations do not touch the design at all, but the design will be off center by 50% or more of a superb centered stamp.

Very Fine—The design will be off center by less than 50% of a superb stamp. The off centered design will be visibly noticeable.

Extra Fine—The design will be almost perfectly centered. The margin will be off by less than 25% of a superb stamp.

Superb—This design will be perfectly centered with all four margins exactly the same. On early imperforate issues, superb specimens will have four clear margins that do not touch the design at any point.

Average
Centering

Fine
Centering

Very Fine
Centering

Extra Fine
Centering

Superb
Centering

GRADE—STAMP GUM

Original Gum—This stamp will have the same gum on it that it had the day it was issued.

Regummed—This stamp will have new gum applied to it as compared to an original gummed stamp. Regummed stamps are worth no more than those with gum missing.

No Gum—This stamp will have had its gum removed or it may have not been issued with gum.

Never Hinged—This stamp has never been hinged so the gum should not have been disturbed in any way.

Lightly Hinged—This stamp has had a hinge applied. A lightly wetted or peelable hinge would do very little damage to the gum when removed.

Heavily Hinged—This stamp has had a hinge applied in such a manner as to secure it to the stamp extremely well. Removal of this hinge usually proves to be disastrous, in most cases, since either part of the hinge remains on the stamp or part of the stamp comes off on the hinge, causing thin spots on the stamp.

GRADE—STAMP FAULTS

Any fault in a stamp such as thin paper, bad perforations, creases, tears, stains, ink marks, pin holes, etc., and depending upon the seriousness of the fault, usually results in grading the stamp to a lower condition.

OTHER STAMP CONSIDERATIONS

CANCELLATIONS

Light Cancel—This stamp has been postally cancelled but the wording and lines are very light and almost unreadable.

Normal Cancel—This stamp has been postally cancelled with just the right amount of pressure. Usually the wording and lines are not distorted and can be made out.

Heavy Cancel—This stamp has been postally cancelled. In the process excessive pressure was used, and the wording and lines are extremely dark and sometimes smeared and in most cases unreadable.

PERFORATIONS

Not to be overlooked in the appearance of a stamp are its perforations. The philatelist might examine these "tear apart" holes with a magnifying glass or microscope to determine the cleanliness of the separations. One must also consider that the different types of paper, upon which the stamp was printed, will sometimes make a difference in the cleanliness of the separations. The term "pulled perf" is used to denote a badly separated stamp in which the perforations are torn or ragged.

COLOR

Other important factors such as color affect the appearance and value of stamps. An expert will have a chart of stamp colors. Chemical changes often occur in inks. Modern printing sometimes uses metallic inks. These "printings" will oxidize upon contact with the natural secretions from animal skin.

The color of certain stamps has been deliberately altered by chemicals to produce a rare shade. Overprints can be eliminated. Postmarks may be eradicated. Replacing gum is a simple process. Some stamps have been found to bear forged watermarks. The back of the paper was cut away and then the stamps rebacked with appropriately watermarked paper.

There are stamp experts who earn a living in the business of stamp repairing. They are craftsmen of the first order. A thin spot on a stamp can be repaired by gluing it on a new layer of paper. Missing perforations can be added. Torn stamps can be put back together. Pieces of stamps may be joined.

In some countries it is accepted practice for an expert, upon examination of a stamp, to certify the authenticity by affixing his signature to the back of the stamp. If the stamp is not genuine, it is his right and duty to so designate on the stamp; but these signatures can also be faked.

REPAIRS, FAKES, AND OTHER UNDESIRABLES

Philately, like most hobbies, is not without its pitfalls. The collector who buys from reputable dealers runs very little risk, as today's stamp pros have high principles and are hard to fool. Buying from auction sales and small dealers, who may not have expert knowledge, is another matter. Here the collector must call into play his own expertise and learn to distinguish the bad from the good.

In the early years of philately, stamps provided a playground for fakers and swindlers. They took advantage of the public's gullibility and the general lack of published information about stamps. Copies were printed of rare stamps, as well as of stamps that never existed in the first place. Cancels were bleached from used specimens to make them appear unused. Fake margins were added to imperforates, to allow ordinary copies to be sold as "superb with jumbo margins." Perforated stamps were reperforated to make them better centered. Thin spots in the paper were filled in, tears closed, missing portions of paper replaced. Stamps were doctored and manipulated in more ways than could be imagined, all in the hope of fooling collectors and making anywhere from a few extra cents to thousands of dollars on them. One of the favorite tricks of fakers was to apply bogus overprints or surcharges. By merely using a rubber handstamp and a pad of ink, they could stamp out a hundred or more "rarities" in a few minutes, turning ordinary British or other issues into varieties not found in any catalog. It was all a great game and proved very profitable, until collectors and the philatelic public at large became wary of such practices. Even though most of these fakes from the hobby's pioneer years have disappeared out of circulation, a few still turn up and must be guarded against.

United States stamps have not been faked nearly so extensively as those of many other nations, notably South America and Japan. Still, the collector should learn to watch for fakes and also repaired specimens.

Total Fake. The counterfeit stamp always varies somewhat from a genuine specimen, though the difference may be very slight. Detection can usually be made if the suspect stamp is examined alongside one known to be genuine. By using a magnifier, the lines of engraving and paper quality can be compared. The ink on a fake is likely to have a fresher appearance and will lie on the surface as a result of being printed at a later date and on less sophisticated equipment; however, this is not always the case. Experts say that when a stamp appears to be a fake, or a reprint, the odds are very good that it is. Some experience is necessary before anyone can get a first glance reaction to a stamp. The presence or absence of a cancel has no bearing on the likelihood of a stamp being a fake, as cancels can be faked too.

Faked Cancel. Faked cancels are very rare on U.S. stamps, as nearly all are worth more unused than used. One notable exception is the 90¢ 1857–1861. These are applied either with a fake handstamp or simply drawn with pen and ink. Skillfully drawn faked cancels can be very deceptive. Faked cancels are *much more numerous* on covers than loose stamps.

Removed Cancels. So-called cleaned copies of used stamps, sold as unused, were once very plentiful and are still encountered from time to time. The faker, of course, chooses lightly cancelled specimens from which the obliteration can be removed without leaving telltale evidence. In the case of imperforates he may trim down the margins to remove part of the cancel. Rarely will he attempt to clean a stamp whose cancel falls across the face or any important portion of the stamp. Holding the stamp to a strong light may reveal the cancel lines. X-ray examination provides positive proof.

Added Margin(s). When margins have been added to an imperforate stamp, the paper fibers are woven together (after moistening) along the back and at the front where the margin extends beyond the stamp's design. They can usually be detected by looking closely for a seam or joint at the point where the design ends and the margin begins. A magnifying glass will be necessary for this. When held against a light, the reverse side will probably show evidence of the weaving operation. Sometimes the added margins are of a slightly different grade of paper.

Reperforated. A stamp that has been reperforated to improve its centering will usually be slightly smaller than a normal specimen, and this can be revealed by placing it atop an untampered copy.

Filled In Thin Spots. If held to a light and examined with a good magnifier, filled in thin spots will normally appear darker than the remainder of the stamp. Such spots are often mistaken for discoloration by beginners. Thin spots are filled in by making a paste of paper pulp and glue and applying it gradually to the injured area. After drying, the stamp is placed in a vise so that no telltale hills or valleys are left. This is not really considered forgery but honest repair work; it becomes forgery only if done with the intent of selling the stamp as undamaged.

Closed Tears. These are almost always visible against a light with a magnifier, even if small. A routine examination of any rare stamp should include a check of its margins for possible closed or open tears.

HOW TO USE THIS BOOK

The main section of this book lists all U.S. stamps with the exception of special issues such as airmail, revenues, etc. Special issues are grouped separately in sections of their own. Please refer to the Table of Contents.

Before pricing your stamps, be sure they are correctly identified. Use the photo section as an aid. In some cases, two or more stamp issues are very similar in appearance and can be distinguished only by minor details. These are always noted in the text. Sometimes the evidence is obvious. If a stamp has perforations, it cannot be earlier than 1857.

Prices are given in columns for used and unused specimens, usually in two grades of condition. You need only refer to the column that applies to your stamp and its condition grade.

Prices shown in this book are actual selling prices, so one should not necessarily expect to receive a discount when buying from dealers.

When a dash (—) appears in place of a price, this indicates that the item is either unavailable in that condition grade or is so seldom available that its price is open to question. It should not be assumed, however, that such items are invariably more valuable than those for which prices are shown.

Prices are given for hinged stamps that have been in collections. In today's stamp market a premium value is placed on stamps that have never been hinged. To determine the premium on any stamp, refer to the premium percentages shown on every page.

The stated values are general guides only and cannot reflect the price of occasional superb specimens, such as imperforates with four wide margins, which may sell considerably higher.

A small box has been provided to the left of each listing for keeping a record of the stamps in your collection.

IMPORTANT

Because of the space limitation on each page we have not been able to include very fine, extra fine, never hinged, or lightly hinged pricing on each stamp. To determine these prices please use the following procedure.

Very Fine Pricing—Prior to 1941: *Double the average price quoted.*

Very Fine Pricing—After 1941: *Add 25% to the fine price.*

Extra Fine Pricing—Prior to 1941: *Triple the average price quoted.*

Never Hinged Pricing—Prior to 1941: *Add the percentage indicated at the right of the issue to any price listed. Example: (N-H add 5%).*

Never Hinged Pricing—After 1941: *Add 15% to any price listed.*

Lightly Hinged Pricing—*Add one half of the N-H percentage indicated for each issue to any price listed.*

DEALER BUYING PRICES

Buying prices will vary greatly depending upon condition, rarity, and existing dealers' stock of a particular stamp. With these facts in mind, a dealer can be expected to buy stamps between 40 percent and 50 percent of their quoted prices; but this will depend upon supply and demand.

EQUIPMENT

To collect stamps properly a collector will need some "tools of the trade." These need not be expensive and need not all be bought at the very outset. That might, in fact, be the worst thing to do. Many a beginning collector has spent his budget on equipment, only to have little or nothing left for stamps and then loses interest in the hobby.

It may be economical in the long run to buy the finest quality accessories, but few collectors, just starting out, have a clear idea of what they will and will not be needing. It is just as easy to make impulse purchases of accessories as of stamps and just as unwise. Equipment must be purchased on the basis of what sort of collection is being built *now,* rather than on what the collection may be in the future. There is no shame in working up from an elementary album.

Starter Kits. Starter or beginner outfits are sold in just about every variety shop, drugstore, etc. These come in attractive boxes and contain a juvenile or beginner's album; some stamps, which may be on paper and in need of removal; a packet of gummed hinges; tongs; a pocket stockbook or file; and often other items such as a perforation gauge, booklet on stamp collecting, magnifier, and watermark detector. These kits are specially suited to young collectors and can provide a good philatelic education.

Albums. When the hobby began, more than a century ago, collectors mounted their stamps in whatever albums were at hand. Scrapbooks, school exercise tablets and diaries all were used, as well as homemade albums. Today a number of firms specialize in printing albums of all kinds for philatelists, ranging from softbounds for the cautious type to huge multi-volume sets that cost hundreds of dollars. There are general worldwide albums, country albums, U.N. albums, and albums for mint sheets, covers, and every other conceivable variety of philatelic material. Choose your album according to the specialty you intend to pursue. It is not necessary, however, to buy a printed album at all. Many collectors feel there is not enough room for creativity in a printed album and prefer to use a binder with unprinted sheets. This allows items to be arranged at will on the page, rather than following the publisher's format, and for a personal write-up to be added. Rod-type binders will prove more durable and satisfactory than ring binders for heavy collections. The pages of an album should not be too thin, unless only one side is used. The presence of tiny crisscrossing lines (quadrilled sheets) is intended as an aid to correct alignment. Once items have been mounted and written up, these lines are scarcely visible and do not interfere with the attractiveness of the page.

Hinges. These are small rectangular pieces of lightweight paper, usually clear or semiopaque, gummed and folded. One side is moistened and affixed to the back of the stamp and the other to the album page. Hinges are sold in packets of 1,000 and are very inexpensive. Though by far the most popular device for mounting stamps, the hobbyist has his choice of a number of other products if hinges are not satisfactory to him. These include cello mounts, which encase the stamp in clear sheeting and have a black background to provide a kind of frame. These are self-sticking. Their cost is much higher than hinges. The chief advantage of cello mounts is that they prevent injuries to the stamp and eliminate the moistening necessary in using hinges; however, they add considerably to the weight of each page, making flipping through an album less convenient, and become detached from the page more readily than hinges.

Glassine Interleaving. These are sheets made of thin semitransparent glassine paper, the same used to make envelopes in which stamps are stored. They come punched to fit albums of standard size and are designed to be placed between each set of sheets, to prevent stamps on one page from becoming entangled with those on the facing page. Glassine interleaving is not necessary if cello mounts are used, but any collection mounted with conventional hinges should be interleaved. The cost is small. Glassine interleaving is sold in packets of 100 sheets.

Magnifier. A magnifier is a necessary tool for *most* stamp collectors, excepting those who specialize in first day covers or other items that would not likely require study by magnification. There are numerous types and grades on the market, ranging in price from about $1 to more than $20. The quality of magnifier to buy should be governed by the extent to which it is likely to be used, and the collector's dependence upon it for identification and study. A collector of plate varieties ought to have the best magnifier he can afford, and carry it whenever visiting dealers, shows or anywhere that he may wish to examine specimens. A good magnifier is also necessary for a specialist in grilled stamps and for collectors of Civil War and other nineteenth-century covers. Those with built-in illumination are best in these circumstances.

Tongs. Beginners have a habit of picking up stamps with their fingers, which can cause injuries, smudges and grease stains. Efficient handling of tongs is not difficult to learn, and the sooner the better. Do not resort to ordinary tweezers, but get a pair of philatelic tongs which are specially shaped and of sufficiently large size to be easily manipulated.

Perforation Gauge. A very necessary inexpensive article, as the identification of many stamps depends upon a correct measuring of their perforations.

TIPS ON STAMP BUYING

There are many ways to buy stamps: packets, poundage mixtures, approvals, new issue services, auctions and a number of others. To buy wisely, a collector must get to know the language of philately and the techniques used by dealers and auctioneers in selling stamps.

Packets of all different worldwide stamps are sold in graduated sizes from 1,000 up to 50,000. True to their word, they contain no duplicates. The stamps come from all parts of the world and date from the 1800s to the present. Both mint and used are included. When you buy larger quantities of most things, a discount is offered; with stamp packets, it works in reverse. The larger the packet, the higher its price per stamp. This is because the smaller packets are filled almost exclusively with low-grade material.

Packets are suitable only as a collection base. A collector should never count on them to build his entire collection. The contents of one worldwide packet are much like that of another. Country packets are sold in smaller sizes, but there are certain drawbacks with packets.

1. Most packets contain some cancelled-to-order stamps, which are not very desirable for a collection. These are stamps released with postmarks already on them, and are classified as used but have never gone through the mail. Eastern Europe and Russia are responsible for many C.T.O.'s.

2. The advertised value of packets bears little relation to the actual value. Packet makers call attention to the catalog values of their stamps, based on prices listed in standard reference works. The lowest sum at which a stamp can be listed in these books is 2¢, therefore, a packet of 1,000 automatically has a minimum catalog value of $20. If the retail price is $3 this seems like a terrific buy when, in fact, most of those thousand stamps are so common they are almost worthless.

Poundage mixtures are very different than packets. Here the stamps are all postally used (no C.T.O.'s) and still attached to small fragments of envelopes or parcel wrappings. Rather than sold by count, poundage mixtures are priced by the pound or ounce and quite often by kilos. Price varies depending on the grade, and the grade depends on where the mixture was assembled. Bank mixtures are considered the best, as banks receive a steady flow of foreign registered mail. Mission mixtures are also highly rated. Of course, the mixture should be sealed and unpicked. Unless a mixture is advertised as unpicked, the high values have been removed. The best poundage mixtures are sold only by mail. Those available in shops are of medium or low quality. Whatever the grade, poundage mixtures can be counted on to contain duplicates.

If you want to collect the stamps of a certain country, you can leave a standing order for its new releases with a new issue service. Whenever that government puts out stamps, they will be sent to the collector along with a bill. Usually the service will supply only mint copies. The price charged is not the face value, but the face value with a surcharge added to meet the costs of importing, handling and the like. New issue services are satisfactory only if the collector is positive he wants all the country's stamps, no matter what. Remember that its issues could include semipostals, long and maybe expensive sets, and extra high values.

By far the most popular way to buy stamps is via approvals. There is nothing new about approvals, as they go back to the Victorian era. Not all services are alike, though. Some offer sets, while others sell penny approvals. Then there are remainder approvals, advanced approvals, and seconds on approval. Penny approvals are really a thing of the past, though the term is still used. Before inflation, dealers would send a stockbook containing several thousand stamps, all priced at a penny each. If all the stamps were kept, the collector got a discount plus the book! Today the same sort of service can be found, but instead of 1¢ per stamp, the price is anywhere from 3¢ to 10¢. Remainder approvals are made up from collection remainders. Rather than dismount and sort stamps from incoming collections, the approval merchant saves himself time by sending them out right on the album pages. The collector receives leaves from someone else's collection with stamps mounted just as he arranged them. Seconds on approval are slightly defective specimens of scarce stamps, which would cost more if perfect. Advanced approvals are designed for specialized collectors who know exactly what they want and have a fairly substantial stamp budget.

In choosing an approval service you should know the ground rules of approval buying and not be unduly influenced by promotional offers. Most approval merchants allow the selections to be kept for ten days to two weeks. The unbought stamps are then returned along with payment for those kept. As soon as the selection is received back, another is mailed. This will go on, regardless of how much or how little is bought, until the company is notified to refrain from sending further selections. The reputable services will always stop when told.

Approval ads range from splashy full pagers in the stamp publications to small three line classified announcements in magazines and newspapers. Most firms catering to beginners offer loss leaders, or stamps on which they take a loss for the sake of getting new customers. If an approval dealer offers 100 pictorials for a dime, it is obvious he is losing money on that transaction, as 10¢ will not even pay the postage. It is very tempting to order these premiums. Remember that when ordering approvals. What sort of service is it? Will it offer the kind of stamps desired? Will prices be high to pay for the loss leaders? Be careful of confusing advertisements. Sometimes the premium offers seem to promise more than they actually do. A rare, early stamp may be pictured. Of course you do not receive the stamp, but merely a modern commemorative picturing it.

Auction Sales. Stamp auctions are held all over the country and account for millions of dollars in sales annually. Buying at auction is exciting and can be economical. Many sleepers turn up—stamps that can be bought at less than their actual value. To be a good auction buyer, the philatelist must know stamps and their prices pretty well, and know the ropes of auctions. An obvious drawback of auctions is that purchases are not returnable. A dealer will take back a stamp that proves not to a collector's liking, but an auctioneer will not. Also, auctioneers require immediate payment while a dealer may extend credit.

Stamps sold at auction come from private collections and the stocks of dealers; not necessarily defunct dealers, but those who want to get shelf space. Because they were brought together from a variety of sources, the nature and condition will vary. In catalog descriptions the full book value will be given for each stamp, but of course defective stamps will sell for much less than these figures. A bidder must calculate how much less. Other lots which can be difficult for the bidder to evaluate are those containing more than one stamp. Sometimes a superb specimen will be lotted along with a defective one. Then there are bulk lots which contain odds and ends from collections and such. It is usual in auctioning a collection for the better stamps to be removed and sold separately. The remainder is then offered in a single lot, which may consist of thousands or even tens of thousands of stamps. By all means examine lots before bidding. A period of inspection is always allowed before each sale, usually for several days. There may or may not be an inspection on sale day. If the bidder is not able to make a personal examination but must bid on strength of the catalog description, he should scale his bids for bulk lots much lower than for single stamp lots. He might bid $50 on a single stamp lot with a catalog value of $100, if the condition is listed as top notch, but to bid one-half catalog value on a bulk lot would not be very wise. These lots are not scrutinized very carefully by the auctioneers and some stamps are bound to be disappointing. There may be some heavily canceled, creased, torn, etc. Also, there will very likely be duplication. A bid of one-fifth the catalog value on a bulk lot is considered high. Often a one-tenth bid is successful.

The mechanics of stamp auctions may strike the beginner as complicated. They are run no differently than other auctions. All material to be sold is lotted by the auctioneer; that is, broken down into lots or units and bidding is by lot. Everything in the lot must be bid on, even if just one of the stamps is desired. The motive of bulk lotting is to save time and give each lot a fair sales value.

Before the sale a catalog is published listing all the lots, describing the contents and sometimes picturing the better items. Catalogs are in the mail about 30 days before the sale date. If a bid is to be mailed, it must be sent early. Bids that arrive after the sale are disqualified, even if they would have been successful.

When the bid is received it is entered into a bidbook, along with the bidder's name and address. On sale day each lot opens on the floor at one level above the second highest mail bid. Say the two highest mail bids are $30 and $20. The floor bidding would begin at $25. If the two highest bids are $100 and $500, the opening bid would probably be $150. The larger the amounts involved, the bigger will be the advances. The auctioneer will not accept an advance of $5 on a $500 lot; but on low value lots even dollar advances are sometimes made. Then it becomes a contest of floor versus book. The auctioneer acts as an agent, bidding for the absentee until his limit is reached. If the floor tops him, he has lost. If the floor does not get as high as his bid, he wins the lot at one advance over the highest floor bid.

When a collector buys stamps by mail from a dealer, he should choose one who belongs to the American Stamp Dealers' Association or A.S.D.A. The emblem is carried in their ads.

SELLING YOUR STAMPS

Almost every collector becomes a stamp seller sooner or later. Duplicates are inevitably accumulated, no matter how careful one may be in avoiding them. Then there are the G and VG stamps that have been replaced with F and VF specimens, and have become duplicates by intent. In addition to duplicates, a more advanced collector is likely to have stamps that are not duplicates but for which he has no further use. These will be odds and ends, sometimes quite valuable ones, that once suited the nature of his collection but are now out of place. Collectors' tastes change. The result is a stockpile of stamps that can be converted back to cash.

The alternative to selling the stamps you no longer need or want is trading them with a collector who does want them, and taking his unwanted stamps in return. All stamp clubs hold trading sessions. Larger national stamp societies operate trade-by-mail services for their members. The APS (American Philatelic Society) keeps $8,000,000 worth of stamps constantly circulating in its trading books or "circuit" books. Trading can be an excellent way of disposing of surplus stamps. In most cases it takes a bit longer than selling. Another potential drawback, especially if you are not a club member, is finding the right person with the right stamps.

The nature and value of the material involved may help in deciding whether to sell outright or trade. Also, there are your own personal considerations. If you're not going to continue in the stamp hobby, or need cash for some purpose other than stamp buying, trading is hardly suitable. Likewise, if you have developed an interest in some very exotic group of stamps or other philatelic items it may be impossible to find someone to trade with.

Once you have decided to sell, if indeed you do make that decision, the matter revolves upon how. To a stamp shop? To another collector? Through an auction house? Possibly by running your own advertisements and issuing price lists, if you have enough stamps and spare time to make this worthwhile?

While some individuals have an absolute horror at the prospect of selling anything, stamp collectors tend to enjoy selling. It is difficult to say why. Some enjoy it so much they keep right on selling stamps, as a business, long after their original objective is achieved. Nearly all professional stamp dealers were collectors before entering the trade.

Selling your stamps outright to a dealer, especially a local dealer whom you can personally visit, is not necessarily the most financially rewarding but it is quick and very problem-free. Of course it helps if the dealer knows you and it's even better if he knows some of your stamps. Dealers have no objection to repurchasing stamps they've sold to you. You will find that the dealers encourage their customers to sell to them just as much as they encourage them to buy. The dealers are really anxious to get your stamps if you have good salable material from popular countries. In fact most dealers would prefer buying from the public rather than any other source.

The collector selling stamps to a dealer has to be reasonable in his expectations. A dealer may not be able to use all the stamps you have. It is simply not smart business for a dealer to invest money in something he may not be able to sell. So, if you have esoteric or highly specialized items for sale, it might be necessary to find a specialist who deals in those particular areas rather than selling to a neighborhood stamp shop.

The local stamp shop will almost certainly want to buy anything you can offer in the way of medium to better grade United States stamps of all kinds, including the so-called "back of the book" items. He may not want plate blocks or full sheets of commemoratives issued within the past 20 years. Most dealers are well supplied with material of this nature and have opportunities to buy more of it every day. The same is true of first day covers, with a few exceptions, issued from the 1960s to the present. The dealers either have these items abundantly or can get them from a wholesaler at rock-bottom prices. They would rather buy stamps that are a bit harder to get from the wholesalers, or for which the wholesalers charge higher prices. On the whole you will meet with a favorable reception when offering U.S. stamps to a local dealer. With foreign stamps it becomes another matter: what do you have and how flexible are you in price? Nearly all the stamp shops in this country do stock foreign stamps to one extent or another. They do not, as a rule, attempt to carry comprehensive or special-ized stocks of them. In the average shop you will discover that the selection of general foreign consists of a combination of modern mint sets, topicals, souvenir sheets, packets, which come from the wholesaler, and a small sprinkling of older material, usually pre-1900. The price range of this older material will be $5 to $50. Non-specialist collectors of foreign stamps buy this type of item and that is essentially who the local shop caters to. When a local dealer buys rare foreign stamps or a large foreign collection, it is not for himself. He buys with the intent of passing them along to another dealer who has the right customers lined up. He acts only as a middleman or go-between. Therefore the price you receive for better grade foreign stamps tends to be lower than for better grade U.S., which the dealer buys for his own use.

What is a fair price to get for your stamps? This is always difficult to say, as many variable factors are involved. Consider their condition. Think in terms of what the dealer could reasonably hope to charge for them at retail and stand a good chance of selling them. Some of your stamps may have to be discounted because of no gum, poor centering, bent perfs, hinge remnants, repairs, or other problems. But even if your stamps are primarily F or VF, a dealer cannot pay book values for them. If you check his selling prices on his specimens of those same stamps, you can usually count on receiving from 40 to 50 percent of those prices. Considering the discount made from book values by the dealer in pricing his stock, your payment may work out to about 25 percent of book values. For rare United States stamps in top condition you can do better than 25 percent, but on most stamps sold to a dealer this is considered a fair offer. Keep in mind that the difference between a dealer's buying and selling prices is not just "profit margin." Most of the markup goes toward operating costs, for without this markup, there would be no stamp dealers.

THE AMERICAN PHILATELIC SOCIETY

The American Philatelic Society is an internationally recognized association of stamp experts and enthusiasts that offers a number of services and educational opportunities for stamp collectors. The APS is the national representative to the Federation Internationale de Philatelie and is affiliated with more than 700 local stamp clubs (APS Chapters) and almost 200 "specialty groups" (APS Affiliates).

The services that are available with an APS membership include a subscription to *The American Philatelist,* one of the premier stamp magazines in the world, as well as numerous other brochures and publications that are available at a discount to members. The APS Sales Division provides an opportunity for collectors to buy or sell stamps through the mail. Members may request "circuits" of stamps or covers in more than 150 categories of countries and topics. Selections of circuit books are mailed at intervals, and members can choose any items they wish to purchase, and then mail the books on to the next APS member on the circuit. The items are priced by the submitting members, and most range from under $1.00 to $5.00.

The APS also provides an insurance program for members living in the United States and Canada. The insurance policy does not require a detailed inventory, only a general description of a collection and a value estimate, and may be applied for along with a membership application.

The Society also runs the American Philatelic Research Library, with a wide range of resource material including thousands of books, journals, auction catalogs, and other material that are loaned or photocopied and available to members by mail for a nominal fee. The APRL also publishes the *Philatelic Literature Review,* a quarterly journal covering literature of interest to collectors. The magazine is available by separate subscription.

The APS offers, in association with Pennsylvania State University, correspondence courses ranging from "Beginning Collecting" to "Printing Techniques" and week-long summer seminars on philately that feature hands-on instruction by prominent experts. In addition, the APS Education Department produces many brochures and other materials and answers inquiries from beginner and intermediate collectors on various "how-to" aspects of the hobby.

Other APS services include identification of members' stamps by the APS Expert Committee, estate advice, a translation service for international trading, and an annual convention-exhibition stamp show.

THE AMERICAN PHILATELIST

The Society's monthly magazine, which is included in the membership fee, features a monthly column for beginning stamp collectors; regular columns on stamp clubs, exhibitions, topical collecting, and more; articles by experienced philatelists; how-to columns on using the Society's Sales Division; commentary on important issues to collectors from the state of the stamp market to insights on stamp condition and auctions; and detailed listings of all new stamps and postal stationery issued by the U.S. Postal Service.

MEMBERSHIP INFORMATION

The APS offers a variety of memberships including special rates for spouses and children, foreign members, and lifetime memberships. The Society operates on a calendar year, and membership fees are pro-rated on a quarterly basis and include a $3.00 admission fee. The 1991 schedule of membership fees is listed below.

Application received by APS National Headquarters	Admission Fee	Membership Fee	Total		
			U.S.	Canada	Foreign
October, November, December	$3.00	$18.00	$21.00	$24.00	$27.00
January, February, March	3.00	13.50	16.50	18.75	21.00
April, May, June	3.00	9.00	12.00	13.50	15.00
July, August, September	3.00	4.50	7.50	8.25	9.00

For more information, call or write the American Philatelic Society at:

APS
P.O. Box 8000, Dept. HC
State College, PA 16803
(814) 237-3803

IMPORTANT NOTICE: On stamps issued before 1890, prices of unused specimens are for ones without original gum. Specimens with original gum can be expected to command a premium of as much as 50 percent. Beware of regummed specimens

Scott No.		Fine Unused Each	Ave. Unused Each	Fine Used Each	Ave. Used Each
GENERAL ISSUES					
1847. FIRST ISSUE					
☐1	5¢ Red Brown	—	3000.00	600.00	400.00
☐2	10¢ Black	—	11000.00	1800.00	1100.00
1875. REPRODUCTIONS OF 1847 ISSUE					
☐3	5¢ Red Brown	1200.00	1000.00	—	—
☐4	10¢ Black	1700.00	1050.00	—	—
1851–1856. REGULAR ISSUE—IMPERFORATE					
☐5A	1¢ Blue (1b)	—	—	4000.00	2500.00
☐6	1¢ Blue (1a)	—	—	5200.00	3100.00
☐7	1¢ Blue (II)	500.00	300.00	125.00	90.00
☐8	1¢ Blue (III)	—	—	1300.00	800.00
☐8A	1¢ Blue (IIIa)	—	1400.00	600.00	400.00
☐9	1¢ Blue (IV)	800.00	200.00	110.00	60.00
☐10	3¢ Orange Brown (I)	—	800.00	50.00	40.00
☐11	3¢ Dull Red (I)	110.00	75.00	10.00	7.00
☐12	5¢ Red Brown (I)	—	—	1100.00	700.00
☐13	10¢ Green (I)	—	—	700.00	410.00
☐14	10¢ Green (II)	—	800.00	275.00	170.00
☐15	10¢ Green (III)	—	1100.00	290.00	180.00
☐16	10¢ Green (IV)	—	—	1400.00	900.00
☐17	12¢ Black	—	1300.00	260.00	175.00
1857–1861. SAME DESIGNS AS 1851–1856 ISSUE—PERF. 15					
☐18	1¢ Blue (I)	700.00	415.00	370.00	210.00
☐19	1¢ Blue (Ia)	—	—	2100.00	1450.00
☐20	1¢ Blue (II)	500.00	300.00	140.00	75.00
☐21	1¢ Blue (III)	—	2100.00	1150.00	690.00
☐22	1¢ Blue (IIIa)	700.00	360.00	230.00	150.00
☐23	1¢ Blue (IV)	—	1100.00	290.00	180.00
☐24	1¢ Blue (V)	140.00	70.00	38.00	24.00
☐25	3¢ Rose (I)	—	350.00	40.00	29.00
☐26	3¢ Dull Red (II)	60.00	34.00	5.00	2.50
☐26A	3¢ Dull Red (IIa)	130.00	80.00	25.00	17.00
☐27	5¢ Brick Red (I)	—	4000.00	850.00	500.00
☐28	5¢ Red Brown (I)	—	800.00	300.00	175.00
☐28A	5¢ Indian Red (I)	—	—	1700.00	1100.00
☐29	5¢ Brown (I)	700.00	400.00	200.00	135.00
☐30	5¢ Orange Brown (II)	750.00	400.00	820.00	500.00
☐30A	5¢ Brown (II)	400.00	220.00	200.00	110.00
☐31	10¢ Green (I)	—	2700.00	500.00	290.00
☐32	10¢ Green (II)	1700.00	930.00	170.00	110.00

Scott No.			Fine Unused Each	Ave. Unused Each	Fine Used Each	Ave. Used Each
☐33	10¢	Green (III)	1700.00	950.00	180.00	110.00
☐34	10¢	Green (IV)	—	—	1500.00	825.00
☐35	10¢	Green (V)	180.00	100.00	60.00	50.00
☐36	12¢	Black (I)	310.00	185.00	90.00	50.00
☐36b	12¢	Black (II)	300.00	160.00	110.00	62.00
☐37	24¢	Gray Lilac	600.00	300.00	200.00	150.00
☐38	30¢	Orange	700.00	400.00	290.00	160.00
☐39	90¢	Blue	1100.00	700.00	—	—

1875. REPRINTS OF 1857–1861 ISSUE

☐40	1¢	Bright Blue	600.00	370.00	—	—
☐41	3¢	Scarlet	3000.00	1750.00	—	—
☐42	5¢	Orange Brown	1000.00	675.00	—	—
☐43	10¢	Blue Green	2200.00	1500.00	—	—
☐44	12¢	Greenish Black	2200.00	1750.00	—	—
☐45	24¢	Blackish Violet	2300.00	1800.00	—	—
☐46	30¢	Yellow Orange	2400.00	1880.00	—	—
☐47	90¢	Deep Blue	4000.00	2900.00	—	—

1861. FIRST DESIGNS—PERF. 12

☐56	3¢	Brown Red	700.00	450.00	—	—
☐62B	10¢	Dark Green	—	—	500.00	300.00

1861–1862. SECOND DESIGNS

☐63	1¢	Blue	140.00	75.00	21.00	12.00
☐63b	1¢	Dark Blue	160.00	100.00	29.00	24.00
☐64	3¢	Pink	—	1900.00	300.00	145.00
☐64b	3¢	Rose Pink	270.00	180.00	45.00	26.00
☐65	3¢	Rose	62.00	36.00	3.00	2.00
☐66	3¢	Lake	—	1100.00	—	—
☐67	5¢	Buff	—	2500.00	400.00	200.00
☐68	10¢	Yellow Green	230.00	150.00	29.00	18.00
☐69	12¢	Black	450.00	300.00	52.00	32.00
☐70	24¢	Red Lilac	575.00	320.00	80.00	42.00
☐70b	24¢	Steel Blue	—	—	280.00	160.00
☐70c	24¢	Violet	—	1700.00	500.00	300.00
☐71	30¢	Orange	465.00	270.00	70.00	40.00
☐72	90¢	Blue	1200.00	650.00	250.00	145.00

1861–1866. NEW VALUES OR NEW COLORS

☐73	2¢	Black	100.00	45.00	26.00	16.00
☐74	3¢	Scarlet	3600.00	2300.00	1500.00	975.00
☐75	5¢	Red Brown	1250.00	710.00	215.00	125.00
☐76	5¢	Brown	310.00	200.00	50.00	32.00
☐77	15¢	Black	500.00	290.00	70.00	40.00
☐78	24¢	Lilac	265.00	150.00	50.00	35.00

Scott No.		Fine Unused Each	Ave. Unused Each	Fine Used Each	Ave. Used Each
1867. SAME DESIGNS AS 1861-1866 ISSUE					
GRILL WITH POINTS UP					
A. GRILL COVERING ENTIRE STAMP					
☐79	3¢ Rose	1800.00	920.00	450.00	210.00
C. GRILL ABOUT 13 x 16 MM.					
☐83	3¢ Rose	1675.00	1100.00	380.00	210.00
GRILL WITH POINTS DOWN					
D. GRILL ABOUT 12 x 14 MM.					
☐84	2¢ Black	2500.00	1650.00	1000.00	600.00
☐85	3¢ Rose	1500.00	800.00	400.00	230.00
Z. GRILL ABOUT 11 x 14 MM.					
☐85B	2¢ Black	1300.00	650.00	330.00	190.00
☐85C	3¢ Rose	2500.00	1900.00	900.00	480.00
☐85E	12¢ Black	1600.00	1000.00	520.00	300.00
E. GRILL ABOUT 11 x 13 MM.					
☐86	1¢ Blue	750.00	400.00	240.00	150.00
☐87	2¢ Black	325.00	190.00	65.00	40.00
☐88	3¢ Rose	260.00	140.00	11.00	8.00
☐89	10¢ Green	1300.00	750.00	175.00	96.00
☐90	12¢ Black	1400.00	800.00	190.00	100.00
☐91	15¢ Black	2900.00	1500.00	400.00	240.00
F. GRILL ABOUT 9 x 13 MM.					
☐92	1¢ Blue	390.00	190.00	95.00	57.00
☐93	2¢ Black	150.00	68.00	32.00	18.00
☐94	3¢ Red	92.00	52.00	4.50	3.00
☐95	5¢ Brown	850.00	500.00	215.00	120.00
☐96	10¢ Yellow Green	700.00	375.00	100.00	62.00
☐97	12¢ Black	700.00	400.00	110.00	68.00
☐98	15¢ Black	700.00	390.00	120.00	68.00
☐99	24¢ Gray Lilac	1250.00	700.00	500.00	255.00
☐100	30¢ Orange	1400.00	800.00	350.00	200.00
☐101	90¢ Blue	3500.00	2200.00	900.00	500.00
1875. RE-ISSUE OF 1861-1866 ISSUES					
☐102	1¢ Blue	—	370.00	—	500.00
☐103	2¢ Black	—	1800.00	—	2500.00
☐104	3¢ Brown Red	—	2200.00	—	3000.00
☐105	5¢ Light Brown	—	1400.00	—	1800.00
☐106	10¢ Green	—	1500.00	—	2400.00
☐107	12¢ Black	—	2400.00	—	2800.00
☐108	15¢ Black	—	2100.00	—	3000.00
☐109	24¢ Deep Violet	—	2100.00	—	3600.00
☐110	30¢ Brownish Orange	—	3000.00	—	4300.00
☐111	90¢ Blue	—	4000.00	—	10000.00

Scott No.		Fine Unused Each	Ave. Unused Each	Fine Used Each	Ave. Used Each
1869. PICTORIAL ISSUES					
GRILL ABOUT 9½ x 9½ MM.					
☐ 112	1¢ Buff	215.00	130.00	70.00	40.00
☐ 113	2¢ Brown	160.00	100.00	30.00	16.00
☐ 114	3¢ Ultramarine	150.00	75.00	7.00	5.00
☐ 115	6¢ Ultramarine	700.00	400.00	90.00	60.00
☐ 116	10¢ Yellow	750.00	420.00	95.00	52.00
☐ 117	12¢ Green	700.00	400.00	100.00	70.00
☐ 118	15¢ Brown & Blue (I)	1600.00	900.00	275.00	160.00
☐ 119	15¢ Brown & Blue (II)	800.00	500.00	145.00	84.00
☐ 120	24¢ Green & Violet	2100.00	1200.00	450.00	300.00
☐ 121	30¢ Blue & Carmine	2000.00	1100.00	300.00	150.00
☐ 122	90¢ Carmine & Black	6000.00	3000.00	1100.00	700.00
1875. RE-ISSUE OF 1869 ISSUE. HARD WHITE PAPER—					
WITHOUT GRILL					
☐ 123	1¢ Buff	310.00	175.00	215.00	130.00
☐ 124	2¢ Brown	400.00	200.00	300.00	185.00
☐ 125	3¢ Blue	2600.00	1900.00	1200.00	900.00
☐ 126	6¢ Blue	—	700.00	—	400.00
☐ 127	10¢ Yellow	—	800.00	—	800.00
☐ 128	12¢ Green	—	1200.00	—	900.00
☐ 129	15¢ Brown & Blue (III)	—	1100.00	—	420.00
☐ 130	24¢ Green & Violet	—	1000.00	—	390.00
☐ 131	30¢ Blue & Carmine	—	1250.00	—	760.00
☐ 132	90¢ Carmine & Black	—	3800.00	—	4000.00
1880. SAME AS ABOVE—SOFT POROUS PAPER					
☐ 133	1¢ Buff	200.00	110.00	130.00	95.00
1870–1871. PRINTED BY NATIONAL BANK NOTE CO.—GRILLED					
☐ 134	1¢ Ultramarine	470.00	260.00	60.00	34.00
☐ 135	2¢ Red Brown	340.00	193.00	32.00	22.00
☐ 136	3¢ Green	270.00	157.00	11.00	7.00
☐ 137	6¢ Carmine	1500.00	800.00	230.00	140.00
☐ 138	7¢ Vermilion	1100.00	650.00	225.00	130.00
☐ 139	10¢ Brown	1350.00	750.00	380.00	225.00
☐ 140	12¢ Light Violet	—	—	2200.00	900.00
☐ 141	15¢ Orange	1410.00	710.00	660.00	400.00
☐ 142	24¢ Purple	—	—	—	6300.00
☐ 143	30¢ Black	—	2400.00	750.00	450.00
☐ 144	90¢ Carmine	—	3000.00	700.00	400.00
1870–1871. SAME AS ABOVE—WITHOUT GRILL					
☐ 145	1¢ Ultramarine	160.00	100.00	7.00	4.50
☐ 146	2¢ Red Brown	68.00	40.00	6.00	3.00
☐ 147	3¢ Green	120.00	63.00	150.00	1.00
☐ 148	6¢ Carmine	235.00	130.00	12.00	8.50
☐ 149	7¢ Vermilion	315.00	180.00	50.00	30.00
☐ 150	10¢ Brown	240.00	125.00	14.00	8.00

Scott No.		Fine Unused Each	Ave. Unused Each	Fine Used Each	Ave. Used Each
☐ 151	12¢ Dull Violet	500.00	300.00	56.00	36.00
☐ 152	15¢ Bright Orange	460.00	260.00	60.00	34.00
☐ 153	24¢ Purple	580.00	315.00	85.00	45.00
☐ 154	30¢ Black	950.00	520.00	90.00	52.00
☐ 155	90¢ Carmine	1175.00	670.00	170.00	99.00

1873. SAME DESIGNS AS 1870–1871 ISSUE—WITH SECRET MARKS
PRINTED BY THE CONTINENTAL BANK NOTE CO.
THIN HARD GRAYISH WHITE PAPER

☐ 156	1¢ Ultramarine	59.00	34.00	3.00	1.50
☐ 157	2¢ Brown	145.00	90.00	9.00	5.00
☐ 158	3¢ Green	48.00	28.00	.25	.20
☐ 159	6¢ Dull Pink	190.00	115.00	10.00	7.00
☐ 160	7¢ Orange Vermilion	380.00	222.00	61.00	32.00
☐ 161	10¢ Brown	185.00	120.00	10.00	7.00
☐ 162	12¢ Black Violet	500.00	300.00	68.00	40.00
☐ 163	15¢ Yellow Orange	500.00	290.00	56.00	36.00
☐ 165	30¢ Gray Black	500.00	300.00	56.00	36.00
☐ 166	90¢ Rose Carmine	1100.00	670.00	170.00	106.00

1875. REGULAR ISSUE

☐ 178	2¢ Vermilion	152.00	90.00	6.00	3.00
☐ 179	5¢ Blue	170.00	96.00	10.00	5.50

1879. SAME DESIGNS AS 1870–1875 ISSUES
PRINTED BY THE AMERICAN BANK NOTE CO.
SOFT POROUS YELLOWISH WHITE PAPER

☐ 182	1¢ Dark Ultramarine	112.00	66.00	1.50	1.00
☐ 183	2¢ Vermilion	55.00	35.00	1.50	1.00
☐ 184	3¢ Green	46.00	28.00	.25	.15
☐ 185	5¢ Blue	200.00	120.00	8.00	4.50
☐ 186	6¢ Pink	450.00	280.00	11.50	7.50
☐ 187	10¢ Brown (no secret mark)	700.00	400.00	15.00	8.75
☐ 188	10¢ Brown (secret mark)	460.00	250.00	19.00	9.00
☐ 188b	10¢ Black Brown	650.00	360.00	65.00	30.00
☐ 189	15¢ Red Orange	172.00	88.00	18.00	9.00
☐ 190	30¢ Full Black	450.00	260.00	30.00	17.00
☐ 191	90¢ Carmine	950.00	600.00	150.00	90.00

1882. REGULAR ISSUE

☐ 205	5¢ Yellow Brown	110.00	60.00	6.00	3.00

1881–1882. DESIGNS OF 1873 ISSUE RE-ENGRAVED (N-H ADD 95%)

☐ 206	1¢ Gray Blue	35.00	20.00	.90	.50
☐ 207	3¢ Blue Green	40.00	22.00	.30	.19
☐ 208	6¢ Rose	205.00	115.00	50.00	30.00
☐ 208a	6¢ Brown Red	200.00	110.00	60.00	32.00

Scott No.		Fine Unused Each	Ave. Unused Each	Fine Used Each	Ave. Used Each
☐ 209	10¢ Brown	90.00	42.00	3.00	1.50
☐ 209b	10¢ Black Brown	115.00	52.00	8.00	5.00

1883. REGULAR ISSUE

☐ 210	2¢ Red Brown	28.00	16.00	.20	.15
☐ 211	4¢ Blue Green	135.00	75.00	7.50	4.50

1887. REGULAR ISSUE

☐ 212	1¢ Ultramarine	60.00	30.00	.80	.50
☐ 213	2¢ Green	28.00	22.00	.16	.14
☐ 214	3¢ Vermilion	52.00	36.00	33.00	21.00

1888. SAME DESIGNS AS 1870–1883 ISSUES

☐ 215	4¢ Carmine	170.00	65.00	11.00	7.00
☐ 216	5¢ Indigo	170.00	75.00	7.00	4.00
☐ 217	30¢ Orange Brown	390.00	180.00	75.00	42.00
☐ 218	90¢ Purple	800.00	400.00	130.00	75.00

IMPORTANT NOTICE: From this point onward, values of unused stamps and blocks are for specimens with original gum. Prices given for **blocks** are for blocks of 4, **without** plate number.

Scott No.		Fine Unused Block	Ave. Unused Block	Fine Unused Each	Ave. Unused Each	Fine Used Each	Ave. Used Each
1890–1893. SMALL DESIGN (N-H ADD 95%)							
☐ 219	1¢ Dull Blue	200.00	110.00	24.00	10.00	.16	.14
☐ 219D	2¢ Lake	850.00	650.00	160.00	75.00	.60	.30
☐ 220	2¢ Carmine	135.00	90.00	18.00	9.00	.16	.12
☐ 220a	2¢ Carmine (Cap on left 2)	300.00	250.00	55.00	26.00	1.10	.75
☐ 220c	2¢ Carmine (Cap both 2's)	1000.00	700.00	140.00	60.00	7.50	4.25
☐ 221	3¢ Purple	550.00	330.00	65.00	25.00	4.50	3.75
☐ 222	4¢ Dark Brown	610.00	400.00	65.00	26.00	2.00	1.10
☐ 223	5¢ Chocolate	900.00	400.00	65.00	28.00	2.00	1.10
☐ 224	6¢ Brown Red	600.00	375.00	65.00	28.00	15.00	8.50
☐ 225	8¢ Lilac	400.00	300.00	50.00	20.00	8.00	6.00
☐ 226	10¢ Green	750.00	600.00	115.00	50.00	210.00	1.75
☐ 227	15¢ Indigo	1100.00	700.00	170.00	70.00	19.00	8.50
☐ 228	30¢ Black	1400.00	1000.00	260.00	90.00	20.00	11.50
☐ 229	90¢ Orange	3700.00	2600.00	390.00	160.00	100.00	49.00
1893. COLUMBIAN ISSUE (N-H ADD 95%)							
☐ 230	1¢ Blue	185.00	110.00	25.00	18.00	.40	.30
☐ 231	2¢ Violet	185.00	110.00	26.00	13.00	.16	.15
☐ 231c	2¢ "Broken Hat"	400.00	300.00	75.00	48.00	.60	.36
☐ 232	3¢ Green	315.00	250.00	52.00	37.00	16.00	9.00
☐ 233	4¢ Ultramarine	590.00	490.00	82.00	49.00	6.00	5.00
☐ 234	5¢ Chocolate	615.00	490.00	85.00	55.00	7.00	5.00
☐ 235	6¢ Purple	615.00	490.00	80.00	52.00	21.00	12.00
☐ 236	8¢ Magenta	610.00	440.00	40.00	29.00	9.00	5.00
☐ 237	10¢ Black Brown	900.00	500.00	119.00	75.00	7.00	4.00
☐ 238	15¢ Dark Green	2000.00	1500.00	200.00	135.00	60.00	32.00

Scott No.		Fine Unused Block	Ave. Unused Block	Fine Unused Each	Ave. Unused Each	Fine Used Each	Ave. Used Each
☐ 239	30¢ Orange Brown	3000.00	2200.00	370.00	160.00	90.00	46.00
☐ 240	50¢ Slate Blue	3000.00	2500.00	410.00	210.00	160.00	85.00
☐ 241	$1 Salmon	—	—	1100.00	650.00	500.00	310.00
☐ 242	$2 Brown Red	—	—	1250.00	700.00	450.00	290.00
☐ 243	$3 Yellow Green	—	—	2600.00	1400.00	900.00	540.00
☐ 244	$4 Crimson Lake	—	—	3700.00	1700.00	1200.00	710.00
☐ 245	$5 Black	—	—	3800.00	1900.00	1400.00	850.00

1894. UNWATERMARKED (N-H ADD 95%)

Scott No.		Fine Unused Block	Ave. Unused Block	Fine Unused Each	Ave. Unused Each	Fine Used Each	Ave. Used Each
☐ 246	1¢ Ultramarine	170.00	130.00	21.00	14.00	3.70	2.00
☐ 247	1¢ Blue	360.00	210.00	50.00	30.00	2.00	1.00
☐ 248	2¢ Pink, Type I	110.00	80.00	19.00	10.00	2.00	1.10
☐ 249	2¢ Carmine Lake, Type I	700.00	600.00	100.00	70.00	1.30	1.00
☐ 250	2¢ Carmine, Type I	200.00	170.00	20.00	14.00	.30	.16
☐ 251	2¢ Carmine, Type II	1300.00	1300.00	160.00	90.00	3.00	2.00
☐ 252	2¢ Carmine, Type III	500.00	315.00	87.00	53.00	3.00	1.75
☐ 253	3¢ Purple	500.00	315.00	70.00	45.00	7.00	4.00
☐ 254	4¢ Dark Brown	600.00	410.00	80.00	48.00	4.00	1.60
☐ 255	5¢ Chocolate	550.00	400.00	69.00	42.00	4.00	2.00
☐ 256	6¢ Dull Brown	1000.00	710.00	140.00	74.00	16.00	8.50
☐ 257	8¢ Violet Brown	900.00	620.00	100.00	60.00	11.00	6.00
☐ 258	10¢ Dark Green	1600.00	1200.00	160.00	90.00	8.00	4.50
☐ 259	15¢ Dark Blue	2000.00	1600.00	215.00	140.00	42.00	28.00
☐ 260	50¢ Orange	2500.00	2000.00	300.00	200.00	70.00	38.00
☐ 261	$1 Black (I)	6000.00	4600.00	600.00	400.00	230.00	130.00
☐ 261A	$1 Black (II)	—	—	1500.00	900.00	410.00	270.00
☐ 262	$2 Blue	—	—	1800.00	1100.00	600.00	350.00
☐ 263	$5 Dark Green	—	—	2600.00	1600.00	900.00	600.00

1895. DOUBLE LINE WATERMARKED "U.S.P.S." PERF. 12 (N-H ADD 95%)

Scott No.		Fine Unused Block	Ave. Unused Block	Fine Unused Each	Ave. Unused Each	Fine Used Each	Ave. Used Each
☐ 264	1¢ Blue	48.00	38.00	6.00	4.00	.18	.15
☐ 265	2¢ Carmine, Type I	220.00	180.00	21.00	14.00	.80	.50
☐ 266	2¢ Carmine, Type II	290.00	200.00	20.00	17.00	3.00	1.90
☐ 267	2¢ Carmine, Type III	45.00	30.00	5.00	3.00	.16	.15
☐ 268	3¢ Purple	300.00	180.00	30.00	19.00	1.40	.75
☐ 269	4¢ Dark Brown	310.00	210.00	32.00	20.00	1.50	.70
☐ 270	5¢ Chocolate	300.00	210.00	31.00	18.00	2.00	1.10
☐ 271	6¢ Dull Brown	400.00	300.00	50.00	32.00	4.00	2.10
☐ 272	8¢ Violet Brown	260.00	160.00	36.00	25.00	1.25	.65
☐ 273	10¢ Dark Green	380.00	210.00	50.00	30.00	1.50	.80
☐ 274	15¢ Dark Blue	850.00	700.00	160.00	85.00	9.00	5.00
☐ 275	50¢ Dull Orange	1200.00	1100.00	200.00	130.00	20.00	12.00
☐ 276	$1 Black (I)	2700.00	1850.00	500.00	300.00	60.00	40.00
☐ 276A	$1 Black (II)	—	—	1100.00	750.00	115.00	75.00
☐ 277	$2 Blue	—	—	800.00	650.00	260.00	145.00
☐ 278	$5 Dark Green	—	—	1600.00	1000.00	400.00	225.00

Scott No.		Fine Unused Block	Ave. Unused Block	Fine Unused Each	Ave. Unused Each	Fine Used Each	Ave. Used Each
1898. REGULAR ISSUE PERF. (N-H ADD 95%)							
☐279	1¢ Deep Green	72.00	45.00	8.00	5.00	.16	.14
☐279B	2¢ Red	70.00	45.00	12.00	5.00	.16	.14
☐279C	2¢ Rose Carmine	650.00	610.00	140.00	80.00	35.00	21.00
☐279D	2¢ Orange Red	70.00	50.00	13.00	10.00	.25	.16
☐280	4¢ Rose Brown	200.00	130.00	30.00	19.00	1.75	.72
☐281	5¢ Dark Blue	210.00	160.00	37.00	21.00	1.75	.72
☐282	6¢ Lake	350.00	210.00	42.00	24.00	2.70	1.30
☐282a	6¢ Purplish Lake	500.00	310.00	50.00	28.00	3.10	1.60
☐282C	10¢ Brown (I)	860.00	600.00	140.00	85.00	3.00	1.50
☐283	10¢ Orange Brown (II)	710.00	510.00	100.00	62.00	2.60	1.30
☐284	15¢ Olive Green	810.00	580.00	110.00	74.00	8.00	4.60
1898. TRANS-MISSISSIPPI EXPOSITION ISSUE (N-H ADD 90%)							
☐285	1¢ Yellow Green	240.00	130.00	30.00	15.00	6.00	3.50
☐286	2¢ Copper Red	240.00	110.00	22.00	14.00	2.00	.90
☐287	4¢ Orange	900.00	600.00	120.00	80.00	26.00	12.00
☐288	5¢ Dull Blue	900.00	600.00	110.00	75.00	21.00	12.00
☐289	8¢ Violet Brown	1000.00	700.00	160.00	85.00	40.00	22.00
☐290	10¢ Gray Violet	1400.00	1000.00	190.00	100.00	21.00	15.00
☐291	50¢ Sage Green	—	—	600.00	400.00	160.00	95.00
☐292	$1 Black	—	—	1600.00	900.00	500.00	350.00
☐293	$2 Orange Brown	—	—	2100.00	1900.00	800.00	450.00
1901. PAN-AMERICAN ISSUE (N-H ADD 75%)							
☐294	1¢ Green & Black	150.00	110.00	18.00	11.00	5.00	3.00
☐295	2¢ Carmine & Black	140.00	110.00	20.00	10.00	1.40	.70
☐296	4¢ Chocolate & Black	700.00	400.00	90.00	50.00	18.00	11.00
☐297	5¢ Ultramarine & Black	700.00	500.00	90.00	55.00	18.00	10.00
☐298	8¢ Brown Violet Black	950.00	700.00	110.00	70.00	60.00	40.00
☐299	10¢ Yellow Brown Black	1250.00	1000.00	200.00	100.00	30.00	19.00
1902–1903. PERF. 12 (N-H ADD 80%)							
☐300	1¢ Blue Green	75.00	55.00	12.00	5.00	.16	.14
☐301	2¢ Carmine	100.00	62.00	12.00	6.00	.16	.14
☐302	3¢ Violet	460.00	310.00	50.00	25.00	3.50	2.00
☐303	4¢ Brown	470.00	310.00	58.00	26.00	1.20	.60
☐304	5¢ Blue	610.00	390.00	60.00	30.00	1.10	.60
☐305	6¢ Claret	610.00	450.00	60.00	30.00	2.50	1.40
☐306	8¢ Violet Black	310.00	260.00	42.00	21.00	2.00	1.10
☐307	10¢ Red Brown	710.00	610.00	60.00	35.00	1.70	.90
☐308	13¢ Purple Black	290.00	190.00	40.00	21.00	9.00	6.00
☐309	15¢ Olive Green	1100.00	700.00	150.00	75.00	6.00	4.00
☐310	50¢ Orange	3800.00	2700.00	500.00	200.00	26.00	15.00
☐311	$1 Black	5000.00	4000.00	600.00	400.00	50.00	30.00
☐312	$2 Dark Blue	—	—	1100.00	500.00	200.00	110.00
☐313	$5 Dark Green	—	—	2400.00	1100.00	600.00	340.00

Scott No.		Fine Unused Block	Ave. Unused Block	Fine Unused Each	Ave. Unused Each	Fine Used Each	Ave. Used Each
1906–1908. IMPERFORATED (N-H ADD 70%)							
☐314	1¢ Blue Green	175.00	115.00	32.00	21.00	21.00	16.00
☐315	5¢ Blue	4000.00	3000.00	600.00	475.00	310.00	210.00
1903. PERF. 12 (N-H ADD 50%)							
☐319	2¢ Carmine	64.00	41.00	9.50	5.00	.18	.14
☐319a	2¢ Lake	90.00	62.00	10.00	6.00	.21	.16
1906. IMPERFORATED (N-H ADD 70%)							
☐320	2¢ Carmine	190.00	115.00	26.00	18.00	18.00	11.00
☐320a	2¢ Lake	390.00	275.00	68.00	42.00	38.00	23.00
1904. LOUISIANA PURCHASE ISSUE							
PERF. 12 (N-H ADD 75%)							
☐323	1¢ Green	200.00	150.00	30.00	16.00	6.00	3.00
☐324	2¢ Carmine	200.00	150.00	28.00	13.00	2.00	1.10
☐325	3¢ Violet	500.00	380.00	86.00	42.00	30.00	20.00
☐326	5¢ Dark Blue	600.00	600.00	100.00	50.00	21.00	14.00
☐327	10¢ Red Brown	1500.00	1000.00	200.00	110.00	30.00	21.00
1907. JAMESTOWN EXPOSITION ISSUE (N-H ADD 75%)							
☐328	1¢ Green	200.00	175.00	20.00	14.00	5.00	2.00
☐329	2¢ Carmine	210.00	160.00	26.00	15.00	5.00	2.10
☐330	5¢ Blue	1100.00	800.00	140.00	75.00	28.00	16.00
1908–1909. DOUBLE LINE WATERMARKED "U.S.P.S."							
PERF. 12 (N-H ADD 50%)							
☐331	1¢ Green	44.00	29.00	7.00	5.00	.16	.14
☐332	2¢ Carmine	42.00	29.00	7.00	5.00	.16	.14
☐333	3¢ Violet	300.00	200.00	28.00	18.00	3.00	1.90
☐334	4¢ Orange Brown	270.00	170.00	30.00	19.00	1.20	.75
☐335	5¢ Blue	310.00	250.00	42.00	25.00	2.30	1.40
☐336	6¢ Red Orange	400.00	300.00	50.00	30.00	5.00	3.00
☐337	8¢ Olive Green	310.00	160.00	29.00	22.00	3.00	1.80
☐338	10¢ Yellow	460.00	310.00	60.00	38.00	1.90	.90
☐339	13¢ Blue Green	410.00	240.00	38.00	22.00	26.00	18.00
☐340	15¢ Pale Ultramarine	420.00	300.00	60.00	36.00	7.00	4.50
☐341	50¢ Violet	1500.00	1200.00	250.00	150.00	17.00	10.00
☐342	$1 Violet Black	2400.00	1600.00	400.00	260.00	75.00	50.00
IMPERFORATE (N-H ADD 65%)							
☐343	1¢ Green	58.00	38.00	8.00	5.00	4.00	3.00
☐344	2¢ Carmine	100.00	65.00	12.00	6.00	4.00	3.00
☐345	3¢ Deep Violet	190.00	100.00	22.00	13.00	16.00	9.50
☐346	4¢ Orange Brown	380.00	240.00	36.00	22.00	21.00	12.00
☐347	5¢ Blue	460.00	280.00	58.00	32.00	30.00	21.00

Scott No.		Fine Unused Line Pair	Ave. Unused Line Pair	Fine Unused Each	Ave. Unused Each	Fine Used Each	Ave. Used Each

1908–1910. COIL STAMPS
PERF. 12 HORIZONTALLY (N-H ADD 70%)

☐ 348	1¢ Green	175.00	125.00	22.00	14.00	12.00	7.50
☐ 349	2¢ Carmine	200.00	130.00	50.00	30.00	8.00	5.00
☐ 350	4¢ Orange Brown	7.00	390.00	110.00	60.00	70.00	43.00
☐ 351	5¢ Blue	725.00	400.00	120.00	60.00	85.00	55.00

PERF. 12 VERTICALLY (N-H ADD 70%)

☐ 352	1¢ Green	290.00	175.00	60.00	26.00	26.00	17.00
☐ 353	2¢ Carmine	275.00	160.00	51.00	25.00	8.50	6.00
☐ 354	4¢ Orange Brown	600.00	500.00	120.00	65.00	50.00	30.00
☐ 355	5¢ Blue	700.00	550.00	130.00	65.00	65.00	42.00
☐ 356	10¢ Yellow	—	—	1300.00	800.00	600.00	400.00

Scott No.		Fine Unused Block	Ave. Unused Block	Fine Unused Each	Ave. Unused Each	Fine Used Each	Ave. Used Each

1909. BLUISH GRAY PAPER
PERF. 12 (N-H ADD 70%)

☐ 357	1¢ Green	700.00	450.00	110.00	65.00	100.00	55.00
☐ 358	2¢ Carmine	700.00	440.00	110.00	68.00	85.00	50.00
☐ 359	3¢ Violet	—	—	1400.00	900.00	—	—
☐ 360	4¢ Orange Brown	—	—	10000.00	8000.00	—	—
☐ 361	5¢ Blue	—	—	3000.00	1900.00	—	—
☐ 362	6¢ Orange	—	—	1000.00	700.00	—	—
☐ 363	8¢ Olive Green	—	—	1200.00	700.00	—	—
☐ 364	10¢ Yellow	—	—	1100.00	650.00	—	—
☐ 365	13¢ Blue Green	—	—	2000.00	1200.00	—	—
☐ 366	15¢ Pale Ultramarine	—	—	900.00	650.00	—	—

1909. LINCOLN MEMORIAL ISSUE (N-H ADD 75%)

☐ 367	2¢ Carmine	90.00	89.00	9.00	5.00	3.00	2.00
☐ 368	2¢ Carmine, Impf.	200.00	170.00	35.00	25.00	28.00	12.00
☐ 369	2¢ Carmine (On B.G. Paper)	1400.00	1100.00	250.00	160.00	200.00	125.00

1909. ALASKA-YUKON ISSUE (N-H ADD 70%)

☐ 370	2¢ Carmine	200.00	185.00	10.00	7.00	2.50	—
☐ 371	2¢ Carmine, Impf.	280.00	200.00	36.00	28.00	32.00	18.00

1909. HUDSON-FULTON ISSUE (N-H ADD 70%)

☐ 372	2¢ Carmine	190.00	170.00	14.00	8.50	5.00	3.00
☐ 373	2¢ Carmine, Impf.	375.00	280.00	50.00	32.00	32.00	20.00

1910–1911. SINGLE LINE WATERMARKED "U.S.P.S."
PERF. 12 (N-H ADD 75%)

☐ 374	1¢ Green	70.00	48.00	7.00	6.00	.16	.14
☐ 375	2¢ Carmine	65.00	38.00	7.00	5.00	.16	.14
☐ 376	3¢ Deep Violet	110.00	100.00	17.00	12.00	1.80	1.10
☐ 377	4¢ Brown	160.00	120.00	26.00	16.00	.55	.36

Scott No.		Fine Unused Block	Ave. Unused Block	Fine Unused Each	Ave. Unused Each	Fine Used Each	Ave. Used Each
☐ 378	5¢ Blue	200.00	140.00	26.00	16.00	.50	.30
☐ 379	6¢ Red Orange	310.00	180.00	32.00	21.00	.80	.50
☐ 380	8¢ Olive Green	600.00	400.00	95.00	60.00	14.00	8.00
☐ 381	10¢ Yellow	500.00	400.00	90.00	60.00	4.00	3.00
☐ 382	15¢ Ultramarine	1300.00	1000.00	210.00	150.00	14.00	9.00

IMPERFORATE (N-H ADD 70%)

☐ 383	1¢ Green	41.00	32.00	5.00	3.00	3.00	2.00
☐ 384	2¢ Carmine	100.00	92.00	7.00	3.50	1.70	1.25

Scott No.		Fine Unused Line Pair	Ave. Unused Line Pair	Fine Unused Each	Ave. Unused Each	Fine Used Each	Ave. Used Each

1910–1913. COIL STAMPS
PERF. 12 HORIZONTALLY (N-H ADD 70%)

☐ 385	1¢ Green	200.00	128.00	26.00	16.00	15.00	8.00
☐ 386	2¢ Carmine	375.00	240.00	35.00	21.00	14.00	7.00

PERF. 12 VERTICALLY (N-H ADD 70%)

☐ 387	1¢ Green	300.00	175.00	65.00	35.00	26.00	16.00
☐ 388	2¢ Carmine	2800.00	2000.00	450.00	360.00	115.00	65.00

PERF. 8½ HORIZONTALLY (N-H ADD 70%)

☐ 390	1¢ Green	28.00	18.00	6.00	3.00	4.00	2.10
☐ 391	2¢ Carmine	200.00	110.00	32.00	17.00	9.00	6.00

PERF. 8½ VERTICALLY (N-H ADD 70%)

☐ 392	1¢ Green	100.00	65.00	17.00	10.00	15.00	10.00
☐ 393	2¢ Carmine	180.00	110.00	35.00	21.00	6.00	5.00
☐ 394	3¢ Violet	280.00	160.00	45.00	30.00	37.00	23.00
☐ 395	4¢ Brown	275.00	160.00	45.00	30.00	29.00	18.00
☐ 396	5¢ Blue	210.00	160.00	44.00	30.00	29.00	17.00

Scott No.		Fine Unused Block	Ave. Unused Block	Fine Unused Each	Ave. Unused Each	Fine Used Each	Ave. Used Each

1913–1915. PANAMA-PACIFIC ISSUE
PERF. 12 (N-H ADD 80%)

☐ 397	1¢ Green	125.00	88.00	15.00	10.00	2.00	1.10
☐ 398	2¢ Carmine	225.00	150.00	16.00	11.00	.80	.50
☐ 399	5¢ Blue	500.00	400.00	60.00	40.00	12.00	6.00
☐ 400	10¢ Orange Yellow	800.00	600.00	130.00	85.00	28.00	15.00
☐ 400A	10¢ Orange	1400.00	1100.00	190.00	110.00	21.00	12.00

PERF. 10 (N-H ADD 80%)

☐ 401	1¢ Green	260.00	170.00	21.00	16.00	8.00	5.00
☐ 402	2¢ Carmine	400.00	300.00	70.00	45.00	2.00	1.25
☐ 403	5¢ Blue	1600.00	1100.00	160.00	100.00	16.00	12.00
☐ 404	10¢ Orange	6000.00	4000.00	900.00	600.00	70.00	45.00

1912–1914. REGULAR ISSUE
PERF. 12 (N-H ADD 70%)

Scott No.		Fine Unused Block	Ave. Unused Block	Fine Unused Each	Ave. Unused Each	Fine Used Each	Ave. Used Each
☐405	1¢ Green	85.00	50.00	7.00	4.00	.17	.14
☐406	2¢ Carmine	100.00	70.00	7.00	4.00	.17	.14
☐407	7¢ Black	510.00	410.00	80.00	50.00	7.00	5.00

IMPERFORATE (N-H ADD 70%)

☐408	1¢ Green	17.00	13.00	1.50	1.00	.65	.55
☐409	2¢ Carmine	35.00	26.00	1.50	1.00	.65	.55

1912. COIL STAMPS
PERF. 8½ HORIZONTALLY (N-H ADD 70%)

Scott No.		Fine Unused Line Pair	Ave. Unused Line Pair	Fine Unused Each	Ave. Unused Each	Fine Used Each	Ave. Used Each
☐410	1¢ Green	60.00	40.00	6.00	5.00	3.50	2.00
☐411	2¢ Carmine	60.00	40.00	9.00	6.00	3.00	2.00

PERF. 8½ VERTICALLY (N-H ADD 80%)

☐412	1¢ Green	110.00	60.00	18.00	12.00	5.00	3.00
☐413	2¢ Carmine	160.00	100.00	28.00	18.00	.90	.50

1912–1914. SINGLE LINE WATERMARKED "U.S.P.S."
PERF. 12 (N-H ADD 75%)

Scott No.		Fine Unused Block	Ave. Unused Block	Fine Unused Each	Ave. Unused Each	Fine Used Each	Ave. Used Each
☐414	8¢ Olive Green	200.00	110.00	34.00	24.00	1.50	1.00
☐415	9¢ Salmon Red	210.00	160.00	42.00	26.00	14.00	8.00
☐416	10¢ Orange Yellow	210.00	160.00	35.00	24.00	50.00	.25
☐417	12¢ Claret Brown	275.00	160.00	36.00	25.00	4.00	3.00
☐418	15¢ Gray	475.00	600.00	60.00	40.00	4.00	2.00
☐419	20¢ Ultramarine	1100.00	700.00	160.00	95.00	15.00	8.50
☐420	30¢ Orange Red	800.00	600.00	100.00	70.00	15.00	8.50
☐421	50¢ Violet	2600.00	1600.00	400.00	240.00	16.00	9.75

1912. DOUBLE LINE WATERMARKED "U.S.P.S." (N-H ADD 75%)

☐422	50¢ Violet	1600.00	1200.00	210.00	140.00	17.00	10.00
☐423	$1 Violet Black	3000.00	2000.00	500.00	300.00	60.00	40.00

1914–1915. SINGLE LINE WATERMARKED "U.S.P.S."
PERF. 10 (N-H ADD 55%)

☐424	1¢ Green	35.00	25.00	3.00	2.00	.16	.14
☐425	2¢ Carmine	26.00	17.00	3.50	2.10	.16	.14
☐426	3¢ Deep Violet	110.00	65.00	12.00	8.00	1.75	1.00
☐427	4¢ Brown	230.00	80.00	27.00	18.00	.60	.40
☐428	5¢ Blue	230.00	170.00	26.00	16.00	.60	.35
☐429	6¢ Orange	230.00	130.00	32.00	20.00	1.40	.90

Scott No.		Fine Unused Block	Ave. Unused Block	Fine Unused Each	Ave. Unused Each	Fine Used Each	Ave. Used Each
☐ 430	7¢ Black	400.00	300.00	80.00	50.00	5.00	3.00
☐ 431	8¢ Olive Green	270.00	190.00	30.00	22.00	2.00	1.10
☐ 432	9¢ Salmon Red	400.00	300.00	40.00	26.00	8.00	5.00
☐ 433	12¢ Orange Yellow	330.00	200.00	35.00	25.00	.35	.20
☐ 434	11¢ Dark Green	160.00	100.00	18.00	12.00	6.50	4.50
☐ 435	12¢ Claret Brown	200.00	135.00	20.00	13.00	4.00	2.50
☐ 435a	12¢ Copper Red	200.00	140.00	24.00	15.00	4.00	2.70
☐ 437	15¢ Gray	800.00	600.00	95.00	60.00	7.00	4.00
☐ 438	20¢ Ultramarine	1100.00	800.00	200.00	115.00	5.00	2.80
☐ 439	30¢ Orange Red	1200.00	900.00	215.00	150.00	18.00	9.00
☐ 440	50¢ Violet	3000.00	2500.00	600.00	400.00	18.00	11.00

Scott No.		Fine Unused Line Pair	Ave. Unused Line Pair	Fine Unused Each	Ave. Unused Each	Fine Used Each	Ave. Used Each
1914. COIL STAMPS							
PERF. 10 HORIZONTALLY (N-H ADD 75%)							
☐ 441	1¢ Green	7.00	5.00	1.10	.75	1.00	.60
☐ 442	2¢ Carmine	45.00	32.00	9.00	6.00	8.00	5.00
PERF. 10 VERTICALLY (N-H ADD 70%)							
☐ 443	1¢ Green	90.00	67.00	20.00	12.00	6.00	4.00
☐ 444	2¢ Carmine	150.00	95.00	30.00	17.00	1.50	1.50
☐ 445	3¢ Violet	1100.00	1000.00	200.00	130.00	100.00	65.00
☐ 446	4¢ Brown	500.00	350.00	110.00	80.00	35.00	21.00
☐ 447	5¢ Blue	180.00	120.00	40.00	22.00	20.00	13.00
1914–1916. ROTARY PRESS COIL STAMPS							
PERF. 10 HORIZONTALLY (N-H ADD 70%)							
☐ 448	1¢ Green	42.00	26.00	7.00	5.00	3.00	2.00
☐ 449	2¢ Red (I)	—	—	1700.00	1000.00	200.00	160.00
☐ 450	2¢ Carmine (III)	60.00	38.00	10.00	7.00	3.00	2.10
PERF. 10 VERTICALLY (N-H ADD 70%)							
☐ 452	1¢ Green	70.00	40.00	10.00	6.50	2.00	1.10
☐ 453	2¢ Red (I)	600.00	300.00	100.00	65.00	4.50	3.00
☐ 454	2¢ Carmine (II)	500.00	300.00	110.00	70.00	12.00	8.00
☐ 455	2¢ Carmine (III)	80.00	50.00	8.00	7.00	1.10	.80
☐ 456	3¢ Violet	1000.00	700.00	240.00	150.00	100.00	70.00
☐ 457	4¢ Brown	135.00	85.00	32.00	17.00	18.00	11.00
☐ 458	5¢ Blue	130.00	95.00	38.00	21.00	18.00	12.00
IMPERFORATE (N-H ADD 60%)							
☐ 459	2¢ Carmine	1800.00	1200.00	410.00	325.00	—	—

Scott No.		Fine Unused Block	Ave. Unused Block	Fine Unused Each	Ave. Unused Each	Fine Used Each	Ave. Used Each

1915. DOUBLE LINE WATERMARKED "U.S.P.S." PERF. 10 (N-H ADD 60%)

| ☐ 460 | $1 Violet Black .... | 4100.00 | 3700.00 | 800.00 | 500.00 | 90.00 | 55.00 |

1915. SINGLE LINE WATERMARKED "U.S.P.S." PERF. 11 (N-H ADD 60%)

| ☐ 461 | 2¢ Pale Carmine Rose ... | 300.00 | 120.00 | 80.00 | 70.00 | 50.00 | — |

1916–1917. UNWATERMARKED PERF. 10 (N-H ADD 70%)

☐ 462	1¢ Green	100.00	70.00	8.00	5.00	.40	.20
☐ 463	2¢ Carmine	100.00	62.00	4.00	3.00	.18	.15
☐ 464	3¢ Violet	400.00	290.00	70.00	50.00	15.00	10.00
☐ 465	4¢ Orange Brown	400.00	250.00	45.00	28.00	2.10	1.50
☐ 466	5¢ Blue	425.00	300.00	70.00	45.00	2.10	1.50
☐ 467	5¢ Carmine (error)	—	900.00	600.00	500.00	—	—
☐ 468	6¢ Red Orange	500.00	350.00	80.00	50.00	7.00	5.00
☐ 469	7¢ Black	600.00	450.00	110.00	70.00	15.00	8.00
☐ 470	58¢ Olive Green	410.00	320.00	48.00	32.00	6.00	4.00
☐ 471	9¢ Salmon Red	340.00	200.00	50.00	32.00	15.00	8.00
☐ 472	12¢ Orange Yellow	600.00	400.00	100.00	70.00	1.10	.60
☐ 473	11¢ Dark Green	230.00	165.00	30.00	18.00	16.00	11.00
☐ 474	12¢ Claret Brown	385.00	250.00	40.00	30.00	6.00	5.00
☐ 475	15¢ Gray	1000.00	800.00	135.00	130.00	11.00	7.00
☐ 476	20¢ Ultramarine	2400.00	1800.00	200.00	150.00	12.00	8.00
☐ 477	50¢ Light Violet	6200.00	4600.00	1100.00	700.00	70.00	45.00
☐ 478	$1 Violet Black	4300.00	2700.00	700.00	500.00	20.00	12.00

1916–1917. DESIGN OF 1902–1903 PERF. 10 (N-H ADD 70%)

| ☐ 479 | $2 Dark Blue .... | 2400.00 | 1800.00 | 450.00 | 260.00 | 42.00 | 28.00 |
| ☐ 480 | $5 Light Green .... | 2300.00 | 1700.00 | 400.00 | 210.00 | 50.00 | 30.00 |

IMPERFORATE (N-H ADD 70%)

☐ 481	1¢ Green	12.00	9.00	1.00	.70	.85	.60
☐ 482	2¢ Carmine	22.00	16.00	2.00	.90	1.60	.85
☐ 483	3¢ Violet (I)	130.00	100.00	16.00	9.00	8.00	5.00
☐ 484	3¢ Violet (II)	92.00	70.00	10.00	7.00	5.00	3.10

Scott No.		Fine Unused Line Pair	Ave. Unused Line Pair	Fine Unused Each	Ave. Unused Each	Fine Used Each	Ave. Used Each

1916–1922. ROTARY PRESS COIL STAMPS PERF. 10 HORIZONTALLY (N-H ADD 60%)

☐ 486	1¢ Green	5.00	4.00	.90	.50	.24	.15
☐ 487	2¢ Carmine (II)	110.00	80.00	18.00	9.00	3.00	2.00
☐ 488	2¢ Carmine (III)	18.00	12.00	4.00	2.00	2.00	1.00
☐ 489	3¢ Violet	32.00	20.00	5.00	3.00	1.50	.80

Scott No.		Fine Unused Line Pair	Ave. Unused Line Pair	Fine Unused Each	Ave. Unused Each	Fine Used Each	Ave. Used Each
PERF. 10 VERTICALLY (N-H ADD 60%)							
☐ 490	1¢ Green	5.00	4.00	.70	.50	.22	.16
☐ 491	2¢ Carmine (II)	—	—	1250.00	830.00	390.00	245.00
☐ 492	2¢ Carmine (III)	50.00	36.00	9.00	6.00	.18	.14
☐ 493	3¢ Violet (I)	110.00	70.00	16.00	11.00	3.00	1.60
☐ 494	3¢ Violet (II)	65.00	45.00	11.00	7.00	.70	.50
☐ 495	4¢ Orange Brown	75.00	50.00	11.00	7.00	4.00	2.00
☐ 496	5¢ Blue	32.00	20.00	5.00	3.00	1.00	.50
☐ 497	10¢ Orange Yellow	110.00	80.00	21.00	16.00	9.00	7.00

Scott No.		Fine Unused Block	Ave. Unused Block	Fine Unused Each	Ave. Unused Each	Fine Used Each	Ave. Used Each
1917–1919. FLAT PLATE PRINTING							
PERF. 11 (N-H ADD 60%)							
☐ 498	1¢ Green	13.00	9.00	.50	.35	.16	.14
☐ 499	2¢ Rose (I)	11.00	7.00	.50	.30	.16	.14
☐ 500	2¢ Deep Rose (Ia)	1500.00	1100.00	210.00	140.00	105.00	68.00
☐ 501	3¢ Violet (I)	140.00	86.00	13.00	10.00	.20	.14
☐ 502	3¢ Violet (II)	140.00	95.00	15.00	10.00	.35	.21
☐ 503	4¢ Brown	130.00	95.00	11.00	7.00	.24	.14
☐ 504	5¢ Blue	115.00	80.00	9.00	6.00	.16	.14
☐ 505	5¢ Rose (error)	—	—	400.00	300.00	—	—
☐ 506	6¢ Red Orange	160.00	105.00	14.00	8.00	.40	.20
☐ 507	7¢ Black	215.00	150.00	27.00	19.00	1.40	.70
☐ 508	8¢ Olive Bistre	142.00	100.00	13.00	7.00	.75	.50
☐ 509	9¢ Salmon Red	145.00	96.00	14.00	10.00	3.00	1.45
☐ 510	10¢ Orange Yellow	180.00	130.00	17.00	11.00	.20	.16
☐ 511	11¢ Light Green	105.00	70.00	10.00	6.00	4.00	2.00
☐ 512	12¢ Claret Brown	115.00	78.00	9.00	6.00	.60	.35
☐ 513	13¢ Apple Green	110.00	72.00	10.00	7.00	7.00	4.00
☐ 514	15¢ Gray	460.00	310.00	40.00	25.00	1.00	.65
☐ 515	20¢ Ultramarine	550.00	400.00	46.00	30.00	.35	.21
☐ 516	30¢ Orange Red	500.00	330.00	45.00	25.00	1.00	.60
☐ 517	50¢ Red Violet	600.00	410.00	85.00	50.00	.90	.50
☐ 518	$1 Violet Brown	800.00	500.00	70.00	50.00	2.00	1.10
☐ 518b	$1 Deep Brown	2900.00	2100.00	700.00	460.00	350.00	220.00
1917. DOUBLE LINE WATERMARKED "U.S.P.S."							
DESIGN OF 1908–1909							
PERF. 11 (N-H ADD 60%)							
☐ 519	2¢ Carmine	1250.00	1000.00	210.00	150.00	200.00	120.00
1918. UNWATERMARKED							
PERF. 11 (N-H ADD 55%)							
☐ 523	$2 Orange Red & Black ..	7500.00	5800.00	800.00	600.00	200.00	115.00
☐ 524	$5 Deep Green & Black ..	3000.00	2100.00	400.00	250.00	30.00	17.00

Scott No.		Fine Unused Block	Ave. Unused Block	Fine Unused Each	Ave. Unused Each	Fine Used Each	Ave. Used Each

1918–1920. OFFSET PRINTING
PERF. 11 (N-H ADD 60%)

Scott No.		Fine Unused Block	Ave. Unused Block	Fine Unused Each	Ave. Unused Each	Fine Used Each	Ave. Used Each
☐ 525	1¢ Gray Green	21.00	13.00	2.00	1.25	.70	.50
☐ 526	2¢ Carmine (IV)	190.00	140.00	26.00	16.00	4.00	2.50
☐ 527	2¢ Carmine (V)	110.00	80.00	14.00	9.00	1.00	.60
☐ 528	2¢ Carmine (Va)	55.00	40.00	8.00	5.00	.21	.18
☐ 528A	2¢ Carmine (VI)	260.00	200.00	41.00	26.00	1.00	.65
☐ 528B	2¢ Carmine (VII)	120.00	85.00	16.00	11.00	.16	.14
☐ 529	3¢ Violet (III)	50.00	28.00	3.00	2.00	.17	.16
☐ 530	3¢ Purple (IV)	11.00	7.00	.90	.60	.16	.14

IMPERFORATE (N-H ADD 60%)

Scott No.		Fine Unused Block	Ave. Unused Block	Fine Unused Each	Ave. Unused Each	Fine Used Each	Ave. Used Each
☐ 531	1¢ Gray Green	95.00	55.00	9.00	7.00	11.00	7.00
☐ 532	2¢ Carmine (IV)	340.00	200.00	40.00	32.00	32.00	21.00
☐ 533	2¢ Carmine (V)	1400.00	900.00	200.00	140.00	65.00	45.00
☐ 534	2¢ Carmine (Va)	110.00	72.00	11.00	8.00	9.00	6.50
☐ 534A	2¢ Carmine (VI)	325.00	175.00	40.00	26.00	28.00	20.00
☐ 534B	2¢ Carmine (VII)	—	—	1400.00	1100.00	400.00	290.00
☐ 535	3¢ Violet	75.00	51.00	9.00	6.00	7.00	5.00

PERF. 12½ (N-H ADD 65%)

Scott No.		Fine Unused Block	Ave. Unused Block	Fine Unused Each	Ave. Unused Each	Fine Used Each	Ave. Used Each
☐ 536	1¢ Gray Green	130.00	82.00	13.00	8.00	12.00	8.00

IMPORTANT NOTICE: Beginning here, prices of **blocks** are for blocks of 4 with **plate number attached.** Ordinary blocks of 4 bring lower prices. Plate blocks consisting of more than 4 stamps would sell higher than these sums. Always check the **headings** of price columns to accurately value your stamps.

Scott No.		Fine Unused Plate Blk	Ave. Unused Plate Blk	Fine Unused Each	Ave. Unused Each	Fine Used Each	Ave. Used Each

1919. VICTORY ISSUE (N-H ADD 45%)

Scott No.		Fine Unused Plate Blk	Ave. Unused Plate Blk	Fine Unused Each	Ave. Unused Each	Fine Used Each	Ave. Used Each
☐ 537	3¢ Violet	100.00	78.00	8.00	7.00	4.00	2.50

1919–1921. REGULAR ISSUE
ROTARY PRESS PRINTING
PERF. 11 x 10 (N-H ADD 70%)

Scott No.		Fine Unused Plate Blk	Ave. Unused Plate Blk	Fine Unused Each	Ave. Unused Each	Fine Used Each	Ave. Used Each
☐ 538	1¢ Green	78.00	52.00	12.00	7.00	9.00	6.00
☐ 538a	Same Impf. Horiz. Pair	—	—	50.00	35.00	—	—
☐ 539	2¢ Carmine Rose (II)	—	—	2200.00	1310.00	600.00	400.00
☐ 540	2¢ Carmine Rose (III)	78.00	60.00	13.00	8.60	9.00	6.00
☐ 540a	Same Impf. Horiz. Pair	—	—	65.00	32.00	—	—
☐ 541	3¢ Violet	300.00	210.00	40.00	21.00	32.00	21.00

PERF. 10 x 11 (N-H ADD 70%)

Scott No.		Fine Unused Plate Blk	Ave. Unused Plate Blk	Fine Unused Each	Ave. Unused Each	Fine Used Each	Ave. Used Each
☐ 542	1¢ Green	125.00	83.00	9.00	6.00	1.00	.70

PERF. 10 x 10 (N-H ADD 70%)

Scott No.		Fine Unused Plate Blk	Ave. Unused Plate Blk	Fine Unused Each	Ave. Unused Each	Fine Used Each	Ave. Used Each
☐ 543	1¢ Green	18.00	10.00	.60	.40	.16	.15

Scott No.		Fine Unused Plate Blk	Ave. Unused Plate Blk	Fine Unused Each	Ave. Unused Each	Fine Used Each	Ave. Used Each
PERF. 11 x 11 (N-H ADD 70%)							
☐544	1¢ Green	—	—	—	—	1650.00	1300.00
☐545	1¢ Green	800.00	700.00	120.00	80.00	120.00	70.00
☐546	2¢ Carmine Rose	500.00	450.00	80.00	60.00	78.00	48.00
FLAT PLATE PRINTING							
PERF. 11 (N-H ADD 60%)							
☐547	$2 Carmine & Black	—	—	400.00	210.00	38.00	24.00
1920. PILGRIM ISSUE (N-H ADD 55%)							
☐548	1¢ Green	45.00	35.00	5.00	4.00	3.00	2.00
☐549	2¢ Carmine Rose	70.00	50.00	7.00	6.00	2.00	1.50
☐550	5¢ Deep Blue	500.00	400.00	45.00	26.00	16.00	10.00
1922–1925. PERF. FLAT PLATE PRINTING							
PERF. 11 (N-H ADD 55%)							
☐551	½¢ Olive Brown	7.00	6.00	.25	.21	.18	.13
☐552	1¢ Deep Green	26.00	16.00	2.00	1.10	.15	.11
☐553	1½¢ Yellow Brown	40.00	25.00	4.00	2.00	.35	.18
☐554	2¢ Carmine	26.00	15.00	1.50	1.00	.17	.13
☐555	3¢ Violet	160.00	110.00	16.00	11.00	1.30	.70
☐556	4¢ Yellow Brown	170.00	120.00	18.00	11.00	.22	.14
☐557	5¢ Dark Blue	180.00	160.00	18.00	11.00	.18	.13
☐558	6¢ Red Orange	425.00	300.00	34.00	21.00	.90	.60
☐559	7¢ Black	70.00	50.00	8.00	6.00	.85	.50
☐560	8¢ Olive Green	500.00	400.00	43.00	28.00	.90	.60
☐561	9¢ Rose	160.00	115.00	18.00	11.00	1.20	.75
☐562	10¢ Orange	210.00	150.00	20.00	13.00	.20	.14
☐563	11¢ Blue	36.00	22.00	2.00	1.60	.40	.21
☐564	12¢ Brown Violet	80.00	60.00	7.00	4.50	.17	.14
☐565	14¢ Dark Blue	50.00	40.00	6.00	4.00	.90	.60
☐566	15¢ Gray	280.00	160.00	24.00	14.00	.16	.14
☐567	20¢ Carmine Rose	285.00	140.00	23.00	17.00	.17	.14
☐568	25¢ Green	210.00	130.00	21.00	14.00	.60	.36
☐569	30¢ Olive Brown	350.00	200.00	32.00	25.00	.50	.29
☐570	50¢ Lilac	700.00	600.00	60.00	46.00	.20	.16
☐571	$1 Violet Black	500.00	300.00	42.00	32.00	.50	.26
☐572	$2 Deep Blue	1400.00	1100.00	110.00	80.00	11.00	7.00
☐573	$5 Carmine & Blue	9000.00	5500.00	250.00	200.00	15.00	9.00
IMPERFORATE (N-H ADD 45%)							
☐575	1¢ Green	80.00	60.00	7.00	8.00	4.00	2.50
☐576	1½¢ Yellow Brown	21.00	18.00	2.00	1.50	2.00	1.50
☐577	2¢ Carmine	30.00	21.00	2.50	1.60	2.00	1.50
1923–1926. ROTARY PRESS PRINTING							
PERF. 11 x 10 (N-H ADD 55%)							
☐578	1¢ Green	600.00	500.00	70.00	42.00	65.00	38.00
☐579	2¢ Carmine	400.00	225.00	50.00	38.00	45.00	31.00

Scott No.		Fine Unused Plate Blk	Ave. Unused Plate Blk	Fine Unused Each	Ave. Unused Each	Fine Used Each	Ave. Used Each
PERF. 10 (N-H ADD 55%)							
□ 581	1¢ Green	95.00	70.00	8.00	5.00	.90	.60
□ 582	1½¢ Brown	40.00	26.00	4.00	3.00	.90	.50
□ 583	2¢ Carmine	26.00	16.00	2.00	1.30	.20	.15
□ 584	3¢ Violet	210.00	150.00	28.00	18.00	2.50	1.20
□ 585	4¢ Yellow Brown	150.00	110.00	15.00	9.00	.60	.28
□ 586	5¢ Blue	140.00	100.00	16.00	9.00	.30	.20
□ 587	6¢ Red Orange	65.00	50.00	7.00	5.00	.60	.36
□ 588	7¢ Black	90.00	60.00	9.00	7.00	5.00	3.00
□ 589	8¢ Olive Green	200.00	180.00	25.00	18.00	4.00	2.10
□ 590	9¢ Rose	50.00	30.00	5.00	3.00	2.50	1.50
□ 591	10¢ Orange	600.00	400.00	60.00	41.00	.18	.15
PERF. 11							
□ 595	2¢ Carmine	1500.00	1000.00	200.00	110.00	200.00	115.00

Scott No.		Fine Unused Line Pair	Ave. Unused Line Pair	Fine Unused Each	Ave. Unused Each	Fine Used Each	Ave. Used Each
1923–1929. ROTARY PRESS COIL STAMPS							
PERF. 10 VERTICALLY (N-H ADD 55%)							
□ 597	1¢ Green	2.00	2.00	.40	.25	.16	.13
□ 598	1½¢ Deep Brown	6.00	4.00	.65	.42	.16	.16
□ 599	2¢ Carmine (I)	2.00	2.00	.40	.25	.16	.13
□ 599A	2¢ Carmine (II)	600.00	400.00	110.00	62.00	13.00	7.00
□ 600	3¢ Deep Violet	36.00	21.00	7.00	5.00	.18	.14
□ 601	4¢ Yellow Brown	35.00	25.00	4.00	3.00	.50	.31
□ 602	5¢ Dark Blue	12.00	7.00	1.20	1.20	.20	.16
□ 603	10¢ Orange	26.00	17.00	5.00	2.10	.17	.14
PERF. 10 HORIZONTALLY (N-H ADD 55%)							
□ 604	1¢ Green	4.00	2.00	.26	.20	.16	.12
□ 605	1½¢ Yellow Brown	3.00	2.00	.26	.20	.17	.13
□ 606	2¢ Carmine	3.00	1.50	.26	.20	.16	.14

Scott No.		Fine Unused Plate Blk	Ave. Unused Plate Blk	Fine Unused Each	Ave. Unused Each	Fine Used Each	Ave. Used Each
1923. HARDING MEMORIAL ISSUE (N-H ADD 45%)							
□ 610	2¢ Black, pf. 11	30.00	18.00	.60	.50	.20	.13
□ 611	2¢ Black, imperf.	110.00	75.00	7.00	7.00	5.00	3.50
□ 612	2¢ Black, pf. 10 rotary . . .	300.00	200.00	12.00	10.00	2.50	1.60
1924. HUGUENOT-WALLOON ISSUE (N-H ADD 45%)							
□ 614	1¢ Green	40.00	35.00	5.00	2.50	4.00	2.50
□ 615	2¢ Carmine Rose	80.00	50.00	8.00	6.00	3.00	2.00
□ 616	5¢ Dark Blue	360.00	250.00	32.00	26.00	21.00	13.00

Scott No.		Fine Unused Plate Blk	Ave. Unused Plate Blk	Fine Unused Each	Ave. Unused Each	Fine Used Each	Ave. Used Each
1925. LEXINGTON-CONCORD SESQUICENTENNIAL (N-H ADD 45%)							
☐617	1¢ Green	50.00	30.00	5.00	3.50	3.50	2.10
☐618	2¢ Carmine Rose	80.00	60.00	7.00	6.00	3.00	2.00
☐619	5¢ Dark Blue	400.00	250.00	31.00	25.00	18.00	11.00
1925. NORSE-AMERICAN ISSUE (N-H ADD 40%)							
☐620	2¢ Carmine & Black	180.00	120.00	7.00	4.00	5.00	2.50
☐621	5¢ Dark Blue & Black	600.00	425.00	26.00	18.00	21.00	12.00
1925–1926.							
☐622	13¢ Green	140.00	110.00	16.00	9.00	.76	.50
☐623	17¢ Black	200.00	140.00	17.00	13.00	.36	.31
1926–1927. COMMEMORATIVES							
1926. SESQUICENTENNIAL EXPOSITION (N-H ADD 50%)							
☐627	2¢ Carmine Rose	40.00	30.00	4.00	3.00	.72	.50
1926. ERICSSON MEMORIAL ISSUE (N-H ADD 50%)							
☐628	5¢ Gray Lilac	85.00	66.00	8.00	6.00	4.50	2.60
1926. BATTLE OF WHITE PLAINS (N-H ADD 45%)							
☐629	2¢ Carmine Rose	—	40.00	3.50	2.00	3.00	1.50
☐630	2¢ Souv. Sheet of 25	—	—	450.00	360.00	—	—
1926–1928. DESIGNS OF 1922–1925							
ROTARY PRESS PRINTING IMPERFORATE (N-H ADD 40%)							
☐631	1½¢ Brown	60.00	50.00	2.10	2.00	2.10	1.20
PERF. 11 x 10½ (N-H ADD 50%)							
☐632	1¢ Green	2.50	2.00	.22	.20	.16	.13
☐633	1½¢ Yellow Brown	80.00	60.00	3.00	3.10	.16	.12
☐634	2¢ Carmine (I)	2.00	1.10	.24	.20	.16	.13
☐634A	2¢ Carmine (II)	—	—	300.00	160.00	16.00	11.00
☐635	3¢ Violet	7.00	4.00	.50	.30	.16	.13
☐636	4¢ Yellow Brown	82.00	60.00	3.00	2.20	.16	.13
☐637	5¢ Dark Blue	20.00	14.00	2.50	1.90	.16	.13
☐638	6¢ Red Orange	20.00	14.00	2.50	1.90	.16	.13
☐639	7¢ Black	20.00	14.00	2.50	1.90	.16	.13
☐640	8¢ Olive Green	20.00	14.00	2.50	1.90	.16	.13
☐641	9¢ Orange Red	20.00	14.00	2.50	1.90	.16	.13
☐642	10¢ Orange	38.00	30.00	6.00	3.60	.16	.13
1927. VERMONT SESQUICENTENNIAL (N-H ADD 45%)							
☐643	2¢ Carmine Rose	40.00	35.00	2.00	1.10	1.40	.80
1927. BURGOYNE CAMPAIGN ISSUE (N-H ADD 45%)							
☐644	2¢ Carmine	42.00	32.00	4.00	2.75	3.00	2.00
1928. VALLEY FORGE ISSUE (N-H ADD 45%)							
☐645	2¢ Carmine	40.00	25.00	1.20	1.00	.75	.42
1928. BATTLE OF MONMOUTH (N-H ADD 45%)							
☐646	2¢ Carmine	42.00	28.00	1.10	.95	1.10	.76

Scott No.	Fine Unused Plate Blk	Ave. Unused Plate Blk	Fine Unused Each	Ave. Unused Each	Fine Used Each	Ave. Used Each
1928. DISCOVERY OF HAWAII (N-H ADD 40%)						
☐ 647 2¢ Carmine Rose	160.00	100.00	5.00	3.50	4.00	3.00
☐ 648 5¢ Blue	400.00	200.00	18.00	10.00	19.00	9.80
1928. AERONAUTICS CONFERENCE (N-H ADD 40%)						
☐ 649 2¢ Carmine	20.00	15.00	1.50	1.00	1.40	1.00
☐ 650 5¢ Blue	100.00	70.00	6.00	4.50	4.50	3.00
1929. GEORGE ROGERS CLARK (N-H ADD 40%)						
☐ 651 2¢ Carmine & Black	16.00	11.00	.90	.50	.85	.60
1929. DESIGNS OF 1922–1925						
ROTARY PRESS PRINTING—PERF. 11 x 10½ (N-H ADD 40%)						
☐ 653 ½¢ Olive Brown	2.10	1.50	.25	.20	.16	.14
1929. EDISON COMMEMORATIVE						
FLAT PLATE PRINTING—PERF. 11 (N-H ADD 40%)						
☐ 654 2¢ Carmine Rose	48.00	30.00	1.25	.70	.90	.60
ROTARY PRESS PRINTING—PERF. 11 x 10½ (N-H ADD 40%)						
☐ 655 2¢ Carmine Rose	85.00	50.00	.80	.60	.40	.26

Scott No.	Fine Unused Line Pair	Ave. Unused Line Pair	Fine Unused Each	Ave. Unused Each	Fine Used Each	Ave. Used Each
ROTARY PRESS COIL STAMPS—PERF. 10 VERTICALLY (N-H ADD 40%)						
☐ 656 2¢ Carmine Rose	75.00	56.00	14.00	10.00	2.60	1.35

Scott No.	Fine Unused Plate Blk	Ave. Unused Plate Blk	Fine Unused Each	Ave. Unused Each	Fine Used Each	Ave. Used Each
1929. SULLIVAN EXPEDITION (N-H ADD 40%)						
☐ 657 2¢ Carmine Rose	32.00	19.00	1.10	.75	.80	.58
1929. 632–42 OVERPRINTED (KANS.) (N-H ADD 45%)						
☐ 658 1¢ Green	40.00	21.00	2.10	1.50	1.90	1.10
☐ 659 1½¢ Brown	52.00	28.00	3.50	2.00	3.40	1.80
☐ 660 2¢ Carmine	58.00	24.00	3.70	2.00	1.10	.60
☐ 661 3¢ Violet	190.00	110.00	16.00	12.00	12.00	7.00
☐ 662 4¢ Yellow Brown	200.00	110.00	16.00	13.00	9.00	5.00
☐ 663 5¢ Deep Blue	160.00	100.00	14.00	9.00	9.00	6.00
☐ 664 6¢ Red Orange	430.00	210.00	27.00	17.00	15.00	9.00
☐ 665 7¢ Black	450.00	200.00	28.00	16.00	22.00	14.00
☐ 666 8¢ Olive Green	750.00	550.00	80.00	50.00	65.00	42.00
☐ 667 9¢ Light Rose	205.00	165.00	12.00	10.00	10.00	9.00
☐ 668 10¢ Orange Yellow	340.00	250.00	21.00	16.00	11.00	6.50
1929. 632–42 OVERPRINTED (NEBR.) (N-H ADD 45%)						
☐ 669 1¢ Green	35.00	24.00	2.80	1.75	2.40	1.35
☐ 670 1½¢ Brown	60.00	32.00	3.40	2.45	2.80	1.75

Scott No.		Fine Unused Plate Blk	Ave. Unused Plate Blk	Fine Unused Each	Ave. Unused Each	Fine Used Each	Ave. Used Each
☐671	2¢ Carmine	48.00	25.00	2.10	1.80	1.10	.45
☐672	3¢ Violet	210.00	110.00	12.00	10.00	11.00	4.50
☐673	4¢ Brown	200.00	150.00	20.00	13.00	11.00	7.00
☐674	5¢ Blue	240.00	170.00	20.00	13.00	12.00	7.00
☐675	6¢ Orange	480.00	300.00	40.00	24.00	25.00	14.00
☐676	7¢ Black	250.00	190.00	25.00	10.00	14.00	8.00
☐677	8¢ Olive Green	290.00	220.00	30.00	17.00	18.00	7.00
☐678	9¢ Rose	400.00	230.00	38.00	21.00	25.00	14.00
☐679	10¢ Orange Yellow	700.00	600.00	100.00	70.00	22.00	12.00

1929. BATTLE OF FALLEN TIMBERS (N-H ADD 35%)

☐680	2¢ Carmine Rose	40.00	21.00	1.60	.70	.85	.65

1929. OHIO RIVER CANALIZATION (N-H ADD 30%)

☐681	2¢ Carmine Rose	24.00	18.00	2.00	.75	.80	.50

1930–1931. COMMEMORATIVES

1930. MASSACHUSETTS BAY COLONY (N-H ADD 35%)

☐682	2¢ Carmine Rose	42.00	28.00	.75	.60	.60	.40

1930. CAROLINA-CHARLESTON ISSUE (N-H ADD 35%)

☐683	2¢ Carmine Rose	60.00	48.00	1.50	1.10	1.60	1.10

1930. REGULAR ISSUE
ROTARY PRESS PRINTING—PERF. 11 x 10½ (N-H ADD 35%)

☐684	1½¢ Brown	4.00	3.50	.50	.32	.16	.14
☐685	4¢ Brown	12.00	8.00	1.00	.62	.16	.14

Scott No.		Fine Unused Line Pair	Ave. Unused Line Pair	Fine Unused Each	Ave. Unused Each	Fine Used Each	Ave. Used Each

ROTARY PRESS COIL STAMPS
PERF. 10 VERTICALLY (N-H ADD 40%)

☐686	1½¢ Brown	12.00	9.00	2.00	1.00	.16	.13
☐687	4¢ Brown	17.00	12.00	4.00	2.00	.55	.25

Scott No.		Fine Unused Plate Blk	Ave. Unused Plate Blk	Fine Unused Each	Ave. Unused Each	Fine Used Each	Ave. Used Each

1930. BATTLE OF BRADDOCK'S FIELD (N-H ADD 40%)

☐688	2¢ Carmine Rose	60.00	35.00	1.10	1.00	1.30	1.10

1930. VON STEUBEN ISSUE (N-H ADD 40%)

☐689	2¢ Carmine Rose	34.00	21.00	.75	.60	.60	.40

1931. PULASKI ISSUE (N-H ADD 40%)

☐690	2¢ Carmine Rose	24.00	21.00	.30	.27	.24	.15

1931. DESIGNS OF 1922–1926
ROTARY PRESS PRINTING—PERF. 11 x 10½ (N-H ADD 40%)

☐692	11¢ Light Blue	30.00	18.00	4.00	2.00	.20	.14
☐693	12¢ Brown Violet	44.00	30.00	5.00	4.00	.16	.13

Scott No.		Fine Unused Plate Blk	Ave. Unused Plate Blk	Fine Unused Each	Ave. Unused Each	Fine Used Each	Ave. Used Each
☐ 694	13¢ Yellow Green	21.00	15.00	2.00	2.00	.24	.15
☐ 695	14¢ Dark Blue	30.00	20.00	4.00	2.50	.60	.25
☐ 696	15¢ Gray	60.00	38.00	9.00	6.00	.16	.13

PERF. 10½ x 11 (N-H ADD 40%)

☐ 697	17¢ Black	30.00	21.00	6.00	3.00	.45	.20
☐ 698	20¢ Carmine Rose	45.00	32.00	10.00	8.00	.15	.12
☐ 699	25¢ Blue Green	45.00	30.00	9.00	6.00	.17	.13
☐ 700	30¢ Brown	80.00	60.00	18.00	9.00	.16	.13
☐ 701	50¢ Lilac	210.00	150.00	45.00	38.00	.16	.13

1931. RED CROSS ISSUE (N-H ADD 40%)

☐ 702	2¢ Black & Red	3.20	2.10	.28	.19	.17	.15

1931. SURRENDER OF YORKTOWN (N-H ADD 40%)

☐ 703	2¢ Carmine Rose & Black	4.00	3.00	.60	.51	.54	.35

1932. WASHINGTON BICENTENNIAL (N-H ADD 40%)

☐ 704	½¢ Olive Brown	5.00	4.00	.16	.17	.16	.11
☐ 705	1¢ Green	6.00	5.00	.18	.17	.15	.11
☐ 706	1½¢ Brown	17.00	15.00	.40	.17	.16	.12
☐ 707	2¢ Carmine	2.10	2.00	.15	.17	.15	.12
☐ 708	3¢ Purple	13.00	10.00	.75	.50	.14	.12
☐ 709	4¢ Light Brown	6.00	5.00	.36	.21	.16	.12
☐ 710	5¢ Blue	12.00	10.00	2.00	1.10	.15	.13
☐ 711	6¢ Orange	60.00	46.00	5.00	3.00	.15	.14
☐ 712	7¢ Black	8.00	6.00	.40	.38	.22	.16
☐ 713	8¢ Olive Bistre	50.00	45.00	4.00	3.00	.90	.55
☐ 714	9¢ Pale Red	40.00	25.00	3.00	2.00	.30	.16
☐ 715	10¢ Orange Yellow	110.00	85.00	16.00	8.00	.16	.14

1932. COMMEMORATIVES

1932. OLYMPIC WINTER GAMES (N-H ADD 30%)

☐ 716	2¢ Carmine Rose	14.00	10.00	.55	.38	.28	.20

1932. ARBOR DAY ISSUE (N-H ADD 30%)

☐ 717	2¢ Carmine Rose	8.00	7.00	.22	.20	.16	.14

1932. OLYMPIC SUMMER GAMES (N-H ADD 30%)

☐ 718	3¢ Purple	15.00	12.00	2.00	2.10	.17	.14
☐ 719	5¢ Blue	24.00	19.00	3.00	3.00	.32	.21

Scott No.		Fine Unused Line Pair	Ave. Unused Line Pair	Fine Unused Each	Ave. Unused Each	Fine Used Each	Ave. Used Each

1932. ROTARY PRESS COIL STAMPS

☐ 720	3¢ Deep Violet	2.00	1.50	.24	.19	.14	.11

PERF. 10 VERTICALLY (N-H ADD 30%)

☐ 721	3¢ Deep Violet	8.00	5.00	3.00	2.10	.16	.11

Scott No.		Fine Unused Line Pair	Ave. Unused Line Pair	Fine Unused Each	Ave. Unused Each	Fine Used Each	Ave. Used Each
PERF. 10 HORIZONTALLY (N-H ADD 30%)							
☐ 722	3¢ Deep Violet	5.00	4.00	2.00	.90	.70	.50
DESIGN OF 1922–1925—PERF. 10 VERTICALLY (N-H ADD 30%)							
☐ 723	6¢ Deep Orange	60.00	40.00	12.00	8.00	.26	.16

Scott No.		Fine Unused Plate Blk	Ave. Unused Plate Blk	Fine Unused Each	Ave. Unused Each	Fine Used Each	Ave. Used Each
1932. WILLIAM PENN ISSUE (N-H ADD 30%)							
☐ 724	3¢ Violet	14.00	10.00	.38	.28	.24	.16
1932. DANIEL WEBSTER ISSUE (N-H ADD 30%)							
☐ 725	3¢ Violet	32.00	18.00	.50	.40	.36	.30
1933. COMMEMORATIVES							
1933. GEORGIA BICENTENNIAL (N-H ADD 30%)							
☐ 726	3¢ Violet	21.00	12.00	.30	.28	.21	.16
1933. PEACE SESQUICENTENNIAL (N-H ADD 30%)							
☐ 727	3¢ Violet	7.00	4.00	.24	.20	.16	.12
1933. CENTURY OF PROGRESS EXPOSITION (N-H ADD 30%)							
☐ 728	1¢ Yellow Green	3.00	2.50	.22	.18	.16	.12
☐ 729	3¢ Purple	5.00	3.00	.22	.17	.15	.12
1933. A.P.S. CONVENTION AND EXHIBITION AT CHICAGO IMPERFORATE—UNGUMMED (N-H ADD 30%)							
☐ 730	1¢ Yellow Green, Sheet of 25	—	—	40.00	30.00	—	—
☐ 730a	1¢ Yellow Green, sgl.	—	—	.80	.65	.60	.40
☐ 731	3¢ Violet Sheet of 25	—	—	28.00	—	30.00	
☐ 731a	3¢ Violet, single	—	—	.70	.50	.50	.35
1933. N.R.A. ISSUE (N-H ADD 25%)							
☐ 732	3¢ Violet	3.00	2.50	.22	.19	.16	.13
1933. BYRD ANTARCTIC EXPEDITION (N-H ADD 30%)							
☐ 733	3¢ Dark Blue	16.00	14.00	.90	.50	.70	.60
1933. KOSCIUSZKO ISSUE (N-H ADD 30%)							
☐ 734	5¢ Blue	40.00	30.00	.70	.60	.40	.24
1934. NATIONAL PHILATELIC EXHIBITION IMPERFORATE—UNGUMMED (N-H ADD 30%)							
☐ 735	3¢ Dark Blue Sheet of 6	—	—	20.00	—	18.00	14.00
☐ 735a	3¢ Dark Blue, sgl.	—	—	3.00	2.00	2.10	2.00
1934. COMMEMORATIVES							
1934. MARYLAND TERCENTENARY (N-H ADD 30%)							
☐ 736	3¢ Rose	13.00	9.00	.22	.20	.16	.14

Scott No.		Fine Unused Plate Blk	Ave. Unused Plate Blk	Fine Unused Each	Ave. Unused Each	Fine Used Each	Ave. Used Each

1934. MOTHER'S DAY ISSUE
ROTARY PRESS PRINTING—PERF. 11 x 10½ (N-H ADD 30%)

| ☐ 737 | 3¢ Deep Violet .... | 2.10 | 1.50 | .20 | .18 | .14 | .12 |

FLAT PRESS PRINTING-PERF. 11 (N-H ADD 30%)

| ☐ 738 | 3¢ Deep Violet .... | 6.00 | 5.00 | .32 | .20 | .24 | .18 |

1934. WISCONSIN TERCENTENARY (N-H ADD 30%)

| ☐ 739 | 3¢ Deep Violet .... | 5.00 | 4.00 | .27 | .20 | .17 | .13 |

1934. NATIONAL PARKS ISSUE (N-H ADD 25%)

☐ 740	1¢ Green	2.10	1.50	.22	.16	.16	.13
☐ 741	2¢ Red	2.00	1.50	.21	.16	.16	.13
☐ 742	3¢ Purple	3.00	2.00	.24	.20	.16	.13
☐ 743	4¢ Brown	9.00	7.00	.50	.35	.50	.30
☐ 744	5¢ Blue	12.00	8.00	1.00	.70	.80	.50
☐ 745	6¢ Indigo	24.00	18.00	1.20	.85	1.10	.70
☐ 746	7¢ Black	18.00	11.00	.80	.60	1.00	.65
☐ 747	8¢ Green	31.00	15.00	2.00	1.70	2.00	1.50
☐ 748	9¢ Salmon	20.00	16.00	2.50	1.60	.70	.55
☐ 749	10¢ Gray Black	34.00	30.00	4.00	3.00	1.40	.70

1934. A.P.S. CONVENTION AND EXHIBITION AT ATLANTIC CITY
IMPERFORATE SOUVENIR SHEET (N-H ADD 25%)

| ☐ 750 | 3¢ Purple, sheet of 6 .... | — | — | 35.00 | — | 37.00 | 26.00 |
| ☐ 750a | 3¢ Purple, single .... | — | — | 5.00 | 3.00 | 4.50 | 3.00 |

1934. TRANS-MISSISSIPPI PHILATELIC EXPOSITION AND
CONVENTION AT OMAHA
IMPERFORATE SOUVENIR SHEET (N-H ADD 25%)

| ☐ 751 | 1¢ Green, sheet of 6 .... | — | — | 32.00 | — | 15.00 | 9.00 |
| ☐ 751a | 1¢ Green, single .... | — | — | 2.00 | 1.80 | 1.75 | 1.40 |

Scott No.		Plate Block	Block Plain	Mint Each	Used Each

1935. "FARLEY SPECIAL PRINTINGS"
DESIGNS OF 1933–1934
PERF. 10½ x 11—UNGUMMED (N-H ADD 25%)

| ☐ 752 | 3¢ Violet .... | 20.00 | 3.00 | .20 | .14 |

PERF. 11—GUMMED (N-H ADD 25%)

| ☐ 753 | 3¢ Dark Blue .... | 21.00 | 4.00 | .62 | .60 |

IMPERFORATE—UNGUMMED (N-H ADD 25%)

| ☐ 754 | 3¢ Deep Violet .... | 21.00 | 4.00 | .75 | .65 |
| ☐ 755 | 3¢ Deep Violet .... | 21.00 | 5.00 | .70 | .60 |

NATIONAL PARKS
IMPERFORATE—UNGUMMED (N-H ADD 25%)

| ☐ 756 | 1¢ Green .... | 6.50 | 1.50 | .20 | .18 |
| ☐ 757 | 2¢ Red .... | 7.00 | 1.70 | .30 | .22 |

Scott No.		Plate Block	Block Plain	Mint Each	Used Each
☐ 758	3¢ Deep Violet	20.00	3.50	.70	.60
☐ 759	4¢ Brown	24.00	9.00	1.10	1.10
☐ 760	5¢ Blue	26.00	17.00	2.10	1.90
☐ 761	6¢ Dark Blue	50.00	17.00	3.00	2.50
☐ 762	7¢ Black	40.00	16.00	2.00	1.80
☐ 763	8¢ Sage Green	50.00	15.00	2.50	1.90
☐ 764	9¢ Red Orange	50.00	15.00	2.50	2.00
☐ 765	10¢ Gray Black	60.00	31.00	4.00	3.50

IMPERFORATE—UNGUMMED (N-H ADD 25%)

☐ 766a	1¢ Yellow Green	—	14.00	.90	.50
☐ 767a	3¢ Violet	—	14.00	.90	.50
☐ 768a	3¢ Dark Blue	—	20.00	3.00	3.00
☐ 769a	1¢ Green	—	12.00	1.90	1.60
☐ 770a	3¢ Deep Violet	—	20.00	3.40	3.00

DESIGN OF CE 1 (N-H ADD 30%)

☐ 771	16¢ Dark Blue	90.00	18.00	3.00	3.00

1935–1936. COMMEMORATIVES

Scott No.		Fine Unused Plate Blk	Ave. Unused Plate Blk	Mint Each	Used Each
1935. CONNECTICUT TERCENTENARY (N-H ADD 25%)					
☐ 772	3¢ Red Violet	2.40	2.00	.20	.11
1935. CALIFORNIA PACIFIC EXPOSITION (N-H ADD 25%)					
☐ 773	3¢ Purple	2.40	1.80	.20	.12
1935. BOULDER DAM ISSUE (N-H ADD 25%)					
☐ 774	3¢ Purple	2.00	1.65	.19	.12
1935. MICHIGAN CENTENARY (N-H ADD 25%)					
☐ 775	3¢ Purple	2.40	1.60	.18	.12
1936. TEXAS CENTENNIAL (N-H ADD 25%)					
☐ 776	3¢ Purple	2.25	1.65	.20	.16
1936. RHODE ISLAND TERCENTENARY (N-H ADD 25%)					
☐ 777	3¢ Purple	2.40	1.60	.27	.15
1936. THIRD INTL. PHILATELIC EXHIBITION "TIPEX" IMPERFORATE SOUVENIR SHEET DESIGNS OF 772, 773, 775, 776 (N-H ADD 25%)					
☐ 778	3¢ Red Violet, sheet of 4	—	—	3.50	3.00
☐ 778a	3¢ Red Violet, single	—	—	.90	.75
☐ 778b	3¢ Red Violet, single	—	—	.90	.75
☐ 778c	3¢ Red Violet, single	—	—	.90	.75
☐ 778d	3¢ Red Violet, single	—	—	.90	.75
1936. ARKANSAS CENTENNIAL (N-H ADD 25%)					
☐ 782	3¢ Purple	2.00	1.70	.19	.12

Scott No.		Fine Unused Plate Blk	Ave. Unused Plate Blk	Fine Unused Each	Ave. Unused Each	Fine Used Each	Ave. Used Each
1936. OREGON TERRITORY CENTENNIAL (N-H ADD 25%)							
☐ 783	3¢ Purple	1.80	1.40	.19	.18	.16	.12
1936. SUFFRAGE FOR WOMEN ISSUE (N-H ADD 25%)							
☐ 784	3¢ Dark Violet	1.20	1.00	.19	.15	.16	.12
1936–1937. ARMY AND NAVY ISSUE							
ARMY COMMEMORATIVES (N-H ADD 20%)							
☐ 785	1¢ Green	1.50	1.10	.18	.14	.16	.12
☐ 786	2¢ Carmine	1.60	1.50	.20	.15	.16	.12
☐ 787	3¢ Purple	2.00	1.90	.25	.21	.18	.14
☐ 788	4¢ Gray	18.00	16.00	.70	.50	.25	.16
☐ 789	5¢ Ultramarine	21.00	16.00	.90	.60	.30	.16
NAVY COMMEMORATIVES (N-H ADD 25%)							
☐ 790	1¢ Green	—	.90	.18	.20	.16	.12
☐ 791	2¢ Carmaine	1.60	1.20	.21	.20	.16	.13
☐ 792	3¢ Purple	1.80	1.20	.24	.22	.18	.15
☐ 793	4¢ Gray	20.00	15.00	.70	.40	.30	.17
☐ 794	5¢ Ultramarine	21.00	15.00	.80	.60	.40	.17
1937. COMMEMORATIVES							
1937. NORTHWEST ORDINANCE ISSUE (N-H ADD 25%)							
☐ 795	3¢ Violet	2.00	1.70	.25	.17	.19	.12
1937. VIRGINIA DARE ISSUE (N-H ADD 20%)							
☐ 796	5¢ Gray Blue	12.00	8.00	.40	.26	.21	.16
1937. S.P.A. CONVENTION ISSUE (N-H ADD 25%)							
DESIGN OF 749 IMPERFORATE SOUVENIR SHEET							
☐ 797	10¢ Blue Green	—	—	1.40	—	.80	.58
1937. CONSTITUTIONAL SESQUICENTENNIAL (N-H ADD 25%)							
☐ 798	3¢ Red Violet	1.70	1.10	.23	.18	.20	.13
1937. TERRITORIAL PUBLICITY ISSUE (N-H ADD 25%)							
☐ 799	3¢ Violet	2.60	2.00	.21	.17	.19	.12
☐ 800	3¢ Violet	2.60	2.00	.21	.17	.19	.12
☐ 801	3¢ Bright Violet	2.60	2.00	.21	.17	.19	.12
☐ 802	3¢ Light Violet	2.60	2.00	.21	.17	.19	.12
1938. PRESIDENTIAL SERIES							
ROTARY PRESS PRINTING—PERF. 11 x 10½ (N-H ADD 25%)							
☐ 803	½¢ Red Orange	.80	.50	.15	.13	.19	.13
☐ 804	1¢ Green	.40	.38	.18	.12	.19	.13
☐ 805	1½¢ Bistre Brown	.40	.38	.18	.13	.19	.13
☐ 806	2¢ Rose Carmine	.60	.50	.21	.14	.19	.13
☐ 807	3¢ Deep Violet	.55	.42	.19	.12	.19	.13
☐ 808	4¢ Red Violet	2.10	1.60	.34	.21	.19	.13
☐ 809	4½¢ Dark Gray	2.00	1.60	.21	.21	.19	.13

Scott No.		Fine Unused Plate Blk	Ave. Unused Plate Blk	Fine Unused Each	Ave. Unused Each	Fine Used Each	Ave. Used Each
☐810	5¢ Bright Blue	2.00	1.90	.27	.24	.19	.12
☐811	6¢ Red Orange	2.50	2.00	.34	.30	.24	.12
☐812	7¢ Sepia	2.50	2.00	.42	.30	.36	.12
☐813	8¢ Olive Green	3.00	3.00	.60	.42	.16	.12
☐814	9¢ Rose Pink	3.00	2.90	.75	.45	.16	.12
☐815	10¢ Brown Red	2.00	1.90	.60	.30	.16	.12
☐816	11¢ Ultramarine	5.00	4.00	.90	.50	.18	.14
☐817	12¢ Bright Violet	14.00	7.00	1.20	.70	.18	.14
☐818	13¢ Blue Green	14.00	8.00	1.40	.75	.19	.14
☐819	14¢ Blue	7.00	6.00	1.50	.60	.19	.14
☐820	15¢ Blue Gray	4.00	3.00	.96	.60	.17	.12
☐821	16¢ Black	11.00	7.00	1.20	.60	.60	.42
☐822	17¢ Rose Red	11.00	7.00	1.30	.60	.19	.13
☐823	18¢ Brown Carmine	16.00	10.00	3.00	1.20	.17	.12
☐824	19¢ Bright Violet	14.00	10.00	1.50	1.00	.80	.60
☐825	20¢ Bright Blue Green	8.00	7.00	1.35	.70	.16	.12
☐826	21¢ Dull Blue	16.00	10.00	2.00	2.00	.31	.14
☐827	22¢ Vermilion	18.00	12.00	1.40	.80	.70	.55
☐828	24¢ Gray Black	31.00	28.00	4.00	4.00	.31	.24
☐829	25¢ Deep Red Lilac	8.00	6.00	2.00	.70	.16	.12
☐830	30¢ Deep Ultramarine ...	46.00	30.00	7.00	6.00	.15	.12
☐831	50¢ Light Red Violet	50.00	40.00	10.00	7.00	.15	.12

FLAT PLATE PRINTING—PERF. 11 (N-H ADD 20%)

☐832	$1 Purple & Black	60.00	40.00	14.00	10.00	.20	.12
☐832b	$1 Watermarked	—	—	300.00	275.00	80.00	75.00
☐832c	$1 Dry Printing, Thick Paper (1954)	50.00	41.00	12.00	7.00	.22	.15
☐833	$2 Green & Black	210.00	170.00	34.00	26.00	8.50	7.00
☐834	$5 Carmine & Black	700.00	500.00	150.00	120.00	7.00	5.00

1938–1939. COMMEMORATIVES

1938. CONSTITUTION RATIFICATION (N-H ADD 25%)

☐835	3¢ Deep Violet	6.00	5.00	.29	.21	.20	.12

1938. SWEDISH-FINNISH TERCENTENARY (N-H ADD 25%)

☐836	3¢ Red Violet	6.00	4.00	.29	.21	.20	.13

1938. NORTHWEST COLONIZATION (N-H ADD 25%)

☐837	3¢ Bright Violet	16.00	11.00	.30	.25	.20	.13

1938. IOWA TERRITORY CENTENNIAL (N-H ADD 25%)

☐838	3¢ Violet	12.00	9.00	.30	.25	.19	.13

Scott No.		Fine Unused Line Pair	Ave. Unused Line Pair	Fine Unused Each	Ave. Unused Each	Fine Used Each	Ave. Used Each

1939. ROTARY PRESS COIL STAMPS
PERF. 10 VERTICALLY (N-H ADD 25%)

		Fine Unused Line Pair	Ave. Unused Line Pair	Fine Unused Each	Ave. Unused Each	Fine Used Each	Ave. Used Each
☐ 839	1¢ Green	1.25	1.00	.40	.30	.16	.12
☐ 840	1½¢ Bistre Brown	2.00	1.40	.40	.30	.16	.12
☐ 841	2¢ Rose Carmine	2.00	1.50	.60	.40	.14	.12
☐ 842	3¢ Deep Violet	2.00	1.50	.62	.50	.16	.12
☐ 843	4¢ Red Violet	30.00	20.00	12.00	8.00	.60	.44
☐ 844	4½¢ Dark Gray	7.00	5.00	1.00	.60	.75	.44
☐ 845	5¢ Bright Blue	30.00	20.00	9.00	5.50	.45	.36
☐ 846	6¢ Red Orange	8.00	7.00	2.00	1.10	.27	.14
☐ 847	10¢ Brown Red	50.00	40.00	22.00	12.00	.12	.65

PERF. 10 HORIZONTALLY (N-H ADD 25%)

☐ 848	1¢ Green	3.00	2.10	.90	.72	.15	.12
☐ 849	1½¢ Bistre Brown	4.00	3.10	1.65	1.30	.58	.46
☐ 850	2¢ Rose Carmine	6.00	4.50	2.80	2.70	.70	.50
☐ 851	3¢ Deep Violet	7.00	5.00	2.80	2.30	.65	.48

Scott No.		Fine Unused Plate Blk	Ave. Unused Plate Blk	Fine Unused Each	Ave. Unused Each	Fine Used Each	Ave. Used Each

1939. GOLDEN GATE INTERNATIONAL EXPOSITION (N-H ADD 25%)

☐ 852	3¢ Bright Purple	2.40	1.60	.25	.20	.15	.12

1939. NEW YORK WORLD'S FAIR (N-H ADD 20%)

☐ 853	3¢ Deep Purple	2.40	1.80	.27	.20	.15	.13

1939. WASHINGTON INAUGURATION SESQUICENTENNIAL (N-H ADD 20%)

☐ 854	3¢ Bright Red Violet	5.00	3.50	.50	.30	.19	.12

1939. BASEBALL CENTENNIAL (N-H ADD 20%)

☐ 855	3¢ Violet	4.00	3.00	1.00	.60	.16	.12

1939. 25TH ANNIVERSARY PANAMA CANAL (N-H ADD 20%)

☐ 856	3¢ Deep Red Violet	5.00	3.50	.30	.21	.17	.13

1939. COLONIAL PRINTING TERCENTENARY (N-H ADD 20%)

☐ 857	3¢ Rose Violet	2.00	1.75	.23	.16	.15	.13

1939. 50TH ANNIVERSARY OF STATEHOOD (N-H ADD 20%)

☐ 858	3¢ Rose Violet	2.10	1.80	.21	.17	.15	.13

1940. FAMOUS AMERICANS SERIES
AMERICAN AUTHORS (N-H ADD 20%)

☐ 859	1¢ Bright Blue Green	2.00	1.50	.18	.13	.15	.12
☐ 860	2¢ Rose Carmine	2.10	1.70	.20	.18	.17	.12
☐ 861	3¢ Bright Red Violet	2.50	1.80	.20	.18	.16	.12
☐ 862	5¢ Ultramarine	20.00	13.00	.35	.32	.40	.35
☐ 863	10¢ Dark Brown	60.00	48.00	2.10	2.00	2.00	1.70

Scott No.		Fine Unused Plate Blk	Ave. Unused Plate Blk	Fine Unused Each	Ave. Unused Each	Fine Used Each	Ave. Used Each
AMERICAN POETS (N-H ADD 20%)							
☐864	1¢ Bright Blue Green	2.80	2.10	.26	.24	.20	.12
☐865	2¢ Rose Carmine	3.50	2.90	.26	.24	.20	.12
☐866	3¢ Bright Red Violet	4.00	3.00	.25	.24	.20	.12
☐867	5¢ Ultramarine	18.00	12.00	.70	.50	.40	.34
☐868	10¢ Dark Brown	50.00	38.00	2.60	2.10	2.00	2.10
AMERICAN EDUCATORS (N-H ADD 20%)							
☐869	1¢ Bright Blue Green	300.00	2.40	.20	.16	.14	.12
☐870	2¢ Rose Carmine	300.00	2.40	.20	.16	.14	.12
☐871	3¢ Bright Red Violet	4.50	3.00	.30	.22	.14	.12
☐872	5¢ Ultramarine	16.00	12.00	.60	.50	.40	.32
☐873	10¢ Dark Brown	42.00	34.00	2.00	1.10	1.75	1.60
AMERICAN SCIENTISTS (N-H ADD 20%)							
☐874	1¢ Bright Blue Green	2.00	1.75	.20	.16	.14	.12
☐875	2¢ Rose Carmine	1.50	1.40	.20	.16	.14	.11
☐876	3¢ Bright Red Violet	1.80	1.50	.20	.16	.14	.11
☐877	5¢ Ultramarine	12.00	10.00	.35	.30	.30	.24
☐878	10¢ Dark Brown	35.00	28.00	2.00	1.65	1.80	1.25
AMERICAN COMPOSERS (N-H ADD 20%)							
☐879	1¢ Bright Blue Green	1.75	1.50	.20	.18	.16	.12
☐880	2¢ Rose Carmine	1.75	1.50	.20	.18	.16	.12
☐881	3¢ Bright Red Violet	2.00	1.75	.20	.18	.17	.15
☐882	5¢ Ultramarine	15.00	12.00	.70	.48	.30	.30
☐883	10¢ Dark Brown	48.00	40.00	6.00	4.00	1.90	1.75
AMERICAN ARTISTS (N-H ADD 20%)							
☐884	1¢ Bright Blue Green	1.50	1.25	.20	.16	.15	.12
☐885	2¢ Rose Carmine	1.50	1.25	.20	.16	.15	.12
☐886	3¢ Bright Red Violet	1.50	1.25	.25	.18	.14	.12
☐887	5¢ Ultramarine	18.00	14.00	.75	.60	.35	.30
☐888	10¢ Dark Brown	40.00	35.00	2.60	1.90	2.00	1.50
AMERICAN INVENTORS (N-H ADD 20%)							
☐889	1¢ Bright Blue Green	4.20	3.10	.22	.16	.15	.12
☐890	2¢ Rose Carmine	2.10	1.30	.22	.16	.15	.12
☐891	3¢ Bright Red Violet	3.60	2.30	.40	.20	.15	.12
☐892	5¢ Ultramarine	35.00	26.00	1.60	.90	.50	.40
☐893	10¢ Dark Brown	170.00	135.00	15.00	11.00	3.00	2.25

1940. COMMEMORATIVES

1940. 80TH ANNIVERSARY OF PONY EXPRESS (N-H ADD 20%)

☐894	3¢ Henna Brown	5.00	4.00	.40	.30	.19	.16

1940. 50TH ANNIVERSARY OF PAN-AMERICAN UNION (N-H ADD 20%)

☐895	3¢ Light Violet	5.00	4.00	.25	.20	.16	.12

Scott No.		Fine Unused Plate Blk	Ave. Unused Plate Blk	Fine Unused Each	Ave. Unused Each	Fine Used Each	Ave. Used Each
1940. 50TH ANNIVERSARY OF IDAHO (N-H ADD 20%)							
☐896	3¢ Bright Violet	2.00	1.80	.24	.17	.16	.12
1940. 50TH ANNIVERSARY OF WYOMING (N-H ADD 20%)							
☐897	3¢ Brown Violet	2.00	1.80	.24	.18	.16	.12
1940. 400TH ANNIVERSARY OF COLORADO EXPEDITION (N-H ADD 20%)							
☐898	3¢ Violet	2.00	1.80	.24	.18	.16	.12
1940. NATIONAL DEFENSE ISSUE (N-H ADD 20%)							
☐899	1¢ Bright Blue Green	.60	.50	.24	.18	.16	.12
☐900	2¢ Rose Carmine	.60	.50	.24	.18	.16	.12
☐901	3¢ Bright Violet	.60	.50	.24	.18	.16	.12
1940. 75TH ANNIVERSARY EMANCIPATION AMENDMENT (N-H ADD 20%)							
☐902	3¢ Deep Violet	5.00	4.00	.28	.24	.21	.16

IMPORTANT NOTICE: Values for mint sheets are provided for the following listings. To command the stated prices, sheets must be complete as issued with the plate number (or numbers) intact.

Scott No.		Mint Sheet	Plate Block	Fine Unused Each	Fine Used Each
1941–1943. COMMEMORATIVES					
1941. VERMONT STATEHOOD					
☐903	3¢ Light Violet	12.00	2.75	.21	.13
1942. KENTUCKY SESQUICENTENNIAL ISSUE					
☐904	3¢ Violet	8.00	2.00	.21	.13
1942. WIN THE WAR ISSUE					
☐905	3¢ Violet	14.00	.85	.21	.13
1942. CHINA ISSUE					
☐906	5¢ Bright Blue	22.00	13.00	.40	.30
1943. ALLIED NATIONS ISSUE					
☐907	2¢ Rose Carmine	7.00	.60	.21	.13
1943. FOUR FREEDOMS ISSUE					
☐908	1¢ Green	7.00	.80	.21	.13
1943–1944. OVERRUN COUNTRIES SERIES					
☐909	5¢ (Poland)	18.00	8.00	.21	.13
☐910	5¢ (Czechoslovakia)	16.00	4.50	.21	.13
☐911	5¢ (Norway)	8.50	2.00	.21	.13
☐912	5¢ (Luxembourg)	8.50	1.80	.21	.13
☐913	5¢ (Netherlands)	8.50	1.80	.21	.13
☐914	5¢ (Belgium)	8.50	1.80	.21	.13
☐915	5¢ (France)	8.50	1.80	.21	.13
☐916	5¢ (Greece)	38.00	15.00	.55	.45

*No hinge pricing from 1941 to date is figured at (N-H ADD 15%)

Scott No.		Mint Sheet	Plate Block	Fine Unused Each	Fine Used Each
☐ 917	5¢ (Yugoslavia)	28.00	9.00	.40	.30
☐ 918	5¢ (Albania)	26.00	9.00	.30	.20
☐ 919	5¢ (Austria)	20.00	8.00	.30	.18
☐ 920	5¢ (Denmark)	24.00	9.00	.30	.20
☐ 921	5¢ (Korea)	15.00	7.00	.21	.20

1944. COMMEMORATIVES

1944. RAILROAD ISSUE
☐ 922	3¢ Violet	15.00	1.75	.25	.14

1944. STEAMSHIP ISSUE
☐ 923	3¢ Violet	7.00	1.75	.21	.13

1944. TELEGRAPH ISSUE
☐ 924	3¢ Bright Red Violet	6.00	1.50	.21	.13

1944. CORREGIDOR ISSUE
☐ 925	3¢ Deep Violet	6.00	1.60	.21	.13

1944. MOTION PICTURE ISSUE
☐ 926	3¢ Deep Violet	8.00	1.60	.18	.12

1945. COMMEMORATIVES

1945. FLORIDA ISSUE
☐ 927	3¢ Bright Red Violet	6.00	1.00	.21	.13

1945. PEACE CONFERENCE ISSUE
☐ 928	5¢ Ultramarine	6.00	.90	.21	.13

1945. IWO JIMA ISSUE
☐ 929	3¢ Yellow Green	6.00	.70	.21	.13

1945–1946. ROOSEVELT MEMORIAL ISSUE
☐ 930	1¢ Blue Green	2.50	.27	.14	.12
☐ 931	2¢ Carmine Rose	3.00	.35	.14	.12
☐ 932	3¢ Purple	5.50	.68	.21	.12
☐ 933	5¢ Bright Blue	7.00	.68	.21	.12

1945. ARMY ISSUE
☐ 934	3¢ Olive Gray	6.00	.70	.21	.13

1945. NAVY ISSUE
☐ 935	3¢ Blue	5.50	.70	.21	.13

1945. COAST GUARD ISSUE
☐ 936	3¢ Bright Blue Green	5.50	.70	.21	.13

1945. ALFRED SMITH ISSUE
☐ 937	3¢ Purple	12.00	.70	.21	.13

1945. TEXAS CENTENNIAL ISSUE
☐ 938	3¢ Blue	5.50	.70	.21	.13

*No hinge pricing from 1941 to date is figured at (N-H ADD 15%)

Scott No.		Mint Sheet	Plate Block	Fine Unused Each	Fine Used Each

1946–1947. COMMEMORATIVES

1946. MERCHANT MARINE ISSUE
| ☐939 | 3¢ Blue Green | 5.50 | .70 | .20 | .12 |

1946. HONORABLE DISCHARGE EMBLEM ISSUE
| ☐940 | 3¢ Dark Violet | 11.00 | .70 | .20 | .12 |

1946. TENNESSEE ISSUE
| ☐941 | 3¢ Dark Violet | 5.50 | .70 | .20 | .12 |

1946. IOWA STATEHOOD ISSUE
| ☐942 | 3¢ Deep Blue | 5.50 | .70 | .20 | .12 |

1946. SMITHSONIAN INSTITUTION ISSUE
| ☐943 | 3¢ Violet Brown | 5.50 | .70 | .20 | .12 |

1946. NEW MEXICO ISSUE
| ☐944 | 3¢ Brown Violet | 5.50 | .70 | .20 | .12 |

1947. EDISON ISSUE
| ☐945 | 3¢ Bright Red Violet | 7.50 | .70 | .20 | .12 |

1947. PULITZER PRIZE
| ☐946 | 3¢ Purple | 5.50 | .70 | .20 | .12 |

1947. U.S. POSTAGE STAMP CENTENARY
| ☐947 | 3¢ Deep Blue | 5.50 | .70 | .20 | .12 |

1947. "CIPEX" SOUVENIR SHEET
☐948	5¢ & 10¢ Sheet of 2	—	—	.90	.70
☐948a	5¢ Blue, sgl. stp.	—	—	.35	.25
☐948b	10¢ Brown Orange, sgl. stp.	—	—	.48	.34

1947. DOCTORS ISSUE
| ☐949 | 3¢ Brown Violet | 5.50 | .70 | .21 | .12 |

1947. UTAH ISSUE
| ☐950 | 3¢ Dark Violet | 5.50 | .70 | .21 | .12 |

1947. U.S.F. CONSTITUTION ISSUE
| ☐951 | 3¢ Blue Green | 5.50 | .70 | .21 | .12 |

1947. EVERGLADES ISSUE
| ☐952 | 3¢ Bright Green | 5.50 | .70 | .21 | .12 |

1948. COMMEMORATIVES

1948. CARVER ISSUE
| ☐953 | 3¢ Red Violet | 7.50 | .70 | .21 | .12 |

1948. GOLD RUSH ISSUE
| ☐954 | 3¢ Dark Violet | 5.50 | .70 | .21 | .12 |

1948. MISSISSIPPI TERRITORY ISSUE
| ☐955 | 3¢ Brown Violet | 5.50 | .70 | .21 | .12 |

*No hinge pricing from 1941 to date is figured at (N-H ADD 15%)

Scott No.		Mint Sheet	Plate Block	Fine Unused Each	Fine Used Each
1948. FOUR CHAPLAINS ISSUE					
□ 956	3¢ Gray Black	5.50	.70	.20	.13
1948. WISCONSIN CENTENNIAL ISSUE					
□ 957	3¢ Dark Violet	5.50	.70	.20	.13
1948. SWEDISH PIONEER ISSUE					
□ 958	5¢ Deep Blue	6.50	.70	.20	.13
1948. 100 YEARS PROGRESS OF WOMEN					
□ 959	3¢ Dark Violet	5.50	.70	.20	.13
1948. WILLIAM ALLEN WHITE ISSUE					
□ 960	3¢ Red Violet	6.50	.70	.20	.13
1948. U.S.-CANADA FRIENDSHIP					
□ 961	3¢ Blue	5.50	.70	.20	.13
1948. FRANCIS SCOTT KEY ISSUE					
□ 962	3¢ Rose Pink	5.50	.70	.20	.13
1948. SALUTE TO YOUTH ISSUE					
□ 963	3¢ Deep Blue	5.50	.70	.20	.13
1948. OREGON TERRITORY ISSUE					
□ 964	3¢ Brown Red	5.50	.70	.20	.13
1948. HARLAN FISKE STONE					
□ 965	3¢ Bright Red Violet	6.50	.80	.21	.14
1948. MT. PALOMAR OBSERVATORY					
□ 966	3¢ Blue	8.00	.80	.21	.14
1948. CLARA BARTON ISSUE					
□ 967	3¢ Rose Pink	5.50	.70	.20	.13
1948. POULTRY ISSUE					
□ 968	3¢ Sepia	5.50	.70	.20	.13
1948. GOLD STAR MOTHERS					
□ 969	3¢ Orange Yellow	5.50	.70	.20	.13
1948. FORT KEARNY ISSUE					
□ 970	3¢ Violet	5.50	.70	.20	.13
1948. VOLUNTEER FIREMEN					
□ 971	3¢ Bright Rose Carmine	5.50	.70	.20	.13
1948. INDIAN CENTENNIAL					
□ 972	3¢ Dark Brown	5.50	.70	.20	.13
1948. ROUGH RIDERS					
□ 973	3¢ Violet Brown	5.50	.70	.20	.13
1948. JULIETTE LOW					
□ 974	3¢ Blue Green	5.50	.70	.20	.13

*No hinge pricing from 1941 to date is figured at (N-H ADD 15%)

Scott No.		Mint Sheet	Plate Block	Fine Unused Each	Fine Used Each
1948. WILL ROGERS					
☐975	3¢ Bright Red Violet	10.00	.70	.20	.13
1948. FORT BLISS					
☐976	3¢ Henna Brown	8.00	.70	.20	.13
1948. MOINA MICHAEL					
☐977	3¢ Rose Pink	5.50	.70	.20	.13
1948. GETTYSBURG ADDRESS					
☐978	3¢ Bright Blue	5.50	.70	.20	.13
1948. AMERICAN TURNERS					
☐979	3¢ Carmine	5.50	.70	.20	.13
1948. JOEL CHANDLER HARRIS					
☐980	3¢ Bright Red Violet	7.50	.70	.20	.13
1949–1950. COMMEMORATIVES					
1949. MINNESOTA CENTENNIAL					
☐981	3¢ Blue Green	5.50	.70	.20	.13
1949. WASHINGTON & LEE UNIVERSITY					
☐982	3¢ Ultramarine	5.50	.70	.20	.13
1949. PUERTO RICO ISSUE					
☐983	3¢ Green	5.50	.70	.20	.13
1949. ANNAPOLIS TERCENTENARY					
☐984	3¢ Aquamarine	5.50	.70	.20	.13
1949. G.A.R. ISSUE					
☐985	3¢ Bright Rose Carmine	5.50	.70	.20	.13
1950. EDGAR ALLAN POE					
☐986	3¢ Bright Red Violet	7.50	.70	.20	.13
1950. BANKERS ASSOCIATION					
☐987	3¢ Yellow Green	5.50	.70	.20	.13
1950. SAMUEL GOMPERS					
☐988	3¢ Bright Red Violet	6.00	.70	.20	.13
1950. WASHINGTON SESQUICENTENNIAL					
☐989	3¢ Bright Blue	5.50	.70	.20	.13
☐990	3¢ Deep Green	6.50	.70	.20	.13
☐991	3¢ Light Violet	6.50	.70	.20	.13
☐992	3¢ Rose Violet	6.50	.70	.20	.13
1950. RAILROAD ENGINEERS					
☐993	3¢ Violet Brown	5.50	.70	.20	.13
1950. KANSAS CITY CENTENARY					
☐994	3¢ Violet	5.50	.70	.20	.13

*No hinge pricing from 1941 to date is figured at (N-H ADD 15%)

Scott No.		Mint Sheet	Plate Block	Fine Unused Each	Fine Used Each
1950. BOY SCOUTS ISSUE					
☐995	3¢ Sepia	5.50	.70	.20	.13
1950. INDIANA SESQUICENTENNIAL					
☐996	3¢ Bright Blue	5.50	.70	.20	.13
1950. CALIFORNIA STATEHOOD					
☐997	3¢ Yellow Orange	5.50	.70	.20	.13
1951–1952. COMMEMORATIVES					
1951. UNITED CONFEDERATE VETERANS					
☐998	3¢ Gray	5.50	.70	.20	.13
1951. NEVADA SETTLEMENT					
☐999	3¢ Light Olive Green	5.50	.70	.20	.13
1951. LANDING OF CADILLAC					
☐1000	3¢ Bright Blue	5.50	.70	.20	.13
1951. COLORADO STATEHOOD					
☐1001	3¢ Violet Blue	5.50	.70	.20	.13
1951. AMERICAN CHEMICAL SOCIETY					
☐1002	3¢ Violet Brown	5.50	.70	.20	.13
1951. BATTLE OF BROOKLYN ISSUE					
☐1003	3¢ Violet	5.50	.70	.20	.13
1952. BETSY ROSS ISSUE					
☐1004	3¢ Carmine Rose	5.60	.70	.20	.13
1952. 4-H CLUB ISSUE					
☐1005	3¢ Blue Green	5.60	.70	.20	.13
1952. BALTIMORE & OHIO RAILROAD					
☐1006	3¢ Bright Blue	6.00	.70	.20	.13
1952. AMERICAN AUTOMOBILE ASSOCIATION (AAA)					
☐1007	3¢ Deep Blue	5.60	.70	.20	.13
1952. NORTH ATLANTIC TREATY ORGANIZATION					
☐1008	3¢ Deep Violet	11.00	.70	.20	.13
1952. GRAND COULEE DAM ISSUE					
☐1009	3¢ Blue Green	5.50	.70	.20	.13
1952. ARRIVAL OF LAFAYETTE					
☐1010	3¢ Ultramarine	5.50	.70	.20	.13
1952. MOUNT RUSHMORE					
☐1011	3¢ Blue Green	5.50	.70	.20	.13
1952. SOCIETY OF CIVIL ENGINEERS					
☐1012	3¢ Violet Blue	5.50	.70	.20	.13

*No hinge pricing from 1941 to date is figured at (N-H ADD 15%)

Scott No.		Mint Sheet	Plate Block	Fine Unused Each	Fine Used Each

1952. WOMEN IN ARMED FORCES
| ☐ 1013 | 3¢ Deep Blue | 5.50 | .70 | .20 | .13 |

1952. GUTENBERG PRINTING
| ☐ 1014 | 3¢ Violet | 5.50 | .70 | .20 | .13 |

1952. NEWSPAPERBOYS
| ☐ 1015 | 3¢ Violet | 5.50 | .70 | .20 | .13 |

1952. INTERNATIONAL RED CROSS
| ☐ 1016 | 3¢ Deep Blue & Carmine | 5.50 | .70 | .20 | .13 |

1953–1954. COMMEMORATIVES

1953. NATIONAL GUARD
| ☐ 1017 | 3¢ Bright Blue | 5.50 | .70 | .20 | .13 |

1953. OHIO STATEHOOD
| ☐ 1018 | 3¢ Chocolate | 8.00 | .70 | .20 | .13 |

1953. WASHINGTON TERRITORY
| ☐ 1019 | 3¢ Green | 5.50 | .70 | .20 | .13 |

1953. LOUISIANA PURCHASE
| ☐ 1020 | 3¢ Violet Brown | 5.50 | .70 | .20 | .13 |

1953. OPENING OF JAPAN
| ☐ 1021 | 3¢ Green | 7.00 | 1.50 | .20 | .13 |

1953. AMERICAN BAR ASSOCIATION
| ☐ 1022 | 3¢ Rose Violet | 5.50 | .70 | .20 | .13 |

1953. SAGAMORE HILL
| ☐ 1023 | 3¢ Yellow Green | 5.50 | .70 | .20 | .13 |

1953. FUTURE FARMERS
| ☐ 1024 | 3¢ Deep Blue | 5.50 | .70 | .20 | .13 |

1953. TRUCKING INDUSTRY
| ☐ 1025 | 3¢ Violet | 5.50 | .70 | .20 | .13 |

1953. GENERAL PATTON
| ☐ 1026 | 3¢ Blue Violet | 7.00 | .70 | .20 | .13 |

1953. NEW YORK CITY
| ☐ 1027 | 3¢ Bright Red Violet | 5.50 | .70 | .20 | .13 |

1953. GADSDEN PURCHASE
| ☐ 1028 | 3¢ Copper Brown | 5.50 | .70 | .20 | .13 |

1954. COLUMBIA UNIVERSITY
| ☐ 1029 | 3¢ Blue | 5.50 | .70 | .20 | .13 |

1954–1961. LIBERTY SERIES
☐ 1030	½¢ Red Orange	5.50	.70	.20	.13
☐ 1031	1¢ Dark Green	5.50	.70	.20	.13
☐ 1031A	1¼¢ Turquoise	5.50	.80	.20	.13

*No hinge pricing from 1941 to date is figured at (N-H ADD 15%)

	Scott No.		Mint Sheet	Plate Block	Fine Unused Each	Fine Used Each
☐ 1032	1½¢	Brown	7.50	3.00	.20	.13
☐ 1033	2¢	Rose Carmine	5.50	.70	.20	.13
☐ 1034	2½¢	Dark Blue	7.50	.70	.20	.13
☐ 1035	3¢	Deep Violet	7.00	.70	.20	.13
☐ 1036	4¢	Red Violet	9.00	.75	.20	.13
☐ 1037	4½¢	Green	10.00	.80	.20	.13
☐ 1038	5¢	Deep Blue	14.00	.70	.20	.13
☐ 1039	6¢	Orange Red	34.00	1.80	.40	.13
☐ 1040	7¢	Deep Carmine	36.00	1.85	.40	.13
☐ 1041	8¢	Dark Violet Blue, Carmine	28.00	3.00	.24	.13
☐ 1042	8¢	Violet Blue, Carmine (Re-engraved)	26.00	1.50	.26	.13
☐ 1042A	8¢	Brown	26.00	1.50	.30	.13
☐ 1043	9¢	Rose Lilac	40.00	2.10	.50	.13
☐ 1044	10¢	Rose Lake	29.00	1.40	.30	.13
☐ 1044A	11¢	Carmine, Violet Blue	34.00	1.60	.40	.13
☐ 1045	12¢	Red	41.00	2.10	.45	.13
☐ 1046	15¢	Maroon	100.00	3.00	.90	.13
☐ 1047	20¢	Ultramarine	65.00	3.00	.60	.13
☐ 1048	25¢	Green	170.00	8.00	1.75	.13
☐ 1049	30¢	Black	120.00	6.00	1.35	.13
☐ 1050	40¢	Brown Carmine	250.00	12.00	2.10	.13
☐ 1051	50¢	Bright Violet	200.00	9.00	2.50	.13
☐ 1052	$1	Deep Violet	1000.00	35.00	7.50	.13
☐ 1053	$5	Black	12,000.00	400.00	100.00	8.75

1954–1965. ROTARY PRESS COIL STAMPS
PERF. 10 VERTICALLY OR HORIZONTALLY

	Scott No.		Fine Unused Line Pair	Ave. Unused Line Pair	Fine Unused Each	Ave. Unused Each	Fine Used Each	Ave. Used Each
☐ 1054	1¢	Deep Green	1.25	.90	.30	.21	.16	.13
☐ 1055	2¢	Rose Carmine	.75	.50	.21	.20	.16	.13
☐ 1056	2½¢	Gray Blue	6.00	4.00	.21	.20	.30	.25
☐ 1057	3¢	Deep Violet	.80	.60	.21	.20	.16	.13
☐ 1058	4¢	Red Violet	.90	.70	.30	.24	.16	.13
☐ 1059	4½¢	Green	18.00	15.00	1.80	1.30	1.50	1.10
☐ 1059A	25¢	Green	3.00	2.50	.80	.50	.80	.24

	Scott No.		Mint Sheet	Plate Block	Fine Unused Each	Fine Used Each

1954. NEBRASKA TERRITORY
☐ 1060	3¢ Violet	5.50	.70	.21	.12

1954. KANSAS TERRITORY
☐ 1061	3¢ Brown Orange	5.50	.70	.21	.12

1954. GEORGE EASTMAN ISSUE
☐ 1062	3¢ Violet Brown	7.75	.70	.21	.12

*No hinge pricing from 1941 to date is figured at (N-H ADD 15%)

Scott No.		Mint Sheet	Plate Block	Fine Unused Each	Fine Used Each
1954. LEWIS & CLARK EXPEDITION					
☐ 1063	3¢ Dark Brown	5.50	.70	.21	.13
1955. COMMEMORATIVES					
1955. PENNSYLVANIA ACADEMY OF FINE ARTS					
☐ 1064	3¢ Rose Brown	5.50	.70	.21	.13
1955. LAND GRANT COLLEGES					
☐ 1065	3¢ Green	5.50	.70	.21	.13
1955. ROTARY INTERNATIONAL ISSUE					
☐ 1066	8¢ Deep Blue	10.00	1.50	.24	.15
1955. ARMED FORCES RESERVE					
☐ 1067	3¢ Red Violet	5.50	.70	.21	.13
1955. OLD MAN OF THE MOUNTAINS					
☐ 1068	3¢ Blue Green	5.50	.70	.21	.13
1955. SOO LOCKS CENTENNIAL					
☐ 1069	3¢ Blue	5.50	.70	.21	.13
1955. ATOMS FOR PEACE					
☐ 1070	3¢ Blue	5.50	.70	.21	.13
1955. FORT TICONDEROGA BICENTENNIAL					
☐ 1071	3¢ Sepia	5.50	.70	.21	.13
1955. ANDREW MELLON ISSUE					
☐ 1072	3¢ Deep Carmine	6.50	.70	.21	.13
1956. COMMEMORATIVES					
1956. 250TH ANNIVERSARY FRANKLIN'S BIRTH					
☐ 1073	3¢ Rose Carmine	5.50	.70	.21	.13
1956. BOOKER T. WASHINGTON ISSUE					
☐ 1074	3¢ Deep Blue	5.50	.70	.21	.13
1956. FIFTH INTL. PHILATELIC EXHIBITION DESIGNS OF 1035 & 1041 IN IMPERF. SOUVENIR SHEET					
☐ 1075	3¢ & 8¢ Sheet of 2	—	—	3.50	2.25
1956. FIFTH INTL. PHILATELIC EXHIBITION					
☐ 1076	3¢ Deep Violet	5.50	.70	.21	—
1956. WILDLIFE CONSERVATION ISSUE					
☐ 1077	3¢ Rose Lake	5.50	.75	.21	.13
☐ 1078	3¢ Brown	5.50	.75	.21	.13
☐ 1079	3¢ Green	5.50	.75	.21	.13
1956. PURE FOOD & DRUG ACT					
☐ 1080	3¢ Dark Blue Green	5.50	.75	.21	.13
1956. HOME OF PRESIDENT BUCHANAN					
☐ 1081	3¢ Black Brown	5.50	.75	.21	.13

*No hinge pricing from 1941 to date is figured at (N-H ADD 15%)

Scott No.	Mint Sheet	Plate Block	Fine Unused Each	Fine Used Each
1956. LABOR DAY ISSUE				
☐ 1082 3¢ Deep Blue	5.50	.70	.20	.13
1956. NASSAU HALL—PRINCETON				
☐ 1083 3¢ Black on Orange	5.50	.70	.20	.13
1956. DEVIL'S TOWER				
☐ 1084 3¢ Purple	5.50	.70	.20	.13
1956. CHILDREN'S ISSUE				
☐ 1085 3¢ Dark Blue	5.50	.70	.20	.13
1957. COMMEMORATIVES				
1957. ALEXANDER HAMILTON ISSUE				
☐ 1086 3¢ Rose Red	5.50	.70	.20	.13
1957. POLIO ISSUE				
☐ 1087 3¢ Light Purple	5.50	.70	.20	.13
1957. COAST & GEODETIC SURVEY				
☐ 1088 3¢ Dark Blue	5.50	.70	.20	.13
1957. ARCHITECTS ISSUE				
☐ 1089 3¢ Red Lilac	5.50	.70	.20	.13
1957. STEEL INDUSTRY CENTENNIAL				
☐ 1090 3¢ Bright Ultra	5.50	.70	.20	.13
1957. INTERNATIONAL NAVAL REVIEW				
☐ 1091 3¢ Blue Green	5.50	.70	.20	.13
1957. OKLAHOMA STATEHOOD				
☐ 1092 3¢ Dark Blue	5.50	.70	.20	.13
1957. SCHOOL TEACHERS				
☐ 1093 3¢ Rose Lake	5.50	.70	.20	.13
1957. U.S. FLAG ISSUE				
☐ 1094 4¢ Blue & Red	5.50	.70	.20	.13
1957. 350TH SHIPBUILDING ANNIVERSARY				
☐ 1095 3¢ Purple	7.75	.70	.21	.14
1957. PHILIPPINES—CHAMPION OF LIBERTY				
☐ 1096 8¢ Red, Blue & Gold	9.00	1.00	.25	.13
1957. BIRTH OF LAFAYETTE				
☐ 1097 3¢ Maroon	5.50	.70	.21	.13
1957. WILDLIFE CONSERVATION ISSUE				
☐ 1098 3¢ Blue, Green & Yellow	5.50	.70	.21	.13
1957. RELIGIOUS FREEDOM				
☐ 1099 3¢ Black	5.50	.70	.21	.13

*No hinge pricing from 1941 to date is figured at (N-H ADD 15%)

Scott No.		Mint Sheet	Plate Block	Fine Unused Each	Fine Used Each

1958. COMMEMORATIVES

1958. GARDENING & HORTICULTURE
| ☐ 1100 | 3¢ Deep Green .... | 5.50 | .70 | .20 | .13 |

1958. BRUSSELS EXHIBITION
| ☐ 1104 | 3¢ Deep Claret .... | 5.50 | .70 | .20 | .13 |

1958. JAMES MONROE BICENTENNIAL
| ☐ 1105 | 3¢ Purple .... | 8.00 | .70 | .20 | .13 |

1958. MINNESOTA STATEHOOD
| ☐ 1106 | 3¢ Green .... | 5.50 | .70 | .20 | .13 |

1958. INTERNATIONAL GEOPHYSICAL YEAR
| ☐ 1107 | 3¢ Black & Orange .... | 5.50 | .70 | .20 | .13 |

1958. GUNSTON HALL BICENTENARY
| ☐ 1108 | 3¢ Light Green .... | 5.50 | .70 | .20 | .13 |

1958. MACKINAC BRIDGE ISSUE
| ☐ 1109 | 3¢ Bluish Green .... | 5.50 | .70 | .20 | .13 |

1958. SOUTH AMERICA—CHAMPION OF LIBERTY
| ☐ 1110 | 4¢ Olive Bistre .... | 8.00 | .70 | .20 | .13 |
| ☐ 1111 | 8¢ Red, Blue & Gold .... | 16.00 | 2.10 | .30 | .22 |

1958. ATLANTIC CABLE CENTENNIAL
| ☐ 1112 | 4¢ Reddish Purple .... | 6.00 | .70 | .20 | .13 |

1958–1959. LINCOLN COMMEMORATIVE ISSUE
☐ 1113	1¢ Green	3.00	.50	.22	.14
☐ 1114	3¢ Rust Brown	5.00	.70	.20	.13
☐ 1115	4¢ Sepia	6.50	.70	.20	.13
☐ 1116	4¢ Blue	6.50	.70	.20	.13

1958. HUNGARY—CHAMPION OF LIBERTY
| ☐ 1117 | 4¢ Bluish Green .... | 8.50 | .70 | .20 | .13 |
| ☐ 1118 | 8¢ Red, Blue & Gold .... | 14.00 | 2.00 | .24 | .16 |

1958. FREEDOM OF THE PRESS
| ☐ 1119 | 4¢ Black .... | 5.50 | .70 | .20 | .13 |

1958. OVERLAND MAIL CENTENNIAL
| ☐ 1120 | 4¢ Crimson Rose .... | 6.50 | .70 | .20 | .13 |

1958. NOAH WEBSTER
| ☐ 1121 | 4¢ Dark Carmine Rose .... | 8.75 | .70 | .20 | .13 |

1958. FOREST CONSERVATION
| ☐ 1122 | 4¢ Yellow, Brown & Green .... | 6.50 | .70 | .20 | .13 |

1958. FORT DUQUESNE BICENTENNIAL
| ☐ 1123 | 4¢ Blue .... | 6.50 | .70 | .20 | .13 |

*No hinge pricing from 1941 to date is figured at (N-H ADD 15%)

Scott No.		Mint Sheet	Plate Block	Fine Unused Each	Fine Used Each
1959. COMMEMORATIVES					
1959. OREGON STATEHOOD					
☐ 1124	4¢ Blue Green	6.00	.70	.20	.13
1959. ARGENTINA & CHILE—CHAMPION OF LIBERTY					
☐ 1125	4¢ Blue	8.00	.70	.20	.13
☐ 1126	8¢ Red, Blue & Gold	14.00	1.25	.28	.15
1959. 10TH ANNIVERSARY N.A.T.O.					
☐ 1127	4¢ Blue	8.00	.70	.20	.13
1959. ARCTIC EXPLORATIONS					
☐ 1128	4¢ Blue	6.00	.70	.20	.13
1959. WORLD PEACE & TRUST					
☐ 1129	8¢ Maroon	10.00	1.75	.28	.15
1959. SILVER DISCOVERY CENTENNIAL					
☐ 1130	4¢ Black	6.00	.70	.20	.13
1959. ST. LAWRENCE SEAWAY ISSUE					
☐ 1131	4¢ Red & Blue	6.00	.70	.20	.13
1959. 49-STAR FLAG ISSUE					
☐ 1132	4¢ Blue, Red & Yellow	6.00	.70	.20	.13
1959. SOIL CONSERVATION					
☐ 1133	4¢ Yellow, Green & Blue	6.00	.70	.20	.13
1959. PETROLEUM INDUSTRY CENTENNIAL					
☐ 1134	4¢ Brown	5.50	.70	.20	.13
1959. DENTAL HEALTH ISSUE					
☐ 1135	4¢ Green	5.50	.70	.20	.13
1959. GERMANY—CHAMPION OF LIBERTY					
☐ 1136	4¢ Gray	8.00	.75	.20	.13
☐ 1137	8¢ Red, Blue & Gold	15.00	2.10	.28	.15
1959. DR. EPHRAIM McDOWELL					
☐ 1138	4¢ Maroon	8.00	.70	.20	.13
1960–1961. CREDO OF AMERICA SERIES					
☐ 1139	4¢ Dark Violet, Blue & Carmine	6.50	.70	.20	.13
☐ 1140	4¢ Olive Bistre & Green	6.50	.70	.20	.13
☐ 1141	4¢ Gray & Red	6.50	.75	.20	.13
☐ 1142	4¢ Red & Blue	6.50	.75	.20	.13
☐ 1143	4¢ Violet & Green	8.00	.75	.20	.13
☐ 1144	4¢ Green & Brown	8.00	.75	.20	.13
1960. COMMEMORATIVES					
1960. BOY SCOUTS GOLDEN JUBILEE					
☐ 1145	4¢ Red, Khaki & Blue	6.00	.70	.20	.13

*No hinge pricing from 1941 to date is figured at (N-H ADD 15%)

Scott No.		Mint Sheet	Plate Block	Fine Unused Each	Fine Used Each
1960. WINTER OLYMPIC GAMES					
☐ 1146	4¢ Blue	6.50	.70	.20	.13
1960. CZECHOSLOVAKIA—CHAMPION OF LIBERTY					
☐ 1147	4¢ Blue	6.50	.70	.20	.13
☐ 1148	8¢ Yellow, Blue & Red	14.00	1.40	.25	.14
1960. WORLD REFUGEE YEAR					
☐ 1149	4¢ Gray Black	6.00	.70	.20	.13
1960. WATER CONSERVATION					
☐ 1150	4¢ Blue, Green & Orange Brown	6.00	.70	.20	.13
1960. SOUTHEAST ASIA TREATY ORGANIZATION					
☐ 1151	4¢ Blue	8.00	.70	.20	.13
1960. HONORING AMERICAN WOMEN					
☐ 1152	4¢ Violet	6.00	.70	.20	.13
1960. 50-STAR FLAG ISSUE					
☐ 1153	4¢ Red & Blue	6.00	.70	.20	.13
1960. PONY EXPRESS CENTENNIAL					
☐ 1154	4¢ Sepia	6.00	.70	.20	.13
1960. EMPLOY THE HANDICAPPED					
☐ 1155	4¢ Blue	6.00	.70	.20	.13
1960. WORLD FORESTRY CONGRESS					
☐ 1156	4¢ Green	6.00	.70	.20	.13
1960. MEXICAN INDEPENDENCE SESQUICENTENNIAL					
☐ 1157	4¢ Red & Green	6.00	.70	.20	.13
1960. UNITED STATES–JAPAN TREATY CENTENNIAL					
☐ 1158	4¢ Blue & Pink	6.00	.70	.20	.13
1960. POLAND—CHAMPION OF LIBERTY					
☐ 1159	4¢ Blue	8.00	.70	.20	.13
☐ 1160	8¢ Red & Blue & Gold	14.00	1.80	.30	.15
1960. ROBERT A. TAFT MEMORIAL ISSUE					
☐ 1161	4¢ Dull Violet	8.00	.70	.20	.13
1960. WHEELS OF FREEDOM					
☐ 1162	4¢ Dark Blue	6.50	.70	.20	.13
1960. BOYS' CLUBS OF AMERICA					
☐ 1163	4¢ Indigo, Slate & Red	6.50	.70	.20	.13
1960. FIRST AUTOMATED POST OFFICE					
☐ 1164	4¢ Dark Blue & Carmine	6.50	.70	.20	.13
1960. FINLAND—CHAMPION OF LIBERTY					
☐ 1165	4¢ Blue	8.00	.70	.20	.13
☐ 1166	8¢ Red, Blue & Gold	14.00	1.60	.30	.16

*No hinge pricing from 1941 to date is figured at (N-H ADD 15%)

Scott No.		Mint Sheet	Plate Block	Fine Unused Each	Fine Used Each
1960. CAMP FIRE GIRLS					
☐ 1167	4¢ Dark Blue & Red	6.00	.70	.20	.13
1960. ITALY—CHAMPION OF LIBERTY					
☐ 1168	4¢ Green	8.00	.70	.20	.13
☐ 1169	8¢ Red, Blue & Gold	14.00	1.50	.35	.16
1960. WALTER F. GEORGE MEMORIAL ISSUE					
☐ 1170	4¢ Dull Violet	8.00	.75	.20	.13
1960. ANDREW CARNEGIE					
☐ 1171	4¢ Deep Claret	8.00	.75	.20	.13
1960. JOHN FOSTER DULLES MEMORIAL ISSUE					
☐ 1172	4¢ Dull Violet	8.00	.70	.20	.13
1960. "ECHO I" SATELLITE					
☐ 1173	4¢ Deep Violet	12.00	.90	.35	.15
1961. COMMEMORATIVES					
1961. INDIA—CHAMPION OF LIBERTY					
☐ 1174	4¢ Red Orange	8.00	.70	.21	.13
☐ 1175	8¢ Red, Blue & Gold	14.00	1.50	.25	.15
1961. RANGE CONSERVATION					
☐ 1176	4¢ Blue, Slate & Brown Orange	6.00	.70	.20	.13
1961. HORACE GREELEY					
☐ 1177	4¢ Dull Violet	8.00	.70	.20	.13
1961–1965. CIVIL WAR CENTENNIAL SERIES					
1961. FORT SUMTER					
☐ 1178	4¢ Light Green	11.00	1.00	.21	.13
1962. BATTLE OF SHILOH					
☐ 1179	4¢ Black on Peach	7.50	.80	.22	.13
1963. BATTLE OF GETTYSBURG					
☐ 1180	5¢ Blue & Gray	9.00	.80	.22	.13
1964. BATTLE OF THE WILDERNESS					
☐ 1181	5¢ Dark Red & Black	9.00	1.00	.22	.13
1965. APPOMATTOX					
☐ 1182	5¢ Black & Blue	20.00	1.75	.22	.13
1961. KANSAS STATEHOOD					
☐ 1183	4¢ Brown, Dark Red & Green on Yellow Paper	6.00	.75	.21	.13
1961. GEORGE W. NORRIS BIRTH CENTENARY					
☐ 1184	4¢ Blue Green	6.00	.75	.21	.13
1961. NAVAL AVIATION GOLDEN JUBILEE					
☐ 1185	4¢ Blue	6.00	.75	.21	.14

*No hinge pricing from 1941 to date is figured at (N-H ADD 15%)

Scott No.		Mint Sheet	Plate Block	Fine Unused Each	Fine Used Each

1961. WORKMEN'S COMPENSATION LAW
| ☐ 1186 | 4¢ Ultramarine | 6.50 | .70 | .20 | .13 |

1961. F. REMINGTON BIRTH CENTENNIAL
| ☐ 1187 | 4¢ Blue, Red & Yellow | 6.50 | .80 | .20 | .13 |

1961. REPUBLIC OF CHINA ISSUE
| ☐ 1188 | 4¢ Blue | 6.50 | .70 | .20 | .13 |

1961. DR. J. NAISMITH—BASKETBALL FOUNDER
| ☐ 1189 | 4¢ Brown | 6.50 | .80 | .20 | .13 |

1961. NURSING PROFESSION
| ☐ 1190 | 4¢ Blue, Red, Black & Green | 6.50 | .75 | .20 | .13 |

1962. COMMEMORATIVES

1962. NEW MEXICO STATEHOOD
| ☐ 1191 | 4¢ Blue, Maroon, Bistre | 6.50 | .70 | .21 | .12 |

1962. ARIZONA STATEHOOD
| ☐ 1192 | 4¢ Red, Deep Blue, Green | 6.50 | .70 | .21 | .12 |

1962. PROJECT MERCURY
| ☐ 1193 | 4¢ Dark Blue & Yellow | 6.50 | .80 | .21 | .12 |

1962. MALARIA ERADICATION
| ☐ 1194 | 4¢ Blue & Bistre | 6.50 | .75 | .20 | .12 |

1962. CHARLES EVANS HUGHES BIRTH CENTENNIAL
| ☐ 1195 | 4¢ Black on Buff | 6.00 | .70 | .20 | .12 |

1962. SEATTLE WORLD'S FAIR
| ☐ 1196 | 4¢ Red & Dark Blue | 6.00 | .70 | .20 | .12 |

1962. LOUISIANA STATEHOOD
| ☐ 1197 | 4¢ Blue, Green, Red | 6.00 | .70 | .20 | .12 |

1962. THE HOMESTEAD ACT
| ☐ 1198 | 4¢ Slate | 6.50 | .70 | .19 | .13 |

1962. GIRL SCOUTS 50TH ANNIVERSARY
| ☐ 1199 | 4¢ Red | 6.00 | .70 | .19 | .13 |

1962. BRIEN McMAHON MEMORIAL ISSUE
| ☐ 1200 | 4¢ Purple | 6.50 | .75 | .19 | .13 |

1962. NATIONAL APPRENTICESHIP ACT
| ☐ 1201 | 4¢ Black on Buff | 6.00 | .70 | .19 | .13 |

1962. SAM RAYBURN MEMORIAL ISSUE
| ☐ 1202 | 4¢ Brown & Blue | 6.00 | .70 | .19 | .13 |

1962. DAG HAMMARSKJOLD MEMORIAL
| ☐ 1203 | 4¢ Yellow, Brown & Black | 6.00 | .70 | .19 | .13 |
| ☐ 1204 | 4¢ Yellow Color Inverted | 12.50 | 2.00 | .25 | .21 |

*No hinge pricing from 1941 to date is figured at (N-H ADD 15%)

Scott No.		Mint Sheet	Plate Block	Fine Unused Each	Fine Used Each
1962. CHRISTMAS TREE					
☐ 1205	4¢ Green & Red	12.00	.75	.20	.12
1962. HIGHER EDUCATION					
☐ 1206	4¢ Green & Black	6.50	.75	.20	.13
1962. WINSLOW HOMER					
☐ 1207	4¢ Brown & Blue	6.50	.75	.22	.13
1963. 50-STAR FLAG					
☐ 1208	5¢ Red & Blue	12.00	.75	.20	.13
1962–1963. REGULAR ISSUE					
☐ 1209	1¢ Green	6.00	.35	.20	.13
☐ 1213	5¢ Dark Blue Gray	12.50	.80	.22	.13

1962–1963. ROTARY PRESS COIL STAMPS PERF. 10 VERTICALLY

Scott No.		Fine Unused Plate Blk	Ave. Unused Plate Blk	Fine Unused Each	Ave. Unused Each	Fine Used Each	Ave. Used Each
☐ 1225	1¢ Green	1.60	1.00	.35	.26	.20	.16
☐ 1229	5¢ Dark Blue Gray	4.00	3.00	1.60	1.10	.20	.16

Scott No.		Mint Sheet	Plate Block	Fine Unused Each	Fine Used Each
1963. COMMEMORATIVES					
1963. CAROLINA CHARTER TERCENTENARY					
☐ 1230	5¢ Dark Carmine & Brown	6.80	.75	.20	.13
1963. FOOD FOR PEACE—FREEDOM FROM HUNGER					
☐ 1231	5¢ Green, Buff & Red	6.80	.75	.20	.13
1963. WEST VIRGINIA STATEHOOD					
☐ 1232	5¢ Green, Red & Black	6.80	.75	.20	.12
1963. EMANCIPATION PROCLAMATION					
☐ 1233	5¢ Black, Blue & Red	6.80	.75	.20	.12
1963. ALLIANCE FOR PROGRESS					
☐ 1234	5¢ Bright Blue & Green	6.80	.75	.20	.12
1963. CORDELL HULL					
☐ 1235	5¢ Blue Green	6.80	.75	.20	.12
1963. ELEANOR ROOSEVELT					
☐ 1236	5¢ Light Purple	6.80	.75	.20	.12
1963. THE SCIENCES					
☐ 1237	5¢ Blue & Black	6.80	.75	.21	.12
1963. CITY MAIL DELIVERY					
☐ 1238	5¢ Red, Blue & Gray	6.80	.75	.20	.12

*No hinge pricing from 1941 to date is figured at (N-H ADD 15%)

Scott No.		Mint Sheet	Plate Block	Fine Unused Each	Fine Used Each
1963. INTERNATIONAL RED CROSS CENTENARY					
☐ 1239	5¢ Slate & Carmine	6.50	.70	.20	.13
1963. CHRISTMAS ISSUE					
☐ 1240	5¢ Dark Blue, Blue Black & Red	12.00	.70	.20	.13
1963. JOHN JAMES AUDUBON					
☐ 1241	5¢ Blue, Brown, Bistre	7.00	.70	.21	.13
1964. COMMEMORATIVES					
1964. SAM HOUSTON					
☐ 1242	5¢ Black	7.00	.70	.21	.13
1964. CHARLES M. RUSSELL					
☐ 1243	5¢ Indigo, Red Brown & Olive	7.00	.70	.21	.13
1964. NEW YORK WORLD'S FAIR					
☐ 1244	5¢ Green	7.00	.70	.21	.13
1964. JOHN MUIR—CONSERVATIONIST					
☐ 1245	5¢ Brown, Green & Olive	7.00	.70	.20	.13
1964. JOHN F. KENNEDY MEMORIAL					
☐ 1246	5¢ Blue Gray	7.00	.70	.20	.13
1964. NEW JERSEY TERCENTENARY					
☐ 1247	5¢ Ultramarine	7.00	.70	.21	.13
1964. NEVADA STATEHOOD					
☐ 1248	5¢ Red, Yellow & Blue	7.00	.70	.20	.13
1964. REGISTER AND VOTE					
☐ 1249	5¢ Dark Blue & Red	7.00	.70	.20	.13
1964. WILLIAM SHAKESPEARE					
☐ 1250	5¢ Brown on Tan	7.00	.70	.20	.13
1964. DOCTORS MAYO					
☐ 1251	5¢ Green	7.00	.70	.20	.13
1964. AMERICAN MUSIC					
☐ 1252	5¢ Red, Black & Blue	7.00	.70	.20	.13
1964. AMERICAN HOMEMAKERS					
☐ 1253	5¢ Multicolored	7.00	.70	.20	.13
1964. CHRISTMAS ISSUE					
☐ 1254	5¢ Red & Green	—	—	1.40	.13
☐ 1255	5¢ Red & Green	—	—	1.40	.13
☐ 1256	5¢ Red & Green	—	—	1.00	.13
☐ 1257	5¢ Red & Green	—	—	.17	.13
1964. VERRAZANO–NARROWS BRIDGE					
☐ 1258	5¢ Green	7.00	.70	.22	.13

*No hinge pricing from 1941 to date is figured at (N-H ADD 15%)

Scott No.		Mint Sheet	Plate Block	Fine Unused Each	Fine Used Each
1964. STUART DAVIS—MODERN ART		7.00	.70	.21	.13
☐ 1259	5¢ Ultramarine, Black & Red				
1964. RADIO AMATEURS		7.50	.70	.21	.13
☐ 1260	5¢ Red Lilac				
1965. COMMEMORATIVES					
1965. BATTLE OF NEW ORLEANS		6.50	.70	.20	.13
☐ 1261	5¢ Carmine, Blue & Gray				
1965. PHYSICAL FITNESS—SOKOL CENTENNIAL		6.50	.70	.20	.13
☐ 1262	5¢ Maroon & Black				
1965. CRUSADE AGAINST CANCER		6.50	.70	.20	.13
☐ 1263	5¢ Black, Purple, Orange				
1965. SIR WINSTON CHURCHILL MEMORIAL		6.50	.75	.20	.13
☐ 1264	5¢ Black				
1965. MAGNA CARTA 750TH ANNIVERSARY		6.50	.70	.20	.13
☐ 1265	5¢ Black, Ochre, Red Lilac				
1965. INTERNATIONAL COOPERATION YEAR		6.50	.70	.20	.13
☐ 1266	5¢ Dull Blue & Black				
1965. SALVATION ARMY		6.50	.75	.20	.13
☐ 1267	5¢ Red, Black & Blue				
1965. DANTE ALIGHIERI		6.50	.70	.20	.12
☐ 1268	5¢ Maroon on Tan				
1965. HERBERT HOOVER		6.50	.70	.20	.12
☐ 1269	5¢ Red Rose				
1965. ROBERT FULTON BIRTH BICENTENNIAL		6.50	.70	.20	.12
☐ 1270	5¢ Black & Blue				
1965. FLORIDA SETTLEMENT QUADRICENTENNIAL		6.50	.75	.20	.12
☐ 1271	5¢ Red, Yellow & Black				
1965. TRAFFIC SAFETY		6.50	.75	.20	.12
☐ 1272	5¢ Green, Black, Red				
1965. JOHN SINGLETON COPLEY—ARTIST		7.00	.75	.20	.12
☐ 1273	5¢ Black, Brown, Olive				
1965. INTERNATIONAL TELECOMMUNICATION UNION		30.00	10.00	.50	.22
☐ 1274	11¢ Black, Carmine, Bistre				
1965. ADLAI E. STEVENSON MEMORIAL		6.00	.80	.20	.12
☐ 1275	5¢ Light & Dark Blue, Black & Red				
1965. CHRISTMAS ISSUE		12.00	.80	.20	.12
☐ 1276	5¢ Red, Green & Yellow				

*No hinge pricing from 1941 to date is figured at (N-H ADD 15%)

Scott No.		Mint Sheet	Plate Block	Fine Unused Each	Fine Used Each

1965–1968. PROMINENT AMERICANS SERIES

		Mint Sheet	Plate Block	Fine Unused Each	Fine Used Each
☐ 1278	1¢ Green	6.00	.70	.20	.12
☐ 1279	1¼¢ Green	21.00	14.00	.20	.13
☐ 1280	2¢ Slate Blue	6.00	.65	.20	.12
☐ 1281	3¢ Purple	8.00	.70	.20	.12
☐ 1282	4¢ Black	10.00	.70	.20	.12
☐ 1283	5¢ Blue	12.00	.70	.20	.12
☐ 1283B	5¢ Blue	12.00	.70	.20	.12
☐ 1284	6¢ Gray Brown	17.00	.70	.20	.12
☐ 1285	8¢ Violet	22.00	1.10	.30	.12
☐ 1286	10¢ Lilac	25.00	1.25	.30	.15
☐ 1286A	12¢ Black	30.00	1.50	.32	.12
☐ 1287	13¢ Brown	32.00	2.00	.32	.12
☐ 1288	15¢ Rose Claret	36.00	4.00	.36	.12
☐ 1288A	15¢ Rose Claret II	34.00	4.00	.35	.15
☐ 1289	20¢ Olive Green	45.00	3.00	.60	.12
☐ 1290	25¢ Rose Lake	50.00	3.00	.65	.12
☐ 1291	30¢ Light Purple	60.00	3.50	.75	.12
☐ 1292	40¢ Dark Blue	86.00	4.50	1.00	.14
☐ 1293	50¢ Maroon	100.00	5.00	1.25	.12
☐ 1294	$1 Purple	210.00	11.00	2.10	.16
☐ 1295	$5 Gray	1000.00	48.00	11.00	2.50

Scott No.		Fine Unused Line Pair	Ave. Unused Line Pair	Fine Unused Each	Ave. Unused Each	Fine Used Each	Ave. Used Each

PERF. 10 HORIZONTALLY

		Fine Unused Line Pair	Ave. Unused Line Pair	Fine Unused Each	Ave. Unused Each	Fine Used Each	Ave. Used Each
☐ 1297	3¢ Purple	.75	.60	.22	.21	.20	.12
☐ 1298	6¢ Gray Brown	1.60	1.20	.21	.20	.20	.12

PERF. 10 VERTICALLY

☐ 1299	1¢ Green	.50	.30	.21	.20	.20	.12
☐ 1303	4¢ Black	1.00	.85	.21	.20	.20	.12
☐ 1304	5¢ Blue	.70	.60	.21	.20	.20	.12
☐ 1305	6¢ Gray Brown	1.10	.80	.21	.20	.20	.12
☐ 1305C	$1 Purple	6.00	4.00	2.00	1.80	2.00	.90

Scott No.		Mint Sheet	Plate Block	Fine Unused Each	Fine Used Each

1966. COMMEMORATIVES

1966. MIGRATORY BIRD TREATY

		Mint Sheet	Plate Block	Fine Unused Each	Fine Used Each
☐ 1306	5¢ Red, Blue, Black	7.00	.70	.20	.12

1966. HUMANE TREATMENT OF ANIMALS

☐ 1307	5¢ Orange Brown & Black	7.00	.70	.20	.12

1966. INDIANA STATEHOOD

☐ 1308	5¢ Ochre, Brown & Violet Blue	7.00	.70	.20	.12

*No hinge pricing from 1941 to date is figured at (N-H ADD 15%)

Scott No.	Mint Sheet	Plate Block	Fine Unused Each	Fine Used Each
1966. AMERICAN CIRCUS				
☐ 1309 5¢ Red, Blue, Pink, Black	7.00	.70	.20	.13
1966. SIXTH INTL. PHILATELIC EXHIBITION "SIPEX"				
☐ 1310 5¢ Multicolored	7.00	.70	.21	.13
IMPERFORATE SOUVENIR SHEET				
☐ 1311 5¢ Multicolored	—	—	.21	.20
1966. BILL OF RIGHTS				
☐ 1312 5¢ Red, Dark & Light Blue	8.00	.70	.20	.12
1966. POLISH MILLENNIUM				
☐ 1313 5¢ Red	7.00	.70	.20	.12
1966. NATIONAL PARK SERVICE				
☐ 1314 5¢ Yellow, Black & Green	7.00	.70	.20	.12
1966. MARINE CORPS RESERVE				
☐ 1315 5¢ Black, Red, Blue, Olive	7.00	.70	.20	.12
1966. GENERAL FEDERATION OF WOMEN'S CLUBS				
☐ 1316 5¢ Blue, Pink, Black	7.00	.70	.20	.12
1966. AMERICAN FOLKLORE—JOHNNY APPLESEED				
☐ 1317 5¢ Red, Black, Green	7.00	.70	.20	.12
1966. BEAUTIFICATION OF AMERICA				
☐ 1318 5¢ Emerald, Pink, Black	7.00	.75	.20	.12
1966. GREAT RIVER ROAD				
☐ 1319 5¢ Yellow, Red, Blue, Green	7.00	.75	.21	.12
1966. SERVICEMEN & SAVINGS BONDS				
☐ 1320 5¢ Red, Light Blue, Dark Blue	7.00	.75	.20	.12
1966. CHRISTMAS ISSUE				
☐ 1321 5¢ Multicolored	12.00	.75	.20	.12
1966. MARY CASSATT—ARTIST				
☐ 1322 5¢ Multicolored	9.00	2.00	.21	.12
1967. COMMEMORATIVES				
1967. NATIONAL GRANGE CENTENARY				
☐ 1323 5¢ Orange, Yellow, Black, Brown & Green	7.00	.70	.20	.12
1967. CANADA CENTENNIAL				
☐ 1324 5¢ Green, Light & Dark Blue, Black	7.00	.70	.20	.12
1967. ERIE CANAL SESQUICENTENNIAL				
☐ 1325 5¢ Light & Dark Blue, Red & Black	7.00	.70	.20	.12
1967. SEARCH FOR PEACE—LIONS INTL.				
☐ 1326 5¢ Red, Blue & Black	7.00	.70	.20	.12
1967. HENRY DAVID THOREAU				
☐ 1327 5¢ Black, Red & Green	7.00	.70	.20	.12

*No hinge pricing from 1941 to date is figured at (N-H ADD 15%)

Scott No.		Mint Sheet	Plate Block	Fine Unused Each	Fine Used Each
1967. NEBRASKA STATEHOOD CENTENNIAL					
☐ 1328	5¢ Yellow Green & Brown	7.00	.75	.20	.12
1967. VOICE OF AMERICA					
☐ 1329	5¢ Red, Blue & Black	7.00	.75	.20	.12
1967. AMERICAN FOLKLORE—DAVY CROCKETT					
☐ 1330	5¢ Green & Black	7.00	.75	.20	.12
1967. SPACE ACCOMPLISHMENTS					
☐ 1331	5¢ Light & Dark Blue, Red, Black	—	—	1.00	.26
☐ 1332	5¢ Light & Dark Blue, Red, Black	—	—	1.00	.26
1967. URBAN PLANNING					
☐ 1333	5¢ Blue & Black	7.00	.75	.20	.12
1967. FINNISH INDEPENDENCE					
☐ 1334	5¢ Blue	7.00	.75	.20	.12
1967. THOMAS EAKINS—ARTIST					
☐ 1335	5¢ Gold & Multicolored	7.00	.75	.20	.12
1967. CHRISTMAS ISSUE					
☐ 1336	5¢ Multicolored	7.00	.75	.20	.12
1967. MISSISSIPPI STATEHOOD					
☐ 1337	5¢ Multicolored	7.00	.80	.20	.12
1968–1971. REGULAR ISSUES					
1968. FLAG ISSUE					
☐ 1338	6¢ Red, Blue, Green	14.00	.75	.20	.11
1968. COMMEMORATIVES					
1968. ILLINOIS STATEHOOD					
☐ 1339	6¢ Black, Gold, Pink	7.00	.75	.21	.11
1968. HEMISFAIR '68					
☐ 1340	6¢ Indigo, Carmine, White	7.00	.75	.21	.11
1968. AIRLIFT TO SERVICEMEN					
☐ 1341	$1 Multicolored	150.00	26.00	4.00	2.00
1968. SUPPORT OUR YOUTH (ELKS)					
☐ 1342	6¢ Red & Blue	7.00	.90	.22	.12
1968. LAW AND ORDER					
☐ 1343	6¢ Blue & Black	7.00	.90	.22	.12
1968. REGISTER & VOTE					
☐ 1344	6¢ Black & Gold	7.00	.90	.22	.12
1968. HISTORIC AMERICAN FLAGS					
☐ 1345	6¢ Dark Blue	—	—	.70	.40
☐ 1346	6¢ Red & Dark Blue	—	—	.70	.40

*No hinge pricing from 1941 to date is figured at (N-H ADD 15%)

Scott No.		Mint Sheet	Plate Block	Fine Unused Each	Fine Used Each
☐ 1347	6¢ Dark, Blue, Olive Green	—	—	.65	.50
☐ 1348	6¢ Dark Blue & Red	—	—	.65	.40
☐ 1349	6¢ Black, Yellow, Red	—	—	.65	.40
☐ 1350	6¢ Dark Blue & Red	—	—	.65	.40
☐ 1351	6¢ Blue, Olive Green, Red	—	—	.65	.40
☐ 1352	6¢ Dark Blue & Red	—	—	.65	.40
☐ 1353	6¢ Blue, Yellow, Red	—	—	.65	.40
☐ 1354	6¢ Blue Red, Yellow				

1968. WALT DISNEY
| ☐ 1355 | 6¢ Multicolored | 28.00 | 1.50 | .60 | .16 |

1968. FATHER MARQUETTE—EXPLORATIONS
| ☐ 1356 | 6¢ Black, Brown, Green | 10.00 | 1.00 | .22 | .12 |

1968. AMERICAN FOLKLORE—DANIEL BOONE
| ☐ 1357 | 6¢ Brown, Yellow, Black, Red | 7.00 | .70 | .22 | .12 |

1968. ARKANSAS RIVER NAVIGATION
| ☐ 1358 | 6¢ Black & Blue | 7.00 | .70 | .22 | .12 |

1968. LEIF ERIKSON
| ☐ 1359 | 6¢ Dark Brown on Brown | 7.00 | .70 | .22 | .12 |

1968. CHEROKEE STRIP LAND RUSH
| ☐ 1360 | 6¢ Brown | 7.00 | .80 | .22 | .12 |

1968. JOHN TRUMBULL PAINTING
| ☐ 1361 | 6¢ Yellow Red, Black | 7.00 | .75 | .22 | .12 |

1968. WILDLIFE CONSERVATION—DUCKS
| ☐ 1362 | 6¢ Multicolored | 11.00 | 1.10 | .22 | .12 |

1968. CHRISTMAS ISSUE
| ☐ 1363 | 6¢ Multicolored | 7.00 | 1.75 | .22 | .12 |

1968. AMERICAN INDIAN
| ☐ 1364 | 6¢ Multicolored | 11.00 | 1.10 | .25 | .13 |

1969. COMMEMORATIVES

1969. BEAUTIFICATION OF AMERICA
☐ 1365	6¢ Multicolored	—	—	1.00	.16
☐ 1366	6¢ Multicolored	—	—	1.00	.16
☐ 1367	6¢ Multicolored	—	—	1.00	.16
☐ 1368	6¢ Multicolored	—	—	1.00	.16

1969. AMERICAN LEGION
| ☐ 1369 | 6¢ Red, Blue, Black | 7.00 | .70 | .22 | .12 |

1969. GRANDMA MOSES PAINTING
| ☐ 1370 | 6¢ Multicolored | 8.00 | .75 | .22 | .12 |

1969. APOLLO 8 MOON ORBIT
| ☐ 1371 | 6¢ Black, Blue, Ochre | 12.00 | 2.10 | .22 | .13 |

*No hinge pricing from 1941 to date is figured at (N-H ADD 15%)

Scott No.		Mint Sheet	Plate Block	Fine Unused Each	Fine Used Each

1969. W. C. HANDY—MUSICIAN

☐ 1372   6¢ Multicolored .... 10.00   .95   .21   .12

1969. SETTLEMENT OF CALIFORNIA

☐ 1373   6¢ Multicolored .... 7.00   .70   .21   .12

1969. MAJOR JOHN WESLEY POWELL—GEOLOGIST

☐ 1374   6¢ Multicolored .... 7.00   .70   .21   .12

1969. ALABAMA STATEHOOD

☐ 1375   6¢ Red, Yellow, Brown .... 7.00   .70   .21   .12

1969. XI INTL. BOTANICAL CONGRESS

☐ 1376   6¢ Multicolored .... —   —   1.40   .22
☐ 1377   6¢ Multicolored .... —   —   1.40   .22
☐ 1378   6¢ Multicolored .... —   —   1.40   .22
☐ 1379   6¢ Multicolored .... —   —   1.40   .22

1969. DARTMOUTH COLLEGE CASE

☐ 1380   6¢ Green .... 7.00   .70   .24   .12

1969. PROFESSIONAL BASEBALL CENTENARY

☐ 1381   6¢ Multicolored .... 36.00   3.50   .65   .12

1969. INTERCOLLEGIATE FOOTBALL CENTENARY

☐ 1382   6¢ Red & Green .... 14.00   1.50   .34   .12

1969. DWIGHT D. EISENHOWER MEMORIAL

☐ 1383   6¢ Blue, Black & Red .... 5.00   .75   .24   .12

1969. CHRISTMAS ISSUE

☐ 1384   6¢ Multicolored .... 7.00   1.75   .24   .12

1969. HOPE FOR THE CRIPPLED

☐ 1385   6¢ Multicolored .... 7.50   .75   .24   .12

1969. WILLIAM M. HARNETT PAINTING

☐ 1386   6¢ Multicolored .... 5.00   .70   .24   .12

1970. COMMEMORATIVES

1970. NATURAL HISTORY

☐ 1387   6¢ Multicolored .... —   —   .25   .14
☐ 1388   6¢ Multicolored .... —   —   .25   .14
☐ 1389   6¢ Multicolored .... —   —   .25   .14
☐ 1390   6¢ Multicolored .... —   —   .25   .14

1970. MAINE STATEHOOD SESQUICENTENNIAL

☐ 1391   6¢ Multicolored .... 7.50   .90   .25   .14

1970. WILDLIFE CONSERVATION—BUFFALO

☐ 1392   6¢ Black on Tan .... 7.00   .75   .25   .14

1970–1974. REGULAR ISSUE

☐ 1393   6¢ Blue Gray .... 14.00   1.10   .20   .13
☐ 1393D   7¢ Light Blue .... 16.50   1.10   .20   .13

*No hinge pricing from 1941 to date is figured at (N-H ADD 15%)

Scott No.			Mint Sheet	Plate Block	Fine Unused Each	Fine Used Each
☐ 1394	8¢	Black, Blue, Red	19.00	1.00	.22	.13
☐ 1395	8¢	Rose Violet	—	—	.22	.13
☐ 1396	8¢	Multicolored	19.00	4.50	.32	.13
☐ 1397	14¢	Brown	30.00	1.70	.38	.13
☐ 1398	16¢	Orange Brown	36.00	1.60	.42	.13
☐ 1399	18¢	Purple	40.00	1.80	.50	.13
☐ 1400	21¢	Green	48.00	2.10	.50	.18

Scott No.			Fine Unused Line Pair	Ave. Unused Line Pair	Fine Unused Each	Ave. Unused Each	Fine Used Each	Ave. Used Each
1970–1971. ROTARY PRESS COIL STAMPS—PERF. 10 VERTICALLY								
☐ 1401	6¢	Blue Gray	.75	.60	.25	.60	.21	.13
☐ 1402	8¢	Rose Violet	.75	.60	.25	.60	.21	.13

Scott No.			Mint Sheet	Plate Block	Fine Unused Each	Fine Used Each
1970. EDGAR LEE MASTERS—POET						
☐ 1405	6¢	Black & Olive Bistre	7.00	.70	.22	.13
1970. 50TH ANNIVERSARY WOMEN'S SUFFRAGE						
☐ 1406	6¢	Blue	7.00	.70	.22	.13
1970. SOUTH CAROLINA TERCENTENARY						
☐ 1407	6¢	Multicolored	7.00	.70	.22	.13
1970. STONE MOUNTAIN MEMORIAL						
☐ 1408	6¢	Gray Black	7.00	.70	.22	.13
1970. FORT SNELLING						
☐ 1409	6¢	Multicolored	7.00	.70	.22	.13
1970. ANTI-POLLUTION						
☐ 1410	6¢	Multicolored	—	—	.35	.16
☐ 1411	6¢	Multicolored	—	—	.35	.16
☐ 1412	6¢	Multicolored	—	—	.35	.16
☐ 1413	6¢	Multicolored	—	—	.35	.16
1970. CHRISTMAS ISSUE						
☐ 1414	6¢	Multicolored	7.00	2.10	.22	.14
☐ 1415	6¢	Multicolored	—	—	.50	.14
☐ 1416	6¢	Multicolored	—	—	.50	.14
☐ 1417	6¢	Multicolored	—	—	.50	.14
☐ 1418	6¢	Multicolored	—	—	.50	.14
1970. PRECANCELLED CHRISTMAS ISSUE						
☐ 1414a	6¢	Multicolored	8.50	3.00	.35	.15
☐ 1415a	6¢	Multicolored	—	—	1.25	.18
☐ 1416a	6¢	Multicolored	—	—	1.25	.18
☐ 1417a	6¢	Multicolored	—	—	1.25	.18
☐ 1418a	6¢	Multicolored	—	—	1.25	.18

*No hinge pricing from 1941 to date is figured at (N-H ADD 15%)

Scott No.		Mint Sheet	Plate Block	Fine Unused Each	Fine Used Each
1970. UNITED NATIONS 25TH ANNIVERSARY					
☐ 1419	6¢ Black, Red, Blue	7.00	.80	.22	.13
1970. PILGRIM LANDING 350TH ANNIVERSARY					
☐ 1420	6¢ Multicolored	7.00	.80	.22	.13
1970. DISABLED AMERICAN VETERANS AND SERVICEMEN ISSUE					
☐ 1421	6¢ Blue, Black, Red	—	—	.35	.18
☐ 1422	6¢ Blue, Black, Red	—	—	.25	.17
1971. COMMEMORATIVES					
1971. ADVENT OF SHEEP TO AMERICA					
☐ 1423	6¢ Multicolored	7.00	.70	.21	.13
1971. GENERAL DOUGLAS MacARTHUR					
☐ 1424	6¢ Red, Blue, Black	7.00	.70	.21	.13
1971. BLOOD DONORS PROGRAM					
☐ 1425	6¢ Light Blue, Scarlet, Indigo	7.00	.70	.21	.13
1971. MISSOURI STATEHOOD					
☐ 1426	8¢ Multicolored	9.50	2.00	.28	.15
1971. WILDLIFE CONSERVATION					
☐ 1427	8¢ Multicolored	—	—	.55	.15
☐ 1428	8¢ Multicolored	—	—	.22	.15
☐ 1429	8¢ Multicolored	—	—	.22	.15
☐ 1430	8¢ Multicolored	—	—	.22	.15
1971. ANTARCTIC TREATY					
☐ 1431	8¢ Red & Blue	9.50	1.30	.30	.12
1971. AMERICAN REVOLUTION BICENTENNIAL					
☐ 1432	8¢ Red, Blue, Black	11.00	2.40	1.20	.12
1971. JOHN SLOAN PAINTING					
☐ 1433	8¢ Multicolored	10.50	1.10	.30	.12
1971. DECADE OF SPACE ACHIEVEMENTS					
☐ 1434	8¢ Multicolored	—	—	.26	.12
☐ 1435	8¢ Multicolored	—	—	.26	.12
1971. EMILY DICKINSON—POET					
☐ 1436	8¢ Multicolored	9.50	1.00	.21	.13
1971. SAN JUAN 450TH ANNIVERSARY					
☐ 1437	8¢ Brown, Carmine, Blk.	9.50	1.00	.22	.13
1971. DRUG ADDICTION					
☐ 1438	8¢ Blue & Black	9.50	1.50	.22	.12
1971. CARE ANNIVERSARY					
☐ 1439	8¢ Multicolored	9.50	2.00	.24	.12
☐ 1440	8¢ Dark Brown & Ochre	—	—	.27	.13

*No hinge pricing from 1941 to date is figured at (N-H ADD 15%)

Scott No.		Mint Sheet	Plate Block	Fine Unused Each	Fine Used Each
☐ 1441	8¢ Dark Brown & Ochre	—	—	.31	.14
☐ 1442	8¢ Dark Brown & Ochre	—	—	.31	.14
☐ 1443	8¢ Dark Brown & Ochre	—	—	.31	.14

1971. CHRISTMAS
☐ 1444	8¢ Multicolored	9.50	2.75	.26	.13
☐ 1445	8¢ Multicolored	9.50	2.75	.26	.13

1972. COMMEMORATIVES

1972. SIDNEY LANIER—POET
☐ 1446	8¢ Multicolored	10.00	1.10	.26	.12

1972. PEACE CORPS
☐ 1447	8¢ Red & Blue	10.00	1.50	.26	.12

1972. NATIONAL PARKS CENTENNIAL
☐ 1448	2¢ Multicolored	—	—	.16	.14
☐ 1449	2¢ Multicolored	—	—	.16	.14
☐ 1450	2¢ Multicolored	—	—	.16	.14
☐ 1451	2¢ Multicolored	—	—	.16	.14
☐ 1452	6¢ Multicolored	7.00	.80	.21	.13
☐ 1453	8¢ Multicolored	6.50	1.10	.22	.13
☐ 1454	15¢ Multicolored	17.00	1.75	.38	.40

1972. FAMILY PLANNING
☐ 1455	8¢ Multicolored	9.50	1.10	.21	.12

1972. AMERICAN REVOLUTION BICENTENNIAL—COLONIAL CRAFTSMEN
☐ 1456	8¢ Deep Brown, Yellow	—	—	.26	.14
☐ 1457	8¢ Deep Brown, Yellow	—	—	.26	.14
☐ 1458	8¢ Deep Brown, Yellow	—	—	.26	.14
☐ 1459	8¢ Deep Brown, Yellow	—	—	.26	.14

1972. OLYMPIC GAMES
☐ 1460	6¢ Multicolored	8.00	2.00	.30	.14
☐ 1461	8¢ Multicolored	9.50	2.50	.30	.13
☐ 1462	15¢ Multicolored	17.00	4.25	.50	.26

1972. PARENT TEACHER ASSOCIATION
☐ 1463	8¢ Black & Yellow	9.50	1.00	.23	.13
☐ 1463a	8¢ Black & Yellow, Reversed Pl. No.	—	1.10	—	—

1972. WILDLIFE CONSERVATION
☐ 1464	8¢ Multicolored	—	—	.25	.14
☐ 1465	8¢ Multicolored	—	—	.25	.14
☐ 1466	8¢ Multicolored	—	—	.25	.14
☐ 1467	8¢ Multicolored	—	—	.25	.14

1972. MAIL ORDER BUSINESS
☐ 1468	8¢ Multicolored	9.50	2.00	.22	.13

*No hinge pricing from 1941 to date is figured at (N-H ADD 15%)

Scott No.		Mint Sheet	Plate Block	Fine Unused Each	Fine Used Each
1972. OSTEOPATHIC MEDICINE					
☐1469	8¢ Yellow Orange, Brown	9.50	1.80	.24	.13
1972. TOM SAWYER—AMERICAN FOLKLORE					
☐1470	8¢ Multicolored	9.50	1.10	.24	.13
1972. CHRISTMAS					
☐1471	8¢ Multicolored	9.50	3.00	.24	.13
☐1472	8¢ Multicolored	9.50	3.00	.24	.13
1972. PHARMACY					
☐1473	8¢ Multicolored	9.50	1.10	.24	.13
1972. STAMP COLLECTING					
☐1474	8¢ Multicolored	8.50	1.10	.24	.14
1973. COMMEMORATIVES					
1973. LOVE—"FOR SOMEONE SPECIAL"					
☐1475	8¢ Red, Green, Blue	8.50	1.60	.24	.12
1973. COLONIAL COMMUNICATIONS					
☐1476	8¢ Black, Red, Blue	8.50	1.10	.27	.13
☐1477	8¢ Blue, Red, Brown	8.50	1.10	.26	.14
☐1478	8¢ Multicolored	8.50	1.10	.26	.12
☐1479	8¢ Multicolored	8.50	1.10	.26	.14
1973. BOSTON TEA PARTY					
☐1480	8¢ Multicolored	—	—	.25	.14
☐1481	8¢ Multicolored	—	—	.25	.14
☐1482	8¢ Multicolored	—	—	.25	.14
☐1483	8¢ Multicolored	—	—	.25	.14
1973. GEORGE GERSHWIN—COMPOSER					
☐1484	8¢ Multicolored	10.00	3.75	.25	.13
1973. ROBINSON JEFFERS—POET					
☐1485	8¢ Multicolored	8.00	3.00	.25	.13
1973. HENRY OSSAWA TANNER—ARTIST					
☐1486	6¢ Multicolored	8.00	3.00	.25	.13
1973. WILLA CATHER—NOVELIST					
☐1487	8¢ Multicolored	8.00	3.00	.25	.13
1973. NICOLAUS COPERNICUS					
☐1488	8¢ Black & Orange	9.50	1.10	.25	.13
1973. POSTAL PEOPLE					
☐1489	8¢ Multicolored	—	—	.22	.13
☐1490	8¢ Multicolored	—	—	.22	.13
☐1491	8¢ Multicolored	—	—	.22	.13
☐1492	8¢ Multicolored	—	—	.22	.13
☐1493	8¢ Multicolored	—	—	.22	.14
☐1494	8¢ Multicolored	—	—	.22	.14

*No hinge pricing from 1941 to date is figured at (N-H ADD 15%)

Scott No.		Mint Sheet	Plate Block	Fine Unused Each	Fine Used Each
☐ 1495	8¢ Multicolored	—	—	.24	.13
☐ 1496	8¢ Multicolored	—	—	.24	.13
☐ 1497	8¢ Multicolored	—	—	.24	.13
☐ 1498	8¢ Multicolored	—	—	.24	.13

1973. HARRY S. TRUMAN MEMORIAL

| ☐ 1499 | 8¢ Black, Red, Blue | 7.00 | 1.10 | .25 | .13 |

1973. PROGRESS IN ELECTRONICS

☐ 1500	6¢ Multicolored	7.00	.90	.22	.20
☐ 1501	8¢ Multicolored	9.00	1.10	.23	.14
☐ 1502	15¢ Multicolored	18.00	2.00	.40	.30

1973. LYNDON B. JOHNSON MEMORIAL

| ☐ 1503 | 8¢ Multicolored | 7.00 | 3.00 | .22 | .14 |

1973. ANGUS CATTLE—RURAL AMERICA

| ☐ 1504 | 8¢ Multicolored | 9.00 | 1.00 | .23 | .13 |

1974. CHAUTAUQUA—RURAL AMERICA

| ☐ 1505 | 10¢ Multicolored | 12.50 | 1.40 | .27 | .13 |

1974. WINTER WHEAT—RURAL AMERICA

| ☐ 1506 | 10¢ Multicolored | 12.50 | 1.15 | .27 | .13 |

1973. CHRISTMAS

| ☐ 1507 | 8¢ Multicolored | 9.00 | 3.00 | .23 | .13 |
| ☐ 1508 | 8¢ Multicolored | 9.00 | 3.00 | .23 | .13 |

1973–1974. REGULAR ISSUES

☐ 1509	10¢ Red & Blue	30.00	7.00	.32	.13
☐ 1510	10¢ Blue	25.00	1.25	.30	.13
☐ 1511	10¢ Multicolored	23.00	2.10	.25	.13

Scott No.		Fine Unused Line Pair	Ave. Unused Line Pair	Fine Unused Each	Ave. Unused Each	Fine Used Each	Ave. Used Each
1973–1974. COIL STAMPS—PERF. 10 VERTICALLY							
☐ 1518	63¢ Orange	1.00	.80	.24	.18	.22	.13
☐ 1519	10¢ Red & Blue	—	—	.28	.22	.20	.13
☐ 1520	10¢ Blue	1.00	.80	.28	.22	.20	.13

Scott No.		Mint Sheet	Plate Block	Fine Unused Each	Fine Used Each
1974. COMMEMORATIVES					
1974. VETERANS OF FOREIGN WARS					
☐ 1525	10¢ Carmine & Blue	11.50	1.40	.28	.14
1974. ROBERT FROST—POET					
☐ 1526	10¢ Black	11.50	1.40	.28	.14
1974. EXPO '74—PRESERVE THE ENVIRONMENT					
☐ 1527	10¢ Multicolored	9.00	3.50	.28	.14

*No hinge pricing from 1941 to date is figured at (N-H ADD 15%)

Scott No.		Mint Sheet	Plate Block	Fine Unused Each	Fine Used Each
1974. HORSE RACING					
☐ 1528	10¢ Multicolored	11.50	3.25	.26	.14
1974. SKYLAB PROJECT					
☐ 1529	10¢ Multicolored	11.50	1.10	.26	.14
1974. UNIVERSAL POSTAL UNION CENTENARY					
☐ 1530	10¢ Multicolored	—	—	.26	.14
☐ 1531	10¢ Multicolored	—	—	.26	.14
☐ 1532	10¢ Multicolored	—	—	.26	.14
☐ 1533	10¢ Multicolored	—	—	.26	.14
☐ 1534	10¢ Multicolored	—	—	.26	.14
☐ 1535	10¢ Multicolored	—	—	.26	.14
☐ 1536	10¢ Multicolored	—	—	.26	.14
☐ 1537	10¢ Multicolored	—	—	.26	.14
1974. MINERALS HERITAGE ISSUE					
☐ 1538	10¢ Multicolored	—	—	.24	.14
☐ 1539	10¢ Multicolored	—	—	.24	.14
☐ 1540	10¢ Multicolored	—	—	.24	.14
☐ 1541	10¢ Multicolored	—	—	.24	.14
1974. FORT HARROD BICENTENNIAL					
☐ 1542	10¢ Multicolored	11.50	1.30	.26	.14
1974. CONTINENTAL CONGRESS					
☐ 1543	10¢ Red, Blue, Gray	—	—	.26	.14
☐ 1544	10¢ Red, Blue, Gray	—	—	.26	.14
☐ 1545	10¢ Red, Blue, Gray	—	—	.26	.14
☐ 1546	10¢ Red, Blue, Gray	—	—	.26	.14
1974. ENERGY CONSERVATION					
☐ 1547	10¢ Multicolored	11.50	1.25	.25	.14
1974. LEGEND OF SLEEPY HOLLOW					
☐ 1548	10¢ Multicolored	11.50	1.25	.25	.14
1974. RETARDED CHILDREN					
☐ 1549	10¢ Light & Dark Brown	11.50	1.25	.25	.14
1974. CHRISTMAS					
☐ 1550	10¢ Multicolored	11.50	2.50	.28	.13
☐ 1551	10¢ Multicolored	11.50	3.50	.28	.13
☐ 1552	10¢ Multicolored	11.50	6.00	.28	.13
☐ 1552A	10¢ Multicolored, Plate Block of 12	11.50	4.00	—	—
1975. COMMEMORATIVES—AMERICAN ARTS					
1975. BENJAMIN WEST—ARTIST					
☐ 1553	10¢ Multicolored	11.50	3.00	.26	.13
1975. PAUL LAURENCE DUNBAR—POET					
☐ 1554	10¢ Multicolored	11.50	3.00	.28	.13

*No hinge pricing from 1941 to date is figured at (N-H ADD 15%)

Scott No.		Mint Sheet	Plate Block	Fine Unused Each	Fine Used Each
1975. D. W. GRIFFITH—MOTION PICTURES					
☐ 1555	10¢ Multicolored	14.00	1.25	.32	.13
1975. PIONEER 10 SPACE MISSION					
☐ 1556	10¢ Multicolored	14.00	1.25	.32	.13
1975. MARINER 10 SPACE MISSION					
☐ 1557	10¢ Multicolored	14.00	1.25	.32	.13
1975. COLLECTIVE BARGAINING					
☐ 1558	10¢ Blue, Red, Purple	11.50	1.50	.32	.13
1975. CONTRIBUTORS TO THE CAUSE					
☐ 1559	8¢ Multicolored	9.00	2.50	.22	.18
☐ 1560	10¢ Multicolored	11.00	2.50	.26	.13
☐ 1561	10¢ Multicolored	11.00	2.50	.26	.13
☐ 1562	18¢ Multicolored	24.00	6.00	.50	.20
1975. LEXINGTON AND CONCORD BATTLES BICENTENNIAL					
☐ 1563	10¢ Multicolored	8.50	3.50	.26	.13
1975. BATTLE OF BUNKER HILL					
☐ 1564	10¢ Multicolored	8.50	3.50	.26	.13
1975. CONTINENTAL MILITARY SERVICE UNIFORMS					
☐ 1565	10¢ Multicolored	—	—	.26	.15
☐ 1566	10¢ Multicolored	—	—	.26	.15
☐ 1567	10¢ Multicolored	—	—	.26	.15
☐ 1568	10¢ Multicolored	—	—	.26	.15
1975. U.S.–SOVIET JOINT SPACE MISSION					
☐ 1569	10¢ Multicolored	—	—	.28	.14
☐ 1570	10¢ Multicolored	—	—	.28	.14
1975. INTERNATIONAL WOMEN'S YEAR					
☐ 1571	10¢ Multicolored	11.00	2.00	.26	.14
1975. U.S. POSTAL SERVICE BICENTENNIAL					
☐ 1572	10¢ Multicolored	—	—	.26	.16
☐ 1573	10¢ Multicolored	—	—	.26	.16
☐ 1574	10¢ Multicolored	—	—	.26	.16
☐ 1575	10¢ Multicolored	—	—	.26	.16
1975. WORLD PEACE THROUGH LAW					
☐ 1576	10¢ Blue, Green, Brown	11.75	1.10	.24	.13
1975. BANKING AND COMMERCE					
☐ 1577	10¢ Multicolored	—	—	.24	.13
☐ 1578	10¢ Multicolored	—	—	.24	.13
1975. CHRISTMAS					
☐ 1579	10¢ Multicolored	12.00	3.10	.26	.14
☐ 1580	10¢ Multicolored	12.00	3.10	.26	.14

*No hinge pricing from 1941 to date is figured at (N-H ADD 15%)

Scott No.		Mint Sheet	Plate Block	Fine Unused Each	Fine Used Each
1975–1980. AMERICANA SERIES					
☐ 1581	1¢ Blue on Green	8.00	.70	.21	.13
☐ 1582	2¢ Brown on Green	8.00	.65	.21	.13
☐ 1584	3¢ Olive on Green	9.00	.70	.21	.13
☐ 1585	4¢ Maroon on Green	10.00	.60	.21	.13
☐ 1590	9¢ Slate on Green	—	—	.30	.21
☐ 1591	9¢ Green on Gray	18.00	1.00	.22	.13
☐ 1592	10¢ Purple	23.00	1.10	.22	.13
☐ 1593	11¢ Orange on Gray	24.00	1.20	.26	.14
☐ 1594	12¢ Maroon	25.00	1.90	.26	.14
☐ 1595	13¢ Brown	—	—	.35	.16
☐ 1596	13¢ Multicolored	31.00	5.00	.35	.16
☐ 1597	15¢ Multicolored	34.00	9.00	.36	.16
☐ 1598	15¢ Multicolored	—	—	.50	.20
☐ 1599	16¢ Blue & Black	45.00	2.50	.50	.13
☐ 1603	24¢ Red on Blue	50.00	3.00	.60	.14
☐ 1604	28¢ Brown & Blue	60.00	3.50	.65	.14
☐ 1605	29¢ Blue & Blue	62.00	3.00	.70	.21
☐ 1606	30¢ Green on Blue	55.00	4.00	.65	.16
☐ 1608	50¢ Black & Orange	95.00	5.00	1.20	.16
☐ 1610	$1 Multicolored	200.00	11.00	2.50	.16
☐ 1611	$2 Multicolored	450.00	22.00	5.00	.55
☐ 1612	$5 Multicolored	800.00	45.00	10.50	3.00

Scott No.		Fine Unused Line Pair	Ave. Unused Line Pair	Fine Unused Each	Ave. Unused Each	Fine Used Each	Ave. Used Each
1975–1978. COIL STAMPS							
☐ 1613	3.1¢ Brown on Yellow	1.00	.90	.22	.16	.17	.13
☐ 1614	7.7¢ Gold on Yellow	1.50	1.10	.26	.20	.20	.15
☐ 1615	7.9¢ Red on Yellow	1.00	.90	.26	.20	.17	.13
☐ 1615C	8.4¢ Red on White	2.50	2.00	.26	.21	.20	.16
☐ 1616	9¢ Green on Gray	1.00	.90	.24	.20	.17	.15
☐ 1617	10¢ Purple on Gray	1.00	.90	.27	.24	.16	.15
☐ 1618	13¢ Brown	1.00	.90	.24	.22	.20	.13

Scott No.		Mint Sheet	Plate Block	Fine Unused Each	Fine Used Each
1975–1977. REGULAR ISSUES					
☐ 1622	13¢ Red, Brown, Blue	31.00	8.00	.31	.14
☐ 1623	13¢ Blue, Red	31.00	10.00	.31	.14
☐ 1623c	13¢ Blue, Red, pf 10	—	—	.35	.15

Scott No.		Fine Unused Each	Ave. Unused Each	Fine Used Each	Ave. Used Each
1975. COIL STAMPS					
☐ 1625	13¢ Red, Brown, Blue	.40	.31	.16	.14

*No hinge pricing from 1941 to date is figured at (N-H ADD 15%)

Scott No.		Mint Sheet	Plate Block	Fine Unused Each	Fine Used Each

1976. COMMEMORATIVES—AMERICAN BICENTENNIAL

1976. SPIRIT OF '76

☐ 1629	13¢ Multicolored	—	—	.32	.12
☐ 1630	13¢ Multicolored	—	—	.32	.12
☐ 1631	13¢ Multicolored	—	—	.32	.12

1976. INTERPHIL '76

☐ 1632	13¢ Dark Blue, Red, Ultramarine	15.00	1.50	.36	.13

1976. STATE FLAGS

☐	13¢ All 50 States	24.00	6.00	—	—
☐	13¢ Individual States	—	—	.50	.25

☐ 1633 Delaware	1650 Louisiana	1667 West Virginia	
☐ 1634 Pennsylvania	1651 Indiana	1668 Nevada	
☐ 1635 New Jersey	1652 Mississippi	1669 Nebraska	
☐ 1636 Georgia	1653 Illinois	1670 Colorado	
☐ 1637 Connecticut	1654 Alabama	1671 North Dakota	
☐ 1638 Massachusetts	1655 Maine	1672 South Dakota	
☐ 1639 Maryland	1656 Missouri	1673 Montana	
☐ 1640 South Carolina	1657 Arkansas	1674 Washington	
☐ 1641 New Hampshire	1658 Michigan	1675 Idaho	
☐ 1642 Virginia	1659 Florida	1676 Wyoming	
☐ 1643 New York	1660 Texas	1677 Utah	
☐ 1644 North Carolina	1661 Iowa	1678 Oklahoma	
☐ 1645 Rhode Island	1662 Wisconsin	1679 New Mexico	
☐ 1646 Vermont	1663 California	1680 Arizona	
☐ 1647 Kentucky	1664 Minnesota	1681 Alaska	
☐ 1648 Tennessee	1665 Oregon	1682 Hawaii	
☐ 1649 Ohio	1666 Kansas		

1976. TELEPHONE CENTENNIAL

☐ 1683	13¢ Black, Purple, Red	16.00	1.50	.36	.13

1976. COMMERCIAL AVIATION

☐ 1684	13¢ Multicolored	16.00	3.75	.36	.13

1976. CHEMISTRY

☐ 1685	13¢ Multicolored	16.00	4.50	.36	.13

1976. BICENTENNIAL SOUVENIR SHEETS

☐ 1686	65¢ Sheet of 5	—	—	5.00	4.00
☐ 1686a	13¢ Multicolored	—	—	1.00	.90
☐ 1686b	13¢ Multicolored	—	—	1.00	.90
☐ 1686c	13¢ Multicolored	—	—	1.00	.90
☐ 1686d	13¢ Multicolored	—	—	1.00	.90
☐ 1686e	13¢ Multicolored	—	—	1.00	.90
☐ 1687	90¢ Sheet of 5	—	—	7.00	6.00
☐ 1687a	18¢ Multicolored	—	—	1.50	1.10
☐ 1687b	18¢ Multicolored	—	—	1.50	1.10
☐ 1687c	18¢ Multicolored	—	—	1.50	1.10
☐ 1687d	18¢ Multicolored	—	—	1.50	1.10

*No hinge pricing from 1941 to date is figured at (N-H ADD 15%)

Scott No.		Mint Sheet	Plate Block	Fine Unused Each	Fine Used Each
☐ 1687e	18¢ Multicolored	—	—	1.50	1.10
☐ 1688	1.20 Sheet of 5	—	—	8.50	7.50
☐ 1688a	24¢ Multicolored	—	—	2.00	1.30
☐ 1688b	24¢ Multicolored	—	—	2.00	1.30
☐ 1688c	24¢ Multicolored	—	—	2.00	1.30
☐ 1688d	24¢ Multicolored	—	—	2.00	1.30
☐ 1688e	24¢ Multicolored	—	—	2.00	1.30
☐ 1689	1.55 Sheet of 5	—	—	10.00	9.00
☐ 1689a	31¢ Multicolored	—	—	2.10	1.75
☐ 1689b	31¢ Multicolored	—	—	2.10	1.75
☐ 1689c	31¢ Multicolored	—	—	2.10	1.75
☐ 1689d	31¢ Multicolored	—	—	2.10	1.75
☐ 1689e	31¢ Multicolored	—	—	2.10	1.75

1976. BENJAMIN FRANKLIN

☐ 1690	13¢ Blue & Multicolored	17.00	1.60	.40	.14

1976. DECLARATION OF INDEPENDENCE

☐ 1691	13¢ Multicolored	—	—	.36	.16
☐ 1692	13¢ Multicolored	—	—	.36	.16
☐ 1693	13¢ Multicolored	—	—	.36	.16
☐ 1694	13¢ Multicolored	—	—	.36	.16

1976. OLYMPIC GAMES

☐ 1695	13¢ Multicolored	—	—	.40	.16
☐ 1696	13¢ Multicolored	—	—	.40	.16
☐ 1697	13¢ Multicolored	—	—	.40	.16
☐ 1698	13¢ Multicolored	—	—	.40	.16

1976. CLARA MAASS

☐ 1699	13¢ Multicolored	12.00	4.50	.36	.13

1976. ADOLPH S. OCHS

☐ 1700	13¢ Black, Green & White	10.00	1.50	.30	.13

1976. CHRISTMAS

☐ 1701	13¢ Multicolored	16.00	7.00	.31	.13
☐ 1702	13¢ Multicolored	16.00	6.00	.31	.13
☐ 1703	13¢ Multicolored	16.00	10.00	.31	.13

1977. COMMEMORATIVES

1977. WASHINGTON

☐ 1704	13¢ Multicolored	12.00	4.00	.31	.13

1977. SOUND RECORDING CENTENARY

☐ 1705	13¢ Multicolored	13.00	1.50	.31	.13

1977. PUEBLO ART

☐ 1706	13¢ Multicolored	—	—	.23	.11
☐ 1707	13¢ Multicolored	—	—	.23	.11
☐ 1708	13¢ Multicolored	—	—	.23	.11
☐ 1709	13¢ Multicolored	—	—	.23	.11

*No hinge pricing from 1941 to date is figured at (N-H ADD 15%)

Scott No.		Mint Sheet	Plate Block	Fine Unused Each	Fine Used Each
1977. TRANSATLANTIC FLIGHT		13.00	4.50	.36	.13
☐ 1710	13¢ Multicolored				
1977. COLORADO		13.00	4.50	.36	.13
☐ 1711	13¢ Multicolored				
1977. BUTTERFLIES					
☐ 1712	13¢ Multicolored	—	—	.30	.13
☐ 1713	13¢ Multicolored	—	—	.30	.13
☐ 1714	13¢ Multicolored	—	—	.30	.13
☐ 1715	13¢ Multicolored	—	—	.30	.13
1977. LAFAYETTE		12.00	2.00	.35	.13
☐ 1716	13¢ Multicolored				
1977. SKILLED HANDS					
☐ 1717	13¢ Multicolored	—	—	.32	.13
☐ 1718	13¢ Multicolored	—	—	.32	.13
☐ 1719	13¢ Multicolored	—	—	.32	.13
☐ 1720	13¢ Multicolored	—	—	.32	.13
1977. PEACE BRIDGE		14.00	1.60	.32	.14
☐ 1721	13¢ Blue & White				
1977. BATTLE OF ORISKANY		12.00	3.75	.32	.14
☐ 1722	13¢ Multicolored				
1977. ENERGY CONSERVATION AND DEVELOPMENT					
☐ 1723	13¢ Multicolored	—	—	.32	.12
☐ 1724	13¢ Multicolored	—	—	.32	.12
1977. ALTA, CALIFORNIA BICENTENNIAL		14.00	1.50	.35	.12
☐ 1725	13¢ Multicolored				
1977. ARTICLES OF CONFEDERATION		16.00	1.60	.35	.12
☐ 1726	13¢ Red & Brown on Tan				
1977. TALKING PICTURES		17.00	1.60	.35	.12
☐ 1727	13¢ Multicolored				
1977. SURRENDER AT SARATOGA		12.00	4.50	.35	.12
☐ 1728	13¢ Multicolored				
1977. CHRISTMAS					
☐ 1729	13¢ Multicolored	34.00	7.00	.38	.13
☐ 1730	13¢ Multicolored	30.00	6.00	.38	.13
1978. CARL SANDBURG		16.00	1.50	.33	.13
☐ 1731	13¢ Brown, Black, White				
1978. CAPTAIN COOK ISSUES					
☐ 1732	13¢ Dark Blue	—	1.60	.33	.13
☐ 1733	13¢ Green	—	1.60	.33	.13

*No hinge pricing from 1941 to date is figured at (N-H ADD 15%)

Scott No.		Mint Sheet	Plate Block	Fine Unused Each	Fine Used Each
1978. INDIAN HEAD PENNY					
☐1734	13¢ Brown & Blue Green	45.00	2.00	.34	.15
1978. NONDENOMINATED "A"					
☐1735	15¢ Orange	34.00	2.00	.35	.11
1978. ROSES					
☐1737	15¢ Multicolored	—	—	.38	.11
1980. WINDMILL—VIRGINIA					
☐1738	15¢ Black	—	—	.38	.11
1980. WINDMILL—RHODE ISLAND					
☐1739	15¢ Black	—	—	.40	.11
1980. WINDMILL—MASSACHUSETTS					
☐1740	15¢ Black	—	—	.40	.11
1980. WINDMILL—ILLINOIS					
☐1741	15¢ Black	—	—	.40	.11
1980. WINDMILL—TEXAS					
☐1742	15¢ Black	—	—	.40	.11
1978. HARRIET TUBMAN					
☐1744	13¢ Multicolored	20.00	6.00	.38	.11
1978. AMERICAN FOLK ART ISSUE					
☐1745	13¢ Multicolored	—	—	.36	.13
☐1746	13¢ Multicolored	—	—	.36	.13
☐1747	13¢ Multicolored	—	—	.36	.13
☐1748	13¢ Multicolored	—	—	.36	.13
1978. AMERICAN DANCE ISSUE					
☐1749	13¢ Multicolored	—	—	.36	.13
☐1750	13¢ Multicolored	—	—	.36	.13
☐1751	13¢ Multicolored	—	—	.36	.13
☐1752	13¢ Multicolored	—	—	.36	.13
1978. FRENCH ALLIANCE					
☐1753	13¢ Blue, Black & Red	12.00	1.70	.34	.12
1978. EARLY CANCER DETECTION					
☐1754	13¢ Brown	16.00	1.75	.34	.12
1978. JIMMIE RODGERS					
☐1755	13¢ Multicolored	16.00	2.50	.34	.12
1978. GEORGE M. COHAN					
☐1756	15¢ Multicolored	21.00	2.50	.45	.12
1978. "CAPAX" '78 SOUVENIR SHEET					
☐1757	13¢ Multicolored, set of 6	15.00	—	2.50	2.00
1978. PHOTOGRAPHY					
☐1758	15¢ Multicolored	13.00	5.00	.36	.12

*No hinge pricing from 1941 to date is figured at (N-H ADD 15%)

Scott No.		Mint Sheet	Plate Block	Fine Unused Each	Fine Used Each
1978. VIKING MISSION TO MARS					
☐1759	15¢ Multicolored	20.00	2.00	.42	.14
1978. AMERICAN OWL ISSUE					
☐1760	15¢ Multicolored	—	—	.50	.14
☐1761	15¢ Multicolored	—	—	.50	.14
☐1762	15¢ Multicolored	—	—	.50	.14
☐1763	15¢ Multicolored	—	—	.50	.14
1978. AMERICAN TREES ISSUE					
☐1764	15¢ Multicolored	—	—	.40	.13
☐1765	15¢ Multicolored	—	—	.40	.13
☐1766	15¢ Multicolored	—	—	.40	.13
☐1767	15¢ Multicolored	—	—	.40	.13
1978. CHRISTMAS ISSUES					
☐1768	15¢ Multicolored	30.00	7.00	.36	.13
☐1769	15¢ Multicolored	30.00	7.00	.36	.13
1979. ROBERT F. KENNEDY ISSUE					
☐1770	15¢ Blue	15.00	1.75	.35	.13
1979. MARTIN LUTHER KING ISSUE					
☐1771	15¢ Multicolored	16.00	5.00	.35	.13
1979. INTERNATIONAL YEAR OF THE CHILD					
☐1772	15¢ Light Brown	16.00	1.75	.35	.13
1979. JOHN STEINBECK ISSUE					
☐1773	15¢ Dark Blue	16.00	1.75	.35	.13
1979. ALBERT EINSTEIN ISSUE					
☐1774	15¢ Brown	16.00	1.75	.35	.13
1979. PENNSYLVANIA TOLEWARE ISSUE					
☐1775	15¢ Multicolored	—	—	.42	.12
☐1776	15¢ Multicolored	—	—	.42	.12
☐1777	15¢ Multicolored	—	—	.42	.12
☐1778	15¢ Multicolored	—	—	.42	.12
1979. ARCHITECTURE U.S.A. ISSUE					
☐1779	15¢ Light Blue & Brown	—	—	.45	.13
☐1780	15¢ Light Blue & Brown	—	—	.45	.13
☐1781	15¢ Light Blue & Brown	—	—	.45	.13
☐1782	15¢ Light Blue & Brown	—	—	.45	.13
1979. ENDANGERED FLORA ISSUE					
☐1783	15¢ Multicolored	—	—	.45	.13
☐1784	15¢ Multicolored	—	—	.45	.13
☐1785	15¢ Multicolored	—	—	.45	.13
☐1786	15¢ Multicolored	—	—	.45	.13
1979. SEEING FOR ME ISSUE					
☐1787	15¢ Multicolored	16.00	7.50	.40	.13

*No hinge pricing from 1941 to date is figured at (N-H ADD 15%)

Scott No.	Mint Sheet	Plate Block	Fine Unused Each	Fine Used Each
1979. SPECIAL OLYMPICS				
☐ 1788 15¢ Multicolored	16.00	4.00	.40	.13
1979. JOHN PAUL JONES				
☐ 1789 15¢ Multicolored	18.00	4.50	.42	.13
1979. OLYMPIC DECATHLON				
☐ 1790 10¢ Multicolored	10.00	2.00	.28	.14
1979. OLYMPIC RUNNERS				
☐ 1791 15¢ Multicolored	—	—	.45	.15
1979. OLYMPIC SWIMMERS				
☐ 1792 15¢ Multicolored	—	—	.45	.15
1979. OLYMPIC ROWERS				
☐ 1793 15¢ Multicolored	—	—	.45	.15
1979. OLYMPIC EQUESTRIAN				
☐ 1794 15¢ Multicolored	—	—	.45	.15
1979. OLYMPIC SKATER				
☐ 1795 15¢ Multicolored	—	—	.45	.14
1979. OLYMPIC SKIER				
☐ 1796 15¢ Multicolored	—	—	.45	.14
1979. OLYMPIC SKI JUMPER				
☐ 1797 15¢ Multicolored	—	—	.45	.14
1979. OLYMPIC GOALTENDER				
☐ 1798 15¢ Multicolored	—	—	.45	.14
1979. MADONNA				
☐ 1799 15¢ Multicolored	32.00	5.00	.38	.13
1979. CHRISTMAS				
☐ 1800 15¢ Multicolored	32.00	5.00	.38	.13
1979. WILL ROGERS				
☐ 1801 15¢ Multicolored	18.00	5.50	.42	.13
1979. VIETNAM VETERANS				
☐ 1802 15¢ Multicolored	18.00	4.50	.42	.13
1980. W.C. FIELDS				
☐ 1803 15¢ Multicolored	18.00	5.00	.42	.13
1980. BENJAMIN BANNEKER				
☐ 1804 15¢ Multicolored	16.00	4.75	.36	.13
1980. LETTERS PRESERVE MEMORIES				
☐ 1805 15¢ Violet & Bistre	—	—	.42	.12
1980. PRESERVE MEMORIES—P.S. WRITE SOON				
☐ 1806 15¢ Violet & Pink	—	—	.42	.12

*No hinge pricing from 1941 to date is figured at (N-H ADD 15%)

	Mint Sheet	Plate Block	Fine Unused Each	Fine Used Each
Scott No.				
1980. LETTERS LIFT SPIRITS				
☐ 1807 15¢ Green & Pink & Orange	—	—	.42	.12
1980. LIFT SPIRITS—P.S. WRITE SOON				
☐ 1808 15¢ Green & Yellow Green	—	—	.42	.12
1980. LETTERS SHAPE OPINIONS				
☐ 1809 15¢ Scarlet & Blue	—	—	.42	.12
1980. SHAPE OPINIONS—P.S. WRITE SOON				
☐ 1810 15¢ Scarlet & Blue	—	—	.42	.12
1980. AMERICANA SERIES				
☐ 1811 1¢ Dark Blue & Green	—	.50	.26	.12
☐ 1813 3.5¢ Purple & Yellow	—	1.20	.26	.12
☐ 1816 12¢ Green	—	1.40	.30	.12
1980. NONDENOMINATED "B"				
☐ 1818 18¢ Purple	—	2.10	.46	.12
1980. FRANCIS PERKINS				
☐ 1821 15¢ Blue	16.00	1.60	.36	.12
1980. DOLLY MADISON				
☐ 1822 15¢ Multicolored	49.00	2.00	.36	.14
1980. EMILY BISSELL				
☐ 1823 15¢ Scarlet & Black	16.00	1.60	.36	.12
1980. HELEN KELLER—ANNE SULLIVAN				
☐ 1824 15¢ Multicolored	16.00	1.60	.36	.12
1980. VETERANS ADMINISTRATION				
☐ 1825 15¢ Carmine & Blue	—	—	.36	.12
1980. GENERAL BERNARDO de GALVEZ				
☐ 1826 15¢ Multicolored	—	—	.36	.12
1980. CORAL REEFS—VIRGIN ISLANDS				
☐ 1827 15¢ Multicolored	—	—	.36	.13
1980. CORAL REEFS—FLORIDA				
☐ 1828 15¢ Multicolored	—	—	.36	.13
1980. CORAL REEFS—AMERICAN SAMOA				
☐ 1829 15¢ Multicolored	—	—	.36	.13
1980. CORAL REEFS—HAWAII				
☐ 1830 15¢ Multicolored	—	—	.36	.12
1980. ORGANIZED LABOR				
☐ 1831 15¢ Multicolored	16.00	4.50	.35	.12
1980. EDITH WHARTON				
☐ 1832 15¢ Violet	16.00	2.00	.35	.12
1980. EDUCATION				
☐ 1833 15¢ Multicolored	16.00	2.50	.35	.12

*No hinge pricing from 1941 to date is figured at (N-H ADD 15%)

Scott No.		Mint Sheet	Plate Block	Fine Unused Each	Fine Used Each
1980. INDIAN ARTS					
☐ 1834	15¢ Multicolored	—	—	.40	.13
☐ 1835	15¢ Multicolored	—	—	.40	.13
☐ 1836	15¢ Multicolored	—	—	.40	.13
☐ 1837	15¢ Multicolored	—	—	.40	.13
1980. ARCHITECTURE					
☐ 1838	15¢ Black & Red	—	—	.45	.14
☐ 1839	15¢ Black & Red	—	—	.45	.14
☐ 1840	16¢ Black & Red	—	—	.45	.14
☐ 1841	15¢ Black & Red	—	—	.45	.14
1980. CHRISTMAS ISSUE					
☐ 1842	15¢ Multicolored	14.00	5.00	.36	.12
☐ 1843	15¢ Multicolored	14.00	7.50	.36	.12
1982. DOROTHEA DIX					
☐ 1844	1¢ Black	7.50	2.00	.22	.11
1983. IGOR STRAVINSKY					
☐ 1845	2¢ Brown	8.00	.75	.22	.11
1983. HENRY CLAY					
☐ 1846	3¢ Green	11.00	.75	.22	.11
1983. CARL SCHURZ					
☐ 1847	4¢ Purple	11.00	.60	.22	.11
1983. PEARL BUCK					
☐ 1848	5¢ Reddish Brown	12.00	.70	.24	.12
1985. WALTER LIPPMANN					
☐ 1849	6¢ Orange	11.50	3.10	.24	.12
1985. ABRAHAM BALDWIN					
☐ 1850	7¢ Red	14.00	3.50	.24	.12
1985. HENRY KNOX					
☐ 1851	8¢ Black	20.00	1.20	.26	.12
1985. SYLVANUS THAYER					
☐ 1852	9¢ Green	20.00	5.00	.26	.12
1984. RICHARD RUSSELL					
☐ 1853	10¢ Blue	21.00	6.00	.30	.14
1985. ALDEN PARTRIDGE					
☐ 1854	11¢ Blue	21.00	1.70	.30	.14
1982. CRAZY HORSE					
☐ 1855	13¢ Brown	30.00	1.90	.35	.14
1985. SINCLAIR LEWIS					
☐ 1856	14¢ Green	31.00	7.00	.35	.14

*No hinge pricing from 1941 to date is figured at (N-H ADD 15%)

Scott No.	Mint Sheet	Plate Block	Fine Unused Each	Fine Used Each
1981. RACHEL CARSON				
☐ 1857 17¢ Blue Green	31.00	1.75	.36	.12
1981. GEORGE MASON				
☐ 1858 18¢ Dark Blue	40.00	3.50	.40	.13
1980. SEQUOYAH				
☐ 1859 19¢ Light Brown	41.00	2.75	.40	.13
1982. RALPH BUNCHE				
☐ 1860 20¢ Carmine	47.00	3.10	.45	.13
1983. THOMAS H. GALLAUDET				
☐ 1861 20¢ Green	46.00	3.10	.45	.13
1984. HARRY S. TRUMAN				
☐ 1862 20¢ Black & White	42.00	3.50	.45	.13
1985. JOHN J. AUDUBON				
☐ 1863 22¢ Blue	42.00	3.50	.50	.13
1984. FRANK C. LAUBACH				
☐ 1864 30¢ Dark Green	56.00	4.00	.45	.13
1981. CHARLES DREW				
☐ 1865 35¢ Gray	65.00	4.00	.45	.14
1982. ROBERT MILLIKAN				
☐ 1866 37¢ Blue	68.00	4.00	.55	.14
1985. GRENVILLE CLARK				
☐ 1867 39¢ Reddish Purple	78.00	5.00	.90	.14
1984. LILLIAN M. GILBRETH				
☐ 1868 40¢ Green	76.00	5.00	.80	.14
1985. CHESTER W. NIMITZ				
☐ 1869 50¢ Dark Brown	90.00	6.00	.85	.14
1981. EVERETT M. DIRKSEN				
☐ 1874 ` 15¢ Dark Green	16.00	2.00	.36	.12
1981. WHITNEY M. YOUNG				
☐ 1875 15¢ Multicolored	16.00	2.00	.36	.12
1981. FLOWERS				
☐ 1876 18¢ Multicolored	—	—	.50	.13
☐ 1877 18¢ Multicolored	—	—	.50	.13
☐ 1878 18¢ Multicolored	—	—	.50	.13
☐ 1879 18¢ Multicolored	—	—	.50	.13
1981. AMERICAN WILDLIFE				
☐ 1880 18¢ Light Brown	—	—	.60	.14
☐ 1881 18¢ Light Brown	—	—	.60	.14
☐ 1882 18¢ Light Brown	—	—	.60	.14
☐ 1883 18¢ Light Brown	—	—	.60	.14

*No hinge pricing from 1941 to date is figured at (N-H ADD 15%)

Scott No.		Mint Sheet	Plate Block	Fine Unused Each	Fine Used Each
☐ 1884	18¢ Light Brown	—	—	.60	.14
☐ 1885	18¢ Light Brown	—	—	.60	.14
☐ 1886	18¢ Light Brown	—	—	.60	.14
☐ 1887	18¢ Light Brown	—	—	.60	.14
☐ 1888	18¢ Light Brown	—	—	.60	.14
☐ 1889	18¢ Light Brown	Booklet	9.00	—	—

1981. FLAG—FOR AMBER WAVES OF GRAIN
☐ 1890	18¢ Multicolored	43.00	12.00	.50	.14

1981. FLAG—FROM SEA TO SHINING SEA
☐ 1891	18¢ Multicolored	—PR.	7.00	.50	.14

1981. U.S.A.
☐ 1892	6¢ Carmine & Dark Blue	—	—	.70	.14

1981. FLAG—FOR PURPLE MOUNTAIN MAJESTIES
☐ 1893	18¢ Multicolored	—	—	.42	.14

1982. FLAG OVER SUPREME COURT
☐ 1894	20¢ Carmine & Dark Blue	42.00	9.00	.50	.14

1982. MAIL WAGON
☐ 1900	9.3¢ Carmine	—	—	.28	.14

1984. RAILROAD CABOOSE
☐ 1902	11¢ Red, coil	—	—	.28	.14

1981. ELECTRIC CAR
☐ 1905	17¢ Blue	—LP.	3.00	.32	.12

1981. SURREY
☐ 1906	18¢ Brown	—LP.	3.00	.32	.12

1982. FIRE PUMPER
☐ 1907	20¢ Red Orange	—	—	.50	.14

1981. AMERICAN RED CROSS
☐ 1910	18¢ Multicolored	—	3.00	.50	.14

1981. SAVINGS AND LOAN
☐ 1911	18¢ Multicolored	—	3.00	.50	.14

1981. SPACE ACHIEVEMENT
☐ 1912	18¢ Multicolored	—	—	.50	.15
☐ 1913	18¢ Multicolored	—	—	.50	.15
☐ 1914	18¢ Multicolored	—	—	.50	.15
☐ 1915	18¢ Multicolored	—	—	.50	.15
☐ 1916	18¢ Multicolored	—	—	.50	.15
☐ 1917	18¢ Multicolored	—	—	.50	.15
☐ 1918	18¢ Multicolored	—	—	.50	.15
☐ 1919	18¢ Multicolored	—	—	.50	.15

1981. PROFESSIONAL MANAGEMENT
☐ 1920	18¢ Dark Blue & Black	22.00	2.50	.50	.14

*No hinge pricing from 1941 to date is figured at (N-H ADD 15%)

Scott No.		Mint Sheet	Plate Block	Fine Unused Each	Fine Used Each
1981. PRESERVATION OF WILDLIFE HABITATS					
☐ 1921	18¢ Multicolored	—	—	.45	.13
☐ 1922	18¢ Multicolored	—	—	.45	.13
☐ 1923	18¢ Multicolored	—	—	.45	.13
☐ 1924	18¢ Multicolored	—	—	.45	.13
1981. DISABLED PERSONS					
☐ 1925	18¢ Multicolored	22.00	3.00	.50	.13
1981. EDNA ST. VINCENT MILLAY					
☐ 1926	18¢ Multicolored	22.00	2.50	.50	.13
1981. ALCOHOLISM					
☐ 1927	18¢ Dark Blue	38.00	24.00	.50	.16
1981. ARCHITECTURE					
☐ 1928	18¢ Brown & Black	—	—	.50	.11
☐ 1929	18¢ Brown & Black	—	—	.50	.11
☐ 1930	18¢ Brown & Black	—	—	.50	.11
☐ 1931	18¢ Brown & Black	—	—	.50	.11
1981. BABE ZAHARIAS					
☐ 1932	18¢ Purple	—	3.00	.55	.13
1981. BOBBY JONES					
☐ 1933	18¢ Dark Green	—	3.00	.55	.13
1981. FREDERIC REMINGTON					
☐ 1934	18¢ Light Brown & Green	22.00	3.00	.55	.13
1981. JAMES HOBAN					
☐ 1935	18¢ Multicolored	22.00	2.50	.55	.13
1981. JAMES HOBAN					
☐ 1936	20¢ Multicolored	24.00	2.50	.60	.14
1981. YORKTOWN MAP					
☐ 1937	18¢ Multicolored	—	—	.50	.13
1981. VIRGINIA CAPES MAP					
☐ 1938	18¢ Multicolored	—	—	.60	.14
1981. CHRISTMAS—BOTTICELLI					
☐ 1939	20¢ Multicolored	46.00	3.00	.60	.14
1981. SEASONS GREETINGS					
☐ 1940	20¢ Multicolored	24.00	3.00	.60	.14
1981. JOHN HANSON					
☐ 1941	20¢ Multicolored	27.00	3.00	.60	.14
1981. DESERT PLANTS					
☐ 1942	Multicolored	—	—	.60	.14
☐ 1943	Multicolored	—	—	.60	.14

*No hinge pricing from 1941 to date is figured at (N-H ADD 15%)

HOW TO FIND YOUR STAMP

This new stamp catalog takes the confusion out of finding and identifying individual stamps. A complete, new FULL-COLOR–FAST-FIND PHOTO INDEX is illustrated on the following pages. All of the stamp photographs are arranged in Scott numerical order and date of issue. Below each stamp picture is the Scott number and the page number on which the stamp listing appears.

GENERAL ISSUE—SCOTT NO. 1–116 (1847–1869)

1, 39, 48a
PG 21

2, 4, 948b
PG 21

5, 9, 18–24, 40
PG 21

10, 11, 25, 26
41–PG 21

12, 27–30A
42–PG 21

13–16, 31–35,
43–PG 21

17, 36, 44
PG 21

37, 45
PG 22

38, 46
PG 22

39, 47
PG 22

56, 63, 85, 86
92, 102–PG 22

64–66, 74, 79, 88
94, 104–PG 22

57–67, 75, 76, 80
95, 195–PG 22

58–62B, 68, 85D,
89, 96, 106–PG 22

59, 69, 85E, 90
97, 107–PG 22

60, 70, 78, 99
109–PG 22

61, 71, 81, 100,
110–PG 22

62, 72, 101,
111–PG 22

73, 84, 85B, 87,
93, 103–PG 22

77, 85F, 91, 98,
108–PG 22

112, 123, 133
PG 24

113, 124
PG 24

114, 125
PG 24

115, 126
PG 24

116, 127
PG 24

117, 128
PG 24

118, 119, 129
PG 24

120, 130
PG 24

121, 131
PG 24

122, 132
PG 24

134, 156, 167
182, 206–PG 24

135, 157, 168
203–PG 24

136, 158, 169,
214–PG 24

137, 148, 159,
195, 208–PG 24

138, 149, 160
171, 196–PG 24

139, 150, 161,
197, 209–PG 24

140-151, 162,
173, 198–PG 24

141, 152, 163,
189, 199–PG 24

142, 153, 164,
175, 200–PG 24

143, 154, 165
190, 201, 217–PG 24

144, 155, 166,
202, 218–PG 24

179, 181, 185,
204–PG 25

205, 205C, 216
PG 25

210, 211B, 213,
PG 26

211, 211D, 215
PG 26

212–RG 26

219–PG 26

219D, 220–PG 26

221–PG 26

222–PG 26

223–PG 26   224–PG 26   225–PG 26   226–PG 26   227–PG 26

228–PG 26   229–PG 26   230–PG 26   231–PG 26

232–PG 26   233–PG 26   234–PG 26

235–PG 26   236–PG 26   237–PG 26

238–PG 26   239–PG 27   240–PG 27

241–PG 27

242–PG 27

243–PG 27

244–PG 27

245–PG 27

246, 247, 264,
279–PG 27

248–252, 265–267,
279B–PG 27

253, 268
PG 27

254, 269, 280
PG 27

255, 270, 281
PG 27

256, 271, 282
PG 27

257, 272
PG 27

258, 273, 282C,
283–PG 27

259, 273, 284
PG 27

260, 275
PG 27

261–261A, 276,
276A–PG 27

262, 277
PG 27

263, 278–PG 27

285–PG 28

286–PG 28

287–PG 28

288–PG 28 289–PG 28 290–PG 28

291–PG 28 292–PG 28 293–PG 28

294–PG 28 295–PG 28 296–PG 28 297–PG 28

298–PG 28 299–PG 28 300, 314, 316, 318–PG 28 301–PG 28 302–PG 28

303, 314A PG 28 304, 315, 317 PG 28 305–PG 28 306–PG 28 307–PG 28 308–PG 28

GENERAL ISSUE—SCOTT NO. 309–398 (1903–1913)

309–PG 28 310–PG 28 311–PG 28 312, 479 PG 28 313, 480 PG 28 319–322 PG 29

323–PG 29 324–PG 29 325–PG 29

326–PG 29 327–PG 29 328–PG 29 329–PG 29

330–PG 29 331, 392 PG 29 332–393, 519 PG 29 333–541 PG 29 367, 369 PG 30

370, 371–PG 30 372, 373–PG 30 397, 401–PG 31 398, 402–PG 31

399, 403 PG 31	400, 400A, 404 PG 31	405–545 PG 32	406–546 PG 32	414–518 PG 32
523, 524, 547 PG 35	537–PG 36	548–PG 37	549–PG 37	
550–PG 37	551, 653 PG 37	552, 575, 578, 604, 632–PG 37	553, 576, 598, 605, 633–PG 37	555, 584, 600, 635–PG 37
556–585, 601 636–PG 37	557, 586, 602, 637–PG 37	558, 587, 638, 723–PG 37	559, 588, 639 PG 37	560, 589, 640 PG 37
561, 590, 641 PG 37	562, 591, 603, 641–PG 37	563, 692 PG 37	564, 693 PG 37	565, 695–PG 37

566–696–PG 37 567, 698–PG 37 568, 699–PG 37 569, 700–PG 37 570, 701–PG 37

571–PG 37 572–PG 37 573–PG 37 583, 599–99A 634–34A–PG 38 610–613–PG 38

614–PG 38 615–PG 38 616–PG 38

617–PG 39 618–PG 39 619–PG 39

620–PG 39 621–PG 39 622, 694–PG 39 623, 697–PG 39

627–PG 39 628–PG 39 629–PG 39 643–PG 39

644–PG 39 645–PG 39 646–PG 39 647–PG 40 648–PG 40

649–PG 40 650–PG 40 651–PG 40

654–656–PG 40 657–PG 40 680–PG 41 681–PG 41 682–PG 41

683–PG 41 684, 686–PG 41 685, 687–PG 41 688–PG 41 689–PG 41

690–PG 41   702–PG 42   703–PG 42   704–PG 42   705–PG 42

706–PG 42   707–PG 42   708–PG 42   709–PG 42   710–PG 42   711–PG 42

712–PG 42   713–PG 42   714–PG 42   715–PG 42   716–PG 42

717–PG 42   718–PG 42   719–PG 42   720–722   724–PG 43   725–PG 43
                                        PG 42

726–PG 43   727, 752   728, 730, 766   729, 731, 767   732–PG 43
             PG 43   PG 43   PG 43

733, 735, 753
PG 43

734–PG 43

736–PG 43

737, 738, 754–PG 44

739, 755–PG 44

740, 751, 756,
769–PG 44

741, 757–PG 44

742, 750, 758, 770–PG 44

743, 759–PG 44

744, 760–PG 44

745, 761–PG 44

746, 762–PG 44

747, 763–PG 44

748, 764–PG 44

749, 765, 797–PG 44

772, 778A–PG 45

773, 778B–PG 45

774–PG 45

775, 778C–PG 45

776, 778D–PG 45

777–PG 45

782–PG 45

783–PG 46

784–PG 46

785–PG 46

786–PG 46

787–PG 46

788–PG 46

789–PG 46

790–PG 46

791–PG 46

792–PG 46

793–PG 46

794–PG 46

795–PG 46

796–PG 46

798–PG 46

799–PG 46

800–PG 46

801–PG 46

802–PG 46

803–PG 46 804, 848–PG 46 805, 849–PG 46 806–PG 46 807–PG 46 808, 843–PG 46

809, 844–PG 46 810, 845–PG 47 811, 846–PG 47 812–PG 47 813–PG 47 814–PG 47

815, 847–PG 47 816–PG 47 817–PG 47 818–PG 47 819–PG 47 820–PG 47

821–PG 47 822–PG 47 823–PG 47 824–PG 47 825–PG 47 826–PG 47

827–PG 47 828–PG 47 829–PG 47 830–PG 47 831–PG 47 832–PG 47

833–PG 47 834–PG 47 835–PG 47 836–PG 47

837-PG 47 838-PG 47 852-PG 48 853-PG 48

854-PG 48 855-PG 48 856-PG 48 857-PG 48

858-PG 48 859-PG 48 860-PG 48 861-PG 48

862-PG 48 863-PG 48 864-PG 49 865-PG 49 866-PG 49

867–PG 49	868–PG 49	869–PG 49	870–PG 49	871–PG 49
872–PG 49	873–PG 49	874–PG 49	875–PG 49	876–PG 49
877–PG 49	878–PG 49	879–PG 49	880–PG 49	881–PG 49
882–PG 49	883–PG 49	884–PG 49	885–PG 49	886–PG 49
887–PG 49	888–PG 49	889–PG 49	890–PG 49	891–PG 49

892–PG 49

893–PG 49

894–PG 49

895–PG 49

896–PG 50

897–PG 50

898–PG 50

899–PG 50

900–PG 50

901–PG 50

902–PG 50

903–PG 50

904–PG 50

905–PG 50

906–PG 50

907–PG 50

908-PG 50

909-PG 50

921-PG 51

922-PG 51

923-PG 51

924-PG 51

925-PG 51

926-PG 51

927-PG 51

928-PG 51

929-PG 51

930-PG 51

931-PG 51

932-PG 51

933-PG 51

934–PG 51

935–PG 51

936–PG 51

937–PG 51

938–PG 51

939–PG 52

940–PG 52

941–PG 52

942–PG 52

943–PG 52

944–PG 52

945–PG 52

946–PG 52

947–PG 52

948–PG 52

949–PG 52

950–PG 52

951–PG 52

952–PG 52

953–PG 52

954–PG 52

955–PG 52

956–PG 53

957–PG 53

958–PG 53

959–PG 53

960–PG 53

961–PG 53

962–PG 53

963–PG 53

964–PG 53

965–PG 53

966–PG 53

967–PG 53

968–PG 53

969–PG 53

970–PG 53

971–PG 53

972–PG 53

973–PG 53

974–PG 53

975–PG 54   976–PG 54   977–PG 54   978–PG 54

979–PG 54   980–PG 54   981–PG 54   982–PG 54

983–PG 54   984–PG 54   985–PG 54

986–PG 54   987–PG 54   988–PG 54   989–PG 54

990–PG 54   991–PG 54   992–PG 54

993–PG 54

994–PG 54

995–PG 55

996–PG 55

997–PG 55

998–PG 55

999–PG 55

1000–PG 55

1001–PG 55

1002–PG 55

1003–PG 55

1004–PG 55

1005–PG 55

1006–PG 55

1007–PG 55

1008–PG 55

1009–PG 55

1010–PG 55

1011–PG 55

1012–PG 55

1013–PG 56

1014–PG 56

1015–PG 56

1016–PG 56

1017–PG 56

1018–PG 56

1019–PG 56

1020–PG 56

1021–PG 56

1022–PG 56

1023–PG 56

1024–PG 56

1025–PG 56

GENERAL ISSUE—SCOTT NO. 1026-1050 (1953-1955)

1026–PG 56

1027–PG 56

1028–PG 56

1029–PG 56

1030–PG 56

1031, 1054–PG 56

1031A, 1054A–PG 56

1032–PG 57

1033, 1055–PG 57

1034, 1056–PG 57

1035–1075–PG 57

1036–1058–PG 57

1037, 1059–PG 57

1038–PG 57

1039–PG 57

1040–PG 57

1041, 1075B–PG 57

1042A–PG 57

1043–PG 57

1044A–PG 57

1044–PG 57

1045–PG 57

1046–PG 57

1047–PG 57

1048–PG 57

1049–PG 57

1050–PG 57

GENERAL ISSUE—SCOTT NO. 1051–1072 (1955)

1051–PG 57

1052–PG 57

1053–PG 57

1060–PG 57

1061–PG 57

1062–PG 57

1063–PG 58

1064–PG 58

1065–PG 58

1066–PG 58

1067–PG 58

1068–PG 58

1069–PG 58

1070–PG 58

1071–PG 58

1072–PG 58

1073–PG 58

1074–PG 58

1075–PG 58

1076–PG 58

1077–PG 58

1078–PG 58

1079–PG 58

GENERAL ISSUE—SCOTT NO. 1080–1093 (1956–1957)

1080–PG 58

1081–PG 58

1082–PG 59

1083–PG 59

1084–PG 59

1085–PG 59

1086–PG 59

1087–PG 59

1088–PG 59

1089–PG 59

1090–PG 59

1091–PG 59

1092–PG 59

1093–PG 59

1094–PG 59

1095–PG 59

1096–PG 59

1097–PG 59

1098–PG 59

1099–PG 59

1100–PG 60

1104–PG 60

1105–PG 60

1106–PG 60

1107–PG 60

1108–PG 60

1109–PG 60

1110–PG 60

1111–PG 60

1112–PG 60
1113–PG 60
1114–PG 60
1115–PG 60

1116–PG 60
1117–PG 60
1118–PG 60
1119–PG 60

1120–PG 60
1121–PG 60
1122–PG 60
1123–PG 60

1124–PG 61
1125–PG 61
1126–PG 61
1127–PG 61

1128–PG 61

1129–PG 61

1130–PG 61

1131–PG 61

1132–PG 61

1133–PG 61

1134–PG 61

1135–PG 61

1136–PG 61

1137–PG 61

1138–PG 61

1139–PG 61

1140–PG 61

1141–PG 61

1142–PG 61

1143–PG 61

GENERAL ISSUE—SCOTT NO. 1144–1160 (1960–1961)

1144–PG 61   1145–PG 61   1146–PG 62   1147–PG 62

1148–PG 62   1149–PG 62   1150–PG 62   1151–PG 62

1152–PG 62   1153–PG 62   1154–PG 62   1155–PG 62

1156–PG 62   1157–PG 62   1158–PG 62   1159–PG 62   1160–PG 62

1161–PG 62

1162–PG 62

1163–PG 62

1164–PG 62

1165–PG 62

1166–PG 62

1167–PG 63

1168–PG 63

1169–PG 63

1170–PG 63

1171–PG 63

1172–PG 63

1173–PG 63

1174–PG 63

1175–PG 63

1176–PG 63

1177–PG 63

1178–PG 63

1179–PG 63

1180–PG 63

1181–PG 63

1182–PG 63

1183–PG 63

1184–PG 63

1185–PG 63

1186–PG 64

1187–PG 64

1188–PG 64

1189–PG 64

1190–PG 64

1191–PG 64

1192–PG 64

1193–PG 64

1194–PG 64

1195–PG 64

1196—PG 64

1197—PG 64

1198—PG 64

1199—PG 64

1200—PG 64

1202—PG 64

1201—PG 64

1203—PG 64

1204—PG 64

1205—PG 65

1206—PG 65

1207—PG 65

1208—PG 65

1209, 1225—PG 65

1213—PG 65

1230—PG 65

1231–PG 65

1232–PG 65

1233–PG 65

1234–PG 65

1235–PG 65

1236–PG 65

1237–PG 65

1238–PG 65

1239–PG 66

1240–PG 66

1241–PG 66

1242–PG 66

1243–PG 66

1244–PG 66

GENERAL ISSUE—SCOTT NO. 1245–1261 (1964–1965)

1245–PG 66

1246–PG 66

1247–PG 66

1248–PG 66

1249–PG 66

1250–PG 66

1251–PG 66

1252–PG 66

1253–PG 66

1254–PG 66

1255–PG 66

1256–PG 66

1257–PG 66

1258–PG 66

1259–PG 67

1260–PG 67

1261–PG 67

1262–PG 67

1263–PG 67

1264–PG 67

1265–PG 67

1266–PG 67

1267–PG 67

1268–PG 67

1269–PG 67

1270–PG 67

1271–PG 67

1272–PG 67

1273–PG 67

1274–PG 67

1275–PG 67

1276–PG 67

1278–PG 68

1279–PG 68

1280–PG 68

1281, 1297–PG 68

1282, 1303–PG 68

1283, 1304–PG 68

1283B–PG 68

1284, 1298–PG 68

1285–PG 68

1286–PG 68

1286A–PG 68

1287–PG 68

1288–PG 68

1289–PG 68

1290–PG 68

1291–PG 68

1292–PG 68

1293–PG 68

1294, 1305C–PG 68

1295–PG 68

1305–PG 68

1306–PG 68

1307–PG 68

1308–PG 68

1309–PG 69

1310–PG 69

1311–PG 69

1312–PG 69

1313–PG 69

1314–PG 69

1315–PG 69

1316–PG 69

1317–PG 69

1318–PG 69

1319–PG 69   1320–PG 69   1321–PG 69   1322–PG 69   1323–PG 69

1324–PG 69   1325–PG 69   1326–PG 69

1327–PG 69   1328–PG 70   1329–PG 70   1330–PG 70

1331–PG 70   1332–PG 70   1333–PG 70   1334–PG 70

1335–PG 70

1336–PG 70

1337–PG 70

1338, 1338A
PG 70

1338F, G–PG 70

1339–PG 70

1340–PG 70

1341–PG 70

1342–PG 70

1343–PG 70

1344–PG 70

1345–PG 70

1354–PG 71

1355–PG 71

1356–PG 71

1357–PG 71

1358–PG 71

1359–PG 71

1360–PG 71

1361–PG 71

1362–PG 71

1363–PG 71

1364–PG 71

1365–1368–PG 71

1369–PG 71

1370–PG 71

1371–PG 71

1372-PG 72

1373-PG 72

1374-PG 72

1375-PG 72

1376–1379-PG 72

1380-PG 72

1381-PG 72

1382-PG 72

1383-PG 72

1384-PG 72

1385–PG 72

1386–PG 72

1387–1390–PG 72

1391–PG 72

1392–PG 72

1393–PG 72

1393D–PG 72

1394–PG 73

1395–PG 73

1396–PG 73

1397–PG 73

1398–PG 73

1399–PG 73

1400–PG 73

1405–PG 73

1406–PG 73

1407–PG 73

1408–PG 73

1409–PG 73

1410–1413–PG 73

1414–PG 73

1415–1418–PG 73

1419–PG 74

1420–PG 74

1421–PG 74

1422–PG 74

1423–PG 74

1424–PG 74

1425–PG 74

1426–PG 74

1427-1430–PG 74

1431–PG 74

1432–PG 74

1433–PG 74

1434–PG 74   1435–PG 74

1436–PG 74

1437–PG 74

1438–PG 74

1439–PG 74

1440–1443–PG 74

1444–PG 75

1445–PG 75

1446–PG 75

1447–PG 75

1448–1451–PG 75

1452–PG 75

1453–PG 75

1454–PG 75

1455–PG 75

1456–1459–PG 75

1460–PG 75

1461–PG 75

1462–PG 75

1463–PG 75

1464–1467–PG 75

1468–PG 75

1469–PG 76

1470–PG 76

1471–PG 76

1472–PG 76

1473–PG 76

1474–PG 76

1475–PG 76

1476–PG 76

1477–PG 76

1478–PG 76

1479–PG 76

1480–1483–PG 76

1484–PG 76

1485–PG 76

1486–PG 76

1487–PG 76   1488–PG 76   1489–PG 76   1490–PG 76

1491–PG 76   1492–PG 76   1493–PG 76   1494–PG 76   1495–PG 77

1496–PG 77   1497–PG 77   1498–PG 77   1499–PG 77

1500–PG 77   1501–PG 77   1502–PG 77

GENERAL ISSUE—SCOTT NO. 1503–1529 (1973–1974)

1503–PG 77

1504–PG 77

1505–PG 77

1506F–PG 77

1507–PG 77

1508–PG 77

1509, 1519–PG 77

1510–PG 77

1511–PG 77

1518–PG 77

1525–PG 77

1526–PG 77

1527–PG 77

1528–PG 78

1529–PG 78

1530–PG 78   1531–PG 78   1532–PG 78   1533–PG 78   1534–PG 78

1535–PG 78   1536–PG 78

1538–1539–PG 78
1540–1541–PG 78

1537–PG 78

1543–1546–PG 78

1542–PG 78

1547–PG 78

1548–PG 78

1549–PG 78

1550–PG 78

1551–PG 78

1552–PG 78

1553–PG 78

1554–PG 78

1555–PG 79

1556–PG 79

1557–PG 79

1558–PG 79

1559–PG 79

1560–PG 79

1561–PG 79

1562–PG 79

1563–PG 79

1564–PG 79

1565–PG 79

1566–PG 79

1567–PG 79

1568–PG 79

1569–PG 79

1570–PG 79

1571–PG 79

1572–PG 79

1573–PG 79

1574–PG 79

GENERAL ISSUE—SCOTT NO. 1575–1608 (1975)

1575–PG 79

1577–1578–PG 79

1576–PG 79

1581–PG 80

1582–PG 80

1584–PG 80

1585–PG 80

1579–PG 79

1580–PG 79

1590–PG 80

1592–PG 80

1593–PG 80

1594–PG 80

1595–PG 80

1596–PG 80

1597–1598–PG 80

1599–PG 80

1603–PG 80

1604–PG 80

1605–PG 80

1606–PG 80

1608–PG 80

A-56

1610–PG 80   1611–PG 80   1612–PG 80   1613–PG 80   1614–PG 80

1615–PG 80   1615C–PG 80   1629–1630–1631–PG 81

1622–PG 80   1623–PG 80   1632–PG 81   1633–1682–PG 81

1683–PG 81   1684–PG 81   1685–PG 81

1686–PG 81   1687–PG 81

1688–PG 82

1689–PG 82

1690–PG 82

1691–1692–1693–1694–PG 82

1695–PG 82   1696–PG 82

1697–PG 82   1698–PG 82

1699–PG 82

1700–PG 82

1701–PG 82

1702–1703–PG 82

1704–PG 82

1705–PG 82

1706–PG 82

1707–PG 82

1708–PG 82

1709–PG 82

1710–PG 83

1711–PG 83

1712–PG 83

1713–PG 83

1714–PG 83

1715–PG 83

1716–PG 83

1717–PG 83

1718–PG 83

1719–PG 83

1720–PG 83

1721–PG 83

1722–PG 83

1723–PG 83

1724–PG 83

1725–PG 83

1726–PG 83

1727–PG 83

1728–PG 83

1729–PG 83

1730–PG 83

1731–PG 83

1732–PG 83

1733–PG 83

1734–PG 84

1735–PG 84

1737–PG 84

1738–1739–1740–1741–1742–PG 84

1744–PG 84

1745–PG 84

1746–PG 84

1747–PG 84

1748–PG 84

1749–PG 84

1750–PG 84

1751–PG 84

1752–PG 84

1753–PG 84

1754–PG 84

1755–PG 84

1756–PG 84

Canadian International Philatelic Exhibition

1757–PG 84

1758–PG 84

1759–PG 85

1760–PG 85

1761–PG 85

1762–PG 85

1763–PG 85

1764–PG 85

1765–PG 85

1766–PG 85   1767–PG 85   1768–PG 85   1769–PG 85

1770–PG 85   1771–PG 85   1772–PG 85   1773–PG 85

1774–PG 85   1775–PG 85   1776–PG 85   1777–PG 85

1778–PG 85   1779–PG 85   1780–PG 85   1781–PG 85

GENERAL ISSUE—SCOTT NO. 1782-1800 (1979)

1782–PG 85

1783–PG 85

1784–PG 85

1785–PG 85

1786–PG 85

1787–PG 85

1788–PG 86

1789–PG 86

1790–PG 86

1791–PG 86

1792–PG 86

1793–PG 86

1794–PG 86

1795–PG 86

1796–PG 86

1797–PG 86

1798–PG 86

1799–PG 86

1800–PG 86

1801–PG 86

1802–PG 86

1803–PG 86

1804–PG 86

1805–1806
PG 86

1807–1808
PG 87

1809–1810
PG 87

1811–PG 87

1813–PG 87

1818–PG 87

1821–PG 87

1822
PG 87

1823–PG 87

1824–PG 87

1825–PG 87

1826–PG 87

1827–PG 87

1828–PG 87

1829–PG 87

1830–PG 87

1831–PG 87

1832–PG 87

1833–PG 87

1834–PG 88

1835–PG 88

1836–PG 88

1837–PG 88

1838–PG 88

1839–PG 88

1840–PG 88

1841–PG 88

1842–PG 88

1843–PG 88

1844–PG 88

1845–PG 88

1846–PG 88

1847–PG 88

1848–PG 88

1849–PG 88

1850–PG 88

1851–PG 88

1852–PG 88

1853–PG 88

1854–PG 88

1855–PG 88

1856–PG 88

1857–PG 89

1858–PG 89

1859–PG 89

Ralph Bunche
USA 20c
1860–PG 89

Thomas H Gallaudet
USA 20c
1861–PG 89

Harry S Truman
USA 20c
1862–PG 89

John J. Audubon
USA 22
1863–PG 89

Frank C Laubach
USA 30c
1864–PG 89

Charles R Drew MD
USA 35c
1865–PG 89

Robert Millikan
37c USA
1866–PG 89

Grenville Clark
USA 39
1867–PG 89

Lillian M.Gilbreth
USA 40c
1868–PG 89

Chester W. Nimitz
USA 50
1869–PG 89

Rose USA 18c
1876–PG 89

Camellia USA 18c
1877–PG 89

USA 15c
Everett Dirksen
1874–PG 89

Whitney Moore Young
Black Heritage USA
1875–PG 89

Dahlia USA 18c
1878–PG 89

Lily USA 18c
1879–PG 89

USA 18c
1880–PG 89

USA 18c
1881–PG 89

USA 18c
1882–PG 89

USA 18c
1883–PG 89

USA 18c
1884–PG 90

USA 18c
1885–PG 90

USA 18c
1886–PG 90

USA 18c
1887–PG 90

USA 18c
1888–PG 90

USA 18c
1889–PG 90

USA 18c
...for amber waves of grain
1890–PG 90

USA 18c
.... from sea to shining sea
1891–PG 90

1892–PG 90

1893–PG 90

1894–PG 90

1900–PG 90

1902–PG 90

1905–PG 90

1906–PG 90

1907–PG 90

1910–PG 90

1911–PG 90

1920–PG 90

1912–1916–PG 90
1917–1919–PG 90

1921–PG 91

1922–PG 91

1923–PG 91

1924–PG 91

1925–PG 91

1926–PG 91

1927–PG 91

1928–PG 91

1929–PG 91

1930–PG 91

1931–PG 91

1932–PG 91

1933–PG 91

1934–PG 91

1935–PG 91

1936–PG 91

1937–PG 91

1938–PG 91

1939–PG 91

1949–PG 93

1940–PG 91

1941–PG 91

1946–1948–PG 93

1950–PG 93

1942–1945–PG 91

1951–PG 93

1952–PG 93

2003–PG 93

2004–PG 93

2005–PG 93

1953–2002–PG 93

USA 20c Solar energy Knoxville World's Fair
USA 20c Synthetic fuels Knoxville World's Fair
USA 20c Breeder reactor Knoxville World's Fair
USA 20c Fossil fuels Knoxville World's Fair

2006-2009-PG 93

Horatio Alger
USA 20c
2010-PG 93

THE BARRYMORES
Performing Arts USA 20c
2012-PG 93

Dr. Mary Walker
Army Surgeon
Medal of Honor
USA 20c
2013-PG 93

Aging together
USA 20c
2011-PG 93

International Peace Garden
1932 1982 USA 20c
2014-PG 94

America's
A B C
Libraries
X Y Z
USA 20c
Library of Congress
2015-PG 94

Jackie Robinson
Black Heritage USA 20c
2016-PG 94

Touro
Synagogue
Newport RI 1763
USA 20c
To bigotry,
no sanction.
To persecution,
no assistance.
George Washington
2017-PG 94

2018–PG 94

Architecture USA 20c
Frank Lloyd Wright 1867-1959 Fallingwater Mill Run PA

Architecture USA 20c
Mies van der Rohe 1886-1969 Illinois Inst Tech Chicago

2023–PG 94

Architecture USA 20c
Walter Gropius 1883-1969 Gropius House Lincoln MA

Architecture USA 20c
Eero Saarinen 1910-1961 Dulles Airport Washington DC

2019–2022–PG 94

2024–PG 94

2025–PG 94

Christmas USA 20c
Tiepolo National Gallery of Art

2026–PG 94

Season's Greetings USA 20c

Season's Greetings USA 20c

Season's Greetings USA 20c

Season's Greetings USA 20c

2027–2030–PG 94

Science & Industry USA 20c

2031–PG 94

2032-2035-PG 95

2036-PG 95

2037-PG 95

2038-PG 95

2039-PG 95

2040-PG 95

2041-PG 95

2042-PG 95

2043-PG 95

2044-PG 95

2045-PG 95

2046–PG 95

2048–2051–PG 95

2047–PG 95

2052–PG 96

2053–PG 96

2054–PG 96

2055–PG 96

2056–PG 96

2057–PG 96

2058–PG 96

2059–PG 96

USA 20c

Early electric streetcar, Montgomery, Ala., 1886

2060–PG 96

USA 20c

"Bobtail" horsecar, Sulphur Rock, Ark., 1926

2061–PG 96

USA 20c

St. Charles streetcar, New Orleans, La., 1923

2062–PG 96

Christmas USA 20c

Raphael, 1483-1965, National Gallery

2063–PG 96

Martin Luther

1483-1983 USA 20c

2065–PG 96

Olympics 84
USA 20c

Olympics 84
USA 20c

Season's Greetings USA 20c

2064–PG 96

USA 20c

1959-1984
Alaska Statehood

2066–PG 96

Olympics 84
USA 20c

Olympics 84
USA 20c

2067–2070–PG 96

FEDERAL DEPOSIT
INSURANCE
CORPORATION

2071–PG 97

LO♥E
LO♥E
LO♥E
LO♥E
LO♥E
USA 20c

2072–PG 97

Carter G. Woodson

Black Heritage USA 20c

2073–PG 97

SOIL AND WATER
CONSERVATION

USA 20c

2074–PG 97

GENERAL ISSUE—SCOTT NO. 2075-2092 (1984)

2075–PG 97

2080–PG 97

2076–2079–PG 97

2081–PG 97

2082–2085–PG 97

2086–PG 97

2088–PG 97

2089–PG 98

2090–PG 98

2087–PG 97

2091–PG 98

2092–PG 98

2093-PG 98

2094-PG 98

2095-PG 98

2096-PG 98

2097-PG 98

2098-PG 98

2099-PG 98

2100-PG 98

2101-PG 98

2102-PG 98

2103-PG 98

2104-PG 98

2105-PG 98

2106-PG 98

2107-PG 98

2108-PG 99

GENERAL ISSUE—SCOTT NO. 2109-2136 (1984-1986)

2109–PG 99

2110–PG 99

2111–2113–PG 99

2114–2116–PG 99

2122–PG 99

School Bus 1920s
3.4 USA
2123–PG 99

Buckboard 1880s
USA
4.9
2125–PG 99

Star Route Truck
5.5 USA 1910s
2126–PG 99

Tricycle 1880s
6 USA
2127–PG 99

Ambulance 1860s
8.3 USA
2128–PG 100

Oil Wagon 1890s
10.1 USA
2129–PG 100

Stutz Bearcat 1933
11 USA
2130–PG 100

2117–2121–PG 99

Stanley Steamer 1909
USA
12
2131–PG 100

Iceboat 1880s
USA
14
2134–PG 100

Dog Sled 1920s
17 USA
2135–PG 100

Bread Wagon 1880s
25 USA
2136–PG 100

Pushcart 1880s
12.5
USA
2132–PG 100

2137–PG 100

2138-2141–PG 100

2142–PG 100

2143–PG 100

2144–PG 100

2145–PG 100

2146–PG 100

2147–PG 100

2149–PG 101

2150–PG 101

2152–PG 101

2153–PG 101

2154–PG 101

2155-2158–PG 101

2159–PG 101

A-81

2160–2163–PG 101

2164–PG 101

2166–PG 101

2165–PG 101

2167–PG 101

2168–PG 101

2169–PG 102

2170–PG 102

2171–PG 102

2172–PG 102

2177–PG 102

2179–PG 102

2183–PG 102

2191–PG 102

2194–PG 102

2195–PG 102

2196–PG 102

2198-2201–PG 102

2202–PG 102

2203–PG 102

2204–PG 102

2210–PG 103

2211–PG 103

2205-2209
PG 102-103

2216–PG 103

GENERAL ISSUE—SCOTT NO. 2217–2223 (1986)

2217–PG 103

2218–PG 103

2219–PG 103

2220–2223–PG 103

GENERAL ISSUE—SCOTT NO. 2224-2250 (1986-1987)

2224–PG 103

2239–PG 104

2235–2238–PG 103

2240–2243–PG 104

2244–PG 104

2245–PG 104

2246–PG 104

2247–PG 104

2248–PG 104

2249–PG 104

2250–PG 104

GENERAL ISSUE—SCOTT NO. 2251–2335 (1987)

2251–PG 104

2275–PG 104

2276–PG 104

2286–2335–PG 104

Dec 7, 1787 USA
Delaware 22
2336–PG 104

Dec 12, 1787
Pennsylvania 22
2337–PG 104

Dec 18, 1787 USA
New Jersey 22
2338–PG 104

Friendship
with Morocco
1787-1987
USA 22
2349–PG 105

William Faulkner
2350–PG 105

Lacemaking USA 22
Lacemaking USA 22
Lacemaking USA 22
Lacemaking USA 22
2351–2354–PG 105

The Bicentennial
of the Constitution of
the United States
of America
1787-1987 USA 22

We the people
of the United States,
in order to form
a more perfect Union...
Preamble, U.S. Constitution 22

Establish justice,
insure domestic tranquility,
provide for the common defense,
promote the general welfare...
Preamble, U.S. Constitution 22

And secure
the blessings of liberty
to ourselves
and our posterity...
Preamble, U.S. Constitution USA 22

Do ordain
and establish this
Constitution for the
United States of America.
Preamble, U.S. Constitution USA 22

2355–2359–PG 105

U.S. Constitution
We the People
22
2360–PG 105

CPA
22
USA
2361–PG 105

CHRISTMAS
22
USA
Moroni, National Gallery
2367–PG 105

2368–PG 105

2369–PG 105

2370–PG 105

2371–PG 105

2372–2375–PG 105

2376–PG 106

2377–PG 106

2378–PG 106

2379–PG 106

2380–PG 106

GENERAL ISSUE—SCOTT NO. 2381–2399 (1988)

1928 Locomobile

1929 Pierce-Arrow

1931 Cord

1932 Packard

1935 Duesenberg

2381–2385
PG 106

Nathaniel Palmer

Lt. Charles Wilkes

Richard E. Byrd

Lincoln Ellsworth

2386–2389–PG 106

USA $8.75

2394–PG 106

Happy Birthday 25 USA

2395–PG 107

25 USA
Best Wishes

2396–PG 107

Thinking of you 25 USA

2397–PG 107

Love you 25 USA

2398–PG 107

CHRISTMAS
25 USA
Botticelli, National Gallery

2399–PG 107

2390–2393
PG 106

A-89

GENERAL ISSUE—SCOTT NO. 2400–2416 (1988)

2400–PG 107

2401–PG 107

2402–PG 107

2403–PG 107

2404–PG 107

2410–PG 107

2411–PG 107

2405–2409
PG 107

2412–PG 107

2413–PG 107

2414–PG 108

2416–PG 108

2417–PG 108

2418–PG 108

2419–PG 108

2420–PG 108

2421–PG 108

2422–2425
PG 108

2426–PG 108

2427–PG 108

2428–PG 108

2434–2437–PG 108

2439–PG 108

2440–PG 109

2442–PG 109

2443–PG 109

2444–PG 109

2445–2448
PG 109

2449–PG 109

2452–PG 109

2470–2474-PG 109

2508–2511-PG 110

2496–2500
PG 109

2501–2505-PG 110

2506–2507-PG 110

GENERAL ISSUE—SCOTT NO. 2512–2539 (1990–1991)

2512-PG 110

2513-PG 110

2514-PG 110

2515-PG 110

2517-PG 110

2521-PG 110

2523-PG 110

2524-PG 110

2528-PG 111

2530-PG 111

2531-PG 111

2532-PG 111

2533-PG 111

2534-PG 111

2535-PG 111

2537-PG 111

2538-PG 111

2539-PG 111

A-94

GENERAL ISSUE—SCOTT NO. 2540–2566 (1991)

2540-PG 111

2541-PG 111

2542-PG 111

2545–2549
PG 111

2550-PG 111

2551-PG 111

2558-PG 112

2553–2557-PG 111

2560-PG 112

2561-PG 112

2562–2566-PG 112

2568–2577-PG 112

2567-PG 112

2578-PG 112

2579-PG 112

2582-PG 112

2583-PG 112

2584-PG 112

2585-PG 112

Scott No.		Mint Sheet	Plate Block	Fine Unused Each	Fine Used Each
☐1944	Multicolored	—	—	.60	.14
☐1945	Multicolored	—	—	.60	.14

1981. "C" EAGLE—SINGLE

| ☐1946 | 20¢ Light Brown | 45.00 | 2.75 | .60 | .14 |

1981. "C" EAGLE—COIL SINGLE

| ☐1947 | 20¢ Light Brown | — | | .60 | .14 |

1981. "C" EAGLE—BOOKLET SINGLE

| ☐1948 | 20¢ Light Brown | | | .60 | .14 |

1981. BIGHORN SHEEP

| ☐1949 | 20¢ Dark Blue | — | — | .60 | .14 |

1982. FRANKLIN ROOSEVELT

| ☐1950 | 20¢ Dark Blue | 27.00 | 5.00 | .60 | .14 |

1982. "LOVE" FLOWERS

| ☐1951 | 20¢ Multicolored | 25.00 | 5.00 | .60 | .14 |

1982. GEORGE WASHINGTON

| ☐1952 | 20¢ Multicolored | 27.00 | 2.75 | .60 | .14 |

1982. BIRDS AND FLOWERS

| ☐1953– 2002 | 20¢ Multicolored | 28.00 | 2.75 | .60 | .14 |

1982. THE NETHERLANDS

| ☐2003 | 20¢ Dark Blue & Red | 30.00 | 2.75 | .60 | .14 |

1982. LIBRARY OF CONGRESS

| ☐2004 | 20¢ Rose & Dark Gray | 25.00 | 2.50 | .55 | .14 |

1982. CONSUMER EDUCATION

| ☐2005 | 20¢ Light Blue & Dark Blue | 30.00 | 2.50 | .75 | .14 |

1982. KNOXVILLE WORLD'S FAIR

☐2006	20¢ Multicolored	24.00	2.50	.60	.14
☐2007	20¢ Multicolored	24.00	2.50	.60	.14
☐2008	20¢ Multicolored	24.00	2.50	.60	.14
☐2009	20¢ Multicolored	24.00	2.50	.60	.14

1982. HORATIO ALGER

| ☐2010 | 20¢ Carmine & Black | 25.00 | 2.50 | .60 | .13 |

1982. AGING TOGETHER

| ☐2011 | 20¢ Light Rose | 25.00 | 2.50 | .60 | .13 |

1982. THE BARRYMORES

| ☐2012 | 20¢ Multicolored | 27.00 | 2.50 | .60 | .13 |

1982. DR. MARY WALKER

| ☐2013 | 20¢ Multicolored | 24.00 | 2.50 | .60 | .13 |

*No hinge pricing from 1941 to date is figured at (N-H ADD 15%)

Scott No.		Mint Sheet	Plate Block	Fine Unused Each	Fine Used Each
1982. INTERNATIONAL PEACE GARDEN					
☐ 2014	20¢ Multicolored	23.00	2.50	.55	.14
1982. AMERICA'S LIBRARIES					
☐ 2015	20¢ Orange-Red & Black	23.00	2.50	.55	.14
1982. JACKIE ROBINSON					
☐ 2016	20¢ Multicolored	28.00	3.00	.60	.14
1982. TOURO SYNAGOGUE					
☐ 2017	20¢ Multicolored	26.00	3.00	.60	.14
1982. WOLF TRAP FARM PARK					
☐ 2018	20¢ Multicolored	24.00	2.50	.55	.14
1982. ARCHITECTURE—WRIGHT					
☐ 2019	20¢ Black and Brown	24.00	2.50	.55	.14
1982. ARCHITECTURE—VAN DER ROHE					
☐ 2020	20¢ Black and Brown	24.00	2.50	.60	.14
1982. ARCHITECTURE—GROPIUS					
☐ 2021	20¢ Black and Brown	23.00	2.50	.60	.14
1982. ARCHITECTURE—SAARINEN					
☐ 2022	20¢ Black and Brown	23.00	2.50	.50	.14
☐ Architecture, above four attached		23.00	2.50	.50	.14
1982. FRANCIS OF ASSISI					
☐ 2023	20¢ Multicolored	24.00	2.50	.50	.14
1982. PONCE DE LEON					
☐ 2024	20¢ Multicolored	26.00	3.00	.50	.14
1982. CHRISTMAS ISSUE, CAT AND DOG					
☐ 2025	13¢ Multicolored	15.00	2.50	.40	.14
1982. CHRISTMAS ISSUE, TIEPOLO'S "MADONNA AND CHILD"					
☐ 2026	20¢ Multicolored	28.00	2.50	.55	.14
1982. SEASON'S GREETINGS, SLEDDING					
☐ 2027	20¢ Multicolored	32.00	—	.50	.14
1982. SEASON'S GREETINGS, BUILDING SNOWMAN					
☐ 2028	20¢ Multicolored	—	—	.50	.14
1982. SEASON'S GREETINGS, ICE SKATING					
☐ 2029	20¢ Multicolored	—	—	.50	.14
1982. SEASON'S GREETINGS, TRIMMING TREE					
☐ 2030	20¢ Multicolored	—	—	.50	.14
☐ Season's Greetings, above four attached		32.00	2.50	.50	.14
1982. SCIENCE AND INDUSTRY					
☐ 2031	20¢ Multicolored	32.00	2.50	.50	.14

*No hinge pricing from 1941 to date is figured at (N-H ADD 15%)

Scott No.	Mint Sheet	Plate Block	Fine Unused Each	Fine Used Each
1983. BALLOONING				
☐ 2032 20¢ Multicolored	—	—	.55	.14
1982. BALLOONING				
☐ 2033 20¢ Multicolored	—	—	.55	.14
1982. BALLOONING				
☐ 2034 20¢ Multicolored	—	—	.55	.14
1982. BALLOONING				
☐ 2035 20¢ Multicolored	—	—	.55	.14
☐ Ballooning, above four attached	23.00	2.50	.55	.14
1983. TREATY OF AMITY				
☐ 2036 20¢ Blue and Black	24.00	2.50	.55	.14
1983. CIVILIAN CONSERVATION CORPS				
☐ 2037 20¢ Multicolored	24.00	2.50	.55	.14
1983. JOSEPH PRIESTLEY				
☐ 2038 20¢ Rust Brown	24.00	2.50	.55	.14
1983. VOLUNTEER				
☐ 2039 20¢ Black and Red	26.00	2.50	.60	.14
1983. CONCORD				
☐ 2040 20¢ Beige	23.00	2.50	.60	.14
1983. BROOKLYN BRIDGE				
☐ 2041 20¢ Blue	25.00	2.50	.60	.14
1983. TENNESSEE VALLEY AUTHORITY				
☐ 2042 20¢ Multicolored	28.00	2.50	.60	.14
1983. PHYSICAL FITNESS				
☐ 2043 20¢ Multicolored	26.00	2.50	.60	.14
1982. SCOTT JOPLIN				
☐ 2044 20¢ Multicolored	27.00	2.50	.60	.14
1983. MEDAL OF HONOR				
☐ 2045 20¢ Multicolored	23.00	2.50	.60	.14
1983. BABE RUTH				
☐ 2046 20¢ Blue	30.00	5.00	.70	.20
1983. NATHANIEL HAWTHORNE				
☐ 2047 20¢ Multicolored	26.00	2.50	.50	.14
1983. SUMMER OLYMPICS 1984				
☐ 2048 13¢ Multicolored	—	—	.50	.14
1983. SUMMER OLYMPICS 1984				
☐ 2049 13¢ Multicolored	—	—	.50	.14
1983. SUMMER OLYMPICS 1984				
☐ 2050 13¢ Multicolored	—	—	.50	.14

*No hinge pricing from 1941 to date is figured at (N-H ADD 15%)

Scott No.	Mint Sheet	Plate Block	Fine Unused Each	Fine Used Each
1983. SUMMER OLYMPICS 1984				
☐ 2051 13¢ Multicolored	—	—	.60	.14
1983. TREATY OF PARIS				
☐ 2052 20¢ Multicolored	22.00	2.75	.60	.14
1983. CIVIL SERVICE				
☐ 2053 20¢ Multicolored	26.00	2.75	.60	.14
1983. METROPOLITAN OPERA				
☐ 2054 20¢ Yellow and Brown	24.00	2.75	.60	.14
1983. INVENTORS				
☐ 2055 20¢ Multicolored	26.00	—	.50	.14
1983. INVENTORS				
☐ 2056 20¢ Multicolored	26.00	—	.50	.14
1983. INVENTORS				
☐ 2057 20¢ Multicolored	27.00	—	.50	.14
1983. INVENTORS				
☐ 2058 20¢ Multicolored	27.00	—	.50	.14
1983. STREETCARS				
☐ 2059 20¢ Multicolored	26.00	—	.55	.13
1983. STREETCARS				
☐ 2060 20¢ Multicolored	25.00	—	.55	.13
1983. STREETCARS				
☐ 2061 20¢ Multicolored	25.00	—	.55	.13
1983. STREETCARS				
☐ 2062 20¢ Multicolored	25.00	—	.55	.13
1983. CHRISTMAS, MADONNA				
☐ 2063 20¢ Multicolored	24.00	2.75	.55	.13
1983. CHRISTMAS, SEASON'S GREETINGS				
☐ 2064 20¢ Multicolored	28.00	2.75	.55	.13
1983. MARTIN LUTHER				
☐ 2065 20¢ Multicolored	23.00	2.75	.55	.13
1984. ALASKA STATEHOOD				
☐ 2066 20¢ Multicolored	23.00	2.75	.55	.13
1984. WINTER OLYMPICS 1984				
☐ 2067 20¢ Multicolored	—	—	.55	.13
1984. WINTER OLYMPICS 1984				
☐ 2068 20¢ Multicolored	—	—	.55	.13
1984. WINTER OLYMPICS 1984				
☐ 2069 20¢ Multicolored	—	—	.55	.13

*No hinge pricing from 1941 to date is figured at (N-H ADD 15%)

Scott No.		Mint Sheet	Plate Block	Fine Unused Each	Fine Used Each
1984. WINTER OLYMPICS 1984					
☐ 2070	20¢ Multicolored	—	—	.50	.13
1984. FEDERAL DEPOSIT INSURANCE CORPORATION					
☐ 2071	20¢ Red & Yellow	24.00	2.50	.50	.13
1984. LOVE					
☐ 2072	20¢ Multicolored	26.00	2.50	.50	.13
1984. CARTER G. WOODSON					
☐ 2073	20¢ Multicolored	23.00	2.50	.50	.13
1984. SOIL AND WATER CONSERVATION					
☐ 2074	20¢ Multicolored	23.00	2.50	.50	.13
1984. CREDIT UNION					
☐ 2075	20¢ Multicolored	23.00	2.50	.50	.13
1984. ORCHIDS					
☐ 2076	20¢ Multicolored	28.00	2.60	.50	.13
1984. ORCHIDS					
☐ 2077	20¢ Multicolored	26.00	2.60	.50	.13
1984. ORCHIDS					
☐ 2078	20¢ Multicolored	28.00	2.60	.50	.13
1984. ORCHIDS					
☐ 2079	20¢ Multicolored	28.00	2.60	.50	.13
1984. HAWAII STATEHOOD					
☐ 2080	20¢ Blue & Yellow	27.00	2.60	.60	.13
1984. NATIONAL ARCHIVES					
☐ 2081	20¢ Brown & Black	27.00	2.60	.60	.13
1984. SUMMER OLYMPICS 1984					
☐ 2082	20¢ Multicolored	27.00	2.60	.60	.13
1984. SUMMER OLYMPICS 1984					
☐ 2083	20¢ Multicolored	27.00	2.60	.60	.13
1984. SUMMER OLYMPICS 1984					
☐ 2084	20¢ Multicolored	27.00	2.60	.60	.13
1984. SUMMER OLYMPICS 1984					
☐ 2085	20¢ Multicolored	27.00	2.60	.60	.13
1984. LOUISIANA WORLD'S FAIR					
☐ 2086	20¢ Multicolored	20.00	2.60	.60	.13
1984. HEALTH RESEARCH					
☐ 2087	20¢ Multicolored	26.00	2.60	.60	.13
1984. DOUGLAS FAIRBANKS					
☐ 2088	20¢ Black & White	27.00	2.60	.60	.13

*No hinge pricing from 1941 to date is figured at (N-H ADD 15%)

Scott No.		Mint Sheet	Plate Block	Fine Unused Each	Fine Used Each
1984. JIM THORPE					
☐ 2089	20¢ Black & White	28.00	3.00	.60	.13
1984. JOHN McCORMACK					
☐ 2090	20¢ Multicolored	26.00	2.50	.60	.13
1984. ST. LAWRENCE SEAWAY					
☐ 2091	20¢ Multicolored	26.00	2.50	.60	.13
1984. WATERFOWL PRESERVATION					
☐ 2092	20¢ Multicolored	30.00	2.50	.60	.13
1984. ROANOKE VOYAGES 1584					
☐ 2093	20¢ Multicolored	26.00	2.50	.60	.13
1984. HERMAN MELVILLE					
☐ 2094	20¢ Green	25.00	2.50	.60	.13
1984. HORACE MOSES					
☐ 2095	20¢ Orange & Brown	30.00	2.50	.60	.13
1984. SMOKEY THE BEAR					
☐ 2096	20¢ Multicolored	24.00	2.50	.60	.13
1984. ROBERTO CLEMENTE					
☐ 2097	20¢ Multicolored	30.00	2.50	1.00	.25
1984. DOGS: BEAGLE					
☐ 2098	20¢ Multicolored	23.00	2.50	.60	.13
1984. DOGS: RETRIEVER					
☐ 2099	20¢ Multicolored	23.00	2.50	.60	.13
1984. DOGS: MALAMUTE					
☐ 2100	20¢ Multicolored	21.00	2.50	.60	.13
1984. DOGS: COONHOUND					
☐ 2101	20¢ Multicolored	21.00	2.50	.60	.13
1984. CRIME PREVENTION					
☐ 2102	20¢ Multicolored	23.00	2.50	.60	.13
1984. HISPANIC AMERICANS					
☐ 2103	20¢ Multicolored	21.00	2.50	.60	.13
1984. FAMILY UNITY					
☐ 2104	20¢ Multicolored	28.00	2.50	.60	.13
1984. ELEANOR ROOSEVELT					
☐ 2105	20¢ Blue	24.00	2.50	.60	.13
1984. NATION OF READERS					
☐ 2106	20¢ Brown & Maroon	24.00	2.50	.60	.13
1984. MADONNA AND CHILD					
☐ 2107	20¢ Multicolored	24.00	2.50	.60	.13

*No hinge pricing from 1941 to date is figured at (N-H ADD 15%)

Scott No.		Mint Sheet	Plate Block	Fine Unused Each	Fine Used Each
1984. SANTA CLAUS					
☐2108	20¢ Multicolored	23.00	2.50	.55	.13
1984. VIETNAM MEMORIAL					
☐2109	20¢ Multicolored	22.00	2.50	.55	.13
1985. JEROME KERN					
☐2110	22¢ Multicolored	26.00	2.50	.55	.13
1985. "D" NON-DENOMINATIONAL					
☐2111	22¢ Green	48.00	2.50	.55	.13
1985. "D" NON-DENOMINATIONAL COIL					
☐2112	22¢ Green	—	5.00	.55	.13
1985. "D" NON-DENOMINATIONAL BOOKLET					
☐2113	22¢ Green	—	—	.55	.13
1985. FLAG OVER DOME					
☐2114	22¢ Multicolored	38.00	2.30	.55	.13
1985. FLAG OVER DOME COIL					
☐2115	22¢ Multicolored	—	—	.50	.13
1985. FLAG OVER DOME BOOKLET					
☐2116	22¢ Multicolored	—	—	.50	.13
1985. SEASHELLS: DOGWINKLE					
☐2117	22¢ Brown	—	—	.50	.13
1985. SEASHELLS: HELMET					
☐2118	22¢ Brown	—	—	.50	.13
1985. SEASHELLS: NEPTUNE					
☐2119	22¢ Brown	—	—	.50	.13
1985. SEASHELLS: SCALLOP					
☐2120	22¢ Pink	—	—	.50	.13
1985. SEASHELLS: WHELK					
☐2121	22¢ Brown	—	—	.50	.13
1985. EXPRESS MAIL U.S.A.					
☐2122	$10.75 Multicolored	—	—	23.00	10.00
1985. SCHOOL BUS					
☐2123	3.4¢ Green	—	—	.21	.12
1985. BUCKBOARD					
☐2125	4.9¢ Dark Brown	—	—	.21	.12
1986. STAR ROUTE TRUCK					
☐2126	5.5¢ Carmine	—	—	.21	.12
1985. TRICYCLE 1880s					
☐2127	6¢ Red	—	—	.21	.12

*No hinge pricing from 1941 to date is figured at (N-H ADD 15%)

Scott No.	Mint Sheet	Plate Block	Fine Unused Each	Fine Used Each
1985. AMBULANCE				
☐ 2128 8.3¢ Green	—	—	.21	.12
1985. OIL WAGON 1890s				
☐ 2129 10.1¢ Black	—	—	.21	.12
1985. STUTZ AUTO				
☐ 2130 11¢ Green	—	—	.21	.12
1985. STANLEY STEAMER 1909				
☐ 2131 12¢ Blue	—	—	.21	.12
1985. PUSHCART 1880s				
☐ 2132 12.5¢ Black	—	—	.21	.12
1985. ICEBOAT 1880s				
☐ 2134 14¢ Blue	—	—	.21	.12
1986. DOG SLED 1920s				
☐ 2135 17¢ Blue	—	—	.30	.12
1986. BREAD WAGON 1880s				
☐ 2136 25¢ Brown	—	—	.30	.12
1985. MARY McLEOD BETHUNE				
☐ 2137 22¢ Multicolored	26.00	2.50	.55	.13
1985. DUCKS: BROADBILL				
☐ 2138 22¢ Multicolored	32.00	2.50	.55	.13
1985. DUCKS: MALLARD				
☐ 2139 22¢ Multicolored	26.00	2.50	.55	.13
1985. DUCKS: CANVASBACK				
☐ 2140 22¢ Multicolored	26.00	2.50	.55	.13
1985. DUCKS: REDHEAD				
☐ 2141 22¢ Multicolored	26.00	2.50	.55	.13
1985. WINTER SPECIAL OLYMPICS				
☐ 2142 22¢ Multicolored	20.00	2.40	.55	.13
1985. LOVE				
☐ 2143 22¢ Multicolored	27.00	2.40	.55	.13
1985. RURAL ELECTRIFICATION ADMINISTRATION				
☐ 2144 22¢ Multicolored	25.00	2.40	.55	.13
1985. AMERIPEX SHOW				
☐ 2145 22¢ Multicolored	24.00	2.40	.55	.13
1985. ABIGAIL ADAMS				
☐ 2146 22¢ Multicolored	24.00	2.40	.55	.12
1985. BARTHOLDI, STATUE OF LIBERTY				
☐ 2147 22¢ Multicolored	24.00	2.40	.55	.12

*No hinge pricing from 1941 to date is figured at (N-H ADD 15%)

Scott No.	Mint Sheet	Plate Block	Fine Unused Each	Fine Used Each
1985. GEORGE WASHINGTON				
☐2149 18¢ Multicolored	—	—	.40	.12
1985. ENVELOPES				
☐2150 21.1¢ Multicolored	—	—	.50	.12
1985. KOREAN VETERANS				
☐2152 22¢ Red & Green	26.00	2.40	.55	.13
1985. SOCIAL SECURITY				
☐2153 22¢ Blue	24.00	2.40	.55	.13
1985. WORLD WAR I VETERANS				
☐2154 22¢ Red & Green	26.00	2.40	.55	.13
1985. HORSES: QUARTER HORSE				
☐2155 22¢ Multicolored	36.00	2.40	.55	.13
1985. HORSES: MORGAN				
☐2156 22¢ Multicolored	26.00	2.40	.55	.13
1985. HORSES: SADDLEBRED				
☐2157 22¢ Multicolored	26.00	2.40	.55	.13
1985. HORSES: APPALOOSA				
☐2158 22¢ Multicolored	21.00	2.40	.55	.13
1985. PUBLIC EDUCATION				
☐2159 22¢ Multicolored	21.00	2.40	.55	.13
1985. YOUTH YEAR: Y.M.C.A.				
☐2160 22¢ Multicolored	24.00	2.40	.55	.13
1985. YOUTH YEAR: BOY SCOUTS				
☐2161 22¢ Multicolored	24.00	2.40	.55	.13
1985. YOUTH YEAR: BIG BROTHERS				
☐2162 22¢ Multicolored	24.00	2.40	.55	.13
1985. YOUTH YEAR CAMPFIRE				
☐2163 22¢ Multicolored	—	2.40	.55	.13
1985. HELP END HUNGER				
☐2164 22¢ Multicolored	26.00	2.40	.55	.13
1985. MADONNA				
☐2165 22¢ Multicolored	26.00	2.40	.55	.13
1985. POINSETTIA				
☐2166 22¢ Multicolored	26.00	2.40	.50	.13
1986. ARKANSAS				
☐2167 22¢ Multicolored	26.00	2.40	.50	.13
1986. MARGARET MITCHELL				
☐2168 1¢ Brown	—	—	.21	.11

*No hinge pricing from 1941 to date is figured at (N-H ADD 15%)

Scott No.	Mint Sheet	Plate Block	Fine Unused Each	Fine Used Each
1987. MARY LYON				
☐2169　2¢ Blue	—		.21	.10
1986. PAUL DUDLEY WHITE M.D.				
☐2170　3¢ Blue	—	—	.21	.10
1986. FATHER FLANAGAN				
☐2171　4¢ Blue	—	—	.21	.10
1986. HUGO L. BLACK				
☐2172　5¢ Olive Green	10.00	.70	.21	.10
1987. JULIA WARD HOWE				
☐2177　14¢ Red	26.00	1.50	.24	.10
1986. BELVA ANN LOCKWOOD				
☐2179　17¢ Blue Green	31.00	1.70	.35	.10
1986. JACK LONDON				
☐2183　25¢ Blue	40.00	2.10	.60	.13
1986. JOHN HARVARD				
☐2191　56¢ Brown	—	—	1.00	.13
1986. BERNARD REVEL				
☐2194　$1.00 Green	—	—	2.60	.13
1986. WILLIAM JENNINGS BRYAN				
☐2195　$2.00 Violet	—	—	3.00	.50
1987. BRET HARTE				
☐2196　$5.00 Brown	—	—	7.00	.95
1986. STAMP COLLECTING: AMERICAN PHILATELIC ASSOC.				
☐2198　22¢ Multicolored	—	—	.55	.13
1986. STAMP COLLECTING: LITTLE BOY				
☐2199　22¢ Multicolored	—	—	.55	.13
1986. STAMP COLLECTING: MAGNIFIER				
☐2200　22¢ Multicolored	—	—	.55	.13
1986. STAMP COLLECTING: RUBBER STAMP				
☐2201　22¢ Multicolored	—	—	.55	.13
1986. LOVE				
☐2202　22¢ Multicolored	23.00	2.50	.50	.12
1986. SOJOURNER TRUTH				
☐2203　22¢ Multicolored	26.00	2.50	.50	.12
1986. TEXAS—SAN JACINTO 1836				
☐2204　22¢ Multicolored	29.00	2.50	.50	.12
1986. FISH: MUSKELLUNGE				
☐2205　22¢ Multicolored	—	—	.50	.12

*No hinge pricing from 1941 to date is figured at (N-H ADD 15%)

Scott No.		Mint Sheet	Plate Block	Fine Unused Each	Fine Used Each
1986. FISH: ATLANTIC COD					
☐ 2206	22¢ Multicolored	—	—	.60	.12
1986. FISH: LARGEMOUTH BASS					
☐ 2207	22¢ Multicolored	—	—	.60	.12
1986. FISH: BLUEFIN TUNA					
☐ 2208	22¢ Multicolored	—	—	.60	.12
1986. FISH: CATFISH					
☐ 2209	22¢ Multicolored	—	—	.60	.12
1986. PUBLIC HOSPITALS					
☐ 2210	22¢ Multicolored	22.00	3.00	.55	.12
1986. DUKE ELLINGTON					
☐ 2211	22¢ Multicolored	22.00	3.00	.55	.12
1986. AMERIPEX '86-PRESIDENTS I					
☐ 2216	22¢ Brown & Black	—	—	.55	.12
1986. AMERIPEX '86-PRESIDENTS II					
☐ 2217	22¢ Brown & Black	—	—	.55	.12
1986. AMERIPEX '86-PRESIDENTS III					
☐ 2218	22¢ Brown & Black	—	—	.55	.12
1986. AMERIPEX '86-PRESIDENTS IV					
☐ 2219	22¢ Brown & Black	—	—	.55	.12
1986. POLAR EXPLORERS: KANE					
☐ 2220	22¢ Multicolored	—	—	.55	.12
1986. POLAR EXPLORERS: GREELY					
☐ 2221	22¢ Multicolored	—	—	.55	.12
1986. POLAR EXPLORERS: STEFANSSON					
☐ 2222	22¢ Multicolored	—	—	.55	.12
1986. POLAR EXPLORERS: HENSON					
☐ 2223	22¢ Multicolored	—	—	.55	.12
1986. LIBERTY					
☐ 2224	22¢ Carmine & Blue	24.00	2.50	.55	.12
1986. NAVAJO ART					
☐ 2235	22¢ Multicolored	24.00	2.50	.55	.12
1986. NAVAJO ART					
☐ 2236	22¢ Multicolored	—	—	.55	.12
1986. NAVAJO ART					
☐ 2237	22¢ Multicolored	—	—	.55	.12
1986. NAVAJO ART					
☐ 2238	22¢ Multicolored	—	—	.55	.12

*No hinge pricing from 1941 to date is figured at (N-H ADD 15%)

Scott No.	Mint Sheet	Plate Block	Fine Unused Each	Fine Used Each
1986. T.S. ELIOT				
☐ 2239 22¢ Brown	—	—	.55	.12
1986. FOLK ART: HIGHLANDER				
☐ 2240 22¢ Multicolored	23.00	2.50	.55	.12
1986. FOLK ART: SHIP				
☐ 2241 22¢ Multicolored	—	—	.55	.12
1986. FOLK ART: NAUTICAL				
☐ 2242 22¢ Multicolored	—	—	.55	.12
1986. FOLK ART: CIGAR STORE				
☐ 2243 22¢ Multicolored	—	—	.55	.12
1986. CHRISTMAS: PEROGINO GALLERY				
☐ 2244 22¢ Multicolored	40.00	2.50	.55	.12
1986. CHRISTMAS: GREETINGS				
☐ 2245 22¢ Multicolored	40.00	2.50	.55	.12
1987. MICHIGAN STATEHOOD				
☐ 2246 22¢ Multicolored	25.00	2.50	.55	.12
1987. PAN AMERICAN GAMES				
☐ 2247 22¢ Multicolored	26.00	2.50	.55	.12
1987. LOVE				
☐ 2248 22¢ Multicolored	—	—	.55	.12
1987. JEAN BAPTISTE POINTE DU SABLE				
☐ 2249 22¢ Multicolored	23.00	2.50	.55	.12
1987. ENRICO CARUSO				
☐ 2250 22¢ Multicolored	27.00	2.50	.55	.12
1987. GIRL SCOUTS				
☐ 2251 22¢ Multicolored	24.00	2.50	.55	.12
1987. UNITED WAY UNITING COMMUNITIES				
☐ 2275 22¢ Multicolored	22.00	2.50	.55	.11
1987. AMERICAN FLAG				
☐ 2276 22¢ Multicolored	—	—	.50	.11
1987. AMERICAN WILDLIFE				
☐ 2286– 2335 22¢ Multicolored	23.00	—	.50ea.	.11ea.
1987. DELAWARE				
☐ 2336 22¢ Multicolored	23.00	2.50	.55	.11
1987. PENNSYLVANIA				
☐ 2337 22¢ Multicolored	23.00	2.50	.55	.11
1987. NEW JERSEY				
☐ 2338 22¢ Multicolored	23.00	2.50	.55	.11

*No hinge pricing from 1941 to date is figured at (N-H ADD 15%)

Scott No.		Mint Sheet	Plate Block	Fine Unused Each	Fine Used Each
1987. FRIENDSHIP WITH MOROCCO					
☐2349	22¢ Multicolored	24.00	2.50	.55	.12
1987. WILLIAM FAULKNER					
☐2350	22¢ Green	24.00	2.50	.55	.12
1987. LACEMAKING					
☐2351–					
2354	22¢ Blue	24.00	2.50	.55ea.	.13ea.
1987. CONSTITUTION (BICENTENNIAL)					
☐2355	22¢ Multicolored	—	—	.50	.12
1987. CONSTITUTION (WE THE PEOPLE)					
☐2356	22¢ Multicolored	—	—	.50	.12
1987. CONSTITUTION (ESTABLISH JUSTICE)					
☐2357	22¢ Multicolored	—	—	.50	.12
1987. CONSTITUTION (AND SECURE)					
☐2358	22¢ Multicolored	—	—	.50	.12
1987. CONSTITUTION (DO ORDAIN)					
☐2359	22¢ Multicolored	26.00	2.50	.50	.12
1987. U.S. CONSTITUTION					
☐2360	22¢ Multicolored	26.00	2.50	.50ea.	.12ea.
1987. C.P.A. CERTIFIED PUBLIC ACCOUNTANTS					
☐2361	22¢ Multicolored	26.00	2.50	.50	.12
1987. CHRISTMAS: MARONI, NATIONAL GALLERY					
☐2367	22¢ Multicolored	—	2.25	.50	.12
1987. GREETINGS					
☐2368	22¢ Multicolored	—	2.25	.50	.12
1988. OLYMPICS (WINTER)					
☐2369	22¢ Multicolored	23.00	2.25	.50	.10
1988. AUSTRALIA BICENTENNIAL					
☐2370	22¢ Multicolored	21.00	2.25	.50	.10
1988. J.W. JOHNSON					
☐2371	22¢ Multicolored	23.00	2.25	.50	.10
1988. CATS (SHORT HAIR)					
☐2372	22¢ Multicolored	23.00	2.25	.50	.10
1988. CATS (HIMALAYAN)					
☐2373	22¢ Multicolored	—	—	.50	.10
1988. CATS (BURMESE)					
☐2374	22¢ Multicolored	—	—	.50	.10
1988. CATS (PERSIAN)					
☐2375	22¢ Multicolored	—	—	.50	.10

*No hinge pricing from 1941 to date is figured at (N-H ADD 15%)

Scott No.		Mint Sheet	Plate Block	Fine Unused Each	Fine Used Each
1988. KNUTE ROCKNE					
☐ 2376	22¢ Multicolored	24.00	2.50	.50	.10
1988. FRANCIS OUIMET					
☐ 2377	25¢ Multicolored	24.00	2.50	.50	.10
1988. LOVE					
☐ 2378	25¢ Multicolored	—	2.50	.50	.10
1988. LOVE					
☐ 2379	45¢ Multicolored	36.00	2.50	.50	.10
1988. OLYMPICS (SUMMER)					
☐ 2380	25¢ Multicolored	26.00	2.50	.50	.10
1988. CARS (LOCOMOBILE)					
☐ 2381	25¢ Multicolored	—	—	.50	.10
1988. CARS (PIERCE-ARROW)					
☐ 2382	25¢ Multicolored	—	—	.50	.10
1988. CARS (CORD)					
☐ 2383	25¢ Multicolored	—	—	.50	.10
1988. CARS (PACKARD)					
☐ 2384	25¢ Multicolored	—	—	.50	.10
1988. CARS (DUESENBERG)					
☐ 2385	25¢ Multicolored	—	—	.50	.10
1988. ANTARCTIC: NATHANIEL PALMER					
☐ 2386	25¢ Multicolored	—	—	.60	.14
1988. ANTARCTIC: LT. CHARLES WILKES					
☐ 2387	25¢ Multicolored	—	—	.60	.14
1988. ANTARCTIC: RICHARD E. BYRD					
☐ 2388	25¢ Multicolored	—	—	.60	.14
1988. ANTARCTIC: LINCOLN ELLSWORTH					
☐ 2389	25¢ Multicolored	—	—	.60	.14
1988. CAROUSEL: DEER					
☐ 2390	25¢ Multicolored	—	—	.60	.14
1988. CAROUSEL: HORSE					
☐ 2391	25¢ Multicolored	—	—	.60	.14
1988. CAROUSEL: CAMEL					
☐ 2392	25¢ Multicolored	—	—	.60	.14
1988. CAROUSEL: GOAT					
☐ 2393	25¢ Multicolored	—	—	.60	.14
1988. EXPRESS MAIL					
☐ 2394	$8.75 Multicolored	—	70.00	16.50	8.00

*No hinge pricing from 1941 to date is figured at (N-H ADD 15%)

Scott No.		Mint Sheet	Plate Block	Fine Unused Each	Fine Used Each
1988. OCCASIONS: HAPPY BIRTHDAY					
☐ 2395	25¢ Multicolored	—	—	.60	.14
1988. OCCASIONS: BEST WISHES					
☐ 2396	25¢ Multicolored	—	—	.60	.14
1988. OCCASIONS: THINKING OF YOU					
☐ 2397	25¢ Multicolored	—	—	.60	.14
1988. OCCASIONS: LOVE YOU					
☐ 2398	25¢ Multicolored	—	—	.60	.14
1988. CHRISTMAS (BOTTICELLI)					
☐ 2399	25¢ Multicolored	—	2.00	.60	.12
1988. GREETINGS (CHRISTMAS)					
☐ 2400	25¢ Multicolored	—	2.00	.60	.12
1988. MONTANA					
☐ 2401	25¢ Multicolored	22.00	2.00	.60	.12
1988. A. PHILIP RANDOLPH					
☐ 2402	25¢ Multicolored	22.00	2.00	.60	.12
1988. NORTH DAKOTA					
☐ 2403	25¢ Multicolored	22.00	2.00	.60	.12
1988. WASHINGTON					
☐ 2404	25¢ Multicolored	22.00	2.00	.60	.12
1988. STEAMBOATS: EXPERIMENT					
☐ 2405	25¢ Multicolored	—	—	.60	.13
1988. STEAMBOATS: PHOENIX					
☐ 2406	25¢ Multicolored	—	—	.60	.13
1988. STEAMBOATS: NEW ORLEANS					
☐ 2407	25¢ Multicolored	—	—	.60	.13
1988. STEAMBOATS: WASHINGTON					
☐ 2408	25¢ Multicolored	—	—	.60	.13
1988. STEAMBOATS: WALK IN THE WATER					
☐ 2409	25¢ Multicolored	—	—	.60	.13
1988. WORLD STAMP EXPO '89					
☐ 2410	25¢ Black & Carmine	22.00	2.50	.60	.13
1988. ARTURO TOSCANINI					
☐ 2411	25¢ Multicolored	22.00	2.50	.60	.13
1988. BICENTENNIAL: HOUSE OF REPRESENTATIVES					
☐ 2412	25¢ Multicolored	22.00	2.50	.60	.13
1988. BICENTENNIAL: UNITED STATES SENATE					
☐ 2413	25¢ Multicolored	22.00	2.50	.60	.13

*No hinge pricing from 1941 to date is figured at (N-H ADD 15%)

Scott No.	Mint Sheet	Plate Block	Fine Unused Each	Fine Used Each
1988. BICENTENNIAL: EXECUTIVE BRANCH				
☐ 2414 25¢ Multicolored	22.00	2.75	.60	.13
1988. SOUTH DAKOTA 1889: STATEHOOD				
☐ 2416 25¢ Multicolored	22.00	2.75	.60	.13
1988. LOU GEHRIG				
☐ 2417 25¢ Multicolored	22.00	2.75	.60	.13
1989. ERNEST HEMINGWAY				
☐ 2418 25¢ Multicolored	22.00	2.75	.60	.13
1989. MOON LANDING				
☐ 2419 $2.40 Multicolored	—	22.00	5.00	3.00
1989. LETTER CARRIERS				
☐ 2420 25¢ Multicolored	20.00	2.75	.60	.13
1989. BILL OF RIGHTS				
☐ 2421 25¢ Multicolored	22.00	2.75	.60	.13
1989. DINOSAURS: TYRANNOSAURUS				
☐ 2422 25¢ Multicolored	24.00	2.75	.60	.13
1989. DINOSAURS: PTERANODON				
☐ 2423 25¢ Multicolored	24.00	2.75	.60	.13
1989. DINOSAURS: STEGOSAURUS				
☐ 2424 25¢ Multicolored	24.00	2.75	.60	.13
1989. DINOSAURS: BRONTOSAURUS				
☐ 2425 25¢ Multicolored	24.00	2.75	.60	.13
1989. COLUMBIAN ARTIFACTS				
☐ 2426 25¢ Multicolored	24.00	2.75	.60	.13
1989. CHRISTMAS: MADONNA				
☐ 2427 25¢ Multicolored	24.00	2.75	.60	.13
1989. CHRISTMAS: SLEIGH				
☐ 2428 25¢ Multicolored	24.00	2.75	.60	.13
1989. MAIL DELIVERY: STAGECOACH				
☐ 2434 25¢ Multicolored	24.00	2.75	.60	.13
1989. MAIL DELIVERY: PADDLEWHEEL				
☐ 2435 25¢ Multicolored	24.00	2.75	.60	.13
1989. MAIL DELIVERY: BIPLANE				
☐ 2436 25¢ Multicolored	24.00	2.75	.60	.13
1989. MAIL DELIVERY: AUTOMOBILE				
☐ 2437 25¢ Multicolored	24.00	2.75	.60	.13
1990. IDAHO CENTENARY: BLUEBIRD				
☐ 2439 25¢ Multicolored	24.00	2.75	.60	.13

*No hinge pricing from 1941 to date is figured at (N-H ADD 15%)

Scott No.	Mint Sheet	Plate Block	Fine Unused Each	Fine Used Each
1990. LOVE				
☐ 2440 25¢ Multicolored	24.00	2.75	.60	.13
1990. BLACK HERITAGE. IDA B. WELLS				
☐ 2442 25¢ Multicolored	24.00	2.75	.60	.13
1990. BEACH UMBRELLA				
☐ 2443 25¢ Multicolored	—	2.75	.40	.11
1990. WYOMING CENTENARY—MOUNTAIN				
☐ 2444 25¢ Multicolored	24.00	2.75	.60	.13
1990. CLASSIC FILMS: WIZARD OF OZ				
☐ 2445 25¢ Multicolored	24.00	2.75	.60	.13
1990. CLASSIC FILMS: GONE WITH THE WIND				
☐ 2446 25¢ Multicolored	21.00	2.75	.60	.13
1990. CLASSIC FILMS: BEAU GESTE				
☐ 2447 25¢ Multicolored	21.00	2.75	.60	.13
1990. CLASSIC FILMS: STAGECOACH				
☐ 2448 25¢ Multicolored	21.00	2.75	.60	.13
1990. LITERARY ARTS: MARIANNE MOORE				
☐ 2449 25¢ Multicolored	24.00	2.75	.60	.13
1990. TRANSPORTATION: CIRCUS WAGON				
☐ 2452 5¢ Multicolored	5.00	1.00	.21	.12
1990. LIGHTHOUSES: ADMIRALTY HEAD				
☐ 2470 25¢ Multicolored	—	—	.60	.13
1990. LIGHTHOUSES: CAPE HATTERAS				
☐ 2471 25¢ Multicolored	—	—	.60	.13
1990. LIGHTHOUSES: WEST QUODDY HEAD				
☐ 2472 25¢ Multicolored	—	—	.60	.13
1990. LIGHTHOUSES: AMERICAN SHOALS				
☐ 2473 25¢ Multicolored	—	—	.60	.13
1990. LIGHTHOUSES: SANDY HOOK				
☐ 2474 25¢ Multicolored	—	—	.60	.13
1990. OLYMPIANS: JESSE OWENS				
☐ 2496 25¢ Multicolored	—	4.75	.60	.13
1990. OLYMPIANS: RAY EWRY				
☐ 2497 25¢ Multicolored	—	4.75	.60	.13
1990. OLYMPIANS: HAZEL WIGHTMAN				
☐ 2498 25¢ Multicolored	—	4.75	.60	.13
1990. OLYMPIANS: EDDIE EAGAN				
☐ 2499 25¢ Multicolored	—	4.75	.60	.13

*No hinge pricing from 1941 to date is figured at (N-H ADD 15%)

Scott No.		Mint Sheet	Plate Block	Fine Unused Each	Fine Used Each
1990. OLYMPIANS: HELENE MADISON					
☐ 2500	25¢ Multicolored	—	4.75	.55	.12
1990. INDIAN: ASSINIBOINE					
☐ 2501	25¢ Multicolored	—	—	.55	.12
1990. INDIAN: CHEYENNE					
☐ 2502	25¢ Multicolored	—	—	.55	.12
1990. INDIAN: COMANCHE					
☐ 2503	25¢ Multicolored	—	—	.55	.12
1990. INDIAN: FLATHEAD					
☐ 2504	25¢ Multicolored	—	—	.55	.12
1990. INDIAN: SHOSHONE					
☐ 2505	25¢ Multicolored	—	—	.55	.12
1990. MICRONESIA					
☐ 2506	25¢ Multicolored	—	—	.55	.12
1990. MARSHALL ISLANDS					
☐ 2507	25¢ Multicolored	—	—	.55	.12
1990. SEA CREATURES: KILLER WHALE					
☐ 2508	25¢ Multicolored	—	2.75	.55	.12
1990. SEA CREATURES: NORTHERN SEA LION					
☐ 2509	25¢ Multicolored	—	2.75	.55	.12
1990. SEA CREATURES: SEA OTTER					
☐ 2510	25¢ Multicolored	—	2.75	.55	.12
1990. SEA CREATURES: DOLPHIN					
☐ 2511	25¢ Multicolored	—	2.75	.55	.12
1990. GRAND CANYON					
☐ 2512	25¢ Multicolored	—	—	.55	.12
1990. DWIGHT D. EISENHOWER					
☐ 2513	25¢ Multicolored	—	—	.55	.12
1990. CHRISTMAS: MADONNA					
☐ 2514	25¢ Multicolored	—	—	.55	.12
1990. CHRISTMAS: CHRISTMAS TREE					
☐ 2515	25¢ Multicolored	—	—	.55	.12
1991. "F" FLOWER: TULIP					
☐ 2517	29¢ Multicolored	40.00	3.00	.65	.13
1991. "F" STAMP RATE: EXTRA POSTAGE					
☐ 2521	4¢ Multicolored	7.00	.80	.21	.13
1991. FLAG: MT. RUSHMORE					
☐ 2523	29¢ Multicolored	6.00	4.50	.65	.13
1991. FLOWER: TULIP					
☐ 2524	29¢ Multicolored	40.00	3.00	.65	.13

*No hinge pricing from 1941 to date is figured at (N-H ADD 15%)

Scott No.		Mint Sheet	Plate Block	Fine Unused Each	Fine Used Each
1991. FLAG: OLYMPIC RINGS					
☐ 2528	Multicolored	—	—	.65	.13
1991. BALLOONING					
☐ 2530	Multicolored		—	.50	.13
1991. FLAGS: ON PARADE					
☐ 2531	Multicolored	42.00	3.00	.65	.16
1991. SWITZERLAND: 700TH ANNIVERSARY					
☐ 2532	50¢ Multicolored	36.00	5.00	1.00	.25
1991. VERMONT: BICENTENNIAL					
☐ 2533	29¢ Multicolored	26.00	3.00	.65	.13
1991. SAVINGS BONDS: 50TH ANNIVERSARY					
☐ 2534	29¢ Multicolored	26.00	3.00	.65	.13
1991. LOVE: HEART					
☐ 2535	29¢ Multicolored	26.00	3.00	.65	.13
1991. LOVE: LOVE BIRDS					
☐ 2537	52¢ Multicolored	60.00	5.00	1.10	.13
1991. LITERARY ARTS: WILLIAM SAROYAN					
☐ 2538	29¢ Multicolored	26.00	3.00	.65	.13
1991. USPS: OLYMPIC RINGS					
☐ 2539	$1.00 Multicolored	—	10.00	2.10	.50
1991. EAGLE: OLYMPIC RINGS					
☐ 2540	$2.90 Multicolored	—	28.00	6.00	3.00
1991. DOMESTIC: EXPRESS MAIL					
☐ 2541	9.95 Multicolored	—	80.00	20.00	5.00
1991. INTERNATIONAL: EXPRESS MAIL					
☐ 2542	$14.00 Multicolored	—	90.00	22.00	7.00
1991. FISHING FLIES					
☐ 2545	29¢ Multicolored	—	—	.65	.14
☐ 2546	29¢ Multicolored	—	—	.65	.14
☐ 2547	29¢ Multicolored	—	—	.65	.14
☐ 2548	29¢ Multicolored	—	—	.65	.14
☐ 2549	29¢ Multicolored	—	—	.65	.14
1991. PERFORMING ARTS: COLE PORTER					
☐ 2550	29¢ Multicolored	26.00	3.00	.65	.14
1991. DESERT STORM: SOUTHWEST ASIA					
☐ 2551	29¢ Multicolored	26.00	3.00	.65	.14
1991. 1992 SUMMER OLYMPICS: BARCELONA					
☐ 2553	29¢ Multicolored	—	6.00	.65	.14
☐ 2554	29¢ Multicolored	—	6.00	.65	.14
☐ 2555	29¢ Multicolored	—	6.00	.65	.14
☐ 2556	29¢ Multicolored	—	6.00	.65	.14
☐ 2557	29¢ Multicolored	—	6.00	.65	.14

*No hinge pricing from 1941 to date is figured at (N-H ADD 15%)

Scott No.		Mint Sheet	Plate Block	Fine Unused Each	Fine Used Each
1991. NUMISMATICS: COINS AND NOTES					
☐2558	29¢ Multicolored	—	3.00	.65	.14
1991. BASKETBALL: 100TH ANNIVERSARY					
☐2560	29¢ Multicolored	26.00	3.00	.65	.14
1991. DISTRICT OF COLUMBIA: BICENTENNIAL					
☐2561	29¢ Multicolored	26.00	3.00	.65	.14
1991. COMEDIANS					
☐2562	29¢ Multicolored	—	—	3.00	.15
☐2563	29¢ Multicolored	—	—	3.00	.15
☐2564	29¢ Multicolored	—	—	3.00	.15
☐2565	29¢ Multicolored	—	—	3.00	.15
☐2566	29¢ Multicolored	—	—	3.00	.15
1991. BLACK HERITAGE					
☐2567	29¢ Multicolored	26.00	3.00	.65	.14
1991. SPACE EXPLORATION					
☐2568	29¢ Multicolored	—	—	.65	.14
☐2569	29¢ Multicolored	—	—	.65	.14
☐2570	29¢ Multicolored	—	—	.65	.14
☐2571	29¢ Multicolored	—	—	.65	.14
☐2572	29¢ Multicolored	—	—	.65	.14
☐2573	29¢ Multicolored	—	—	.65	.14
☐2574	29¢ Multicolored	—	—	.65	.14
☐2575	29¢ Multicolored	—	—	.65	.14
☐2576	29¢ Multicolored	—	—	.65	.14
☐2577	29¢ Multicolored	—	—	.65	.14
1991. CHRISTMAS					
☐2578	29¢ Multicolored	—	3.00	.65	.14
☐2579	29¢ Multicolored	—	—	.65	.14
☐2582	29¢ Multicolored	—	—	.65	.14
☐2583	29¢ Multicolored	—	—	.65	.14
☐2584	29¢ Multicolored	—	—	.65	.14
☐2585	29¢ Multicolored	—	—	.65	.14

Scott No.		Fine Unused Plate Blk	Ave. Unused Plate Blk	Fine Unused Each	Ave. Unused Each	Fine Used Each	Ave. Used Each
AIRMAIL STAMPS							
1918. FIRST ISSUE—(N-H ADD 45%)							
☐C1	6¢ Orange	900.00	600.00	100.00	60.00	50.00	22.00
☐C2	16¢ Green	1800.00	1100.00	120.00	100.00	60.00	35.00
☐C3	24¢ Carmine & Blue ...	1600.00	1200.00	120.00	100.00	60.00	38.00

*No hinge pricing from 1941 to date is figured at (N-H ADD 15%)

Scott No.	Fine Unused Plate Blk	Ave. Unused Plate Blk	Fine Unused Each	Ave. Unused Each	Fine Used Each	Ave. Used Each

1923. SECOND ISSUE—(N-H ADD 35%)

☐ C4 8¢ Dark Green	500.00	400.00	40.00	32.00	24.00	15.00
☐ C5 16¢ Dark Blue	2800.00	1800.00	125.00	80.00	42.00	36.00
☐ C6 24¢ Carmine	3600.00	2800.00	160.00	110.00	38.00	28.00

1926–1927. LONG MAP (N-H ADD 35%)

☐ C7 10¢ Dark Blue	45.00	38.00	3.50	3.00	.50	.38
☐ C8 15¢ Olive Brown	65.00	40.00	4.50	3.75	3.00	2.40
☐ C9 20¢ Yellow Green	165.00	98.00	12.00	9.00	2.40	1.90

1927. LINDBERGH TRIBUTE ISSUE (N-H ADD 25%)

☐ C10 10¢ Dark Blue	210.00	120.00	12.00	8.00	3.00	1.40

1928. BEACON (N-H ADD 20%)

☐ C11 5¢ Carmine & Blue	65.00	50.00	5.00	3.50	1.00	.40

1930. WINGED GLOBE—FLAT PRESS (N-H ADD 35%)

☐ C12 5¢ Violet	225.00	175.00	12.00	9.00	.50	.30

1930. GRAF ZEPPELIN ISSUE (N-H ADD 20%)

☐ C13 65¢ Green	2900.00	2800.00	380.00	260.00	340.00	200.00
☐ C14 $1.30 Brown	7600.00	5800.00	800.00	600.00	550.00	450.00
☐ C15 $2.60 Blue	9800.00	7800.00	1400.00	800.00	800.00	650.00

1931–1932.
WINGED GLOBE—ROTARY PRESS (N-H ADD 25%)

☐ C16 5¢ Violet	125.00	80.00	6.50	4.00	.50	.30
☐ C17 8¢ Olive Bistre	35.00	28.00	3.00	2.00	.35	.21

1933. CENTURY OF PROGRESS ISSUE (N-H ADD 25%)

☐ C18 50¢ Green	900.00	700.00	100.00	90.00	80.00	60.00

1934. DESIGN OF 1930 (N-H ADD 25%)

☐ C19 6¢ Orange	34.00	24.00	3.50	2.50	.20	.15

1935–1937. TRANSPACIFIC ISSUE (N-H ADD 10%)

☐ C20 25¢ Blue	30.00	20.00	1.50	1.10	1.00	.60
☐ C21 20¢ Green	120.00	100.00	10.00	8.00	1.90	1.10
☐ C22 50¢ Carmine	130.00	110.00	10.00	8.00	5.50	3.50

1938. EAGLE (N-H ADD 20%)

☐ C23 6¢ Blue & Carmine	10.00	7.00	.50	.35	.15	.12

1939. TRANSATLANTIC (N-H ADD 20%)

☐ C24 30¢ Dull Blue	210.00	165.00	8.00	6.00	1.80	.90

1941–1944. TRANSPORT PLANE (N-H ADD 20%)

☐ C25 6¢ Carmine	1.30	1.10	.22	.20	.13	.11
☐ C26 8¢ Olive Green	2.00	1.65	.20	.21	.13	.12
☐ C27 10¢ Violet	10.00	8.00	1.40	1.00	.15	.12
☐ C28 15¢ Brown Carmine	18.00	9.00	3.50	2.80	.40	.26
☐ C29 20¢ Bright Green	22.00	16.00	2.75	2.00	.36	.30
☐ C30 30¢ Violet	18.00	15.00	3.00	2.00	.40	.28
☐ C31 50¢ Orange	140.00	90.00	12.00	9.00	4.00	3.00

*No hinge pricing from 1941 to date is figured at (N-H ADD 15%)

Scott No.		Mint Sheet	Plate Block	Fine Unused Each	Fine Used Each

1946–1947. DC-4 SKYMASTER

		Mint Sheet	Plate Block	Fine Unused Each	Fine Used Each
☐ C32	5¢ Carmine	7.50	.70	.21	.14
☐ C33	5¢ Carmine	13.00	.70	.21	.14

1947. REGULAR ISSUE

		Mint Sheet	Plate Block	Fine Unused Each	Fine Used Each
☐ C34	10¢ Black	22.00	1.75	.30	.14
☐ C35	15¢ Bright Blue Green	28.00	1.85	.40	.14
☐ C36	25¢ Blue	90.00	5.00	1.10	.14

Scott No.		Fine Unused Line Pair	Ave. Unused Line Pair	Fine Unused Each	Ave. Unused Each	Fine Used Each	Ave. Used Each

1948. DESIGN OF 1947

		Fine Unused Line Pair	Ave. Unused Line Pair	Fine Unused Each	Ave. Unused Each	Fine Used Each	Ave. Used Each
☐ C37	5¢ Carmine	9.00	7.50	1.00	.70	.80	.50

Scott No.		Mint Sheet	Plate Block	Fine Unused Each	Fine Used Each

1948. NEW YORK CITY JUBILEE ISSUE

		Mint Sheet	Plate Block	Fine Unused Each	Fine Used Each
☐ C38	5¢ Red	28.00	6.00	.21	.14

1949. DESIGN OF 1947

		Mint Sheet	Plate Block	Fine Unused Each	Fine Used Each
☐ C39	6¢ Carmine	18.00	.80	.22	.13

1949. ALEXANDRIA BICENTENNIAL

		Mint Sheet	Plate Block	Fine Unused Each	Fine Used Each
☐ C40	6¢ Carmine	9.50	.80	.22	.13

Scott No.		Fine Unused Line Pair	Ave. Unused Line Pair	Fine Unused Each	Ave. Unused Each	Fine Used Each	Ave. Used Each

1949. DESIGN OF 1947

		Fine Unused Line Pair	Ave. Unused Line Pair	Fine Unused Each	Ave. Unused Each	Fine Used Each	Ave. Used Each
☐ C41	6¢ Carmine	16.75	12.00	3.50	2.75	.14	.11

Scott No.		Mint Sheet	Plate Block	Fine Unused Each	Fine Used Each

1949. U.P.U.—UNIVERSAL POSTAL UNION ISSUE

		Mint Sheet	Plate Block	Fine Unused Each	Fine Used Each
☐ C42	10¢ Purple	18.50	1.80	.35	.24
☐ C43	15¢ Ultramarine	27.00	1.75	.40	.30
☐ C44	25¢ Carmine	45.00	7.00	.70	.50

1949. WRIGHT BROTHERS ISSUE

		Mint Sheet	Plate Block	Fine Unused Each	Fine Used Each
☐ C45	6¢ Magenta	12.00	.90	.25	.14

1952. HAWAII—DIAMOND HEAD

		Mint Sheet	Plate Block	Fine Unused Each	Fine Used Each
☐ C46	80¢ Bright Red Violet	550.00	65.00	8.50	1.50

1953. 50TH ANNIVERSARY POWERED FLIGHT

		Mint Sheet	Plate Block	Fine Unused Each	Fine Used Each
☐ C47	6¢ Carmine	7.50	.80	.22	.16

1954. EAGLE IN FLIGHT

		Mint Sheet	Plate Block	Fine Unused Each	Fine Used Each
☐ C48	4¢ Bright Blue	12.00	2.40	.21	.15

*No hinge pricing from 1941 to date is figured at (N-H ADD 15%)

Scott No.				Mint Sheet	Plate Block	Fine Unused Each	Fine Used Each

1957. 50TH ANNIVERSARY AIR FORCE

☐ C49	6¢ Blue	9.50	.90	.23	.15

1958. DESIGN OF 1954

☐ C50	5¢ Red	18.00	1.90	.22	.16

1958. JETLINER SILHOUETTE

☐ C51	7¢ Blue	18.50	.70	.22	.13

Scott No.		Fine Unused Line Pair	Ave. Unused Line Pair	Fine Unused Each	Ave. Unused Each	Fine Used Each	Ave. Used Each
☐ C52	7¢ Blue	17.00	14.00	3.00	1.60	.16	.12

Scott No.				Mint Sheet	Plate Block	Fine Unused Each	Fine Used Each

1959. COMMEMORATIVES

1959. ALASKA STATEHOOD

☐ C53	7¢ Dark Blue	6.50	.80	.22	.13

1959. BALLOON JUPITER FLIGHT

☐ C54	7¢ Dark Blue & Red	7.00	.80	.22	.13

1959. HAWAII STATEHOOD

☐ C55	7¢ Rose Red	7.00	.80	.22	.13

1959. PAN AMERICAN GAMES

☐ C56	10¢ Red & Blue	12.00	1.75	.28	.15

1959–1961. REGULAR ISSUE

☐ C57	10¢ Black & Green	85.00	8.50	2.00	1.00
☐ C58	15¢ Black & Orange	22.00	2.50	.55	.15
☐ C59	25¢ Black & Maroon	27.00	2.75	.65	.15

1960. DESIGN OF 1958

☐ C60	7¢ Carmine	16.00	.85	.22	.14

Scott No.		Fine Unused Line Pair	Ave. Unused Line Pair	Fine Unused Each	Ave. Unused Each	Fine Used Each	Ave. Used Each
☐ C61	7¢ Carmine	45.00	40.00	5.00	4.00	.36	.29

Scott No.				Mint Sheet	Plate Block	Fine Unused Each	Fine Used Each

1961. DESIGNS OF 1959–1960

☐ C62	13¢ Black & Red	21.00	2.50	.60	.16
☐ C63	15¢ Black & Orange	17.00	2.00	.46	.16

1962. JETLINER OVER CAPITOL

☐ C64	8¢ Carmine	21.00	1.10	.26	.12

*No hinge pricing from 1941 to date is figured at (N-H ADD 15%)

Scott No.		Fine Unused Line Pair	Ave. Unused Line Pair	Fine Unused Each	Ave. Unused Each	Fine Used Each	Ave. Used Each
☐ C65	8¢ Carmine	6.00	5.00	.45	.32	.16	.12

Scott No.		Mint Sheet	Plate Block	Fine Unused Each	Fine Used Each

1963. FIRST INTERNATIONAL POSTAL CONFERENCE CENTENARY
☐ C66	15¢ Dull Red, Dark Brown & Blue	32.00	4.50	.80	.60

1963. POSTAL CARD RATE
☐ C67	6¢ Red	18.00	3.00	.28	.16

1963. AMELIA EARHART
☐ C68	8¢ Carmine & Maroon	11.00	1.60	.26	.18

1964. DR. ROBERT H. GODDARD
☐ C69	8¢ Blue, Red, Bistre	28.00	3.00	.65	.18

1967–1969.
1967. ALASKA PURCHASE CENTENARY
☐ C70	8¢ Dark Brown	18.00	2.40	.35	.16

1967.
☐ C71	20¢ Blue, Brown, Bistre	65.00	5.00	1.10	.15

1968.
☐ C72	10¢ Carmine	34.00	1.25	.28	.15

Scott No.		Fine Unused Line Pair	Ave. Unused Line Pair	Fine Unused Each	Ave. Unused Each	Fine Used Each	Ave. Used Each
☐ C73	10¢ Carmine	3.00	2.60	.35	.30	.15	.12

Scott No.		Mint Sheet	Plate Block	Fine Unused Each	Fine Used Each

1968. 50TH ANNIVERSARY AIRMAIL SERVICE
☐ C74	10¢ Black, Blue, Red	20.00	4.00	.40	.20

1968.
☐ C75	20¢ Red, Blue, Black	32.00	3.50	.60	.16

1969. FIRST MAN ON THE MOON
☐ C76	10¢ Red, Blue, Brown	12.00	2.20	.35	.17

1971–1973.
☐ C77	9¢ Red	21.00	1.25	.30	.20
☐ C78	11¢ Carmine	25.00	1.50	.30	.12
☐ C79	13¢ Carmine	32.00	1.70	.45	.14
☐ C80	17¢ Green, Blue, Red	28.00	2.50	.55	.15
☐ C81	21¢ Blue, Red, Black	25.00	2.10	.45	.15

*No hinge pricing from 1941 to date is figured at (N-H ADD 15%)

Scott No.		Fine Unused Line Pair	Ave. Unused Line Pair	Fine Unused Each	Ave. Unused Each	Fine Used Each	Ave. Used Each
☐ C82	11¢ Carmine	1.20	1.00	.42	.30	.14	.12
☐ C83	13¢ Carmine	1.25	1.00	.40	.30	.14	.12

Scott No.		Mint Sheet	Plate Block	Fine Unused Each	Fine Used Each
1972. NATIONAL PARKS CENTENNIAL					
☐ C84	11¢ Multicolored	14.00	1.80	.40	.16
1972. OLYMPIC GAMES					
☐ C85	11¢ Multicolored	14.50	3.10	.40	.16
1973. PROGRESS IN ELECTRONICS					
☐ C86	11¢ Multicolored	14.00	2.00	.40	.16
1974.					
☐ C87	18¢ Red, Blue, Black	28.00	2.50	.55	.40
☐ C88	26¢ Red, Blue, Black	30.00	3.75	.75	.17
1976.					
☐ C89	25¢ Red, Blue, Black	31.00	4.10	.75	.17
☐ C90	31¢ Red, Blue, Black	32.00	4.00	.90	.17
1979.					
☐ C91	31¢ Blue, Brown, Red	79.00	5.00	.90	.17
☐ C92	31¢ Blue, Brown, Red	79.00	5.00	.90	.17
1979.					
☐ C93	21¢ Blue, Brown, Red	90.00	6.00	1.20	.22
☐ C94	21¢ Blue, Brown, Red	90.00	6.00	1.20	.22
1980.					
☐ C95	25¢ Multicolored	130.00	7.00	1.40	.36
☐ C96	25¢ Multicolored	130.00	7.00	1.40	.36
☐ C97	31¢ Multicolored	46.00	17.00	1.35	.36
1981.					
☐ C98	40¢ Multicolored	42.00	12.00	1.50	.20
☐ C99	28¢ Multicolored	34.00	11.00	.80	.20
☐ C100	35¢ Multicolored	39.00	11.00	.85	.20
1983.					
☐ C101	28¢ Multicolored	45.00	5.00	1.10	.30
☐ C102	28¢ Multicolored	45.00	5.00	1.10	.30
☐ C103	28¢ Multicolored	45.00	5.00	1.10	.30
☐ C104	28¢ Multicolored	45.00	5.00	1.10	.30
☐ C105	40¢ Multicolored	60.00	6.00	1.50	.35
☐ C106	40¢ Multicolored	60.00	6.00	1.50	.35
☐ C107	40¢ Multicolored	60.00	6.00	1.50	.35
☐ C108	40¢ Multicolored	60.00	6.00	1.50	.35
☐ C109	35¢ Multicolored	50.00	6.00	1.50	.35
☐ C110	35¢ Multicolored	50.00	6.00	1.50	.35

*No hinge pricing from 1941 to date is figured at (N-H ADD 15%)

Scott No.			Mint Sheet	Plate Block	Fine Unused Each	Fine Used Each
☐C111	35¢	Multicolored	50.00	6.00	1.50	.35
☐C112	35¢	Multicolored	50.00	6.00	1.50	.35
1985.						
☐C113	33¢	Multicolored	35.00	4.00	.80	.30
☐C114	39¢	Multicolored	40.00	5.00	.95	.30
☐C115	44¢	Multicolored	45.00	6.00	1.00	.35
☐C116	44¢	Multicolored	55.00	6.00	1.00	.35
1988.						
☐C117	44¢	Multicolored	52.00	7.00	1.00	.35
☐C118	45¢	Multicolored	50.00	6.00	1.00	.35
☐C119	36¢	Multicolored	40.00	5.00	1.00	.35
1989.						
☐C120	45¢	Multicolored	27.00	5.00	1.00	.35
☐C121	45¢	Multicolored	45.00	5.00	1.00	.35
☐C122	45¢	Multicolored	50.00	6.00	1.25	.50
☐C123	45¢	Multicolored	45.00	6.00	1.00	.40
☐C124	45¢	Multicolored	45.00	6.00	1.00	.40
☐C125	45¢	Multicolored	45.00	6.00	1.00	.40
☐C126	45¢	Multicolored	45.00	6.00	1.00	.40
1990.						
☐C127	45¢	Multicolored	45.00	6.00	1.00	.40
☐C128	50¢	Multicolored	50.00	5.00	1.00	.30
☐C129	40¢	Multicolored	42.00	5.00	1.00	.30
☐C130	50¢	Multicolored	50.00	5.00	1.00	.30
1991.						
☐C131	50¢	Multicolored	50.00	5.00	1.00	.30

Scott No.			Fine Unused Plate Blk	Ave. Unused Plate Blk	Fine Unused Each	Ave. Unused Each	Fine Used Each	Ave. Used Each
AIRMAIL SPECIAL DELIVERY								
☐CE1	16¢	Dark Blue	28.00	21.00	1.25	.76	1.00	.80
☐CE2	16¢	Red & Blue	16.00	12.00	.70	.50	.35	.35
SPECIAL DELIVERY STAMPS								
1885.								
☐E1	10¢	Blue	—	—	225.00	130.00	36.00	27.00
1888.								
☐E2	10¢	Blue	—	—	225.00	130.00	12.00	8.00
1893. (N-H ADD 80%)								
☐E3	10¢	Orange	—	—	130.00	135.00	21.00	14.00
1894. (N-H ADD 80%)								
☐E4	10¢	Blue	—	—	600.00	400.00	23.00	14.00
1895. (N-H ADD 80%)								
☐E5	10¢	Blue	—	—	110.00	90.00	3.50	2.00

*No hinge pricing from 1941 to date is figured at (N-H ADD 15%)

Scott No.	Fine Unused Plate Blk	Ave. Unused Plate Blk	Fine Unused Each	Ave. Unused Each	Fine Used Each	Ave. Used Each
1902. (N-H ADD 55%)						
☐E6 10¢ Ultramarine	—	—	90.00	45.00	3.00	1.75
1908. (N-H ADD 55%)						
☐E7 10¢ Green	—	—	65.00	40.00	33.00	26.00
1911. (N-H ADD 40%)						
☐E8 10¢ Ultramarine	—	—	90.00	50.00	5.00	3.00
1914. (N-H ADD 40%)						
☐E9 10¢ Ultramarine	—	—	170.00	100.00	7.00	4.50
1916. (N-H ADD 40%)						
☐E10 10¢ Pale Ultramarine	—	—	300.00	175.00	21.00	16.00
1917. (N-H ADD 40%)						
☐E11 10¢ Ultramarine	—	—	18.00	10.00	.60	.40
1922–1925. (N-H ADD 30%)						
☐E12 10¢ Deep Ultramarine	400.00	250.00	40.00	26.00	.26	.19
☐E13 10¢ Deep Orange	275.00	175.00	30.00	19.00	1.10	.95
☐E14 20¢ Black	55.00	38.00	3.75	3.00	3.00	2.00
1927–1951. (N-H ADD 30%)						
☐E15 10¢ Gray Violet	8.50	6.00	.90	.75	.21	.16
☐E16 15¢ Orange	6.00	5.00	.90	.75	.21	.14
☐E17 13¢ Blue	5.00	4.00	.85	.60	.21	.14
☐E18 17¢ Yellow	40.00	28.00	5.50	4.50	4.00	2.00
☐E19 20¢ Black	11.00	9.00	2.50	1.90	.21	.12

Scott No.	Mint Sheet	Plate Block	Fine Unused Each	Fine Used Each
1954.				
☐E20 20¢ Blue	36.00	4.00	.85	.15
1957.				
☐E21 30¢ Maroon	45.00	4.50	.88	.15
1969.				
☐E22 45¢ Red & Blue	85.00	11.00	1.80	.15
1971.				
☐E23 60¢ Blue & Red	65.00	7.00	1.65	.15

Scott No.	Fine Unused Plate Blk	Ave. Unused Plate Blk	Fine Unused Each	Ave. Unused Each	Fine Used Each	Ave. Used Each
1911. REGISTRATION STAMPS (N-H ADD 30%)						
☐F1 10¢ Ultramarine	1400.00	900.00	90.00	55.00	6.00	4.00

Scott No.			Mint Sheet	Plate Block	Fine Unused Each	Fine Used Each
☐FA1	15¢ Postman		30.00	8.00	.55	.45

*No hinge pricing from 1941 to date is figured at (N-H ADD 15%)

Scott No.			Name Block 6	Name Block 4	Plain Block 4	Unused Each	Used Each

UNITED NATIONS

1951.

☐1	1¢	Magenta	.90	.55	.35	.21	.14
☐2	1½¢	Blue Green	.90	.55	.40	.21	.14
☐2a	1½¢	Precancelled					20.00
☐3	2¢	Purple	1.10	.60	.50	.21	.14
☐4	3¢	Magenta & Blue	.90	.70	.55	.21	.14
☐5	5¢	Blue	1.75	.70	.60	.22	.14
☐6	10¢	Chocolate	5.00	2.75	1.50	.28	.21
☐7	15¢	Violet & Blue	5.00	2.65	1.50	.28	.21
☐8	20¢	Dark Brown	12.00	8.00	6.50	1.75	.60
☐9	25¢	Olive Gray & Blue	14.00	9.00	6.00	1.75	.60
☐10	50¢	Indigo	100.00	60.00	45.00	10.00	2.00
☐11	$1	Red	30.00	19.00	15.00	3.50	1.40
☐1–11		First Postage Set Complete	240.00	100.00	80.00	21.00	17.00

1952.

☐12	5¢	War Memorial Bldg.	8.00	6.00	4.00	.85	.40
☐13–14	3¢, 5¢	Fourth H.R. Day	21.00	12.00	9.50	2.00	.90

1953.

☐15–16	3¢, 5¢	Refugees	26.00	19.00	14.00	4.00	1.75
☐17–18	3¢, 5¢	U.P.U.	32.00	22.00	19.00	5.00	1.75
☐19–20	3¢, 5¢	Technical Assist	16.00	12.00	10.00	2.00	1.50
☐21–22	3¢, 5¢	Human Rights	26.00	22.00	18.00	5.00	1.50

1954.

☐23–24	3¢, FAO (Agriculture)		30.00	20.00	16.00	4.00	1.20
☐25–26	3¢, 8¢	OIT (Labor Org.)	50.00	40.00	32.00	8.50	1.90
☐27–28	3¢, 8¢	UN Day	60.00	50.00	40.00	11.00	4.00
☐29–30	3¢, 8¢	H.R. Day	150.00	120.00	90.00	26.00	7.00

1955.

☐31–32	3¢, 8¢	I.C.A.O.	60.00	55.00	48.00	12.00	4.25
☐33–34	3¢, 8¢	UNESCO	28.00	20.00	16.00	4.00	1.00
☐35–37	3¢, 4¢, 8¢	UN Day	60.00	50.00	40.00	10.00	2.00
☐38	3¢, 4¢, 8¢	UN Day Sheet	—	—	—	225.00	80.00
☐39–40	3¢, 8¢	Human Rights	18.00	15.00	12.00	3.00	1.40

1956.

☐41–42	3¢, 8¢	Telecommunication	20.00	12.00	10.00	3.00	1.50
☐43–44	3¢, 8¢	World Health	20.00	12.00	10.00	3.00	1.50
☐45–46	3¢, 8¢	UN Day	3.00	1.75	1.25	.35	.28
☐47–48	3¢, 8¢	Human Rights	2.50	1.50	1.00	.30	.22

Scott No.		Name Block 6	Name Block 4	Plain Block 4	Unused Each	Used Each
1957.						
☐ 49–50	3¢, 8¢ W.M.O. Meteorological	2.00	1.50	1.10	.30	.20
☐ 51–52	3¢, 8¢ U.N.E.F. 1st Printing	2.00	1.50	1.10	.30	.20
☐ 53–54	3¢, 8¢ U.N.E.F. 2nd Printing	3.75	2.90	2.00	.50	.28
☐ 55–56	3¢, 8¢ Security Council	2.00	1.50	1.00	.30	.20
☐ 57–58	3¢, 8¢ Human Rights	2.00	1.50	1.00	.30	.20
1958.						
☐ 59–60	3¢, 8¢ Atomic Energy	2.10	1.50	1.00	.30	.21
☐ 61–62	3¢, 8¢ General Assembly	2.10	1.50	1.00	.30	.21
☐ 63–64	4¢, 8¢ Regular Issues	2.10	1.50	1.00	.30	.21
☐ 65–66	4¢, 8¢ Economic Council	2.10	1.50	1.00	.35	.22
☐ 67–68	4¢, 8¢ Human Rights	2.10	1.50	1.00	.35	.22
☐ 69–70	4¢, 8¢ Flushing Meadows	2.25	1.80	1.20	.35	.22
☐ 71–72	4¢, 8¢ E.C.E.	3.00	2.25	1.80	.50	.30
☐ 73–74	4¢, 8¢ Trusteeship	2.80	1.85	2.10	.40	.28
☐ 75–76	4¢, 8¢ World Refugee Year	2.25	1.80	2.10	.40	.28
1960.						
☐ 77–78	4¢, 8¢ Palais de Chaillot	2.10	1.75	1.25	.36	.30
☐ 79–80	4¢, 8¢ Forestry Congress	2.10	1.75	1.25	.36	.30
☐ 83–84	4¢, 8¢ 15th Anniversary	2.10	1.75	1.25	.36	.30
☐ 85	4¢, 8¢ 15th Ann. Souv. Sheet	2.10	1.75	—	4.00	3.50
☐ 86–87	4¢, 8¢ International	2.10	1.75	1.25	.36	.30
1961.						
☐ 88–89	4¢, 8¢ Court of Justice	2.00	1.65	1.10	.36	.30
☐ 90–91	4¢, 7¢ Monetary Fund	2.00	1.65	1.10	.36	.30
☐ 92	30¢ Regular Issue	6.00	4.00	3.00	.90	.65
☐ 93–94	4¢, 11¢ E.C. for Latin Am.	6.50	5.00	4.00	1.10	.65
☐ 95–96	4¢, 11¢ E.C. for Africa	3.00	2.50	2.00	.55	.38
☐ 97–99	3¢, 4¢, 13¢ Children's Fund	4.00	3.40	2.50	.75	.38
1962.						
☐ 100–01	4¢, 7¢ Housing	3.00	2.00	1.75	.45	.35
☐ 102–03	4¢, 11¢ Malaria	4.00	3.00	2.70	.65	.45
☐ 104–07	1¢, 3¢, 5¢, 11¢ Reg. Issue	5.00	4.00	3.00	1.00	.80
☐ 108–09	5¢, 15¢ Hammarskjold	12.00	10.00	8.00	2.00	1.75
☐ 110–11	4¢, 11¢ U.N. Congo	10.00	8.00	6.00	1.80	1.65
☐ 112–13	4¢, 11¢ Peaceful Space Use	3.50	2.50	2.00	.55	.40
1963.						
☐ 114–15	5¢, 11¢ Econ. Development	3.50	2.50	2.00	.60	.35
☐ 116–17	5¢, 11¢ Freedom—Hunger	3.50	2.50	2.00	.60	.35
☐ 118	25¢ UNTEA W. Irian	4.50	3.50	3.00	.70	.50
☐ 119–20	5¢, 11¢, 10th Hdqrs. Anniv.	3.50	2.50	2.00	.55	.32
☐ 121–22	5¢, 11¢, 15th Anniv. H. Rights	3.50	2.50	2.00	.55	.32
1964.						
☐ 123–24	5¢, 11¢ Maritime	3.00	2.50	2.50	.55	.32
☐ 125–27	2¢, 7¢, 10¢ Reg. Issue	3.00	2.50	2.00	.55	.32

Scott No.		Name Block 6	Name Block 4	Plain Block 4	Unused Each	Used Each
☐ 128	50¢ New Regular	6.50	8.00	6.00	.80	.70
☐ 129–30	5¢, 11¢ Trade & Develop	3.00	2.00	1.50	.32	.28
☐ 131–32	5¢, 11¢ Narcotics Control	2.00	2.10	1.80	.50	.40
☐ 133	5¢ Nuclear Tests End	1.80	.60	.45	.20	.16
☐ 134–36	4¢, 5¢, 11¢ Education	1.90	2.10	1.75	.55	.45

1965.

☐ 137–38	5¢, 11¢ Special Fund	2.75	2.10	1.90	.45	.25
☐ 139–40	5¢, 11¢ U.N. in Cyprus	2.75	2.10	1.90	.45	.25
☐ 141–42	5¢, 11¢ I.T.U. (Satellite)	2.75	2.10	1.90	.45	.25
☐ 143–44	5¢, 15¢ Co-operation	3.00	2.25	2.00	.55	.40
☐ 145	5¢, 15¢ Min. Sheet	—	—	—	1.80	1.35
☐ 146–49	1¢, 15¢, 20¢, 25¢ Regular	18.00	11.00	9.00	2.25	3.00
☐ 150	$1 Regular Issue (1966)	26.00	19.00	16.00	3.00	2.00
☐ 151–53	4¢, 5¢, 11¢ Population Trends	3.00	2.25	2.00	.55	.40

1966.

☐ 154–55	5¢, 15¢ World Federation	3.00	2.50	2.00	.55	.40
☐ 156–57	5¢, 11¢ W.H.O. Building	3.00	2.00	1.80	.45	.25
☐ 158–59	5¢, 11¢ Coffee Agreement	3.00	2.25	1.90	.60	.42
☐ 160	15¢ Peacekeeping	2.75	1.80	1.65	.42	.28
☐ 161–63	4¢, 5¢, 11¢ UNICEF Anniv.	3.25	2.50	2.00	.55	.25

1967.

☐ 164–65	5¢, 11¢ Development	3.00	2.10	1.90	.45	.28
☐ 166–67	1½¢, 5¢ Regular Issue	2.00	1.00	.85	.23	.16
☐ 168–69	5¢, 11¢ Independence	3.00	2.10	1.90	.45	.28

1967.

☐ 170–74	4¢, 5¢, 8¢, 10¢, 15¢ EXPO	10.00	8.00	6.00	1.60	1.10
☐ 175–76	5¢, 15¢ Intl. Tourist Year	3.25	2.50	2.00	.55	.45
☐ 177–78	6¢, 13¢ Toward Disarm	4.00	3.00	2.50	.65	.50
☐ 179	6¢ Chagall Sheet of Six	—	—	—	.90	.70
☐ 180	6¢ Chagall Window	1.00	.85	.65	.21	.16

1968.

☐ 181–82	6¢, 13¢, Secretariat	3.50	2.50	2.10	.55	.40
☐ 183–84	6¢, 75¢ Starcke Statue	28.00	21.00	18.00	4.00	2.50
☐ 185–86	6¢, 13¢ ONUDI	3.10	2.25	1.90	.55	.40
☐ 187	6¢ Regular Issue	1.90	.85	.65	.20	.16
☐ 188–89	6¢, 20¢ Weather Watch	4.50	3.50	2.90	.80	.60
☐ 190–91	6¢, 13¢ Int'l. Year Human Rts.	4.50	3.10	2.50	.70	.55

1969.

☐ 192–93	6¢, 13¢ UNITAR	3.10	2.40	2.00	.55	.40
☐ 194–95	6¢, 15¢ ECLA Bldg	3.50	2.80	2.00	.65	.40
☐ 196	13¢, Regular Issue	2.50	1.85	1.55	.40	.26
☐ 197–98	6¢, 13¢ Peace thru Law	3.00	2.25	1.90	.55	.32
☐ 199–00	6¢, 20¢ Labor & Devl	4.25	3.50	2.90	.55	.40
☐ 201–02	6¢, 13¢ Art Series	3.50	2.25	1.90	.55	.40
☐ 203–04	6¢, 25¢ Japan Peace Bell	5.00	4.00	3.00	.90	.65
☐ 205–06	6¢, 13¢ Mekong Basin	3.50	2.25	1.90	.55	.45

Scott No.		Name Block 6	Name Block 4	Plain Block 4	Unused Each	Used Each
☐ 207–08	6¢, 13¢ Cancer	3.00	2.25	2.00	.55	.40
☐ 209–11	6¢, 13¢, 25¢ 25th U.V. Anniv.	8.00	7.00	6.00	1.60	1.25
☐ 212	Same, Souvenir Sheet	—	—	—	1.50	1.25
☐ 213–14	6¢, 13¢ Peace, Just. Prog.	3.75	2.50	2.00	.55	.45
1971.						
☐ 215	6¢ Sea Bed	1.50	.90	.80	.24	.21
☐ 216–17	6¢, 13¢ Refugees	3.50	2.50	2.10	.55	.45
☐ 218	13¢ World Food Prog.	2.50	1.85	1.65	.40	.35
☐ 219	20¢ U.P.U. Building	3.50	2.50	2.25	.55	.45
☐ 220–21	8¢, 13¢ Anti-Discrim.	4.00	3.00	2.50	.65	.50
☐ 222–23	8¢, 60¢ Regular Issue	12.00	10.00	8.00	2.00	1.75
☐ 224–25	8¢, 21¢ Intl. Schools	6.00	4.50	3.75	1.10	.50
1972.						
☐ 226	95¢ Regular Issue	16.00	13.00	10.00	3.00	1.90
☐ 227	8¢, Non-Proliferation	2.00	1.25	.90	.30	.26
☐ 228	15¢ World Health	3.00	2.10	1.75	.45	.32
☐ 229–30	8¢, 15¢ Environment	4.00	3.10	2.50	.60	.46
☐ 231	21¢ E.C. Europe	4.50	3.50	2.60	.70	.50
☐ 232–33	8¢, 15¢ U.N. Art Sert.	4.50	3.40	2.70	.70	.50
1973.						
☐ 234–35	8¢, 15¢ Disarmament	4.50	3.50	3.00	.75	.52
☐ 236–37	8¢, 15¢ Drug Abuse	4.50	3.50	3.00	.75	.52
☐ 238–39	8¢, 21¢ U.N. Volunteers	5.50	4.50	3.75	.90	.65
☐ 240–41	8¢, 15¢ Namibia	5.00	4.00	3.00	.85	.70
☐ 242–43	8¢, 21¢ Human Rights	5.00	4.00	2.90	.85	.70
1974.						
☐ 244–45	10¢, 21¢ ILO Hdqr.	7.50	5.00	4.00	1.10	.80
☐ 246	10¢ UPU Centenary	2.00	1.25	.90	.32	.24
☐ 247–48	10¢, 18¢ Brazil Mural	4.50	3.75	3.00	.90	.65
☐ 249–51	2¢, 10¢, 18¢ Regular	5.00	3.80	3.00	.90	.62
☐ 252–53	10¢, 18¢ Population	5.50	4.50	3.50	.95	.60
☐ 254–55	10¢, 26¢ Law of Sea	6.50	5.00	4.00	1.10	.80
1975.						
☐ 256–57	10¢, 26¢ Space Usage	9.00	5.00	4.00	1.10	.90
☐ 258–59	10¢, 18¢ Women's Year	5.50	4.50	3.50	1.00	.85
☐ 260–61	10¢, 26¢ UN 30th Anniv.	7.50	6.00	5.00	1.00	.85
☐ 262	36¢ Same Souv. Sheet	—	—	—	1.75	1.45
☐ 263–64	10¢, 18¢ Namibia	7.50	4.00	3.00	.85	.65
☐ 265–66	13¢, 26¢ Peacekeeping	7.00	5.50	4.50	1.10	.85
1976.						
☐ 267–71	3¢, 4¢, 9¢, 30¢, 50¢ Regular	18.00	15.00	12.00	3.00	1.65
☐ 272–73	13¢, 26¢ WFUNA	8.00	6.00	5.00	1.40	.85
☐ 274–75	13¢, 31¢ UNCTAD	8.00	6.00	5.00	1.25	.65
☐ 276–77	13¢, 25¢ HABITAT	7.00	5.00	4.00	1.25	.65
☐ 278–79	13¢, 31¢ 25th Postal Anniv.	78.00	50.00	40.00	10.00	7.00
☐ 280	13¢ Food Council	3.00	2.10	1.50	.45	.32

Scott No.			Name Block 6	Name Block 4	Plain Block 4	Unused Each	Used Each
1977.							
☐ 281–82	13¢, 31¢	WIPO	10.00	7.50	6.00	1.50	.80
☐ 283–84	13¢, 25¢	Water Conf.	9.50	6.50	5.50	1.50	.80
☐ 285–86	13¢, 31¢	Security Council	9.00	7.50	6.50	1.50	.80
☐ 287–88	13¢, 25¢	Combat Racism	7.50	6.00	5.00	1.35	.75
☐ 289–90	13¢, 18¢	Atomic Energy	6.00	4.50	3.00	.90	.60
1978.							
☐ 291–93	1¢, 25¢, $1	Regular	26.00	22.00	16.00	4.60	2.90
☐ 294–95	13¢, 31¢	Small Pox	9.50	8.00	6.00	1.40	.75
☐ 296–97	13¢, 18¢	Namibia	6.50	5.00	4.00	1.00	.55
☐ 298–99	13¢, 25¢	ICAO-Air Safety	7.50	6.00	4.50	1.10	.55
☐ 300–01	13¢, 18¢	General Assembly	6.50	5.00	4.00	1.00	.55
☐ 302–03	13¢, 31¢	Technical Cooperation	12.00	9.00	7.00	1.30	.75
1979.							
☐ 304–07	5¢, 14¢, 15¢, 20¢	Regular Issues	13.00	9.00	7.20	1.75	.90
☐ 308–09	15¢, 20¢	UNDRO	8.00	6.00	4.50	1.10	.60
☐ 310–11	15¢, 31¢	Intl. Year of Child	26.00	14.00	11.00	1.90	1.00
☐ 312–13	15¢, 31¢	Namibia	9.00	7.00	5.50	1.50	.90
☐ 314–15	15¢, 31¢	Court of Justice	9.00	7.00	5.50	1.20	.80
1980.							
☐ 316–17	15¢, 31¢	Economic Order	9.00	7.00	5.50	1.50	.80
☐ 318–19	15¢, 20¢	Women's Decade	7.00	6.00	4.00	1.10	.70
☐ 320–21	15¢, 31¢	Peacekeeping	11.00	9.50	6.00	2.00	.75
☐ 322–23	15¢, 31¢	35th Anniversary	10.00	8.00	6.00	1.25	.70
☐ 324	15¢,	Same, Souvenir Sheet	—	—	—	1.50	.70
☐ 325–40	15¢	World Flags	—	26.00	—	6.50	3.50
☐ 325–28	15¢	World Flags	—	8.00	—	1.90	1.00
☐ 329–32	15¢	World Flags	—	8.00	—	1.90	1.00
☐ 333–36	15¢	World Flags	—	8.00	—	1.90	1.00
☐ 337–40	15¢	World Flags	—	8.00	—	1.90	1.00
☐ 341–42	15¢, 20¢	Economic and Social Council	7.50	6.00	5.00	1.20	.90
1981.							
☐ 343	15¢	Palestinian People	3.50	2.50	1.90	.55	.30
☐ 344–45	20¢, 35¢	Disabled Persons	11.00	9.00	7.00	2.00	.70
☐ 346–47	20¢, 31¢	Fresco	—	8.50	7.00	2.00	.70
☐ 348–49	20¢, 40¢	Sources of Energy	12.50	11.00	8.00	2.00	.70
☐ 350–65	1981	World Flags	—	42.00	—	10.00	4.00
☐ 350–53	20¢	World Flags	—	12.00	—	3.00	1.00
☐ 358–61	20¢	World Flags	—	12.00	—	3.00	1.00
☐ 354–57	15¢, 20¢	World Flags	—	12.00	—	3.00	1.00
☐ 362–65	20¢	World Flags	—	12.00	—	3.00	1.00
☐ 366–67	18¢, 28¢	Volunteers Program	—	9.00	7.00	1.75	.90
1982.							
☐ 368–70	17¢, 28¢, 40¢	Definitives	16.00	14.00	10.00	2.25	.80
☐ 371–72	20¢, 40¢	Human Environment	12.00	10.00	8.00	2.10	.80

Scott No.		Name Block 6	Name Block 4	Plain Block 4	Unused Each	Used Each
☐ 373	20¢ Space Exploration	3.50	3.00	1.80	.40	.28
☐ 374–89	World Flags	40.00	22.00	21.00	4.00	3.00
☐ 390–91	20¢, 28¢ Nature Conservation	11.00	10.00	1.90	1.40	.46

1983.

☐ 392–93	20¢, 40¢ Communication	12.00	10.00	2.10	.75	.55
☐ 394–95	20¢, 37¢ Safety at Sea	12.00	10.00	2.25	.75	.55
☐ 396	20¢ World Food	5.00	3.50	1.20	.45	.28
☐ 397–98	20¢, 28¢ Trade	10.00	8.00	8.00	.65	.50
☐ 399–14	World Flags	36.00	22.00	16.00	2.50	1.90
☐ 415–16	20¢, 40¢ Human Rights	16.00	15.00	3.10	.75	.55

1984.

☐ 417–18	20¢, 40¢ Population Conference	12.00	10.00	3.00	2.00	.60
☐ 419–20	20¢, 40¢ World Food Day	12.00	10.00	3.00	2.00	.60
☐ 421–22	20¢, 50¢ Heritage	13.00	11.00	3.10	2.10	.60
☐ 423–24	20¢, 50¢ Refugees	13.00	11.00	3.10	2.10	.65
☐ 425–50	World Flags	26.00	21.00	16.00	4.00	1.90

UNITED NATIONS
1951–1957. AIRMAILS

☐ C1	6¢ Airmail (1951)	24.00	21.00	18.00	.65	.45
☐ C2	10¢ Airmail	24.00	21.00	18.00	.65	.45
☐ C3	15¢ Airmail	24.00	21.00	18.00	.65	.45
☐ C4	25¢ Airmail	24.00	21.00	18.00	.65	.45
☐ C1–4	First Issue Airmails	65.00	50.00	40.00	6.50	.45
☐ C5–7	4¢, 5¢, 7¢ Airmail (1957)	3.00	2.50	2.00	.65	.35

1963–1964. AIRMAILS

☐ C8–10	6¢, 8¢, 13¢ Airmail (1963)	21.00	21.00	16.00	.85	.60
☐ C11–12	15¢, 25¢ Airmail (1964)	21.00	21.00	16.00	1.10	.75

1968–1972. AIRMAILS

☐ C13	20¢ Airmail (1968)	4.00	3.00	2.00	.75	.40
☐ C14	10¢ Airmail (1969)	4.00	3.00	2.00	.75	.40
☐ C15–18	9¢, 11¢, 17¢, 21¢ (1972)	10.00	9.00	7.00	.85	.75

1974–1977. AIRMAILS

☐ C19–21	13¢, 18¢, 26¢ (1974)	11.00	9.00	7.50	1.10	.65
☐ C22–23	25¢, 31¢ (1977)	8.00	7.00	6.50	1.20	.65

UNITED NATIONS SOUVENIR CARDS

		Unused Each	Used Each
☐ 1	WHO, First Printing	6.00	—
☐ 1a	WHO, Second Printing	5.00	—
☐ 2	Art at U.N.	3.00	—
☐ 3	Disarmament	3.00	—
☐ 4	Human Rights	7.00	—
☐ 5	Universal Postal Union	7.00	—
☐ 6	World Population	20.00	—
☐ 7	Outer Space	8.00	—

		Unused Each	Used Each
☐8	Peacekeeping	10.00	—
☐9	World Federation of U.N.	11.00	—
☐10	World Food Council	7.00	—
☐11	World Intellectual Property	4.00	—
☐12	Combat Racism	5.00	—
☐13	Namibia	5.00	—
☐14	ICAO-Air Safety	5.00	—
☐15	International Year of The Child	4.00	—
☐16	Court of Justice	4.00	—
☐17	Women's Decade	25.00	—
☐18	Economic and Social Council	6.50	—
☐19	Disabled Persons	4.50	—
☐20	Energy Sources	5.00	—

Scott No.		Name Block 6	Name Block 4	Plain Block 4	Unused Each	Used Each

UNITED NATIONS—GENEVA, SWITZERLAND
DENOMINATIONS ARE GIVEN IN SWISS CURRENCY
DESIGNS ARE SIMILAR TO U.N. NEW YORK ISSUES
1969–1970.

		Name Block 6	Name Block 4	Plain Block 4	Unused Each	Used Each
☐1–14	5¢ to 10 franc	145.00	100.00	85.00	20.00	15.00
1971.						
☐15	30¢ Sea Bed	2.00	1.50	1.10	.40	.30
☐16	50¢ Refugees	5.00	4.00	3.00	.80	.60
☐17	50¢ World Food Prog.	5.00	4.00	3.00	.90	.70
☐18	75¢ U.P.U. Building	12.00	11.00	9.00	2.25	1.75
☐19–20	30¢, 50¢ Anti-Discrim	10.50	9.00	8.00	1.50	1.00
☐21	1.10 fr. Intl. Schools	17.50	16.00	14.00	3.30	2.00
1972.						
☐22	40¢ Regular Issue	3.50	2.50	2.00	.55	.40
☐23	40¢ Non-Proliferation	9.50	9.00	7.00	1.90	1.10
☐24	80¢ World Health	9.50	9.00	7.00	2.10	1.50
☐25–26	40¢, 80¢ Environment	18.50	18.00	16.00	3.10	2.00
☐27	1.10 fr. E.C. Europe	16.00	15.00	12.00	3.00	2.00
☐28–29	40¢, 80¢ U.N. Art-Sert	19.00	18.00	14.00	3.00	2.00
1973.						
☐30–31	60¢, 1.10 fr. Disarm	19.00	18.00	15.00	2.50	1.90
☐32	60¢ Drug Abuse	7.50	7.00	6.50	1.40	.80
☐33	80¢ U.N. Volunteers	8.75	8.00	6.00	1.50	.90
☐34	60¢ Namibia	8.50	8.00	6.00	1.50	.90
☐35–36	40¢, 80¢ Human Rights	12.00	11.00	9.00	2.50	1.40
1974.						
☐37–38	60¢, 80¢ ILO Hdqrs.	14.00	13.00	11.00	2.50	1.40
☐39–40	30¢, 60¢ UPU Centenary	8.00	7.00	6.00	1.50	.90
☐41–42	60¢, 1 fr. Brazil Mural	15.00	14.00	10.00	3.00	1.80
☐43–44	60¢, 80¢ Population	13.00	12.00	9.00	2.50	1.90
☐45	1.30 fr. Law of Sea	12.00	11.00	9.00	2.00	1.30

Scott No.		Name Block 6	Name Block 4	Plain Block 4	Unused Each	Used Each
1975.						
☐46–47	60¢, 80¢ Space Usage	16.00	12.00	9.00	2.50	1.75
☐48–49	60¢, 90¢ Women's Year	20.00	15.00	12.00	3.20	2.00
☐50–51	60¢, 90¢ U.N. Anniv.	15.00	10.00	8.00	2.70	1.50
☐52	1.50 fr. Same, Souv. Sheet	—	—	—	2.75	1.00
☐53–54	50¢ 1.30 fr. Namibia	14.00	11.00	8.00	2.10	1.50
☐55–56	60¢, 70¢ Peacekeeping	14.00	10.00	8.00	2.60	1.50
1976.						
☐57	90¢ WFUNA	9.50	7.50	6.00	1.70	1.10
☐58	1.10 fr. UNCTAD	10.00	8.00	7.50	1.75	1.10
☐59–60	40¢ 1.50 fr. HABITAT	17.00	13.00	11.00	3.00	1.80
☐61–62	80¢, 1.10 fr. U.N. Postal Anniv.	68.00	60.00	52.00	11.00	3.50
☐63	70¢ World Food Council	8.00	5.00	3.75	1.10	.65
1977.						
☐64	80¢ WIPO	7.00	6.00	5.00	1.40	.90
☐65–66	80¢ 1.10 fr. Water Conf.	14.00	11.00	8.00	2.10	1.00
☐67–68	80¢, 1.10 fr. Security Council	14.00	11.00	8.00	2.10	1.00
☐69–70	40¢, 1.10 fr. Combat Racism	14.00	11.00	8.00	2.00	1.00
☐71–72	80¢, 1.10 fr. Atomic Energy	18.00	14.00	10.00	3.00	1.25
☐73	35¢ Doves	40.00	2.75	2.00	.65	.40
☐74–75	80¢, 1.10 fr. Smallpox	15.00	12.00	8.50	2.75	.90
☐76	80¢ Namibia	8.00	6.00	4.75	1.25	.70
☐77–78	70¢, 80¢ ICAO-Air Safety	14.00	10.00	8.00	2.10	1.00
☐79–80	70¢, 1.10 Fr. General Assembly	15.00	12.00	8.00	2.50	1.00
☐81	80¢ Technical Cooperation	8.50	6.00	4.50	1.10	.75
1979.						
☐82–83	80¢, 1.50 UNDRO	18.00	15.00	13.50	3.10	2.10
☐84–85	80¢, 1.10 Intl. Year of The Child	28.00	20.00	16.00	4.00	1.00
☐86	1.10 fr. Namibia	13.00	8.00	6.50	2.10	1.05
☐87–88	80¢, 1.10 Court of Justice	16.00	13.00	10.00	3.00	1.00
1980.						
☐89	80¢ Economic Order	9.00	7.00	6.00	1.40	.90
☐90–91	40¢, 70¢ Women's Decade	12.00	9.00	7.00	1.50	.85
☐92	1.10 fr. Peacekeeping	11.00	8.00	6.00	1.65	.80
☐93–94	40¢, 70¢, 35th Anniversary	11.00	8.00	6.00	1.65	.80
☐95	40¢, 70¢ Sheet	—	—	—	2.10	.85
☐96–97	40¢, 70¢ Economic and Social Council	11.00	8.00	5.00	1.20	.50
1981.						
☐98	80¢ Palestinian People	8.00	6.50	4.10	1.25	.60
☐99–100	40¢, 1.50 fr., Disabled Persons	16.00	12.00	8.00	3.00	.75
☐101	80¢ Bulgarian Mural	7.50	6.00	4.50	1.40	.60
☐102	1.10 fr. Energy Sources	11.00	9.00	7.50	1.90	.60
☐103–04	40¢, 70¢ Volunteers	11.00	9.00	7.50	1.90	.60
1982.						
☐105–06	1 fr., Definitives	13.00	10.00	8.00	2.10	.60
☐107–08	40¢, 1.20 fr., Human Environment	15.00	12.00	8.00	2.60	.65

Scott No.		Fine	Ave.
UNUSED BOOKLET PANES			
☐319g	2¢ Carmine . . .	110.00	70.00
☐331a	1¢ Green	130.00	90.00
☐332a	2¢ Carmine . . .	100.00	70.00
☐374a	1¢ Green	120.00	75.00
☐375a	2¢ Carmine . . .	100.00	60.00
☐405b	1¢ Green	56.00	40.00
☐406a	2¢ Carmine . . .	65.00	35.00
☐424d	1¢ Green	7.50	4.50
☐425e	2¢ Carmine . . .	19.00	11.00
☐462a	1¢ Green	12.00	7.20
☐463a	2¢ Carmine . . .	90.00	52.00
☐498e	1¢ Green	2.75	2.00
☐499e	2¢ Rose	4.50	2.90
☐501b	3¢ Violet I . . .	100.00	60.00
☐502b	3¢ Violet II . .	68.00	45.00
☐552a	1¢ Dark Green . . .	7.50	5.00
☐554c	2¢ Carmine . . .	8.00	5.00
☐583a	2¢ Carmine . . .	85.00	55.00
☐632a	1¢ Green	6.00	4.00
☐634d	2¢ Carmine . . .	2.90	1.50
☐720b	3¢ Dark Violet . .	46.00	30.00
☐804b	1¢ Green	16.00	3.00
☐806b	2¢ Red Carmine . .	9.00	4.00
☐807a	3¢ Dark Violet . .	14.00	8.00
☐1035a	3¢ Dark Violet . . .	4.00	3.00
☐1036a	4¢ Red Violet. . .	4.00	3.00
☐1213a	5¢ "ZIP"	4.00	2.50
☐1213x	5¢ Mailman	7.50	5.00
☐1213y	5¢ Zone No. . . .	11.00	7.00
☐1278a	1¢ Jeff. (8)	1.50	.90
☐1278ae	1¢ T. Gum (8) . . .	4.00	1.65
☐1278b	1¢ Green-(4) . . .	1.00	.45
☐1280a	2¢ Blue Gray (5) . .	2.00	.80
☐1280c	2¢ Blue Gray (6) . .	1.50	.60
☐1284b	6¢ F.D.R. (8) . . .	2.50	1.50
☐1284c	6¢ F.D.R. (5) . . .	2.50	1.75
☐1393a	6¢ Ike (8)	2.50	1.00
☐1393ae	6¢ T. Gum	3.50	1.40
☐1393b	6¢ Ike (5)	2.10	1.00
☐1395a	8¢ Ike (8)	3.50	1.50
☐1395b	8¢ Ike (6)	3.00	1.80
☐1395c	8¢ Ike (4)	2.25	1.40
☐1395d	8¢ Ike (7)	3.50	2.00

Scott No.		Fine	Ave.
☐1510b	10¢ Mem'l (5)	2.40	1.00
☐1510c	10¢ Mem'l (8)	3.50	1.50
☐1510d	10¢ Mem'l (6)	6.00	3.00
☐1595b	13¢ Bell (6).	3.50	3.00
☐1595c	13¢ Bell (7). . . .	4.00	3.00
☐1595c	13¢ Bell (8). . . .	4.00	3.00
☐1595d	13¢ Bell (5). . . .	3.10	2.90
☐1623a	13¢ (7), 9¢ (1). . . .	4.00	3.00
☐1623c	Same, Perf. 10	48.00	36.00
☐1736a	"A" Eagle (no denomination) .	5.00	3.40
☐1737a	15¢ Multicolored. . .	5.00	3.00
☐1742a	15¢ Multicolored. . .	7.00	3.00
☐C10a	10¢ Lindbergh . .	130.00	85.00
☐C25a	6¢ Carmine	7.00	3.00
☐C39a	6¢ Small.	21.00	15.00
☐C51a	7¢ Blue	18.00	12.00
☐C60a	7¢ Carmine	21.00	18.00
☐C64c	8¢ Carmine "Zip".	2.10	1.50
☐C64bx	8¢ Mailman	12.00	9.00
☐C64by	8¢ Zone No.	48.00	30.00
☐C72b	10¢ Carmine (8) . . .	4.00	2.80
☐C72c	10¢ Carmine (5) . . .	7.00	5.00
☐C78a	11¢ Carmine (4) . . .	1.75	1.50
☐C79a	13¢ Letter (5)	2.50	1.75

Scott No.		Fine
SOUVENIR CARDS		
☐1	Truck w/gum.	100.00
☐	Truck w/o gum	15.00
☐2	Barcelona.	325.00
☐3	SIPEX Scenes	175.00
☐3a	SIPEX Miner	14.00
☐4	EFIMEX.	3.00
☐5	SANDIPEX	60.00
☐	Ana '69	60.00
☐	FRESNO	400.00
☐6	ASDA '69.	18.00
☐7	INTERPEX '70	55.00
☐8	COMPEX '70.	10.00
☐	ANA 1970	100.00
☐9	PHILYMPIA.	3.50
☐10	HAPEX	11.00

Scott No.		Fine	Scott No.		Fine
☐11	INTERPEX '71	2.50	☐	INTERPHIL Program with	
☐12	WESTPEX	2.75		B.E.P. Card	11.00
☐13	NAPEX '71	2.75	☐47	Science BEP	8.00
☐	ANA 1971	3.00	☐48	Science U.S.P.S.	4.50
☐14	TEXANEX	3.00	☐49	Stamp Expo '76	7.50
☐15	EXFILIMA	2.00	☐50	Colorado Statehood	3.00
☐16	ASDA '71	2.50	☐51	HAFNIA '76	3.50
☐17	ANPHILEX	1.50	☐	ANA 1976	8.50
☐18	INTERPEX '72	1.50	☐52	ITALIA '76	3.50
☐19	NOPEX	1.50	☐53	NORDPOSTA '76	3.50
☐20	BELGICA	1.50	☐54	MILCOPEX '77	2.75
☐	ANA 1972	4.00	☐55	ROMPEX '77	3.00
☐21	Olympia Phil. Munchen	1.50	☐56	AMPHILEX '77	3.75
☐22	EXFILBRA	1.50	☐	ANA 1977	5.00
☐23	Postal Forum	1.50	☐57	SAN MARCO	3.00
☐24	SEPAD '72	1.50	☐58	Puripex	2.75
☐25	ASDA '72	1.50	☐59	ASDA '77	3.50
☐26	Stamp Expo '75	1.80	☐60	ROPEX '78	4.00
☐27	INTERPEX '73	2.00	☐	Paper Money Show	5.00
☐28	IBRA	2.00	☐61	NAPOSTA '78	3.00
☐29	COMPEX '73	2.00	☐62	CENTEX '78	4.00
☐30	APEX	1.75	☐63	BRASILIANA '79	4.00
☐	ANA 1973	6.00	☐64	JAPEX '79	4.00
☐31	POLSKA	2.00	☐	ANA '80	50.00
☐32	NAPEX '73	2.10	☐65	LONDON '80	4.00
☐33	ASDA '73	2.10	☐	Money Show '80	8.00
☐34	Stamps Expo '73	2.10	☐66	NORWEX '80	5.00
☐35	Hobby Show Chicago	3.50	☐67	NAPEX '80	12.00
☐36	MILCOPEX '72	3.00	☐	Visitor Center	8.00
☐37	INTERNABA 1974	3.00	☐68	ASDA STAMP	
☐	ANA 1974	15.00		FESTIVAL '80	14.00
☐38	STOCKHOLMIA '74	3.00	☐69	ESSEN '80	4.00
☐39	EXFILMEX '74	3.00	☐70	STAMP EXPO '81	13.00
☐40	ESPANA '75	3.00	☐	Visitor Center	9.00
☐41	NAPEX '75	8.00	☐71	WIPA '81	5.00
☐42	ARPHILA '75	2.50	☐	Paper Money	9.00
☐43	Women's Year	32.00	☐	ANA '81	13.00
☐	ANA 1975	16.00	☐72	STAMP COLLECTORS	
☐44	ASDA '75	42.00		MONTH	4.50
☐45	WERABA '76	4.00	☐73	PHILATOKYO '81	5.00
☐46	INTERPHIL '76	7.00	☐74	NORD POSKTA '81	4.00

Scott No.		Fine Unused Each	Ave. Unused Each	Fine Used Each	Ave. Used Each
POSTAGE DUE STAMPS					
1879. PERFORATED 12 (N-H ADD 80%)					
☐ J1	1¢ Brown	24.00	14.00	7.00	4.50
☐ J2	2¢ Brown	175.00	105.00	6.50	4.00
☐ J3	3¢ Brown	19.00	12.00	3.00	1.90
☐ J4	5¢ Brown	240.00	140.00	25.00	15.00
☐ J5	10¢ Brown	310.00	200.00	10.00	8.00
☐ J6	30¢ Brown	135.00	80.00	25.00	13.00
☐ J7	50¢ Brown	215.00	125.00	42.00	25.00
1884–1889. SAME DESIGN—PERF. 12 (N-H ADD 80%)					
☐ J15	1¢ Red Brown	31.00	18.00	3.50	2.00
☐ J16	2¢ Red Brown	37.00	20.00	3.50	2.00
☐ J17	3¢ Red Brown	410.00	250.00	90.00	55.00
☐ J18	5¢ Red Brown	200.00	110.00	10.00	7.00
☐ J19	10¢ Red Brown	175.00	95.00	6.00	4.00
☐ J20	30¢ Red Brown	100.00	58.00	27.00	16.00
☐ J21	50¢ Red Brown	900.00	550.00	115.00	75.00
1891–1893. SAME DESIGN—PERF. 12 (N-H ADD 80%)					
☐ J22	1¢ Bright Claret	10.00	7.00	.70	.35
☐ J23	2¢ Bright Claret	11.00	7.00	.65	.35
☐ J24	3¢ Bright Claret	25.00	15.00	3.00	2.00
☐ J25	5¢ Bright Claret	26.00	17.00	3.00	2.00
☐ J26	10¢ Bright Claret	60.00	35.00	9.00	5.00
☐ J27	30¢ Bright Claret	200.00	125.00	90.00	55.00
☐ J28	50¢ Bright Claret	220.00	140.00	85.00	55.00
1894. NEW SMALL DESIGN—NO WTMK.—PERF. 12 (N-H ADD 55%)					
☐ J29	1¢ Vermilion	425.00	300.00	90.00	55.00
☐ J30	2¢ Vermilion	210.00	110.00	38.00	21.00
☐ J31	1¢ Claret	18.00	10.00	4.00	2.50
☐ J32	2¢ Claret	16.00	8.00	3.00	1.50
☐ J33	3¢ Claret	65.00	42.00	20.00	10.00
☐ J34	5¢ Claret	70.00	43.00	23.00	15.00
☐ J35	10¢ Claret	65.00	43.00	14.00	9.00
☐ J36	30¢ Claret (Shades)	180.00	100.00	48.00	29.00
☐ J37	50¢ Claret (Shades)	400.00	270.00	100.00	65.00
1895. SAME NEW SMALL DESIGN—D.L. WTMK.—PERF. 12 (N-H ADD 80%)					
☐ J38	1¢ Claret	5.00	3.80	.45	.26
☐ J39	2¢ Claret	5.00	3.80	.35	.21
☐ J40	3¢ Claret	30.00	20.00	1.25	.60
☐ J41	5¢ Claret	28.00	16.00	1.25	.60
☐ J42	10¢ Claret	30.00	18.00	2.50	1.50
☐ J43	30¢ Claret	210.00	140.00	25.00	14.00
☐ J44	50¢ Claret	165.00	100.00	25.00	13.00

Scott No.		Fine Unused Each	Ave. Unused Each	Fine Used Each	Ave. Used Each

1910–1912. SMALL DESIGN—S.L. WTMK.—PERF. 12 (N-H ADD 80%)

☐ J45	1¢ Claret	19.00	11.00	2.50	1.45
☐ J46	2¢ Claret	19.00	11.00	.30	.21
☐ J47	3¢ Claret	310.00	210.00	15.00	9.50
☐ J48	5¢ Claret	50.00	32.00	2.50	1.50
☐ J49	10¢ Claret	65.00	42.00	10.00	5.00
☐ J50	50¢ Claret	550.00	350.00	80.00	48.00

1914–1916. SAME SMALL DESIGN—S.L. WTMK. PERF. 10. (N-H ADD 80%)

☐ J52	1¢ Carmine	36.00	24.00	8.00	5.00
☐ J53	2¢ Carmine	24.00	13.00	.40	.26
☐ J54	3¢ Carmine	390.00	210.00	12.00	6.00
☐ J55	5¢ Carmine	21.00	14.00	2.00	1.25
☐ J56	10¢ Carmine	35.00	20.00	1.25	.60
☐ J57	30¢ Carmine	125.00	80.00	16.00	9.00
☐ J58	50¢ Carmine	4800.00	2400.00	350.00	200.00
☐ J59	1¢ Rose (No Wtmk.)	950.00	500.00	150.00	110.00
☐ J60	2¢ Rose (No Wtmk.)	75.00	40.00	6.00	3.90

Scott No.		Fine Unused Plate Blk	Ave. Unused Plate Blk	Fine Unused Each	Ave. Unused Each	Fine Used Each	Ave. Used Each

1917–1926. SAME SMALL DESIGN—NO WTMK.—PERF. 11 (N-H ADD 40%)

☐ J61	1¢ Carmine Rose	40.00	30.00	3.00	1.60	.20	.16
☐ J62	2¢ Carmine Rose	38.00	29.00	3.00	1.60	.20	.12
☐ J63	3¢ Carmine Rose	100.00	70.00	8.00	4.00	.20	.14
☐ J64	5¢ Carmine Rose	100.00	75.00	8.00	5.00	.20	.14
☐ J65	10¢ Carmine Rose	140.00	100.00	14.00	6.00	.24	.14
☐ J66	30¢ Carmine Rose	400.00	300.00	50.00	32.00	.55	.30
☐ J67	50¢ Carmine Rose	600.00	500.00	60.00	40.00	.22	.14
☐ J68	½¢ Dull Red	14.00	12.00	.80	.45	.22	.14

1930–1931. NEW DESIGN FLAT PRESS—PERF. 11 x 11 (N-H ADD 30%)

☐ J69	½¢ Carmine	59.00	40.00	4.00	2.90	.80	.55
☐ J70	1¢ Carmine	41.00	28.00	2.80	1.75	.25	.21
☐ J71	2¢ Carmine	53.00	38.00	4.00	3.00	.26	.21
☐ J72	3¢ Carmine	250.00	182.00	26.00	20.00	1.50	.90
☐ J73	5¢ Carmine	275.00	182.00	24.00	18.00	1.65	1.10
☐ J74	10¢ Carmine	465.00	370.00	50.00	30.00	.80	.40
☐ J75	30¢ Carmine	1300.00	960.00	135.00	100.00	1.50	.75
☐ J76	50¢ Carmine	1400.00	1075.00	140.00	100.00	.40	.26
☐ J77	$1 Carmine	330.00	250.00	30.00	21.00	.19	.16
☐ J78	$5 Carmine	380.00	270.00	40.00	30.00	.28	.21

Scott No.		Fine Unused Plate Blk	Ave. Unused Plate Blk	Fine Unused Each	Ave. Unused Each	Fine Used Each	Ave. Used Each
1931–1956. SAME DESIGN—ROTARY PRESS—PERF. 11 x 10½ (N-H ADD 20%)							
☐ J79	½¢ Carmine	26.00	20.00	1.50	.90	.21	.12
☐ J80	1¢ Carmine	3.00	2.00	.23	.15	.16	.11
☐ J81	2¢ Carmine	3.00	2.00	.23	.15	.16	.11
☐ J82	3¢ Carmine	4.00	3.00	.40	.30	.16	.11
☐ J83	5¢ Carmine	5.00	3.00	.60	.36	.16	.11
☐ J84	10¢ Carmine	11.00	8.00	1.35	1.00	.17	.12
☐ J85	30¢ Carmine	50.00	40.00	13.00	7.00	.16	.12
☐ J86	50¢ Carmine	60.00	40.00	14.00	8.00	.15	.12
☐ J87	$1 Red (10½x11)	350.00	210.00	60.00	34.00	.26	.16

Scott No.		Mint Sheet	Plate Block	Fine Unused Each	Fine Used Each
1959. NEW SERIES—NEW DESIGN—ROTARY PRESS—PERF. 11 x 10½ (N-H ADD 20%)					
☐ J88	½¢ Red & Black	500.00	250.00	1.90	1.50
☐ J89	1¢ Red & Black	2.75	.67	.12	.09
☐ J90	2¢ Red & Black	4.00	.67	.12	.09
☐ J91	3¢ Red & Black	6.00	.82	.12	.09
☐ J92	4¢ Red & Black	7.00	1.30	.15	.09
☐ J93	5¢ Red & Black	8.50	1.20	.17	.09
☐ J94	6¢ Red & Black	10.00	1.65	.23	.09
☐ J95	7¢ Red & Black	12.00	2.00	.23	.12
☐ J96	8¢ Red & Black	15.00	2.10	.27	.10
☐ J97	10¢ Red & Black	19.00	2.10	.29	.09
☐ J98	30¢ Red & Black	40.00	5.00	.72	.09
☐ J99	50¢ Red & Black	90.00	5.00	1.25	.09
☐ J100	$1 Red & Black	180.00	9.00	2.00	.09
☐ J101	$5 Red & Black	900.00	42.00	13.00	.20
1978. SAME DESIGN, NEW VALUES					
☐ J102	11¢ Red & Black	20.00	4.00	.24	.26
☐ J103	13¢ Red & Black	24.00	3.50	.28	.30
1985. SAME DESIGN, NEW VALUES					
☐ J104	17¢ Red & Black	65.00	25.00	.60	.30

Scott No.		Fine
	U.S. UNUSED ZIP CODE BLOCKS OF FOUR	
☐ 1181	5¢ Battle—Wilderness	1.00
☐ 1182	5¢ Appomattox	1.75
☐ 1242	5¢ Sam Houston	.70
☐ 1243	5¢ Chas. M. Russell	.70
☐ 1244	5¢ N.Y. World's Fair	.70
☐ 1247	5¢ N.J. Tercentenary	.70
☐ 1248	5¢ Nevada Statehood	.70
☐ 1249	5¢ Register & Vote	.70
☐ 1250	5¢ Wm. Shakespeare	.70
☐ 1251	5¢ Mayo Brothers	.70
☐ 1252	5¢ American Music	.70
☐ 1253	5¢ Homemakers	.70
☐ 1254–57	5¢ Christmas, 1964	2.00
☐ 1258	5¢ Verr.—Narr. Bridge	.70
☐ 1259	5¢ Modern Art	.70
☐ 1260	5¢ Radio Amateurs	.70
☐ 1261	5¢ Battle—N. Orleans	.70
☐ 1262	5¢ Physical Fitness	.70
☐ 1263	5¢ Cancer Crusade	.70
☐ 1264	5¢ Churchill Mem'l	.75
☐ 1265	5¢ Magna Carta	.75
☐ 1266	5¢ Intl. Co-op Year	.75
☐ 1267	5¢ Salvation Army	.70
☐ 1268	5¢ Dante Alighieri	.70
☐ 1269	5¢ Herbert Hoover	.70
☐ 1270	5¢ Robert Fulton	.70
☐ 1272	5¢ Traffic Safety	.75
☐ 1273	5¢ John S. Copley	.75
☐ 1274	11¢ Intl. Telecom. Un.	4.00
☐ 1276	5¢ Christmas, 1965	.80
☐ 1278	1¢ Thomas Jefferson	.70
☐ 1280	2¢ F. Lloyd Wright	.65
☐ 1281	3¢ Francis Parkman	.70
☐ 1284	6¢ F.D. Roosevelt	5.00
☐ 1285	8¢ Albert Einstein	.70
☐ 1286	10¢ Andrew Jackson	1.25
☐ 1286A	12¢ Henry Ford	1.50
☐ 1288	15¢ O.W. Holmes	4.00
☐ 1289	20¢ Geo. C. Marshall	3.00
☐ 1290	25¢ F. Douglass	3.00
☐ 1291	30¢ John Dewey	3.50
☐ 1292	40¢ Thomas Paine	4.50
☐ 1293	50¢ Lucy Stone	5.00
☐ 1294	$1 Eugene O'Neill	11.00
☐ 1306	5¢ Migr. Bird Treaty	.70
☐ 1307	5¢ Humane to Animals	.70

Scott No.		Fine
☐ 1308	5¢ Indiana Statehood	.70
☐ 1309	5¢ American Circus	.70
☐ 1310	5¢ 6th Intl. Phil. Exh.	.70
☐ 1312	5¢ Bill of Rights	.70
☐ 1313	5¢ Polish Millennium	.70
☐ 1314	5¢ Natl. Park Service	.70
☐ 1315	5¢ Marine Reserves	.70
☐ 1316	5¢ Women's Clubs	.70
☐ 1317	5¢ Johnny Appleseed	.70
☐ 1318	5¢ Beautify America	.75
☐ 1319	5¢ Great River Road	.75
☐ 1320	5¢ Servicemen-Bonds	.75
☐ 1321	5¢ Christmas, 1966	.75
☐ 1322	5¢ Mary Cassatt	2.00
☐ 1323	5¢ National Grange	.70
☐ 1324	5¢ Canada Centennial	.70
☐ 1325	5¢ Erie Canal	.70
☐ 1326	5¢ Search for Peace	.70
☐ 1327	5¢ Henry D. Thoreau	.70
☐ 1328	5¢ Nebraska Statehood	.75
☐ 1329	5¢ Voice of America	.75
☐ 1330	5¢ Davy Crockett	.75
☐ 1331–32	5¢ Twin Space	10.00
☐ 1333	5¢ Urban Planning	.75
☐ 1334	5¢ Finnish Independ.	.75
☐ 1336	5¢ Christmas, 1967	.75
☐ 1337	5¢ Miss. Statehood	.80
☐ 1338	6¢ American Flag	.75
☐ 1339	6¢ Illinois Statehood	.75
☐ 1341	$1 Airlift	26.00
☐ 1342	6¢ Support Our Youth	.90
☐ 1343	6¢ Law & Order	.90
☐ 1344	6¢ Register & Vote	.90
☐ 1353–54	6¢ Historic Flags	3.50
☐ 1355	6¢ Walt Disney	1.50
☐ 1356	6¢ Fr. Marquette	1.00
☐ 1357	6¢ Daniel Boone	.70
☐ 1358	6¢ Arkansas River	.70
☐ 1359	6¢ Leif Erikson	.70
☐ 1360	6¢ Cherokee Strip	.80
☐ 1361	6¢ Trumbull Painting	.75
☐ 1362	6¢ Wildlife Conserv.	1.10
☐ 1364	6¢ American Indian	1.75
☐ 1365–68	6¢ Beautify America	6.50
☐ 1369	6¢ American Legion	.70
☐ 1370	6¢ Grandma Moses	.75
☐ 1371	6¢ Apollo 8	2.10
☐ 1372	6¢ W.C. Handy	.95
☐ 1373	6¢ California	.70

Scott No.		Fine
☐1374	6¢ J.W. Powell	.70
☐1375	6¢ Alabama	.70
☐1376-79	6¢ Botanical	11.00
☐1380	6¢ Dartmouth Case	.70
☐1381	6¢ Baseball	3.50
☐1382	6¢ Football	1.50
☐1383	6¢ Eisenhower	.75
☐1385	6¢ Rehabilitation	.75
☐1386	6¢ Wm. M. Harnett	.70
☐1387-90	6¢ Natural History	1.50
☐1391	6¢ Maine Statehood	.90
☐1392	6¢ Buffalo	.75
☐1393	6¢ Eisenhower-Reg.	1.10
☐1393D	7¢ Franklin	1.10
☐1394	8¢ Eisenhower	1.00
☐1396	8¢ Postal Service	4.50
☐1397	14¢ F. LaGuardia	1.60
☐1398	16¢ Ernie Pyle	1.60
☐1399	18¢ Dr. E. Blackwell	1.80
☐1400	21¢ A.P. Giannini	2.10
☐1405	6¢ E.L. Masters	.70
☐1406	6¢ Women's Suffrage	.70
☐1407	6¢ So. Carolina	.70
☐1408	6¢ Stone Mountain	.70
☐1409	6¢ Fort Snelling	.70
☐1410-13	6¢ Anti-Pollution	3.00
☐1414	6¢ Nativity	1.10
☐1414a	6¢ Precancelled	1.10
☐1415-18	6¢ Christmas Toys	4.00
☐1415-18a	6¢ Precancelled	12.00
☐1419	6¢ United Nations	.80
☐1420	6¢ Pilgrim Landing	.80
☐1421-22	6¢ D.A.V. & P.O.W.	1.40
☐1423	6¢ Sheep	.70
☐1424	6¢ D. MacArthur	.70
☐1425	6¢ Blood Donors	.70
☐1426	8¢ Mo. Statehood	2.00
☐1427-30	8¢ Wildlife Cons.	2.50
☐1431	8¢ Antarctic Treaty	1.30
☐1432	8¢ Amer. Revolution	2.40
☐1433	8¢ John Sloan	1.10
☐1434-35	8¢ Space Achievement	1.50
☐1436	8¢ Emily Dickinson	1.00
☐1437	8¢ San Juan	1.00
☐1438	8¢ Drug Addiction	1.50
☐1439	8¢ CARE	2.00
☐1440-43	8¢ Historic Pres.	1.50
☐1444	8¢ Nativity	2.00
☐1445	8¢ Partridge	2.00

Scott No.		Fine
☐1446	8¢ Sidney Lanier	1.10
☐1447	8¢ Peace Corps.	1.50
☐1448-51	2¢ Cape Hatteras	.75
☐1452	6¢ Wolf Trap Farm	.80
☐1453	8¢ Yellowstone	1.10
☐1454	15¢ Mt. McKinley	1.75
☐1455	8¢ Family Planning	1.10
☐1456-59	8¢ Colonial Crafts.	1.50
☐1460	6¢ Olympic Games	2.00
☐1461	8¢ Olympic Games	2.50
☐1462	15¢ Olympic Games	3.00
☐1463	8¢ P.T.A.	1.00
☐1464	8¢ Wildlife	1.50
☐1468	8¢ Mail Order	2.00
☐1469	8¢ Osteopathic	1.50
☐1470	8¢ Tom Sawyer	1.10
☐1471	8¢ Xmas-Religious	1.10
☐1472	8¢ Xmas-Santa Claus	1.10
☐1473	8¢ Pharmacy	1.10
☐1474	8¢ Stamp Collectors	1.10
☐1475	8¢ Love	1.10
☐1476	8¢ Pamphlet Printing	1.10
☐1477	8¢ Posting Broadside	1.10
☐1478	8¢ Post Rider	1.10
☐1479	8¢ Drummer	1.10
☐1480-83	8¢ Bost. Tea Party	1.10
☐1484	8¢ George Gershwin	3.75
☐1485	8¢ Robinson Jeffers	1.10
☐1486	8¢ Tanner	1.10
☐1487	8¢ Willa Cather	1.10
☐1488	8¢ N. Copernicus	1.10
☐1500	6¢ Electronics	.90
☐1501	8¢ Electronics	1.10
☐1502	15¢ Electronics	2.00
☐1504	8¢ Angus Cattle	1.00
☐1505	10¢ Chautauqua	1.40
☐1506	10¢ Winter Wheat	1.15
☐1507	8¢ Xmas-Religious	1.10
☐1508	8¢ Xmas-Tree	1.10
☐1510	10¢ Jefferson Mem'l.	1.25
☐1511	10¢ Zip Code	2.00
☐1525	10¢ V.F.W.	1.40
☐1526	10¢ Robert Frost	1.40
☐1527	10¢ EXPO '74–Envir.	1.40
☐1528	10¢ Horse Racing	1.40
☐1529	10¢ Skylab Project	2.00
☐1538-41	10¢ Minerals	1.30
☐1542	10¢ Fort Harrod	1.30
☐1543-46	10¢ Cont. Congress	1.30

Scott No.		Fine
☐1547	10¢ Energy Conserv.	1.25
☐1548	10¢ Sleepy Hollow	1.25
☐1549	10¢ Retarded Children	1.25
☐1550	10¢ Xmas-Religious	1.10
☐1551	10¢ Xmas-Sleigh	1.10
☐1553	10¢ B. West.	1.10
☐1554	10¢ P. Dunbar	1.10
☐1555	10¢ D.W. Griffith	1.25
☐1556	10¢ Pioneer-Jupiter	1.25
☐1557	10¢ Mariner 10	1.25
☐1558	10¢ Collective Barg	1.25
☐1559	8¢ Sybil Ludington	1.15
☐1560	10¢ Salem Poor	1.15
☐1561	10¢ Haym Solomon	1.15
☐1562	18¢ Peter Francisco	2.00
☐1563	10¢ Lex.-Concord	1.75
☐1564	10¢ Bunker Hill	1.75
☐1565–68	10¢ Uniforms	1.75
☐1569–70	10¢ Apollo-Soyuz.	1.75
☐1571	10¢ Women's Year	1.75
☐1572–75	10¢ Postal Service	1.75
☐1576	10¢ World Peace.	1.10
☐1577–78	10¢ Banking & Com..	1.10
☐1579	10¢ Xmas-Religious	1.10
☐1580	10¢ Xmas-Post Card.	3.10
☐1581a	1¢ Ability to Write.	.70
☐1582	2¢ Freedom to Speak	.65
☐1585	4¢ Public that Reads.	.60
☐1591	9¢ Freedom to Assemble	1.10
☐1592	10¢ Justice	1.10
☐1593	11¢ Freedom of Press.	1.20
☐1596	13¢ Eagle & Shield	1.75
☐1603	24¢ Old North Church	3.00
☐1629–31	13¢ Spirit of '76	3.00
☐1632	13¢ Interphil '76	1.60
☐1633–82	13¢ State Flags	1.60
☐1683	13¢ Telephone	1.10
☐1684	13¢ Aviation.	1.10
☐1685	13¢ Chemistry	1.10
☐1690	13¢ Ben Franklin.	1.10
☐1691–94	13¢ Dec. of Indep..	3.00
☐1695–98	13¢ Olympic Games	3.00
☐1699	13¢ Clara Maass	1.80
☐1700	13¢ Adolph Ochs.	1.50
☐1701	13¢ Nativity.	1.40
☐1702	13¢ Winter Pastime	3.00
☐1704	13¢ Wash. at Princeton	1.50
☐1705	13¢ Sound Recording	1.50
☐1706–09	13¢ Pueblo Art (6)	3.50

Scott No.		Fine
☐1710	13¢ Transatlantic Flight	2.00
☐1711	13¢ Colorado	2.00
☐1712	13¢ Butterflies	2.00
☐1716	13¢ Lafayette.	2.00
☐1717–20	20¢, 13¢ Skilled Hands	2.50
☐1721	13¢ Peace Bridge	1.60
☐1722	13¢ Herkimer.	1.60
☐1723–24	24¢, 13¢ Energy	2.00
☐1725	13¢ Alta	1.50
☐1726	13¢ Confederation	1.60
☐1727	13¢ Pictures.	1.60
☐1728	13¢ Saratoga	2.00
☐1730	13¢ Mailbox.	2.00
☐1731	13¢ Sandburg.	1.50
☐1732	13¢ Capt. Cook.	1.60
☐1733	13¢ Capt. Cook R&S	1.60
☐1734	13¢ Indian Cent	1.60
☐1735	15¢ No Value "A" Eagle	1.60
☐1744	13¢ Harriet Tubman	2.00
☐1745–48	13¢ Quilts	3.00
☐1749–52	13¢ Dance	2.50
☐1753	13¢ French Alliance	1.70
☐1754	13¢ Papanicolau	1.75
☐1755	13¢ Jimmie Rodgers.	2.50
☐1756	15¢ George M. Cohan.	2.50
☐1757	13¢ Capex SS	2.50
☐1758	15¢ Photography	2.00
☐1759	15¢ Viking.	2.00
☐1760–63	15¢ Owls	3.00
☐1764–67	15¢ Trees	3.00
☐1768	15¢ Madonna	7.00
☐1769	15¢ Xmas Hobby Horse.	7.00
☐1770	15¢ R.F. Kennedy	1.75
☐1771	15¢ M.L. King.	1.75
☐1772	15¢ Intl. Year of Child	1.75
☐1773	15¢ Steinbeck	1.75
☐1774	15¢ Einstein.	1.75
☐1775–78	15¢ Toleware	3.00
☐1779–82	15¢ Architecture	3.00
☐1783–86	15¢ Endangered Flora.	3.00
☐1788	15¢ Special Olympics	2.00
☐1789	15¢ John Paul Jones	3.00
☐1790	10¢ Olympics	1.60
☐1791–94	15¢ Summer Olympics	2.50
☐1795–98	15¢ Winter Olympics	6.00
☐1799	15¢ Madonna	2.00
☐100	15¢ Xmas Santa	2.00
☐1801	15¢ Will Rogers	2.00
☐1802	15¢ Vietnam Veterans	2.00

Scott No.		Fine
☐1803	15¢ Fields.	1.80
☐1804	15¢ Banneker.	1.80
☐1805–10	15¢ Letter Writing	7.00
☐1811	15¢ Perkins	.70
☐1822	15¢ Madison	2.00
☐1823	15¢ Bissell	1.60
☐1824	15¢ Keller/Sullivan	1.60
☐1825	15¢ Vets. Admin.	1.80
☐1826	15¢ De Galvez	1.80
☐1827–30	15¢ Coral Reefs	7.00
☐1831	15¢ Org. Labor.	1.70
☐1832	15¢ Wharton	2.00
☐1833	15¢ Education	2.50
☐1834–37	15¢ Indian Masks	3.00
☐1838–41	15¢ Architecture	2.40
☐1842	15¢ Christmas Madonna . .	1.70
☐1849	17¢ Rachel Carson	1.70
☐1850	18¢ Geo. Mason	3.50
☐1851	19¢ Sequoyah	1.20
☐1859	35¢ Dr. Charles Drew . . .	1.20
☐1874	15¢ Everett Dirksen	2.00
☐1875	15¢ Whitney Young	2.00
☐1876–79	18¢ Flowers.	3.50
☐1910	18¢ Red Cross	3.00
☐1911	18¢ Savings & Loan	3.00
☐1912–19	18¢ Space Achievement . .	6.50
☐1920	18¢ Management.	3.00
☐1921–24	18¢ Habitats	3.00
☐1925	18¢ Disabled	3.00
☐1926	18¢ Edna St. Vincent Millay .	2.50
☐1928–31	18¢ Architecture	3.50
☐1932	18¢ Babe Zaharias.	3.00
☐1933	18¢ Bobby Jones.	3.00
☐1934	18¢ Remington	3.00
☐1935	18¢ James Hoban	2.50
☐1936	20¢ James Hoban	2.50
☐1937–38	18¢ Yorktown, Virginia. . . .	3.00
☐1939	20¢ Christmas Madonna . .	3.00
☐1940	20¢ Christmas Child Art . . .	3.00
☐1941	20¢ John Hanson	3.00
☐1942–45	20¢ Desert Plants	3.50
☐C69	8¢ Robert H. Goddard . . .	3.00
☐C70	8¢ Alaska Purchase	2.40
☐C71	20¢ Columbia Jays.	5.00
☐C72	10¢ Stars	3.00
☐C74	10¢ 50 Years Airmail	2.50
☐C75	20¢ U.S.A. & Jet.	3.50
☐C76	10¢ Moon Landing.	2.20
☐C77	9¢ Delta Plane	1.25

Scott No.		Fine
☐C78	11¢ Plane Silhouette.	1.50
☐C79	13¢ Letter	1.70
☐C80	17¢ Liberty Head.	2.50
☐C81	21¢ "USA"	2.10
☐C84	11¢ City of Refuge.	1.80
☐C85	11¢ Olympic Games.	1.75
☐C86	11¢ Electronics.	2.00
☐C87	18¢ Statue of Liberty	2.50
☐C88	26¢ Mount Rushmore	3.75
☐C89	5¢ Plane & Globes	4.10
☐C90	31¢ Plane, Flag & Globes. .	4.00
☐C91–2	31¢ Wright Bros.	5.00
☐C93–4	21¢ Chanute	6.00
☐C95–6	25¢ Wiley Post	7.00
☐C97	31¢ Olympics	7.00
☐C98	40¢ Mazzel	5.00
☐C99	28¢ Scott	4.00
☐C100	35¢ Curtiss	4.00
☐E22	45¢ Special Delivery.	11.00
☐E23	60¢ Special Delivery.	7.00

U.S. UNUSED MAIL EARLY INSCRIPTION BLOCKS

Scott No.		Fine
☐1278	1¢ T. Jefferson	.70
☐1280	2¢ F.L. Wright.	.70
☐1281	3¢ Parkman	.70
☐1284	6¢ F.D. Roosevelt	3.00
☐1285	8¢ A. Einstein.	1.10
☐1286	10¢ A. Jackson.	1.25
☐1286A	12¢ Henry Ford.	1.50
☐1288	15¢ O.W. Holmes	4.00
☐1289	20¢ G.C. Marshall	3.00
☐1290	25¢ F. Douglass	3.00
☐1291	30¢ John Dewey	3.50
☐1292	40¢ T. Paine	4.50
☐1293	50¢ Lucy Stone.	5.00
☐1294	$1 E. O'Neill.	11.00
☐1338	6¢ American Flag.	.75
☐1340	6¢ Hemis Fair '68.	.75
☐1341	$1 Airlift	26.00
☐1342	6¢ Support Our Youth . . .	.90
☐1343	6¢ Law & Order.	.90
☐1344	6¢ Register & Vote.	.90
☐1347–49	6¢ Historic Flags	.90
☐1355	6¢ Walt Disney	1.50
☐1356	6¢ Fr. Marquette	1.00
☐1357	6¢ Daniel Boone	.70
☐1358	6¢ Arkansas River	.70
☐1359	6¢ Leif Erikson	.70

Scott No.		Fine	Scott No.		Fine
☐ 1360	6¢ Cherokee Strip	.80	☐ 1432	8¢ Bicentennial	1.50
☐ 1361	6¢ Trumbull Painting	.75	☐ 1433	8¢ J. Sloan Painting	1.40
☐ 1362	6¢ Wildlife Conserv.	1.10	☐ 1434–35	8¢ Space Accomp	1.40
☐ 1364	6¢ American Indian	1.75	☐ 1436	8¢ Emily Dickinson	1.40
☐ 1365–68	6¢ Beautify America	6.00	☐ 1437	8¢ San Juan	1.40
☐ 1369	6¢ American Legion	.70	☐ 1438	8¢ Drug Addiction	1.40
☐ 1370	6¢ Grandma Moses	.75	☐ 1439	8¢ CARE	1.40
☐ 1371	6¢ Apollo 8	2.10	☐ 1440–43	8¢ Historic Press	1.40
☐ 1372	6¢ W.C. Handy	.95	☐ 1444	8¢ Nativity (4)	2.75
☐ 1373	6¢ California	.70	☐ 1445	8¢ Partridge (4)	2.75
☐ 1374	6¢ J.W. Powell	.70	☐ 1446	8¢ Sidney Lanier	1.10
☐ 1375	6¢ Alabama	.70	☐ 1447	8¢ Peace Corps	1.50
☐ 1376–79	6¢ Botanical	12.00	☐ 1448–51	2¢ Hatteras (8)	1.25
☐ 1380	6¢ Dartmouth Case	.70	☐ 1452	6¢ Wolf Trap Farm	.80
☐ 1381	6¢ Baseball	3.50	☐ 1453	8¢ Yellowstone	1.10
☐ 1382	6¢ Football	1.50	☐ 1454	15¢ Mt. McKinley	1.75
☐ 1383	6¢ Eisenhower	.75	☐ 1455	8¢ Family Planning	1.10
☐ 1385	6¢ Rehabilitation	.75	☐ 1456–59	8¢ Craftman	1.90
☐ 1386	6¢ W.M. Harnett	.70	☐ 1460	8¢ Olympic Games	2.00
☐ 1387–90	6¢ Nat. History	1.10	☐ 1461	8¢ Olympic Games	2.50
☐ 1391	6¢ Maine	.90	☐ 1462	15¢ Olympic Games	3.30
☐ 1392	6¢ Buffalo	.75	☐ 1463	8¢ P.T.A.	1.00
☐ 1393	6¢ Eisenhower	1.10	☐ 1464–67	8¢ Wildlife	1.10
☐ 1393D	7¢ B. Franklin	1.10	☐ 1468	8¢ Mail Order (4)	2.00
☐ 1394	8¢ Eisenhower	1.00	☐ 1469	8¢ Osteopathic	1.80
☐ 1396	8¢ Postal Service (4)	4.50	☐ 1470	8¢ Tom Sawyer	1.10
☐ 1397	14¢ F. LaGuardia	1.70	☐ 1471	8¢ Religious	1.40
☐ 1398	16¢ Ernie Pyle	1.60	☐ 1472	8¢ Santa Claus	1.40
☐ 1399	18¢ Dr. E. Blackwell	1.80	☐ 1473	8¢ Pharmacy	1.10
☐ 1400	21¢ A.P. Giannini	2.10	☐ 1474	8¢ Stamp Collector	1.10
☐ 1405	6¢ E.L. Masters	.70	☐ 1475	8¢ Love	1.60
☐ 1406	6¢ Women's Suffrage	.70	☐ 1476	8¢ Pamphlet Printing	1.10
☐ 1407	6¢ South Carolina	.70	☐ 1477	8¢ Posting Broadside	1.10
☐ 1408	6¢ Stone Mountain	.70	☐ 1478	8¢ Post Rider	1.10
☐ 1409	6¢ Fort Snelling	.70	☐ 1479	8¢ Drummer	1.10
☐ 1410–13	6¢ Anti-Pollution	3.75	☐ 1480–83	8¢ Bost. Tea Party	1.35
☐ 1414	6¢ Nativity	2.10	☐ 1488	8¢ Copernicus	1.10
☐ 1414a	6¢ Precancelled	3.00	☐ 1500	6¢ Electronics	.90
☐ 1415–18	6¢ Christmas Toys	5.00	☐ 1501	8¢ Electronics	1.10
☐ 1415a–18a	6¢ Precancelled	10.00	☐ 1502	15¢ Electronics	2.00
☐ 1419	6¢ United Nations	.80	☐ 1504	8¢ Angus Cattle	1.00
☐ 1420	6¢ Pilgrim Landing	.80	☐ 1505	10¢ Chautauqua	1.40
☐ 1421–22	6¢ D.A. & P.O.W.	1.10	☐ 1506	10¢ Winter Wheat	1.15
☐ 1423	6¢ Sheep	.70	☐ 1507	8¢ Religious (4)	3.00
☐ 1424	6¢ Gen. MacArthur	.70	☐ 1508	8¢ Xmas Tree (4)	3.00
☐ 1425	6¢ Blood Donors	.70	☐ 1510	10¢ Jefferson Mem'l.	1.25
☐ 1426	8¢ Missouri (4)	2.00	☐ 1511	10¢ Zip Code	2.10
☐ 1427–30	8¢ Wildlife	1.90	☐ 1525	10¢ V.F.W.	1.40
☐ 1431	8¢ Antarctic	1.30	☐ 1526	10¢ Robert Frost	1.40

Scott No.		Fine
☐1528	10¢ Horse Racing (4)	1.45
☐1529	10¢ Skylab Project	1.60
☐1538–41	10¢ Minerals	1.70
☐1542	10¢ Fort Harrod	1.70
☐1543–46	10¢ Cont. Cong.	1.70
☐1547	10¢ Energy Cons.	1.70
☐1548	10¢ Sleepy Hollow	1.70
☐1549	10¢ Retarded Children	1.70
☐1550	10¢ Xmas-Religious	2.10
☐1551	10¢ Xmas-Sleigh (4)	1.60
☐1553	10¢ Benjamin West	1.85
☐1554	10¢ Paul Dunbar	1.85
☐1555	10¢ D.W. Griffith	1.85
☐1556	10¢ Pioneer-Jupiter	1.85
☐1557	10¢ Mariner 10	1.85
☐1558	10¢ Coll. Bargaining	1.85
☐1559	8¢ Sybil Ludington	1.70
☐1560	10¢ Salem Poor	1.70
☐1561	10¢ Haym Salomon	1.70
☐1562	18¢ Peter Francisco	3.50
☐1565–68	10¢ Uniforms (4)	1.50
☐1571	10¢ Women's Year	1.35
☐1572–75	10¢ Postal Service (4)	1.35
☐1576	10¢ World Peace	1.35
☐1577–78	10¢ Banking & Comm.	1.40
☐1579	10¢ Xmas-Religious	1.40
☐1580	10¢ Xmas Post Card (4)	1.40
☐1581	1¢ Ability Write	.70
☐1582	2¢ Freedom to Speak	.70
☐1584	3¢ Cast A Ballot	.80
☐1585	4¢ Public that Reads	.90
☐1591	9¢ Freedom to Assemble	1.40
☐1593	11¢ Freedom of Press	1.60
☐1596	13¢ Eagle & Shield	1.60
☐1603	24¢ Old North Church	3.00
☐1632	13¢ Interphil '76	2.10
☐1633–82	13¢ State Flags	4.00
☐1683	13¢ Telephone	2.40
☐1684	13¢ Aviation	2.40
☐1685	13¢ Chemistry	1.75
☐1690	13¢ Ben. Franklin	2.25
☐1691–94	13¢ Independence	2.60
☐1695–98	13¢ Olympic Games	3.00
☐1700	13¢ Adolph Ochs	2.10
☐1701	13¢ "Nativity" (4)	2.00
☐1702	13¢ "Winter Pastime"	2.00
☐1705	13¢ Sound Recording	2.00
☐1710	13¢ Transatlantic	2.00
☐1711	13¢ Colorado	1.90

Scott No.		Fine
☐1712–15	13¢ Butterflies	1.60
☐1716	13¢ Lafayette	2.10
☐1717–20	13¢ Skilled Hands (4)	1.80
☐1721	13¢ Peace Bridge	2.10
☐1725	13¢ California	2.10
☐1726	13¢ Articles of Conf.	2.10
☐1727	13¢ Talking Pictures	2.10
☐1730	13¢ Mailbox	2.10
☐1735	15¢ Eagle Issue "A"	2.40
☐1818	18¢ Eagle Issue "B"	2.75
☐C72	10¢ Stars	5.00
☐C74	10¢ Airmail 50th Ann.	4.00
☐C75	20¢ U.S.A. Airmail	4.50
☐C76	10¢ Moon Landing	2.10
☐C77	9¢ Delta Plane	1.75
☐C78	1¢ Silhouette	2.10
☐C79	13¢ Letter	1.90
☐C80	17¢ Liberty Head	3.00
☐C81	21¢ U.S.A. Airmail	3.00
☐C84	11¢ City of Refuge	2.00
☐C85	11¢ Olympic Games	2.00
☐C86	11¢ Electronics	2.00
☐C87	18¢ Liberty	3.00
☐C88	26¢ Mt. Rushmore	4.00
☐C89	25¢ Plane & Globes	4.10
☐C90	31¢ Plane/Flag/Globes	4.50
☐E22	45¢ Arrows	11.00
☐E23	60¢ Arrows	11.00

U.S. UNUSED CENTER LINE AND ARROW BLOCKS

Scott No.		Fine Ctr Line Blk of 4	Fine Arrow Blk of 4
☐314	1¢ Imperforate	290.00	125.00
☐320	2¢ Imperforate	290.00	125.00
☐343	1¢ Imperforate	65.00	50.00
☐344	2¢ Imperforate	90.00	60.00
☐345	3¢ Imperforate	145.00	110.00
☐346	4¢ Imperforate	275.00	200.00
☐347	5¢ Imperforate	375.00	270.00
☐368	2¢ Lincoln, Imp.	300.00	185.00
☐371	2¢ Alaska-Yukon, Imperf.	380.00	260.00
☐373	2¢ Hudson-Fulton, Imperf.	500.00	280.00
☐383	1¢ Imperforate	50.00	24.00
☐384	2¢ Imperforate	90.00	40.00
☐408	1¢ Imperforate	19.00	8.50

Scott No.		Fine Ctr Line Blk of 4	Fine Arrow Blk of 4
☐409	2¢ Imperforate	21.00	13.00
☐481	1¢ Imperforate	14.00	7.00
☐482	2¢ Imperforate	16.00	10.00
☐484	3¢ Imperforate Type II	100.00	80.00
☐524	5¢ Green & Blk	2400.00	2100.00
☐531	1¢ Offset, Imperf.	110.00	90.00
☐532	2¢ Offset, Imperf. Type IV	300.00	250.00
☐534	2¢ Offset, Imperf. Type Va.	100.00	75.00
☐534A	2¢ Offset, Imp. Type VI	300.00	220.00
☐535	3¢ Offset, Imperf.	90.00	60.00
☐547	$2 Carm. & Blk.	2000.00	1500.00
☐573	$5 Carm. & Blk.	1200.00	1000.00
☐575	1¢ Imperforate	65.00	60.00
☐576	1½¢ Imperf.	18.00	9.00
☐577	2¢ Imperforate	19.00	11.00
☐611	2¢ Harding Imperf.	70.00	65.00
☐620	2¢ Norse-Amer'n	40.00	36.00
☐621	5¢ Norse-Amer'n	110.00	110.00
☐631	1½¢ Harding, Rotary Imperf	29.00	19.00
☐703	2¢ Yorktown	3.50	2.40
☐832	$1 Purple & Blk	45.00	46.00
☐833	$2 Yel./Gm./Blk	110.00	110.00
☐834	$5 Red & Blk.	500.00	450.00
☐C1	6¢ Airmail	500.00	450.00
☐C2	16¢ Airmail	600.00	700.00
☐C3	24¢ Airmail	700.00	700.00
☐C23	36¢ Airmail	4.00	3.00
☐CE2	16¢ Spec. Del. Airmail	3.50	3.00

1927–1940. MINT SHEETS

Scott No.		Fine
☐643	2¢ Vermont	350.00
☐644	2¢ Burgoyne	400.00
☐645	2¢ Valley Forge	250.00
☐646	2¢ Molly Pitcher	230.00
☐647	2¢ Hawaii	850.00
☐648	5¢ Hawaii	2300.00
☐649	2¢ Aeronautics	110.00
☐650	5¢ Aeronautics	700.00
☐651	2¢ George R. Clark	80.00
☐654	2¢ Edison-Flat.	210.00

Scott No.		Fine
☐655	2¢ Edison-Rotary	200.00
☐657	2¢ Sullivan	190.00
☐680	2¢ Fallen Timbers	210.00
☐681	2¢ Ohio River Canal	140.00
☐682	2¢ Mass. Bay	150.00
☐683	2¢ Carolina-Charleston	250.00
☐688	2¢ Braddock	230.00
☐689	2¢ Von Steuben	120.00
☐690	2¢ Pulaski	65.00
☐702	2¢ Red Cross	29.00
☐703	2¢ Yorktown	32.00
☐704	½¢ Wash. Bicent'l	19.00
☐705	1¢ Wash. Bicent'l	24.00
☐706	1½¢ Wash. Bicent'l	90.00
☐707	2¢ Wash. Bicent'l	16.00
☐708	3¢ Wash. Bicent'l	110.00
☐709	4¢ Wash. Bicent'l	55.00
☐710	5¢ Wash. Bicent'l	325.00
☐711	6¢ Wash. Bicent'l	600.00
☐712	7¢ Wash. Bicent'l	75.00
☐713	8¢ Wash. Bicent'l	650.00
☐714	9¢ Wash. Bicent'l	500.00
☐715	10¢ Wash. Bicent'l	2400.00
☐716	2¢ Lake Placid	95.00
☐717	2¢ Arbor Day	40.00
☐718	3¢ Olympics	300.00
☐719	5¢ Olympics	450.00
☐724	3¢ Penn	68.00
☐725	3¢ Webster	130.00
☐726	3¢ Oglethorpe	60.00
☐727	3¢ Newburgh	30.00
☐728	1¢ Chicago	20.00
☐729	3¢ Chicago	29.00
☐732	3¢ N.R.A.	23.00
☐733	3¢ Byrd	77.00
☐734	5¢ Kosciuszko	145.00
☐736	3¢ Maryland	41.00
☐737	3¢ Mother's Day (R)	13.00
☐738	3¢ Mother's Day (F)	20.00
☐739	3¢ Wisconsin	17.00
☐740	1¢ Natl. Parks	6.50
☐741	2¢ Natl. Parks	11.00
☐742	3¢ Natl. Parks	12.50
☐743	4¢ Natl. Parks	40.00
☐744	5¢ Natl. Parks	78.00
☐745	6¢ Natl. Parks	100.00
☐746	7¢ Natl. Parks	70.00
☐747	8¢ Natl. Parks	160.00

Scott No.		Fine	Scott No.		Fine
☐748	9¢ Natl. Parks	150.00	☐861	3¢ Emerson	9.00
☐749	10¢ Natl. Parks	250.00	☐862	5¢ Alcott	42.00
☐772	3¢ Connecticut	16.00	☐863	10¢ Clemens	200.00
☐773	3¢ San Diego	10.00	☐864	1¢ Longfellow	10.00
☐774	3¢ Boulder Dam	10.00	☐865	2¢ Whittier	10.00
☐775	3¢ Michigan	10.00	☐866	3¢ Lowell	12.00
☐776	3¢ Texas	11.00	☐867	5¢ Whitman	50.00
☐777	3¢ Rhode Island	16.00	☐868	10¢ Riley	250.00
☐782	3¢ Arkansas	11.00	☐869	1¢ Mann	9.00
☐783	3¢ Oregon	10.00	☐870	2¢ Hopkins	8.00
☐784	3¢ Susan B. Anthony	17.00	☐871	3¢ Elliot	21.00
☐785	1¢ Army	7.00	☐872	5¢ Willard	58.00
☐786	2¢ Army	8.00	☐873	10¢ B.T. Washington	180.00
☐787	3¢ Army	17.00	☐874	1¢ Audubon	8.00
☐788	4¢ Army	46.00	☐875	2¢ Long	8.50
☐789	5¢ Army	60.00	☐876	3¢ Burbank	10.00
☐790	1¢ Navy	7.00	☐877	5¢ Reed	34.00
☐791	2¢ Navy	7.00	☐878	10¢ Addams	160.00
☐792	3¢ Navy	12.00	☐879	1¢ Fosters	7.50
☐793	4¢ Navy	45.00	☐880	2¢ Sousa	12.00
☐794	5¢ Navy	64.00	☐881	3¢ Herbert	12.00
☐795	3¢ N.W. Territory	9.00	☐882	5¢ MacDowell	60.00
☐796	5¢ Virginia Dare	24.00	☐883	10¢ Nevin	470.00
☐798	3¢ Constitution	10.00	☐884	1¢ Sturat	6.00
☐799	3¢ Hawaii	11.00	☐885	2¢ Whistler	7.00
☐800	3¢ Alaska	11.00	☐886	3¢ St. Gaudens	8.00
☐801	3¢ Puerto Rico	10.00	☐887	5¢ French	60.00
☐802	3¢ Virgin Islands	10.00	☐888	10¢ Remington	240.00
☐835	3¢ Ratification	17.00	☐889	1¢ Whitney	11.00
☐836	3¢ Swede-Finn	12.00	☐890	2¢ Morse	11.00
☐837	3¢ N.W. Territory	35.00	☐891	3¢ McCormick	20.00
☐838	3¢ Iowa	21.00	☐892	5¢ Howe	130.00
☐852	3¢ Golden Gate	9.00	☐893	10¢ Bell	1100.00
☐853	3¢ N.Y. Fair	12.00	☐894	3¢ Pony Express	28.00
☐854	3¢ Inauguration	30.00	☐895	3¢ Pan American	25.00
☐855	3¢ Baseball	50.00	☐896	3¢ Idaho	12.00
☐856	3¢ Canal Zone	18.00	☐897	3¢ Wyoming	12.00
☐857	3¢ Printing	9.00	☐898	3¢ Coronado	12.00
☐858	3¢ Four States	9.00	☐899	1¢ Defense	10.00
☐859	1¢ Irving	7.25	☐900	2¢ Defense	11.00
☐860	2¢ Cooper	8.50	☐901	3¢ Defense	13.00
			☐902	3¢ Emancipation	20.00

NOTE: Mint Sheets from 1941 to date are included with individual listing.

Scott No.			Fine Unused Each	Ave. Unused Each	Fine Used Each	Ave. Used Each
OFFICIAL STAMPS						
1873. CONTINENTAL PRINTING (N-H ADD 70%)						
☐ O1	1¢	Agricultural Department	48.00	30.00	32.00	20.00
☐ O2	2¢		34.00	28.00	14.00	10.00
☐ O3	3¢	....	30.00	19.00	4.00	3.00
☐ O4	4¢		42.00	26.00	14.00	8.00
☐ O5	10¢	....	90.00	55.00	48.00	30.00
☐ O6	12¢		125.00	80.00	60.00	42.00
☐ O7	15¢	....	90.00	55.00	48.00	29.00
☐ O8	24¢		100.00	70.00	60.00	35.00
☐ O9	30¢	....	140.00	90.00	80.00	50.00
☐ O10	1¢	Executive Department	220.00	120.00	90.00	50.00
☐ O11	2¢		140.00	90.00	70.00	40.00
☐ O12	3¢	....	150.00	90.00	70.00	38.00
☐ O13	6¢		220.00	150.00	130.00	90.00
☐ O14	10¢	....	225.00	145.00	130.00	90.00
☐ O15	1¢	Interior Department	15.00	9.00	2.30	1.80
☐ O16	2¢		12.00	8.00	2.00	1.00
☐ O17	3¢	....	21.00	12.00	2.00	1.00
☐ O18	6¢		15.00	9.00	2.00	1.00
☐ O19	10¢	....	12.00	8.00	4.00	2.40
☐ O20	12¢		18.00	11.00	3.00	2.00
☐ O21	15¢	....	36.00	22.00	8.00	5.00
☐ O22	24¢		28.00	18.00	6.00	4.00
☐ O23	30¢	....	38.00	23.00	6.00	3.00
☐ O24	90¢		78.00	45.00	12.00	8.00
☐ O25	1¢	Justice Department	34.00	20.00	18.00	11.00
☐ O26	2¢		50.00	32.00	20.00	12.00
☐ O27	3¢	....	60.00	38.00	7.50	4.50
☐ O28	6¢		50.00	31.00	10.00	6.00
☐ O29	10¢	....	58.00	34.00	24.00	15.00
☐ O30	12¢		40.00	24.00	12.00	7.50
☐ O31	15¢	....	90.00	60.00	48.00	28.00
☐ O32	24¢		275.00	150.00	100.00	70.00
☐ O33	30¢	....	240.00	145.00	90.00	50.00
☐ O34	90¢		350.00	200.00	180.00	100.00
☐ O35	1¢	Navy Department	30.00	18.00	11.00	7.00
☐ O36	2¢		20.00	12.00	9.00	5.50
☐ O37	3¢	....	25.00	15.00	3.50	2.00
☐ O38	6¢		20.00	12.00	5.00	3.50
☐ O39	7¢	....	145.00	100.00	65.00	38.00
☐ O40	10¢		30.00	19.00	11.00	6.00
☐ O41	12¢	....	40.00	22.00	9.00	5.00
☐ O42	15¢		70.00	42.00	26.00	15.00
☐ O43	24¢	....	70.00	42.00	32.00	17.00
☐ O44	30¢		58.00	32.00	14.00	8.00
☐ O45	90¢	....	280.00	160.00	100.00	60.00
☐ O47	1¢	Post Office Department	8.00	5.00	4.00	2.00

Scott No.		Fine Unused Each	Ave. Unused Each	Fine Used Each	Ave. Used Each
☐ 048	2¢	8.00	5.00	3.00	1.75
☐ 049	3¢	3.00	1.80	.90	.60
☐ 050	6¢	8.00	5.00	2.00	1.25
☐ 051	10¢	36.00	20.00	20.00	11.00
☐ 052	12¢	18.00	10.00	5.00	2.50
☐ 053	15¢	20.00	12.00	8.00	4.50
☐ 054	24¢	28.00	15.00	9.00	5.00
☐ 055	30¢	26.00	15.00	8.00	5.00
☐ 056	90¢	42.00	26.00	12.00	7.00
☐ 057	1¢ State Department	39.00	20.00	12.00	6.50
☐ 058	2¢	86.00	50.00	30.00	18.00
☐ 059	3¢	38.00	19.00	9.00	5.00
☐ 060	6¢	36.00	18.00	8.50	5.00
☐ 061	7¢	60.00	36.00	18.00	10.00
☐ 062	10¢	65.00	20.00	13.00	8.00
☐ 063	12¢	78.00	43.00	30.00	18.00
☐ 064	15¢	60.00	34.00	18.00	10.00
☐ 065	24¢	150.00	90.00	88.00	50.00
☐ 066	30¢	135.00	80.00	60.00	38.00
☐ 067	90¢	300.00	180.00	118.00	80.00
☐ 068	$2	450.00	300.00	210.00	150.00
☐ 072	1¢ Treasury Department	15.00	7.00	2.00	1.10
☐ 073	2¢	19.00	12.00	2.10	1.15
☐ 074	3¢	13.00	6.00	1.50	.70
☐ 075	6¢	19.00	12.00	1.50	.70
☐ 076	7¢	39.00	22.00	13.00	6.50
☐ 077	10¢	38.00	22.00	4.00	3.10
☐ 078	12¢	39.00	22.00	3.00	1.35
☐ 079	15¢	38.00	23.00	4.50	2.00
☐ 080	24¢	160.00	100.00	60.00	34.00
☐ 081	30¢	50.00	30.00	4.00	3.00
☐ 082	90¢	66.00	35.00	4.00	2.50
☐ 083	1¢ War Department	56.00	33.00	5.00	2.50
☐ 084	2¢	50.00	30.00	7.00	3.00
☐ 085	3¢	45.00	30.00	3.00	.95
☐ 086	6¢	225.00	150.00	4.50	2.10
☐ 087	7¢	45.00	34.00	29.00	16.00
☐ 088	10¢	18.00	11.00	3.50	2.40
☐ 089	12¢	55.00	38.00	3.00	1.80
☐ 090	15¢	18.00	10.00	1.90	1.25
☐ 091	24¢	18.00	10.00	2.25	1.65
☐ 092	30¢	18.00	12.00	2.25	1.40
☐ 093	90¢	38.00	25.00	11.00	6.00

1879. AMERICAN PRINTING—SOFT POROUS PAPER (N-H ADD 80%)

☐ 094	1¢ Agricultural Department	1300.00	700.00	—	—
☐ 095	3¢	160.00	100.00	30.00	25.00

Scott No.			Fine Unused Each	Ave. Unused Each	Fine Used Each	Ave. Used Each
☐ O96	1¢	Interior Department	120.00	79.00	69.00	41.00
☐ O97	2¢		3.00	1.80	1.10	.70
☐ O98	3¢		2.00	1.50	1.00	.65
☐ O99	6¢		3.00	2.00	1.30	.85
☐ O100	10¢		32.00	19.00	20.00	12.00
☐ O101	12¢		60.00	32.00	36.00	21.00
☐ O102	15¢		140.00	85.00	72.00	43.00
☐ O103	24¢		1050.00	700.00	—	—
☐ O106	3¢	Justice Department	48.00	30.00	20.00	13.00
☐ O107	6¢		98.00	64.00	71.00	43.00
☐ O108	3¢	Post Office Department	10.00	6.00	2.00	.90
☐ O109	3¢	Treasury Department	25.00	15.00	3.00	1.80
☐ O110	6¢		50.00	33.00	22.00	13.00
☐ O111	10¢		65.00	42.00	19.00	12.00
☐ O112	30¢		710.00	400.00	140.00	85.00
☐ O113	90¢		710.00	400.00	140.00	85.00
☐ O114	1¢	War Department	2.90	1.60	1.45	.75
☐ O115	2¢		3.00	1.90	1.20	.90
☐ O116	3¢		3.00	1.90	1.00	.65
☐ O117	6¢		3.00	1.90	1.00	.65
☐ O118	10¢		18.00	11.00	8.00	5.00
☐ O119	12¢		14.00	7.00	2.50	1.70
☐ O120	30¢		42.00	26.00	30.00	16.00

1910–1911. POSTAL SAVINGS (N-H ADD 70%)

			Fine Unused Each	Ave. Unused Each	Fine Used Each	Ave. Used Each
☐ O121	2¢	Black, D.L. Wmk	11.00	6.00	1.10	.80
☐ O122	50¢	Dark Green, D.L. Wmk	100.00	70.00	34.00	18.00
☐ O123	$1	Ultramarine, D.L. Wmk	100.00	70.00	12.00	7.00
☐ O124	1¢	Dark Violet, S.L. Wmk	4.00	3.00	1.50	.80
☐ O125	2¢	Black, S.L. Wmk	38.00	21.00	4.00	2.50
☐ O126	10¢	Carmine, S.L. Wmk	8.00	6.00	1.30	.75

Scott No.			Fine Unused Block	Ave. Unused Block	Fine Unused Each	Ave. Unused Each	Fine Used Each	Ave. Used Each
1912. PARCEL POST DUE (N-H ADD 45%)								
☐ JQ1	1¢	Dark Green	125.00	60.00	16.00	9.00	5.00	3.00
☐ JQ2	2¢	Dark Green	600.00	400.00	100.00	68.00	26.00	15.50
☐ JQ3	5¢	Dark Green	125.00	85.00	18.00	11.00	6.00	3.50
☐ JQ4	10¢	Dark Green	1500.00	1000.00	190.00	130.00	50.00	30.00
☐ JQ5	25¢	Dark Green	600.00	450.00	100.00	62.00	6.00	4.00
1912–1913. PARCEL POST STAMPS (N-H ADD 45%)								
☐ Q1	1¢	P.O. Clerk	55.00	32.00	4.00	3.10	1.60	.80
☐ Q2	2¢	City Carrier	62.00	45.00	5.00	3.80	.90	.65
☐ Q3	3¢	Railway Clerk	125.00	95.00	14.00	8.50	6.00	3.50
☐ Q4	4¢	Rural Carrier	150.00	110.00	38.00	22.00	2.90	1.90
☐ Q5	5¢	Mail Train	200.00	140.00	40.00	26.00	2.10	1.25
☐ Q6	10¢	Steamship	225.00	180.00	56.00	38.00	3.00	1.75

Scott No.		Fine Unused Block	Ave. Unused Block	Fine Unused Each	Ave. Unused Each	Fine Used Each	Ave. Used Each
☐Q7	15¢ Mail Truck	420.00	270.00	60.00	48.00	9.00	5.00
☐Q8	20¢ Airplane	750.00	550.00	150.00	90.00	20.00	10.00
☐Q9	25¢ Manufacturing	410.00	280.00	80.00	50.00	6.00	3.50
☐Q10	50¢ Dairying	1600.00	1300.00	220.00	170.00	41.00	28.00
☐Q11	75¢ Harvesting	470.00	400.00	80.00	60.00	40.00	22.00
☐Q12	$1 Fruit Growing	2200.00	1600.00	400.00	210.00	30.00	24.00

1925–1929. SPECIAL HANDLING STAMPS (N-H ADD 35%)

☐QE1	10¢ Yellow Green	30.00	18.00	2.25	1.50	1.50	.75
☐QE2	15¢ Yellow Green	40.00	26.00	2.50	1.90	1.50	.70
☐QE3	20¢ Yellow Green	42.00	26.00	4.00	2.75	2.25	1.00
☐QE4	25¢ Yellow Green	300.00	200.00	30.00	21.00	10.00	4.00
☐QE4A	25¢ Deep Green	350.00	200.00	36.00	26.00	9.00	4.00

1919–1922. U.S. OFFICES IN CHINA (N-H ADD 60%)
SHANGHAI 2¢ CHINA

☐K1	2¢ on 1¢	100.00	70.00	20.00	13.00	21.00	13.00
☐K2	4¢ on 2¢	100.00	70.00	20.00	13.00	21.00	13.00
☐K3	6¢ on 3¢	240.00	150.00	41.00	24.00	42.00	30.00
☐K4	8¢ on 4¢	260.00	180.00	41.00	38.00	45.00	30.00
☐K5	10¢ on 5¢	310.00	210.00	50.00	38.00	58.00	38.00
☐K6	12¢ on 6¢	290.00	215.00	55.00	38.00	58.00	36.00
☐K7	14¢ on 7¢	300.00	220.00	60.00	38.00	60.00	46.00
☐K8	16¢ on 8¢ Olive Bistre	280.00	200.00	55.00	36.00	55.00	34.00
☐K8a	16¢ on 8¢ Olive Green	290.00	200.00	55.00	34.00	55.00	41.00
☐K9	18¢ on 9¢	300.00	190.00	60.00	36.00	55.00	41.00
☐K10	20¢ on 10¢	300.00	190.00	60.00	36.00	56.00	36.00
☐K11	24¢ on 12¢ Br. Car	300.00	190.00	60.00	36.00	56.00	37.00
☐K11a	24¢ on 12¢ Cl. Br.	320.00	270.00	70.00	45.00	70.00	58.00
☐K12	30¢ on 15¢	300.00	220.00	65.00	38.00	70.00	50.00
☐K13	40¢ on 20¢	400.00	300.00	100.00	60.00	80.00	60.00
☐K14	60¢ on 30¢	400.00	300.00	85.00	52.00	80.00	60.00
☐K15	$1 on 50¢	3000.00	1600.00	610.00	360.00	400.00	300.00
☐K16	$2 on $1	2000.00	1400.00	460.00	280.00	325.00	280.00
☐K17	2¢ on 1¢ Loc. Sur	350.00	290.00	90.00	58.00	72.00	45.00
☐K18	4¢ on 2¢ Loc. Sur	340.00	240.00	82.00	52.00	73.00	45.00

Scott No.		Imperforated (a)		Part Perforated (b)		Perforated (c)	
		Fine	Ave.	Fine	Ave.	Fine	Ave.

1862–1971. UNITED STATES REVENUE STAMPS

☐R1	1¢ Express	54.00	36.00	40.00	24.00	1.10	.70
☐R2	1¢ Play Cards	750.00	475.00	385.00	230.00	90.00	55.00
☐R3	1¢ Proprietary	450.00	300.00	90.00	65.00	.40	.35
☐R4	1¢ Telegraph	260.00	175.00	—	—	7.50	4.50
☐R5	2¢ Bank Ck., Blue	.85	.65	1.10	.75	.21	.16
☐R6	2¢ Bank Ck., Orange	—	—	72.00	41.00	.18	.13
☐R7	2¢ Certif., Blue	11.00	6.00	—	—	28.00	14.00
☐R8	2¢ Certif., Orange	—	—	—	—	24.00	13.00

*No hinge pricing from 1941 to date is figured at (N-H ADD 15%)

Scott No.		Imperforated (a)		Part Perforated (b)		Perforated (c)	
		Fine	Ave.	Fine	Ave.	Fine	Ave.
☐R9	2¢ Express, Blue	11.00	6.50	14.00	8.50	.35	.16
☐R10	2¢ Express, Orange	—	—	—	—	6.00	4.00
☐R11	2¢ Ply. Cds., Blue	—	—	125.00	70.00	3.10	1.50
☐R12	2¢ Ply. Cds., Orange ...	—	—	—	—	23.00	16.00
☐R13	2¢ Proprietary, Blue	—	—	90.00	55.00	.35	.21
☐R14	2¢ Proprietary, Orange ...	—	—	—	—	32.00	18.00
☐R15	2¢ U.S.I.R.	—	—	—	—	.16	.14
☐R16	3¢ Foreign Ex.	—	—	140.00	78.00	2.25	1.10
☐R17	3¢ Playing Cds.	—	—	—	—	95.00	55.00
☐R18	3¢ Proprietary	—	—	140.00	90.00	1.80	.85
☐R19	3¢ Telegraph	46.00	29.00	16.00	8.00	2.10	1.25
☐R20	4¢ Inland Exch.	—	—	—	—	1.75	.90
☐R21	4¢ Playing Cards	—	—	—	—	340.00	190.00
☐R22	4¢ Proprietary	—	—	170.00	100.00	2.70	1.30
☐R23	5¢ Agreement	—	—	—	—	.35	.16
☐R24	5¢ Certificate	2.50	1.30	10.00	5.00	.21	.16
☐R25	....	4.00	3.00	5.00	3.10	.35	.20
☐R26	5¢ Foreign Ex.	—	—	—	—	.60	.21
☐R27	5¢ Inland Exch.	3.75	2.20	3.50	2.00	.27	.16
☐R28	5¢ Playing Cds.	—	—	—	—	12.00	6.50
☐R29	5¢ Proprietary	—	—	—	—	18.00	9.00
☐R30	6¢ Inland Exch.	—	—	—	—	1.00	.65
☐R32	10¢ Bill of Ldg.	46.00	32.00	150.00	76.00	.85	.45
☐R33	10¢ Certificate	86.00	60.00	90.00	65.00	.35	.18
☐R34	10¢ Contract Bill	—	—	92.00	65.00	.36	.18
☐R35	10¢ For Ex. Bill	—	—	—	—	4.50	2.65
☐R36	10¢ Inland Exch.	115.00	70.00	3.10	2.10	.36	.18
☐R37	10¢ Power of Aty.	310.00	200.00	22.00	18.00	.40	.22
☐R38	10¢ Proprietary	—	—	—	—	16.00	8.00
☐R39	15¢ Foreign Exch.	—	—	—	—	12.00	8.00
☐R40	15¢ Inland Exch.	26.00	14.00	12.00	7.00	1.20	.60
☐R41	20¢ Foreign Exch.	42.00	30.00	—	—	28.00	16.00
☐R42	20¢ Inland Exch.	13.00	8.00	17.00	10.00	.50	.26
☐R43	25¢ Bond	91.00	56.00	7.00	4.00	2.25	1.10
☐R44	25¢ Certificate	9.50	8.00	7.50	4.10	.35	.18
☐R45	25¢ Entry of Gds.	22.00	14.00	36.00	24.00	1.40	.75
☐R46	25¢ Insurance	11.00	8.00	12.00	7.00	.85	.50
☐R47	25¢ Life Insur.	34.00	26.00	84.00	60.00	4.00	2.10
☐R48	25¢ Power of Atty.	7.50	4.00	20.00	12.00	.70	.36
☐R49	25¢ Protest	24.00	16.00	150.00	120.00	7.00	3.50
☐R50	25¢ Warehouse Rct.	45.00	30.00	150.00	120.00	25.00	16.00
☐R51	30¢ Foreign Exch.	65.00	45.00	310.00	200.00	45.00	20.00
☐R52	30¢ Inland Exch.	39.00	30.00	36.00	24.00	2.75	1.25
☐R53	40¢ Inland Exch.	410.00	260.00	4.00	2.90	3.00	1.40
☐R54	50¢ Convey, Blue	11.00	7.00	1.40	.85	.40	.21
☐R55	50¢ Entry of Gds.	—	—	12.00	6.00	.55	.21
☐R56	50¢ Foreign Exch.	36.00	21.00	34.00	18.00	4.00	2.25
☐R57	50¢ Lease	22.00	12.50	52.00	31.00	6.00	2.90

*No hinge pricing from 1941 to date is figured at (N-H ADD 15%)

Scott No.		Imperforated (a) Fine	Ave.	Part Perforated (b) Fine	Ave.	Perforated (c) Fine	Ave.
☐R58	50¢ Life Insur.	28.00	16.00	51.00	41.00	.80	.45
☐R59	50¢ Mortgage	10.00	7.00	2.10	1.50	.50	.30
☐R60	50¢ Orig. Process	2.50	1.60	—	—	.50	.26
☐R61	50¢ Passage Tkt.	70.00	38.00	100.00	60.00	.70	.30
☐R62	50¢ Prob. of Will	31.00	20.00	41.00	25.00	18.00	10.00
☐R63	50¢ Sty. Bond, Bl.	110.00	65.00	3.00	2.00	.40	.18
☐R64	60¢ Inland Exch.	75.00	42.00	43.00	26.00	5.00	3.00
☐R65	70¢ Foreign Exch.	270.00	160.00	85.00	45.00	5.00	3.00
☐R66	$1 Conveyance	11.00	7.00	240.00	140.00	2.70	1.25
☐R67	$1 Entry of Gds.	25.00	15.00	—	—	1.70	.90
☐R68	$1 Foreign Exch.	50.00	28.00	—	—	.75	.42
☐R69	$1 Inland Exch.	11.00	7.00	210.00	129.00	.70	.30
☐R70	$1 Lease	34.00	18.00	—	—	1.65	.85
☐R71	$1 Life Insur.	135.00	75.00	—	—	4.50	2.60
☐R72	$1 Manifest	50.00	30.00	—	—	22.00	12.00
☐R73	$1 Mortgage	16.00	10.00	—	—	125.00	70.00
☐R74	$1 Passage Tkt.	150.00	90.00	—	—	140.00	70.00
☐R75	$1 Power of Atty.	60.00	38.00	—	—	1.75	1.00
☐R76	$1 Prob. of Will	55.00	28.00	—	—	32.00	16.00
☐R77	$1.30 Foreign Exch.	1400.00	1100.00	—	—	43.00	24.00
☐R78	$1.50 Inland Exch.	24.00	12.00	—	—	3.10	1.80
☐R79	$1.60 Foreign Exch.	600.00	310.00	—	—	90.00	48.00
☐R80	$1.90 Foreign Exch.	1600.00	1000.00	—	—	51.00	30.00
☐R81	$2 Conveyance	95.00	55.00	650.00	370.00	2.00	1.10
☐R82	$2 Mortgage	72.00	41.00	—	—	2.40	1.30
☐R83	$2 Prob. of Will	1600.00	1100.00	—	—	40.00	22.00
☐R84	$2.50 Inland Exch.	900.00	550.00	—	—	3.00	2.00
☐R85	$3 Chart. Pty.	95.00	52.00	—	—	4.00	2.10
☐R86	$3 Manifest	84.00	46.00	—	—	20.00	11.00
☐R87	$3.50 Inland Exch.	650.00	475.00	—	—	42.00	24.00
☐R88	$5 Chtr. Party	200.00	120.00	—	—	6.00	3.00
☐R89	$5 Conveyance	30.00	17.00	—	—	5.00	2.80
☐R90	$5 Manifest	86.00	50.00	—	—	80.00	45.00
☐R91	$5 Mortgage	80.00	50.00	—	—	18.00	9.00
☐R92	$5 Prob. of Will	360.00	200.00	—	—	18.00	9.00
☐R93	$10 Chrt. Party	390.00	220.00	—	—	22.00	13.00
☐R94	$10 Conveyance	80.00	46.00	—	—	60.00	32.00
☐R95	$10 Mortgage	290.00	160.00	—	—	22.00	12.00
☐R96	$10 Prob. of Will	900.00	500.00	—	—	22.00	12.00
☐R97	$15 Mortgage	810.00	450.00	—	—	90.00	55.00
☐R98	$20 Conveyance	57.00	36.00	—	—	34.00	19.00
☐R99	$20 Prob. of Will	800.00	470.00	—	—	750.00	480.00
☐R100	$25 Mortgage	650.00	375.00	—	—	90.00	50.00
☐R101	$50 U.S.I.R.	165.00	95.00	—	—	80.00	50.00
☐R102	$200 U.S.I.R.	1000.00	600.00	—	—	500.00	300.00

*No hinge pricing from 1941 to date is figured at (N-H ADD 15%)

1871. SECOND ISSUE
R103 THROUGH R131
HAVE BLUE FRAMES
AND A BLACK CENTER

Scott No.		Fine Used Each	Ave. Used Each
☐R103	1¢	26.00	15.00
☐R104	2¢	1.20	.60
☐R105	3¢	14.00	8.00
☐R106	4¢	42.00	25.00
☐R107	5¢	1.25	.65
☐R108	6¢	65.00	36.00
☐R109	10¢	.90	.55
☐R110	15¢	24.00	15.00
☐R111	20¢	5.00	3.50
☐R112	25¢	.60	.45
☐R113	30¢	50.00	28.00
☐R114	40¢	28.00	16.00
☐R115	50¢	.70	.40
☐R116	60¢	56.00	31.00
☐R117	70¢	24.00	12.00
☐R118	$1	3.00	1.75
☐R119	$1.30	225.00	120.00
☐R120	$1.50	12.00	7.00
☐R121	$1.60	275.00	160.00
☐R122	$1.90	125.00	72.00
☐R123	$2	11.00	6.00
☐R124	$2.50	21.00	10.00
☐R125	$3	30.00	17.00
☐R126	$3.50	110.00	60.00
☐R127	$5	16.00	9.00
☐R128	$10	85.00	52.00
☐R129	$20	270.00	150.00
☐R130	$25	290.00	140.00
☐R131	$50	260.00	170.00

1871–1872. THIRD ISSUE
SAME DESIGNS AS
SECOND ISSUE

Scott No.		Fine Used Each	Ave. Used Each
☐R134	1¢ Claret & Blk.	22.00	12.00
☐R135	2¢ Org. & Blk.	.18	.20
☐R136	4¢ Bm. & Blk.	28.00	15.00
☐R137	5¢ Org. & Blk.	.35	.16
☐R138	6¢ Rog. & Blk.	27.00	16.00
☐R139	15¢ Bm. & Blk.	10.00	6.00
☐R140	30¢ Org. & Blk.	11.00	6.00
☐R141	40¢ Bm. & Blk.	22.00	13.00
☐R142	60¢ Org. & Blk.	45.00	26.00
☐R143	70¢ Gm. & Blk.	31.00	18.00
☐R144	$1 Gm. & Blk.	1.80	.75
☐R145	$2 Verm'n & Blk.	22.00	12.00
☐R146	$2.50 Claret & Blk.	32.00	16.00
☐R147	$3 Gm. & Blk.	32.00	20.00
☐R148	$5 Verm'n & Blk.	20.00	9.00
☐R149	$10 Gm. & Blk.	75.00	42.00
☐R150	$20 Org. & Blk.	380.00	210.00

1874. FOURTH ISSUE

Scott No.		Fine Used Each	Ave. Used Each
☐R151	2¢ Org. & Blk., Gm. Paper	.16	.13

1875. ISSUE

Scott No.		Fine Used Each	Ave. Used Each
☐R152a	2¢ Blue, Silk Paper	.16	.13
☐R152b	2¢ Blue, Watermarked	.16	.13
☐R152c	2¢ Blue, Rouletted	28.00	16.00

Scott No.		Fine Un-cancelled Each	Ave. Un-cancelled Each	Fine Used Each	Ave. Used Each
1898. POSTAGE AND NEWSPAPER STAMPS SURCHARGED I.R.					
☐R153	1¢ Green, Small I.R.	1.20	.65	.70	.40
☐R154	1¢ Green, Large I.R.	.30	.21	.21	.16
☐R154a	1¢ Green Inverted Surch	8.00	5.00	5.50	3.00
☐R155	2¢ Carmine, Large I.R.	.26	.22	.60	.26
☐R155a	2¢ Carmine, Inverted Surch	1.50	.79	1.10	.70
☐R159	$5 Blue, Surch. down	170.00	100.00	120.00	75.00
☐R160	$5 Blue, Surch. up	84.00	46.00	55.00	30.00
1898. DOCUMENTARY "BATTLESHIP" DESIGN					
☐R161	½¢ Orange	2.00	3.00	6.00	4.00
☐R162	½¢ Dark Gray	.26	.20	.16	.13
☐R163	1¢ Pale Blue	.26	.18	.16	.13
☐R164	2¢ Carmine	.26	.18	.16	.13
☐R165	3¢ Dark Blue	.85	.40	.21	.13
☐R166	4¢ Pale Rose	.40	.26	.18	.13
☐R167	5¢ Lilac	.26	.18	.16	.12
☐R168	10¢ Dark Brown	.40	.21	.18	.12
☐R169	25¢ Purple Brown	.40	.21	.18	.16
☐R170	40¢ Blue Lilac (cut .25)	50.00	25.00	1.15	.90
☐R171	50¢ Slate Violet	3.90	2.10	.18	.15
☐R172	80¢ Bistre (cut .15)	21.00	11.00	.40	.26
1898–1899. DOCUMENTARY STAMPS					
☐R173	$1 Dark Green	3.80	2.10	.22	.18
☐R174	$3 Dark Brown (cut. 18)	7.00	4.00	.46	.35
☐R175	$5 Orange (cut .25)	—	—	1.20	.90
☐R176	$10 Black (cut .75)	—	—	3.00	2.40
☐R177	$30 Red (cut 25.00)	—	—	70.00	42.00
☐R178	$50 Gray Brown (cut 1.50)	—	—	4.00	2.50
☐R179	$100 Brown & Black (cut 12.00)	—	—	32.00	12.00
☐R180	$500 Lake & Black (cut 180.00)	—	—	415.00	290.00
☐R181	$100 Green & Black (cut 100.00)	—	—	310.00	260.00
1900. DOCUMENTARY STAMPS					
☐R182	$1 Carmine (cut .15)	5.00	3.00	.50	.32
☐R183	$3 Lake (cut 8.00)	56.00	34.00	36.00	21.00
1900–1902. SURCHARGED LARGE BLACK NUMERALS					
☐R184	$1 Gray (cut .09)	3.00	1.50	.21	.16
☐R185	$2 Gray (cut .09)	2.65	1.60	.21	.16
☐R186	$3 Gray (cut 1.15)	25.00	16.00	10.00	7.50
☐R187	$5 Gray (cut .40)	17.00	10.00	6.00	4.50
☐R188	$10 Gray (cut 3.25)	40.00	24.00	16.00	6.00
☐R189	$50 Gray (cut 80.00)	510.00	290.00	320.00	185.00
☐R190	$1 Green (cut .35)	7.00	4.00	2.50	1.10
☐R191	$2 Green (cut .30)	6.00	3.00	1.10	1.00
☐R192	$5 Green (cut 1.60)	41.00	23.00	15.00	8.00
☐R193	$10 Green (cut 27.50)	210.00	125.00	140.00	85.00
☐R194	$50 Green (cut 220.00)	900.00	550.00	650.00	400.00

Scott No.		Fine Un-cancelled Each	Ave. Un-cancelled Each	Fine Used Each	Ave. Used Each
1914. DOCUMENTARY SINGLE LINE WATERMARK					
☐R195	½¢ Rose	4.50	3.00	2.00	1.25
☐R196	1¢ Rose	1.50	.75	.26	.16
☐R197	2¢ Rose	1.50	.75	.26	.16
☐R198	3¢ Rose	27.00	19.00	20.00	10.00
☐R199	4¢ Rose	6.00	4.30	.85	.70
☐R200	5¢ Rose	2.15	1.60	.42	.22
☐R201	10¢ Rose	2.10	1.50	.32	.16
☐R202	25¢ Rose	11.00	6.00	.65	.35
☐R203	40¢ Rose	9.00	6.00	.85	.50
☐R204	50¢ Rose	3.50	1.80	.60	.36
☐R205	80¢ Rose	36.00	24.00	6.00	4.00
1914. DOCUMENTARY DOUBLE LINE WATERMARK					
☐R206	½¢ Rose	1.10	.65	.60	.35
☐R207	1¢ Rose	.23	.21	.21	.13
☐R208	2¢ Rose	.23	.21	.21	.13
☐R209	3¢ Rose	.95	.36	.38	.16
☐R210	4¢ Rose	1.80	1.40	.65	.31
☐R211	5¢ Rose	.92	.55	.24	.18
☐R212	10¢ Rose	.75	.50	.18	.12
☐R213	25¢ Rose	3.50	2.10	.95	.40
☐R214	40¢ Rose (cut .60)	30.00	17.00	5.00	3.00
☐R215	50¢ Rose	7.00	3.50	.36	.18
☐R216	80¢ Rose (cut 1.10)	38.00	25.00	8.00	6.00
☐R217	$1 Green (cut .06)	6.50	2.50	.33	.21
☐R218	$2 Carmine (cut .10)	21.00	9.00	.60	.35
☐R219	$2 Carmine (cut .25)	30.00	19.00	2.00	.95
☐R220	$5 Blue (cut .65)	27.00	16.00	2.50	1.75
☐R221	$10 Orange (cut 1.10)	45.00	30.00	7.00	4.00
☐R222	$30 Vermilion (cut 2.35)	120.00	78.00	14.00	9.00
☐R223	$50 Violet (cut 200.00)	800.00	560.00	600.00	400.00
☐R224	$60 Brown (cut 47.50)	—	—	100.00	70.00
☐R225	$100 Green (cut 14.50)	—	—	42.00	26.00
1917–1933. TENTH ISSUE DOCUMENTARY STAMPS—PERF. 11					
☐R228	1¢ Rose	.24	.21	.20	.13
☐R229	2¢ Rose	.18	.17	.16	.11
☐R230	3¢ Rose	.35	.31	.28	.20
☐R231	4¢ Rose	.32	.26	.18	.11
☐R232	5¢ Rose	.32	.26	.18	.11
☐R233	8¢ Rose	1.50	1.00	.24	.15
☐R234	10¢ Rose	.60	.26	.18	.13
☐R235	20¢ Rose	.65	.26	.18	.13
☐R236	25¢ Rose	.70	.26	.18	.14
☐R237	40¢ Rose	.80	.25	.16	.13
☐R238	50¢ Rose	.90	.25	.16	.13
☐R239	80¢ Rose	2.60	2.00	.16	.14

Scott No.		Fine Un-cancelled Each	Ave. Un-cancelled Each	Fine Used Each	Ave. Used Each
☐R240	$1 Green	2.40	2.00	.21	.13
☐R241	$2 Rose	7.00	6.00	.21	.13
☐R242	$3 Violet (cut .15)	22.00	13.00	.40	.04
☐R243	$4 Brown (cut .20)	14.00	7.00	1.10	.85
☐R244	$5 Blue (cut .13)	10.00	7.00	.35	.28
☐R245	$10 Orange (cut .20)	15.00	10.00	.65	.40

1917. DOCUMENTARY STAMPS—PERF. 12

☐R246	$30 Vermilion (cut .80)	27.00	17.00	3.00	2.00
☐R247	$60 Brown (cut 1.00)	36.00	22.00	9.00	4.00
☐R248	$100 Green (cut .45)	25.00	14.00	2.50	.60
☐R249	$500 Blue (cut 9.50)	—	—	34.00	21.00
☐R250	$1000 Orange (cut 3.50)	86.00	50.00	53.00	40.00

1928–1929. DOCUMENTARY STAMPS—PERF. 10

☐R251	1¢ Carmine Rose	1.70	1.10	.65	.50
☐R252	2¢ Carmine Rose	.45	.35	.26	.16
☐R253	4¢ Carmine Rose	5.00	3.00	3.10	1.60
☐R254	5¢ Carmine Rose	.95	.60	.32	.20
☐R255	10¢ Carmine Rose	1.60	.85	.80	.50
☐R256	20¢ Carmine Rose	4.00	2.50	3.20	1.10
☐R257	$1 Green (cut 1.90)	50.00	32.00	28.00	16.50
☐R258	$2 Rose	9.00	7.00	.90	.65
☐R259	$10 Orange (cut 8.00)	60.00	45.00	23.00	18.00

1929–1930. DOCUMENTARY STAMPS—PERF. 11 x 10

☐R260	2¢ Carmine Rose	2.25	1.50	1.25	.65
☐R261	5¢ Carmine Rose	1.90	1.10	.85	.55
☐R262	10¢ Carmine Rose	7.00	4.00	3.25	2.50
☐R263	20¢ Carmine Rose	13.00	7.50	4.00	4.00

Scott No.		Fine Used Each	Ave. Used Each	Fine Used Each	Ave. Used Each
		Violet Paper (a)		Green Paper (b)	

1871–1874. PROPRIETARY (ALL USED)

☐RB1	1¢ Green & Black	4.00	2.00	5.00	3.00
☐RB2	2¢ Green & Black	4.00	2.50	10.00	6.00
☐RB3	3¢ Green & Black	9.50	5.00	33.00	18.00
☐RB4	4¢ Green & Black	6.50	4.00	12.00	7.00
☐RB5	4¢ Green & Black	100.00	60.00	100.00	65.00
☐RB6	6¢ Green & Black	26.00	15.00	80.00	45.00
☐RB7	10¢ Green & Black	150.00	80.00	35.00	21.00
☐RB8	50¢ Green & Black	600.00	400.00	800.00	475.00

Scott No.		Silk Paper (a) Fine	Ave.	Watermarked (b) Fine	Ave.	Rouletted (c) Fine	Ave.

1875–1881. PROPRIETARY STAMPS (ALL USED)

☐RB11	1¢ Green	2.20	2.30	.40	.26	37.00	24.00
☐RB12	2¢ Brown	2.20	2.30	1.25	.90	42.00	26.00

Scott No.		Silk Paper (a) Fine	Ave.	Watermarked (b) Fine	Ave.	Rouletted (c) Fine	Ave.
☐ RB13	3¢ Orange	13.00	6.00	2.00	1.50	52.00	40.00
☐ RB14	4¢ Red Brown	4.50	3.00	3.50	2.10	—	—
☐ RB15	4¢ Red	—	—	3.60	2.10	52.00	32.00
☐ RB16	5¢ Black	86.00	50.00	72.00	38.00	500.00	400.00
☐ RB17	6¢ Violet Blue	21.00	12.00	14.00	8.00	140.00	85.00
☐ RB18	6¢ Violet	—	—	21.00	11.00	170.00	110.00
☐ RB19	10¢ Blue	—	—	175.00	100.00	—	—

Scott No.		Fine Un-cancelled Each	Ave. Un-cancelled Each	Fine Used Each	Ave. Used Each

1898. PROPRIETARY STAMPS (BATTLESHIP)

☐ RB20	⅛¢ Yellow Green	.24	.20	.16	.14
☐ RB21	¼¢ Pale Green	.24	.20	.16	.14
☐ RB22	⅜¢ Deep Orange	.26	.20	.16	.16
☐ RB23	⅝¢ Deep Ultramarine	.26	.20	.16	.16
☐ RB24	1¢ Dark Green	.45	.35	.30	.16
☐ RB25	1¼¢ Violet	.26	.21	.21	.15
☐ RB26	1⅞¢ Dull Blue	2.00	1.50	1.30	.60
☐ RB27	2¢ Violet Brown	.45	.40	.40	.36
☐ RB28	2½¢ Lake	.80	.70	.60	.15
☐ RB29	3¾¢ Olive Gray	8.00	7.00	5.00	1.20
☐ RB30	4¢ Purple	2.60	2.10	2.00	.60
☐ RB31	5¢ Brown Orange	2.60	2.10	2.00	.60

1914. BLACK PROPRIETARY STAMPS—S.L. WTMK.

☐ RB32	⅛¢ Black	.30	.21	.26	.18
☐ RB33	¼¢ Black	1.00	.65	.80	.40
☐ RB34	⅜¢ Black	.30	.21	.21	.18
☐ RB35	⅝¢ Black	2.20	1.30	1.60	.85
☐ RB36	1¼¢ Black	1.50	.80	.80	.42
☐ RB37	1⅞¢ Black	22.00	14.00	14.00	8.10
☐ RB38	2¼¢ Black	2.90	2.00	2.10	1.10
☐ RB39	3⅛¢ Black	56.00	38.00	40.00	28.00
☐ RB40	3¾¢ Black	22.00	12.00	15.00	8.00
☐ RB41	4¢ Black	38.00	22.00	21.00	13.50
☐ RB42	4⅞¢ Black	800.00	400.00	—	—
☐ RB43	5¢ Black	82.00	46.00	50.00	32.00

1914. BLACK PROPRIETARY STAMPS—D.L. WTMK.

☐ RB44	⅛¢ Black	.26	.21	.20	.15
☐ RB45	¼¢ Black	.26	.21	.20	.15
☐ RB46	⅜¢ Black	.70	.55	.50	.45
☐ RB47	½¢ Black	2.10	1.75	1.60	1.35
☐ RB48	⅝¢ Black	.26	.24	.21	.16
☐ RB49	1¢ Black	4.00	2.80	1.75	1.35
☐ RB50	1¼¢ Black	.45	.35	.45	.31
☐ RB51	1½¢ Black	2.50	1.90	1.80	1.45
☐ RB52	1⅞¢ Black	.85	.75	.55	.36
☐ RB53	2¢ Black	5.00	3.50	4.00	2.70

Scott No.		Fine Un-cancelled Each	Ave. Un-cancelled Each	Fine Used Each	Ave. Used Each
☐ RB54	2½¢ Black	1.20	.75	.90	.45
☐ RB55	3¢ Black	2.90	1.75	2.30	1.40
☐ RB56	3⅛¢ Black	3.40	2.00	2.70	1.90
☐ RB57	3¾¢ Black	8.70	6.00	5.00	3.00
☐ RB58	4¢ Black	.42	.21	.30	.18
☐ RB59	4⅜¢ Black	10.00	5.50	6.00	4.00
☐ RB60	5¢ Black	2.10	1.10	1.85	1.00
☐ RB61	6¢ Black	42.00	25.00	30.00	17.00
☐ RB62	8¢ Black	17.00	10.00	9.00	6.00
☐ RB63	10¢ Black	9.00	5.00	5.00	4.50
☐ RB64	20¢ Black	16.00	10.00	11.00	7.00

1919. PROPRIETARY STAMPS

☐ RB65	1¢ Dark Blue	.26	.21	.18	.13
☐ RB66	2¢ Dark Blue	.26	.21	.18	.13
☐ RB67	3¢ Dark Blue	.90	.60	.65	.35
☐ RB68	4¢ Dark Blue	.90	.60	.55	.45
☐ RB69	5¢ Dark Blue	.90	.60	.55	.45
☐ RB70	8¢ Dark Blue	11.00	8.00	7.00	5.00
☐ RB71	10¢ Dark Blue	2.40	1.90	1.65	1.10
☐ RB72	20¢ Dark Blue	4.10	3.10	3.00	1.90
☐ RB73	40¢ Dark Blue	20.00	12.50	7.00	3.00

1918–1934. FUTURE DELIVERY STAMPS

☐ RC1	2¢ Carmine Rose	1.10	.60	.21	.13
☐ RC2	3¢ Carmine Rose (cut 7.50)	28.00	25.00	21.00	12.00
☐ RC3	4¢ Carmine Rose	.90	.70	.21	.13
☐ RC3A	5¢ Carmine Rose	—	—	2.50	1.40
☐ RC4	10¢ Carmine Rose	.55	.45	.21	.13
☐ RC5	20¢ Carmine Rose	.75	.50	.22	.13
☐ RC6	25¢ Carmine Rose (cut .10)	4.00	2.10	.55	.21
☐ RC7	40¢ Carmine Rose (cut .10)	4.00	3.00	.55	.20
☐ RC8	50¢ Carmine Rose	1.10	.80	.35	.18
☐ RC9	80¢ Carmine Rose (cut .75)	10.00	6.00	6.50	2.00
☐ RC10	$1 Green (cut .10)	—	—	.26	.13
☐ RC11	$2 Rose (cut .08)	—	—	.28	.18
☐ RC12	$3 Violet (cut .12)	—	—	.65	.50
☐ RC13	$5 Dark Blue (cut .09)	—	—	.40	.20
☐ RC14	$10 Orange (cut .20)	—	—	.85	.50
☐ RC15	$20 Olive Bistre (cut .50)	—	—	3.50	2.10
☐ RC16	$30 Vermilion (cut .95)	—	—	5.00	2.10
☐ RC17	$50 Olive Green (cut .30)	—	—	.80	.50
☐ RC18	$60 Brown (cut .55)	—	—	3.00	.90
☐ RC19	$100 Yellow Green (cut 5.00)	—	—	21.00	12.00
☐ RC20	$500 Blue (cut 3.00)	—	—	11.00	8.00
☐ RC21	$1000 Orange (cut 1.60)	—	6.00	7.00	4.00
☐ RC22	1¢ Carmine Rose Narrow Overprint	.22	.16	.18	.11
☐ RC23	80¢ Narrow Overprint (cut .20)	—	—	1.10	1.00

Scott No.		Fine Un-cancelled Each	Ave. Un-cancelled Each	Fine Used Each	Ave. Used Each
☐ RC25	$1 Serif Overprint (cut .08)	5.00	2.90	.48	.28
☐ RC26	$10 Serif Overprint (cut 4.50)	—	—	10.00	6.00

1918–1929. STOCK TRANSFER STAMPS—PERF. 11 OR 12

☐ RD1	1¢ Carmine Rose, Perf. 11	.50	.30	.16	.13
☐ RD2	2¢ Carmine Rose, Perf. 11	.30	.21	.16	.13
☐ RD3	4¢ Carmine Rose, Perf. 11	.24	.21	.16	.13
☐ RD4	5¢ Carmine Rose, Perf. 11	.24	.21	.16	.13
☐ RD5	10¢ Carmine Rose, Perf. 11	.24	.21	.16	.13
☐ RD6	20¢ Carmine Rose, Perf. 11	.24	.21	.16	.13
☐ RD7	25¢ Carmine Rose, Perf. 12 (cut .07)	.65	.36	.22	.14
☐ RD8	40¢ Carmine Rose, Perf. 11	.65	.36	.16	.13
☐ RD9	50¢ Carmine Rose, Perf. 11	.42	.22	.16	.13
☐ RD10	80¢ Carmine Rose, Perf. 11 (cut .07)	1.60	.80	.22	.20
☐ RD11	$1 Green, perf. 11, Red Ovpt. (cut .40)	22.00	15.00	12.00	5.00
☐ RD12	$1 Green, Perf. 11, Black Ovpt	1.30	.65	.15	.14
☐ RD13	$2 Rose, Perf. 11	1.20	.40	.18	.14
☐ RD14	$3 Violet, Perf. 11 (cut .17)	4.00	2.70	.90	.30
☐ RD15	$4 Y. Brown, Perf. 11 (cut .07)	2.00	1.25	.18	.14
☐ RD16	$5 Blue, Perf. 11 (cut .07)	2.00	1.25	.18	.14
☐ RD17	$10 Orange, Perf. 11 (cut .07)	3.50	1.90	.45	.15
☐ RD18	$20 Bistre, Perf. 11 (cut 4.25)	23.00	12.00	.18	10.00
☐ RD19	$30 Vermilion (cut 1.05)	22.00	12.00	7.00	2.70
☐ RD20	$50 Olive Green (cut 9.75)	74.00	46.00	36.00	28.00
☐ RD21	$60 Brown (cut 4.60)	60.00	32.00	21.00	12.00
☐ RD22	$100 Green (cut 1.10)	22.00	10.00	4.00	3.00
☐ RD23	$500 Blue (cut 38.00)	—	—	108.00	58.00
☐ RD24	$1000 Orange (cut 10.00)	—	—	70.00	55.00
☐ RD25	2¢ Carmine Rose, Perf. 10	.30	.26	.16	.13
☐ RD26	4¢ Carmine Rose, Perf. 10	.30	.26	.16	.13
☐ RD27	10¢ Carmine Rose, Perf. 10	.40	.26	.16	.13
☐ RD28	20¢ Carmine Rose, Perf. 10	.40	.26	.16	.13
☐ RD29	50¢ Carmine Rose, Perf. 10	.55	.42	.22	.16
☐ RD30	$1 Green, Perf. 10	.30	.28	.16	.13
☐ RD31	$2 Carmine Rose, Perf. 10	.30	.28	.16	.13
☐ RD32	$10 Orange, Perf. 10 (cut .07)	2.25	1.65	.21	.16

1919–1928.
STOCK TRANSFER STAMPS, SERIF OVERPRINT

☐ RD33	2¢ Carmine Rose, Perf. 11	1.60	.80	.70	.40
☐ RD34	10¢ Carmine Rose, Perf. 11	.45	.26	.30	.13
☐ RD35	20¢ Carmine Rose, Perf. 11	.45	.26	.30	.13
☐ RD36	50¢ Carmine Rose, Perf. 11	.70	.60	.36	.26
☐ RD37	$1 Carmine Rose, Perf. 11 (cut. 11)	4.00	2.80	3.00	2.50
☐ RD38	$2 Rose, Perf. 11 (cut .12)	3.00	2.00	2.00	1.10
☐ RD39	2¢ Carmine Rose, Perf. 10	.40	.26	.18	.14
☐ RD40	10¢ Carmine Rose, Perf. 10	.42	.26	.18	.12
☐ RD41	20¢ Carmine Rose, Perf. 10	.60	.31	.18	.12

Scott No.		Fine Unused Block	Ave. Unused Block	Fine Unused Each	Ave. Unused Each	Fine Used Each	Ave. Used Each
CONFEDERATE STATES OF AMERICA (N-H ADD 80%)							
☐1	5¢ J. Davis, Green	—	1000.00	200.00	140.00	110.00	75.00
☐2	10¢ Jefferson, Blue	—	1600.00	300.00	210.00	160.00	160.00
☐3	2¢ Jackson, Green	—	—	550.00	415.00	500.00	600.00
☐4	5¢ J. Davis, Blue	800.00	600.00	110.00	70.00	80.00	70.00
☐5	10¢ Jefferson, Rose	—	—	700.00	600.00	400.00	420.00
☐6	5¢ Davis, Lon. Print	100.00	85.00	12.00	12.00	18.00	14.00
☐7	5¢ Davis, Local Print	150.00	110.00	18.00	16.00	10.00	19.00
1863.							
☐8	2¢ Jackson, Br. Red	600.00	400.00	46.00	56.00	370.00	270.00
☐9	10¢ Davis (len)	—	—	700.00	610.00	640.00	430.00
☐10	10¢ Davis (w fr. lin.)	—	—	2600.00	1800.00	1400.00	700.00
☐11	10¢ Davis (no fr.)	80.00	65.00	17.00	11.00	22.00	14.00
☐12	10¢ Davis (fill. com)	110.00	100.00	20.00	13.00	22.00	19.00
☐13	20¢ Washington	410.00	350.00	64.00	44.00	310.00	250.00
1862.							
☐14	1¢ J.C. Calhoun	1000.00	700.00	110.00	100.00	—	—

Scott No.		Fine Plate Block	Block	Fine Unused Each	Fine Used Each
1935. "FARLEY SPECIAL PRINTINGS"					
☐752	3¢ Newburgh . . . . , . . .	21.00	1.50	.24	.21
☐753	3¢ Byrd, Perf	29.00	3.10	.70	.60
☐754	3¢ Mother's Day	29.00	4.00	.85	.55
☐755	3¢ Wisconsin	29.00	4.00	.85	.60
☐756	1¢ Park	7.00	2.00	.50	.35
☐757	2¢ Park	9.00	3.00	.42	.36
☐758	3¢ Park	25.00	6.00	.80	.70
☐759	4¢ Park	32.00	11.00	1.75	1.50
☐760	5¢ Park	40.00	20.00	3.00	1.90
☐761	6¢ Park	65.00	22.00	3.80	1.90
☐762	7¢ Park	52.00	25.00	2.60	1.90
☐763	8¢ Park	68.00	24.00	3.00	1.90
☐764	9¢ Park	76.00	24.00	3.10	1.90
☐765	10¢ Park	75.00	35.00	5.50	3.50
☐766a	1¢ Chicago	—	5.00	1.05	.80
☐767a	3¢ Chicago	—	6.00	1.05	.65
☐768a	3¢ Byrd	—	28.00	4.00	1.80
☐769a	1¢ Park	—	19.00	1.80	1.70
☐770a	3¢ Park	—	40.00	1.75	3.10
☐771	16¢ Air Spec. Del	110.00	32.00	4.00	3.40

Scott No.		Center Line Block	Fine Arrow Block	Block W/Vert. Line	Pair W/Vert. Line	Block W/Horiz. Line	Fair W/Horiz. Line
1935. FARLEY POSITION ON BLOCKS AND PAIRS							
☐ 752	3¢ Newburgh	49.00	75.00	21.00	10.00	14.00	4.00
☐ 753	3¢ Byrd	100.00	160.00	80.00	48.00	—	1.75
☐ 754	3¢ Mother's Day	13.00	20.00	6.00	2.50	5.00	1.90
☐ 755	3¢ Wisconsin	13.00	20.00	6.00	2.50	5.00	1.90
☐ 756	1¢ Park	5.00	10.00	1.80	1.60	1.10	.80
☐ 757	2¢ Park	6.50	10.00	1.90	1.60	2.10	.90
☐ 758	3¢ Park	8.00	16.00	3.50	2.75	4.00	1.40
☐ 759	4¢ Park	15.00	46.00	8.00	6.00	6.50	3.60
☐ 760	5¢ Park	20.00	50.00	12.00	8.00	12.00	4.00
☐ 761	6¢ Park	27.00	85.00	20.00	6.00	14.00	6.00
☐ 762	7¢ Park	26.00	60.00	19.00	5.00	12.00	4.00
☐ 763	8¢ Park	26.00	62.00	18.00	5.00	16.00	4.00
☐ 764	9¢ Park	28.00	60.00	24.00	6.00	18.00	4.50
☐ 765	10¢ Park	45.00	190.00	32.00	12.00	30.00	12.00
☐ 766a	1¢ Chicago	23.00	—	25.00	9.00	15.00	6.00
☐ 767a	3¢ Chicago	21.00	—	21.00	7.00	12.00	7.00
☐ 768a	3¢ Byrd	24.00	—	19.00	12.00	16.00	8.00
☐ 769a	1¢ Park	19.00	—	18.00	7.00	12.00	5.00
☐ 770a	3¢ Park	38.00	—	21.00	12.00	21.00	14.00
☐ 771	16¢ Air Spec. Del	86.00	110.00	30.00	9.00	21.00	8.00

Scott No.		Fine Plate Block	Ave. Plate Block	Fine Unused Each	Ave. Unused Each	Fine Used Each	Ave. Used Each
HUNTING PERMIT STAMPS							
☐ RW1							
(1934)	$1 Blue	4500.00	3000.00	300.00	200.00	90.00	50.00
☐ RW2							
(1935)	$1 Rose Lake	6000.00	4000.00	300.00	240.00	150.00	85.00
☐ RW3							
(1936)	$1 Brown Blk	2800.00	1800.00	175.00	120.00	75.00	50.00
☐ RW4							
(1937)	$1 Lt. Green	1600.00	1000.00	140.00	80.00	40.00	26.00
☐ RW5							
(1938)	$1 Lt. Violet	1600.00	1000.00	140.00	90.00	35.00	26.00
☐ RW6							
(1939)	$1 Chocolate	1100.00	700.00	110.00	70.00	26.00	18.00
☐ RW7							
(1940)	$1 Sepia	1000.00	650.00	105.00	70.00	26.00	18.00
☐ RW8							
(1941)	$1 Brn. Carmine	900.00	600.00	105.00	70.00	26.00	18.00
☐ RW9							
(1942)	$1 Violet Brn.	850.00	500.00	105.00	70.00	26.00	18.00
☐ RW10							
(1943)	$1 Deep Rose	300.00	210.00	50.00	32.00	24.00	16.00
☐ RW11							
(1944)	$1 Red Org.	290.00	190.00	50.00	32.00	24.00	15.00

Scott No.		Fine Plate Block	Ave. Plate Block	Fine Unused Each	Ave. Unused Each	Fine Used Each	Ave. Used Each
☐ RW12 (1945)	$1 Black	220.00	170.00	32.00	19.00	13.00	10.00
☐ RW13 (1946)	$1 Red Brn	220.00	170.00	22.00	19.00	13.00	9.00
☐ RW14 (1947)	$1 Black	220.00	140.00	23.00	19.00	13.00	9.00
☐ RW15 (1948)	$1 Brt. Blue	210.00	140.00	26.00	19.00	13.00	9.00
☐ RW16 (1949)	$2 Brt. Green	210.00	140.00	38.00	30.00	12.00	9.00
☐ RW17 (1950)	$2 Violet	300.00	200.00	38.00	30.00	9.00	7.00
☐ RW18 (1951)	$2 Gray Blk	300.00	200.00	38.00	30.00	9.00	7.00
☐ RW19 (1952)	$2 Ultramarine	300.00	200.00	38.00	30.00	9.00	7.00
☐ RW20 (1953)	$2 Dk. Rose Brn	300.00	200.00	38.00	30.00	9.00	7.00
☐ RW21 (1954)	$2 Black	320.00	200.00	38.00	30.00	9.00	7.00
☐ RW22 (1955)	$2 Dk. Blue	320.00	200.00	38.00	30.00	9.00	6.00
☐ RW23 (1956)	$2 Black	320.00	200.00	38.00	30.00	9.00	6.00
☐ RW24 (1957)	$2 Emerald	320.00	200.00	38.00	30.00	9.00	6.00
☐ RW25 (1958)	$2 Black	320.00	200.00	38.00	30.00	9.00	6.00
☐ RW26 (1959)	$3 Bl./Ochre/Blk	320.00	200.00	44.00	50.00	9.00	6.00
☐ RW27 (1960)	$3 Red Brn./Bl./Bist	320.00	200.00	44.00	50.00	9.00	6.00
☐ RW28 (1961)	$3 Bl./Bist./Brn	330.00	210.00	44.00	55.00	9.00	6.00
☐ RW29 (1962)	$3 Bl./Brn./Blk	340.00	220.00	54.00	65.00	10.00	7.00
☐ RW30 (1963)	$3 Blk./Bl. Yel./Grn	340.00	220.00	54.00	65.00	10.00	7.00
☐ RW31 (1964)	$3 Bl./Blk./Bist	2000.00	1480.00	54.00	62.00	10.00	7.00
☐ RW32 (1965)	$3 Grn./Blk./Brn	340.00	210.00	54.00	65.00	10.00	7.00
☐ RW33 (1966)	$3 Bl./Grn./Blk	325.00	210.00	54.00	62.00	10.00	7.00
☐ RW34 (1967)	$3 Multicolored	325.00	210.00	54.00	62.00	10.00	7.00
☐ RW35 (1968)	$3 Grn./Blk./Brn	130.00	100.00	54.00	30.00	10.00	7.00

Scott No.		Fine Plate Block	Ave. Plate Block	Fine Unused Each	Ave. Unused Each	Fine Used Each	Ave. Used Each
☐ RW36 (1969)	$3 Multicolored	140.00	110.00	47.00	32.00	7.00	7.00
☐ RW37 (1970)	$3 Multicolored	140.00	110.00	44.00	26.00	7.00	7.00
☐ RW38 (1971)	$3 Multicolored	140.00	110.00	32.00	26.00	7.00	7.00
☐ RW39 (1972)	$5 Multicolored	110.00	95.00	24.00	19.00	7.00	7.00
☐ RW40 (1973)	$5 Multicolored	90.00	70.00	20.00	16.00	6.00	7.00
☐ RW41 (1974)	$5 Multicolored	85.00	52.00	16.00	10.00	6.00	7.00
☐ RW42 (1975)	$5 Multicolored	65.00	50.00	14.00	10.00	6.00	7.00
☐ RW43 (1976)	$5 Emerald & Blk	60.00	50.00	14.00	10.00	6.00	6.00
☐ RW44 (1977)	$5 Multicolored	60.00	50.00	14.00	10.00	6.00	6.00
☐ RW45 (1978)	$5 Multicolored	60.00	50.00	14.00	10.00	6.00	6.00
☐ RW46 (1979)	$7.50 Multicolored	58.00	48.00	16.00	11.00	6.00	6.00
☐ RW47 (1980)	$7.50 Multicolored	60.00	46.00	16.00	11.00	6.00	6.00
☐ RW48 (1981)	$7.50 Multicolored	60.00	46.00	16.00	11.00	6.00	6.00

Scott No.		Fine Unused Each	Ave. Unused Each	Fine Used Each	Ave. Used Each

HAWAIIAN ISSUES
1851–1952. "MISSIONARIES"

		Fine Unused Each	Fine Used Each
☐ 1	2¢ Blue	— 400,000.00	— 190,000.00
☐	On Cover		425,000.00
☐ 2	5¢ Blue	— 34,000.00	16,000.00
☐	On Cover		26,000.00
☐ 3	13¢ Blue	— 18,000.00	9,500.00
☐	On Cover		14,500.00
☐ 4	13¢ Blue	— 44,000.00	— 20,000.00
☐	On Cover		28,000.00

NOTE: Prices on the above classic stamps of Hawaii vary greatly depending on the individual specimen and circumstances of sale.

NOTE: Beware of fake cancels on Hawaiian stamps, when the value is higher used than unused.

Scott No.		Fine Unused Each	Ave. Unused Each	Fine Used Each	Ave. Used Each

1853. KING KAMEHAMEHA III

☐5	5¢ Blue	—	600.00	—	500.00
☐6	13¢ Dark Red	—	500.00	—	400.00
☐7	5¢ on 13¢ Dark Red	—	4000.00	—	4200.00

1857.

☐8	5¢ Blue	—	250.00	—	250.00

1861.

☐9	5¢ Blue	—	115.00	—	100.00

1868. RE-ISSUE

☐10	5¢ Blue	—	25.00	—	—
☐11	13¢ Rose	—	180.00	—	—

1859–1862.

☐12	1¢ Light Blue	—	2600.00	—	2900.00
☐13	2¢ Light Blue	—	2300.00	—	1100.00
☐14	2¢ Black	—	3000.00	—	1400.00

1863.

☐15	1¢ Black	—	200.00	—	300.00
☐16	2¢ Black	—	400.00	—	340.00
☐17	2¢ Dark Blue	—	3800.00	—	2200.00
☐18	2¢ Black	—	670.00	—	1000.00

1864–1865.

☐19	1¢ Black	—	280.00	—	650.00
☐20	2¢ Black	—	360.00	—	500.00
☐21	5¢ Blue	—	250.00	—	250.00
☐22	5¢ Blue	—	200.00	—	300.00

1864. LAID PAPER

☐23	1¢ Black	160.00	120.00	600.00	400.00
☐24	2¢ Black	160.00	120.00	600.00	400.00

1865. WOVE PAPER

☐25	1¢ Blue	175.00	140.00	140.00	120.00
☐26	2¢ Blue	170.00	140.00	140.00	120.00
☐27	2¢ Rose	180.00	150.00	115.00	100.00
☐28	2¢ Rose Vert	180.00	150.00	115.00	100.00

1869. ENGRAVED

☐29	2¢ Red	85.00	50.00	—	—

Scott No.		Fine Unused Each	Ave. Unused Each	Fine Used Each	Ave. Used Each
1864–1871.					
☐30	1¢ Purple	10.00	7.50	7.00	4.50
☐31	2¢ Vermilion	12.00	8.00	7.00	4.50
☐32	5¢ Blue	60.00	38.00	17.00	10.00
☐33	6¢ Green	21.00	14.00	7.00	4.50
☐34	18¢ Rose	86.00	55.00	25.00	9.00
1875.					
☐35	2¢ Brown	7.50	4.00	3.10	1.90
☐36	12¢ Black	42.00	30.00	21.00	14.00
☐37	1¢ Blue	5.00	6.00	8.00	4.50
☐38	2¢ Lilac Rose	85.00	60.00	32.00	18.00
☐39	5¢ Ultramarine	11.00	8.00	2.90	1.90
☐40	10¢ Black	21.00	16.00	16.00	11.00
☐41	15¢ Red Brown	42.00	24.00	21.00	16.00
1883–1886.					
☐42	1¢ Green	3.00	1.90	1.60	.90
☐43	2¢ Rose	4.00	2.50	1.00	.65
☐44	10¢ Red Brown	32.00	15.00	13.00	6.00
☐45	10¢ Vermilion	24.00	12.00	11.00	6.00
☐46	12¢ Red Lilac	50.00	34.00	28.00	21.00
☐47	25¢ Dark Violet	88.00	50.00	40.00	24.00
☐48	50¢ Red	120.00	90.00	68.00	48.00
☐49	$1 Rose Red	190.00	120.00	85.00	50.00
☐50	2¢ Orange	115.00	90.00	—	—
☐51	2¢ Carmine	21.00	15.00	—	—
1890–1891.					
☐52	2¢ Dull Violet	3.75	2.50	1.10	.90
☐52C	5¢ Dark Blue	86.00	68.00	70.00	40.00
1893. PROVISIONAL GOVT. RED OVERPRINT					
☐53	1¢ Purple	4.00	3.00	5.00	2.50
☐54	1¢ Blue	4.00	3.00	6.00	2.50
☐55	1¢ Green	1.60	1.00	2.50	1.80
☐56	2¢ Brown	4.00	2.75	8.00	2.00
☐57	2¢ Dull Violet	1.40	1.10	1.10	.90
☐58	5¢ Dark Blue	9.00	4.50	15.00	3.50
☐59	5¢ Ultramarine	6.00	3.00	3.00	2.40
☐60	6¢ Green	11.00	6.00	18.00	4.50
☐61	10¢ Black	8.00	5.00	9.00	4.00
☐62	12¢ Black	8.00	4.50	11.00	3.75
☐63	12¢ Red Lilac	110.00	54.00	140.00	48.00
☐64	25¢ Dark Violet	21.00	12.00	28.00	9.00

Scott No.		Fine Unused Each	Ave. Unused Each	Fine Used Each	Ave. Used Each
BLACK OVERPRINT					
☐65	2¢ Vermilion	48.00	34.00	50.00	29.00
☐66	2¢ Rose	1.50	.90	2.50	1.40
☐67	10¢ Vermilion	12.00	8.40	18.00	9.00
☐68	10¢ Red Brown	6.75	6.00	9.00	4.00
☐69	12¢ Red Lilac	230.00	135.00	260.00	175.00
☐70	15¢ Red Brown	18.00	13.00	29.00	16.00
☐71	18¢ Dull Rose	23.50	15.00	32.00	17.00
☐72	50¢ Red	58.00	34.00	80.00	35.00
☐73	$1 Rose Red	115.00	70.00	135.00	65.00
☐74	1¢ Yellow	2.00	1.70	1.30	1.20
☐75	2¢ Brown	2.10	1.70	.80	.70
☐76	5¢ Rose Lake	3.90	2.50	1.75	1.60
☐77	10¢ Yellow Green	6.00	3.50	5.00	4.50
☐78	12¢ Blue	11.00	6.90	12.00	7.00
☐79	25¢ Deep Blue	11.00	7.00	13.00	9.00
1899.					
☐80	1¢ Dark Green	1.60	1.00	1.40	.95
☐81	2¢ Rose	1.60	.95	1.00	.95
☐82	5¢ Blue	6.00	3.30	3.25	2.30
1896. OFFICIAL STAMPS					
☐O1	2¢ Green	36.00	30.00	20.00	13.00
☐O2	5¢ Dark Brown	36.00	30.00	20.00	13.00
☐O3	6¢ Deep Ultramarine	54.00	45.00	20.00	13.00
☐O4	10¢ Rose	38.00	30.00	20.00	13.00
☐O5	12¢ Orange	60.00	45.00	20.00	13.00
☐O6	25¢ Gray Violet	110.00	80.00	20.00	13.00

Scott No.		Single	Block Of 4
UNITED STATES FIRST DAY COVERS UNCACHETED			
☐551	½¢ Hale	14.00	15.00
☐552	1¢ Franklin	21.00	50.00
☐553	1½¢ Harding	26.00	60.00
☐554	2¢ Washington . .	32.00	55.00
☐555	3¢ Lincoln.	32.00	300.00
☐556	4¢ Martha Washington . .	38.00	250.00
☐557	5¢ Roosevelt . .	95.00	300.00
☐558	6¢ Garfield	165.00	500.00
☐559	7¢ McKinley . . .	95.00	140.00
☐560	8¢ Grant. . . .	115.00	700.00
☐561	9¢ Jefferson . . .	115.00	300.00
☐562	10¢ Monroe . . .	115.00	300.00
☐563	11¢ Hayes	420.00	50.00
☐564	12¢ Cleveland . .	100.00	125.00
☐565	14¢ Indian	310.00	125.00
☐566	15¢ Statue of Liberty	330.00	—
☐568	25¢ Niagara Falls	500.00	350.00
☐569	30¢ Bison.	600.00	600.00
☐570	50¢ Arlington. .	700.00	1800.00
☐571	$1 Lincoln Memorial . .	5000.00	700.00
☐572	$2 U.S. Capitol	10000.00	—
☐573	$5 America . .	12000.00	—
☐576	1½¢ Harding	42.00	120.00
☐581	1¢ Franklin	1800.00	—
☐582	1½¢ Harding	39.00	65.00
☐583a	2¢ Washington . .	300.00	—
☐584	3¢ Lincoln.	46.00	310.00
☐585	4¢ Martha Washington . .	45.00	210.00
☐586	5¢ Roosevelt . . .	46.00	200.00
☐587	6¢ Garfield . . .	55.00	100.00
☐588	7¢ McKinley . . .	52.00	175.00
☐589	8¢ Grant.	58.00	300.00
☐590	9¢ Jefferson . . .	55.00	52.00
☐591	10¢ Monroe . . .	75.00	800.00
☐597	1¢ Franklin	400.00	32.00
☐598	1½¢ Harding . . .	40.00	30.00
☐599	2¢ Washington .	550.00	—
☐600	3¢ Lincoln.	58.00	30.00
☐602	5¢ Roosevelt . . .	65.00	32.00
☐603	10¢ Monroe	80.00	40.00

Scott No.		Single	Block Of 4
☐604	1¢ Franklin	75.00	40.00
☐605	1½¢ Harding	48.00	40.00
☐606	2¢ Washington . .	95.00	32.00
☐610	2¢ Harding	22.00	40.00
☐611	2¢ Harding	72.00	180.00
☐612	2¢ Harding	100.00	400.00
☐614	1¢ Huguenot-Walloon . . .	22.00	65.00
☐615	2¢ Huguenot-Walloon . . .	24.00	120.00
☐616	5¢ Huguenot-Walloon	45.00	450.00
☐617	1¢ Lexington-Concord. . . .	22.00	85.00
☐618	2¢ Lexington Concord	26.00	140.00
☐619	5¢ Lexington-Concord	55.00	450.00
☐620	2¢ Norse-American	24.00	300.00
☐621	5¢ Norse-American	32.00	850.00
☐622	13¢ Harrison. . . .	24.00	270.00
☐623	17¢ Wilson	24.00	275.00
☐627	2¢ Sesquicenten-nial.	10.00	60.00
☐628	5¢ Erikson	16.00	120.00
☐629	2¢ White Plains . .	7.00	60.00
☐630	2¢ White Plains Sheet	1200.00	—
☐631	1½ Harding	29.00	80.00
☐632	1¢ Franklin	41.00	5.00
☐633	1½¢ Harding	41.00	110.00
☐634	2¢ Washington . .	42.00	3.00
☐635	3¢ Lincoln. . . .	40.00	14.00
☐635a	3¢ Bright Violet. .	18.00	29.00
☐636	4¢ Martha Washington . . .	40.00	120.00
☐637	5¢ Roosevelt . . .	40.00	27.00
☐638	6¢ Garfield	50.00	27.00
☐639	7¢ McKinley . . .	50.00	27.00
☐640	8¢ Grant.	52.00	27.00
☐641	9¢ Jefferson . . .	55.00	32.00
☐642	10¢ Monroe . . .	65.00	40.00
☐643	2¢ Vermont. . . .	6.00	60.00
☐644	2¢ Burgoyne . . .	8.00	70.00
☐645	2¢ Valley Forge . .	5.00	55.00
☐646	2¢ Molly Pitcher .	11.00	50.00
☐647	2¢ Hawaii	13.00	200.00
☐648	5¢ Hawaii	20.00	250.00
☐649	2¢ Aero Conf. . . .	6.00	21.00

Scott No.		Single	Block Of 4
☐650	5¢ Aero Conf. . . .	8.00	100.00
☐651	2¢ Clark.	5.00	16.00
☐653	½¢ Hale	24.00	2.10
☐654	2¢ Electric Light . .	7.00	42.00
☐655	2¢ Electric Light . .	60.00	60.00
☐656	2¢ Electric Light . .	70.00	—
☐657	2¢ Sullivan	4.00	41.00
☐658	1¢ Kansas	24.00	40.00
☐659	1½¢ Kansas	24.00	65.00
☐660	2¢ Kansas	22.00	60.00
☐661	3¢ Kansas	25.00	210.00
☐662	4¢ Kansas	28.00	210.00
☐663	5¢ Kansas	28.00	200.00
☐664	6¢ Kansas	39.00	500.00
☐665	7¢ Kansas	39.00	500.00
☐666	8¢ Kansas	70.00	800.00
☐667	9¢ Kansas	65.00	250.00
☐668	10¢ Kansas	75.00	400.00
☐669	1¢ Nebraska	24.00	40.00
☐670	1½¢ Nebraska	24.00	—
☐671	2¢ Nebraska	24.00	35.00
☐672	3¢ Nebraska	31.00	175.00
☐673	4¢ Nebraska	33.00	230.00
☐674	5¢ Nebraska	34.00	300.00
☐675	6¢ Nebraska	45.00	600.00
☐676	7¢ Nebraska	50.00	350.00
☐677	8¢ Nebraska	50.00	500.00
☐678	9¢ Nebraska	62.00	500.00
☐679	10¢ Nebraska	66.00	1100.00
☐680	2¢ Fallen Timbers .	3.50	40.00
☐681	2¢ Ohio River. . . .	3.50	31.00
☐682	2¢ Massachusetts Bay Colony.	3.50	52.00
☐683	2¢ Carolina-Charleston . . .	3.50	75.00
☐684	1½¢ Harding	4.00	4.00
☐685	4¢ Taft.	5.50	13.00
☐686	1½¢ Harding	3.75	9.00
☐687	4¢ Taft.	22.00	—
☐688	2¢ Braddock	3.00	60.00
☐689	2¢ Von Steuben . .	3.00	38.00
☐690	2¢ Pulaski.	3.00	21.00
☐692	11¢ Hayes	76.00	20.00
☐693	12¢ Cleveland . . .	76.00	32.00
☐694	13¢ Harrison	75.00	20.00
☐695	14¢ Indian	75.00	26.00
☐696	15¢ Liberty	95.00	60.00
☐697	17¢ Wilson	275.00	—
☐698	20¢ Golden Gate	225.00	65.00

Scott No.		Single	Block Of 4
☐699	25¢ Niagara Falls	300.00	60.00
☐700	30¢ Bison.	210.00	100.00
☐701	50¢ Arlington. . .	300.00	300.00
☐702	2¢ Red Cross. . . .	2.40	4.00
☐703	2¢ Yorktown	3.00	5.00
☐704	½¢ Olive Brown. .	12.00	5.00
☐705	1¢ Green	12.00	6.00
☐706	1½¢ Brown	12.00	26.00
☐707	2¢ Carmine Rose	12.00	2.00
☐708	3¢ Deep Violet . .	12.00	20.00
☐709	4¢ Light Brown. .	12.00	7.00
☐710	5¢ Blue	12.00	26.00
☐711	6¢ Red Orange. .	12.00	100.00
☐712	7¢ Black.	14.00	9.00
☐713	8¢ Olive Bistre . .	14.00	100.00
☐714	9¢ Pale Red . . .	14.00	65.00
☐715	10¢ Orange Yellow	14.00	165.00
☐716	2¢ Olympic Winter Games.	17.00	20.00
☐717	2¢ Arbor Day . . .	14.00	12.00
☐718	3¢ Olympic Summer Games.	20.00	24.00
☐719	5¢ Olympic Summer Games.	20.00	41.00
☐720	3¢ Washington . .	30.00	3.00
☐721	3¢ Washington (coil)	32.00	15.00
☐722	3¢ Washington (coil)	32.00	16.00
☐723	6¢ Garfield (coil). .	32.00	16.00
☐724	3¢ William Penn .	12.00	18.00
☐725	3¢ Daniel Webster	12.00	32.00
☐726	3¢ Gen. Oglethorpe . .	12.00	21.00
☐727	3¢ Peace Proclamation.	12.00	9.00
☐728	1¢ Century of Progress. . . .	12.00	4.00
☐729	3¢ Century of Progress. . . .	12.00	5.00
☐730	1¢ American Philatelic Society, full sheet on cover. . .	150.00	15.00
☐730a	1¢ American Philatelic Society . . .	12.00	4.00
☐731	3¢ American Philatelic Society . . .	160.00	—
☐731a	3¢ American Philatelic Society	12.00	4.50

Scott No.		Single	Block Of 4
☐732	3¢ National Recovery Administration	12.00	3.00
☐733	3¢ Byrd Antarctic	21.00	25.00
☐734	5¢ Kosciuszko	15.00	50.00
☐735	3¢ National Exhibition	46.00	—
☐735a	3¢ National Exhibition	12.00	6.00
☐736	3¢ Maryland Tercentenary	9.00	15.00
☐737	3¢ Mothers of America	9.00	3.00
☐738	3¢ Mothers of America	9.00	7.00
☐739	3¢ Wisconsin	9.00	6.00
☐740	1¢ Parks, Yosemite	9.00	3.00
☐741	2¢ Parks, Grand Canyon	9.00	2.75
☐742	3¢ Parks, Mt. Ranier	9.00	3.00
☐743	4¢ Parks, Mesa Verde	9.00	13.00
☐744	5¢ Parks, Yellowstone	9.00	16.00
☐745	6¢ Parks, Crater Lake	9.00	28.00
☐746	7¢ Parks, Acadia	9.00	17.00
☐747	8¢ Parks, Zion	9.00	28.00
☐748	9¢ Parks, Glacier Park	9.00	27.00
☐749	10¢ Parks, Smoky Mountains	9.00	45.00
☐750	3¢ American Philatelic Society, full sheet on cover	48.00	—
☐750a	3¢ American Philatelic Society	9.00	14.00
☐751	1¢ Trans-Mississippi Philatelic Expo, full sheet on cover	48.00	—
☐751a	1¢ Trans-Mississippi Philadelic Expo.	9.00	10.00
☐752	3¢ Peace Commemoration	32.00	20.00
☐753	34¢ Byrd	32.00	20.00
☐754	3¢ Mothers of America	32.00	20.00
☐755	3¢ Wisconsin	32.00	20.00
☐756	1¢ Parks, Yosemite	28.00	5.00

Scott No.		Single	Block Of 4
☐757	2¢ Parks, Grand Canyon	28.00	6.00
☐758	3¢ Parks, Mount Ranier	28.00	15.00
☐759	4¢ Parks, Mesa Verde	28.00	21.00
☐760	5¢ Parks, Yellowstone	28.00	25.00
☐761	6¢ Parks, Crater Lake	28.00	40.00
☐762	7¢ Parks, Acadia	28.00	32.00
☐763	8¢ Parks, Zion	28.00	40.00
☐764	9¢ Parks, Glacier Park	28.00	30.00
☐765	10¢ Parks, Smoky Mountains	28.00	40.00
☐766a	1¢ Century of Progress	32.00	15.00
☐767a	3¢ Century of Progress	32.00	15.00
☐768a	3¢ Byrd	32.00	16.00
☐769	1¢ Parks, Yosemite	32.00	10.00
☐770a	3¢ Parks, Mount Ranier	30.00	24.00
☐771	16¢ Airmail, special delivery	30.00	60.00

UNITED STATES FIRST DAY COVERS CACHETED

Scott No.		Single	Block Of 4
☐610	2¢ Harding	500.00	—
☐617	1¢ Lexington-Concord	135.00	—
☐618	2¢ Lexington-Concord	135.00	—
☐619	5¢ Lexington-Concord	170.00	—
☐623	17¢ Wilson	250.00	—
☐627	2¢ Sesquicenten-nial	60.00	—
☐628	5¢ Erikson	375.00	—
☐629	2¢ White Plains	48.00	—
☐630	2¢ White Plains Sheet	1200.00	—
☐635a	3¢ Bright Violet	42.00	—
☐643	2¢ Vermont	48.00	55.00
☐644	2¢ Burgoyne	50.00	70.00
☐645	2¢ Valley Forge	40.00	50.00

Scott No.		Single	Block Of 4
☐646	2¢ Molly Pitcher .	80.00	—
☐647	2¢ Hawaii	50.00	175.00
☐648	5¢ Hawaii	60.00	350.00
☐649	2¢ Aero Conf. . .	28.00	25.00
☐650	5¢ Aero Conf. . .	34.00	100.00
☐651	2¢ Clark	26.00	16.00
☐654	2¢ Electric Light .	26.00	42.00
☐655	2¢ Electric Light	150.00	60.00
☐656	2¢ Electric Light	170.00	—
☐657	2¢ Sullivan, Auburn, N.Y.	25.00	42.00
☐680	2¢ Fallen Timbers	25.00	42.00
☐681	2¢ Ohio River. . .	25.00	30.00
☐682	2¢ Massachusetts Bay Colony.	28.00	55.00
☐683	2¢ California-Charleston . .	28.00	75.00
☐684	1½¢ Harding	28.00	6.00
☐685	4¢ Taft.	35.00	14.00
☐686	1½¢ Harding	29.00	14.00
☐687	4¢ Taft.	60.00	14.00
☐688	2¢ Braddock . . .	25.00	60.00
☐689	2¢ Von Steuben .	26.00	36.00
☐690	2¢ Pulaski.	26.00	21.00
☐702	2¢ Red Cross. . .	22.00	3.00
☐703	2¢ Yorktown . . .	28.00	6.00
☐704	1½¢ Olive Brown. .	14.00	4.00
☐705	1¢ Green	14.00	6.00
☐706	1½¢ Brown	14.00	26.00
☐707	2¢ Carmine Rose	14.00	2.00
☐708	3¢ Deep Violet . .	14.00	21.00
☐709	4¢ Light Brown . .	14.00	7.00
☐710	5¢ Blue	14.00	26.00
☐711	6¢ Red Orange. .	14.00	90.00
☐712	7¢ Black.	14.00	9.00
☐713	8¢ Olive Bistre . .	17.00	90.00
☐714	9¢ Pale Red . . .	17.00	60.00
☐715	10¢ Orange Yellow	17.00	160.00
☐716	2¢ Olympic Winter Games.	18.00	21.00
☐717	2¢ Arbor Day . . .	16.00	12.00
☐718	3¢ Olympic Summer Games.	20.00	24.00
☐719	5¢ Olympic Summer Games.	20.00	35.00
☐720	3¢ Washington . .	30.00	3.00
☐720b	3¢ Booklet pane	140.00	—
☐721	3¢ Washington (coil)	33.00	—

Scott No.		Single	Block Of 4
☐722	3¢ Washington (coil)	32.00	—
☐723	6¢ Garfield (coil) .	32.00	—
☐724	3¢ William Penn .	14.00	18.00
☐725	3¢ Daniel Webster	14.00	30.00
☐726	3¢ Gen. Oglethorpe	14.00	20.00
☐727	3¢ Peace Proclamation .	14.00	9.00
☐728	1¢ Century of Progress. . . .	14.00	4.00
☐729	3¢ Century of Progress. . . .	14.00	5.00
☐730	1¢ American Philatelic Society, full sheet on cover. . .	160.00	—
☐730a	1¢ American Philatelic Society	14.00	5.00
☐731	3¢ American Philatelic Society	160.00	—
☐731a	3¢ American Philatelic Society	14.00	5.00
☐732	3¢ National Recovery Administration	14.00	3.00
☐733	3¢ Byrd Antarctic	20.00	26.00
☐734	5¢ Kosciuszko . .	16.00	50.00
☐735	3¢ National Exhibition . . .	38.00	—
☐735a	3¢ National Exhibition . . .	14.00	6.00
☐736	3¢ Maryland Tercentenary . .	9.00	14.00
☐737	3¢ Mothers of America	9.00	4.00
☐738	3¢ Mothers of America	9.00	8.00
☐739	3¢ Wisconsin . . .	9.00	6.00
☐740	1¢ Parks, Yosemite	9.00	3.00
☐741	2¢ Parks, Grand Canyon	9.00	3.00
☐742	35¢ Parks, Mt. Rainier.	9.00	3.00
☐743	4¢ Parks, Mesa Verde	9.00	12.00
☐744	5¢ Parks, Yellowstone. .	10.00	16.00
☐745	6¢ Parks, Crater Lake	10.00	30.00
☐746	7¢ Parks, Acadia. .	10.00	18.00
☐747	8¢ Parks, Zion . .	10.00	30.00

Scott No.		Single	Block Of 4
☐748	9¢ Parks, Glacier Park	9.00	30.00
☐749	10¢ Parks, Smoky Mountains	9.00	45.00
☐750	3¢ American Philatelic Society, full sheet on cover	45.00	—
☐750a	3¢ American Philatelic Society	9.00	20.00
☐751	1¢ Trans-Mississippi Philatelic Expo., full sheet on cover	45.00	—
☐751a	1¢ Trans-Mississippi Philatelic Expo.	9.00	14.00
☐752	3¢ Peace Commemoration	32.00	18.00
☐753	3¢ Byrd	32.00	19.00
☐754	3¢ Mothers of America	32.00	19.00
☐755	3¢ Wisconsin Tercentenary	32.00	19.00
☐756	1¢ Parks, Yosemite	28.00	6.00
☐757	2¢ Parks, Grand Canyon	28.00	7.00

Scott No.		Single	Block Of 4
☐758	3¢ Parks, Mount Rainier	28.00	20.00
☐759	4¢ Parks, Mesa Verde	28.00	20.00
☐760	5¢ Parks, Yellowstone	27.00	22.00
☐761	6¢ Parks, Crater Lake	27.00	42.00
☐762	7¢ Parks, Acadia	27.00	32.00
☐763	8¢ Parks, Zion	27.00	42.00
☐764	9¢ Parks, Glacier Park	27.00	42.00
☐765	10¢ Parks, Smoky Mountains	27.00	50.00
☐766a	1¢ Century of Progress	36.00	18.00
☐767a	3¢ Century of Progress	30.00	18.00
☐768a	3¢ Byrd	30.00	20.00
☐769a	1¢ Parks, Yosemite	30.00	20.00
☐770a	3¢ Parks, Mount Rainier	30.00	26.00
☐771	16¢ Airmail, special delivery	30.00	60.00

Scott No.		Single	Block	Plate Block
☐772	3¢ Connecticut Tercentenary	6.25	8.00	14.00
☐773	3¢ California Exposition	6.25	8.00	14.00
☐774	3¢ Boulder Dam	7.00	10.00	14.00
☐775	3¢ Michigan Centenary	6.00	8.00	14.00
☐776	3¢ Texas Centennial	6.00	8.00	14.00
☐777	3¢ Rhode Island Tercentenary	6.00	8.00	14.00
☐778	3¢ TIPEX	14.00	8.00	—
☐782	3¢ Arkansas Centennial	6.00	8.00	14.00
☐783	3¢ Oregon Territory	6.00	8.00	14.00
☐784	3¢ Susan B. Anthony	6.00	9.00	14.00
☐785	1¢ Army	4.00	6.00	10.00
☐786	2¢ Army	4.00	6.00	10.00
☐787	3¢ Army	4.00	6.00	10.00
☐788	5¢ Army	4.00	6.00	10.00
☐790	1¢ Navy	4.00	6.00	10.00
☐791	2¢ Navy	4.00	6.00	10.00
☐792	3¢ Navy	4.00	6.00	10.00
☐793	4¢ Navy	4.00	6.00	10.00
☐794	5¢ Navy	4.00	6.00	10.00
☐795	3¢ Ordinance of 1787	4.00	6.00	12.00
☐796	5¢ Virginia Dare	4.00	6.00	13.00
☐797	10¢ Souvenir Sheet	4.00	—	—

Scott No.			Single	Block	Plate Block
☐ 798	3¢	Constitution	5.75	8.00	14.00
☐ 799	3¢	Hawaii	5.75	8.00	14.00
☐ 800	3¢	Alaska	5.75	8.00	14.00
☐ 801	3¢	Puerto Rico	5.75	8.00	14.00
☐ 802	3¢	Virgin Islands	5.75	8.00	14.00
☐ 803	½¢	Franklin	2.10	3.00	4.75
☐ 804	1¢	Washington	2.10	3.00	4.75
☐ 805	1½¢	Martha Washington	2.10	3.00	4.75
☐ 806	2¢	Adams	2.10	3.00	4.75
☐ 807	3¢	Jefferson	2.10	3.00	4.75
☐ 808	4¢	Madison	2.10	3.00	4.75
☐ 809	4½¢	White House	2.10	3.50	5.00
☐ 810	5¢	Monroe	2.10	3.50	5.00
☐ 811	6¢	Adams	2.10	3.50	5.00
☐ 812	7¢	Jackson	2.10	3.50	5.00
☐ 813	8¢	VanBuren	2.10	3.50	5.00
☐ 814	9¢	Harrison	2.10	3.50	5.00
☐ 815	10¢	Tyler	2.10	4.00	6.00
☐ 816	11¢	Polk	2.40	4.00	6.00
☐ 817	12¢	Taylor	2.40	4.00	6.00
☐ 818	13¢	Fillmore	2.40	4.00	6.00
☐ 819	14¢	Pierce	2.40	4.00	6.00
☐ 820	15¢	Buchanan	2.40	4.00	6.00
☐ 821	16¢	Lincoln	3.00	4.00	7.00
☐ 822	17¢	Johnson	3.00	4.00	7.00
☐ 823	18¢	Grant	3.00	4.00	7.00
☐ 824	19¢	Hayes	3.00	4.00	7.00
☐ 825	20¢	Garfield	3.00	4.00	7.00
☐ 826	21¢	Arthur	3.50	5.00	10.00
☐ 827	22¢	Cleveland	3.50	5.00	10.00
☐ 828	24¢	Harrison	4.00	5.00	10.00
☐ 829	25¢	McKinley	4.00	6.00	11.00
☐ 830	30¢	Roosevelt	5.00	7.00	11.00
☐ 831	50¢	Taft	13.00	16.00	24.00
☐ 832	$1	Wilson	60.00	60.00	84.00
☐ 832c	$1	Wilson	28.00	40.00	60.00
☐ 833	$2	Harding	100.00	180.00	240.00
☐ 834	$5	Coolidge	125.00	210.00	350.00
☐ 835	3¢	Constitution	5.00	8.00	11.00
☐ 836	3¢	Swedes and Finns	5.00	8.00	11.00
☐ 837	3¢	Northwest Sesquicentennial	5.00	8.00	11.00
☐ 838	3¢	Iowa	5.00	8.00	11.00
☐ 852	3¢	Golden Gate Expo	5.00	8.00	11.00
☐ 853	3¢	N.Y. World's Fair	5.00	8.00	11.00
☐ 854	3¢	Washington Inauguration	5.00	8.00	11.00
☐ 855	3¢	Baseball Centennial	20.00	20.00	40.00
☐ 856	3¢	Panama Canal	5.00	8.00	11.00
☐ 857	3¢	Printing Tercentenary	5.00	8.00	11.00

Scott No.		Single	Block	Plate Block
☐ 858	3¢ 50th Statehood Anniversary	5.00	7.00	10.00
☐ 859	1¢ Washington Irving	2.00	3.00	3.50
☐ 860	2¢ James Fenimore Cooper	2.00	3.00	3.50
☐ 861	3¢ Ralph Waldo Emerson	2.00	3.00	3.50
☐ 862	5¢ Louisa May Alcott	2.10	4.50	6.00
☐ 863	10¢ Samuel L. Clemens	5.00	8.00	13.00
☐ 864	1¢ Henry W. Longfellow	2.00	3.00	3.50
☐ 865	2¢ John Greenleaf Whittier	2.00	3.00	3.50
☐ 866	3¢ James Russell Lowell	2.00	3.00	3.50
☐ 867	5¢ Walt Whitman	2.10	4.00	6.00
☐ 868	10¢ James Whitcomb Riley	4.00	8.00	10.00
☐ 869	1¢ Horace Mann	2.00	3.00	3.50
☐ 870	2¢ Mark Hopkins	2.00	3.00	3.50
☐ 871	3¢ Charles W. Eliot	2.00	3.00	3.50
☐ 872	5¢ Frances E. Willard	2.50	4.00	5.50
☐ 873	10¢ Booker T. Washington	5.00	8.00	13.00
☐ 874	1¢ John James Audubon	2.00	3.00	3.50
☐ 875	2¢ Dr. Crawford W. Long	2.00	3.00	3.50
☐ 876	3¢ Luther Burbank	2.00	3.00	3.50
☐ 877	5¢ Dr. Walter Reed	2.90	4.00	6.00
☐ 878	10¢ Jane Addams	4.50	8.00	10.00
☐ 879	1¢ Stephen Collins Foster	2.00	3.00	3.50
☐ 880	2¢ John Philip Sousa	2.00	3.00	3.50
☐ 881	3¢ Victor Herbert	2.00	3.00	3.50
☐ 882	5¢ Edward A MacDowell	2.50	4.00	6.00
☐ 883	10¢ Ethelbert Nevin	4.50	8.00	10.00
☐ 884	1¢ Gilbert Charles Stuart	2.10	3.00	3.50
☐ 885	2¢ James A. McNeill Whistler	2.10	4.00	3.50
☐ 886	3¢ Augustus Saint-Gaudens	2.10	4.00	3.50
☐ 887	5¢ Daniel Chester French	2.90	4.00	5.50
☐ 888	10¢ Frederic Remington	4.50	8.00	10.00
☐ 889	1¢ Eli Whitney	2.10	2.50	3.00
☐ 890	2¢ Samuel F.B. Morse	2.10	2.50	3.00
☐ 891	3¢ Cyrus Hall McCormick	2.10	2.50	3.00
☐ 892	5¢ Elias Howe	2.50	4.00	5.00
☐ 893	10¢ Alexander Graham Bell	7.00	15.00	18.00
☐ 894	3¢ Pony Express	3.50	5.00	10.00
☐ 895	3¢ Pan American Union	3.50	5.00	10.00
☐ 896	3¢ Idaho Statehood	3.50	5.00	10.00
☐ 897	3¢ Wyoming Statehood	3.50	5.00	10.00
☐ 898	3¢ Coronado Expedition	3.50	5.00	10.00
☐ 899	1¢ Defense	2.50	4.50	6.00
☐ 900	2¢ Defense	2.50	4.50	6.00
☐ 901	3¢ Defense	2.50	4.50	6.00
☐ 902	3¢ Thirteenth Amendment	4.00	5.00	9.00
☐ 903	3¢ Vermont Statehood	4.00	5.00	9.00
☐ 904	3¢ Kentucky Statehood	4.00	5.00	9.00
☐ 905	3¢ "Win the War"	3.50	4.50	7.00

Scott No.			Single	Block	Plate Block
☐ 906	5¢	Chinese Commemorative	5.00	7.00	11.00
☐ 907	2¢	United Nations	3.00	5.00	7.00
☐ 908	1¢	Four Freedoms	4.00	4.75	9.00
☐ 909	5¢	Poland	4.00	5.25	10.00
☐ 910	5¢	Czechoslovakia	3.40	5.25	8.50
☐ 911	5¢	Norway	3.40	5.25	8.50
☐ 912	5¢	Luxembourg	3.40	5.25	8.50
☐ 913	5¢	Netherlands	3.40	5.25	8.50
☐ 914	5¢	Belgium	3.40	5.25	8.50
☐ 915	5¢	France	3.40	5.25	8.50
☐ 916	5¢	Greece	3.40	5.25	8.50
☐ 917	5¢	Yugoslavia	3.40	5.25	8.50
☐ 918	5¢	Albany	3.40	5.25	8.50
☐ 919	5¢	Austria	3.40	5.25	8.50
☐ 920	5¢	Denmark	3.40	5.25	8.50
☐ 921	5¢	Korea	3.40	5.25	8.50
☐ 922	3¢	Railroad	4.00	5.00	6.50
☐ 923	3¢	Steamship	2.90	5.00	8.00
☐ 924	3¢	Telegraph	2.90	5.00	8.00
☐ 925	3¢	Philippines	2.90	5.00	8.00
☐ 926	3¢	Motion Picture	2.90	5.00	8.00
☐ 927	3¢	Florida	2.90	5.00	8.00
☐ 928	5¢	United Nations Conference	2.90	5.00	8.00
☐ 929	3¢	Iwo Jima	3.50	5.00	7.00
☐ 930	1¢	Roosevelt	2.90	4.50	5.25
☐ 931	2¢	Roosevelt	2.90	4.50	5.25
☐ 932	3¢	Roosevelt	2.90	4.50	5.25
☐ 933	5¢	Roosevelt	2.90	4.50	5.25
☐ 934	3¢	Army	2.90	4.50	5.25
☐ 935	3¢	Navy	2.90	4.50	5.25
☐ 936	3¢	Coast Guard	2.90	4.50	5.25
☐ 937	3¢	Alfred E. Smith	2.90	4.50	5.25
☐ 938	3¢	Texas	2.90	4.50	5.25
☐ 939	3¢	Merchant Marine	2.25	3.50	4.00
☐ 940	3¢	Honorable Discharge	2.25	3.50	4.00
☐ 941	3¢	Tennessee	2.25	3.50	4.00
☐ 942	3¢	Iowa	2.25	3.50	4.00
☐ 943	3¢	Smithsonian	2.25	3.50	4.00
☐ 944	3¢	Santa Fe	2.25	3.50	4.00
☐ 945	3¢	Thomas A. Edison	2.25	3.50	4.00
☐ 946	3¢	Joseph Pulitzer	2.25	3.50	4.00
☐ 947	3¢	Stamp Centenary	2.25	3.50	4.00
☐ 948	5¢ and 10¢	Centenary Exhibition Sheet	3.50	—	—
☐ 949	3¢	Doctors	2.25	3.50	4.00
☐ 950	3¢	Utah	2.25	3.50	4.00
☐ 951	3¢	"Constitution"	2.25	3.50	4.00
☐ 952	3¢	Everglades Park	2.25	3.50	4.00
☐ 953	3¢	Carver	2.25	3.50	4.00

Scott No.		Single	Block	Plate Block
☐ 954	3¢ California Gold	2.25	3.75	4.50
☐ 955	3¢ Mississippi Territory	2.25	3.75	4.50
☐ 956	3¢ Four Chaplains	2.25	3.75	4.50
☐ 957	3¢ Wisconsin Centennial	2.25	3.75	4.50
☐ 958	5¢ Swedish Pioneers	2.25	3.75	4.50
☐ 959	3¢ Women's Progress	2.25	3.75	4.50
☐ 960	3¢ William Allen White	2.25	3.75	4.50
☐ 961	3¢ U.S.-Canada Friendship	2.25	3.75	4.50
☐ 962	3¢ Francis Scott Key	2.25	3.75	4.50
☐ 963	3¢ Salute to Youth	2.25	3.75	4.50
☐ 964	3¢ Oregon Territory	2.25	3.75	4.50
☐ 965	3¢ Harlan Fiske Stone	2.25	3.75	4.50
☐ 966	3¢ Palomar Observatory	2.50	3.75	4.50
☐ 967	3¢ Clara Barton	2.25	3.75	4.50
☐ 968	3¢ Poultry Industry	2.25	3.75	4.50
☐ 969	3¢ Gold Star Mothers	2.25	3.75	4.50
☐ 970	3¢ Volunteer Fireman	2.25	3.75	4.50
☐ 972	3¢ Indian Centennial	2.25	3.75	4.50
☐ 973	3¢ Rough Riders	2.25	3.50	4.00
☐ 974	3¢ Juliette Low	2.25	3.50	4.00
☐ 975	3¢ Will Rogers	2.25	3.50	4.00
☐ 976	3¢ Fort Bliss	2.25	3.50	4.00
☐ 977	3¢ Moina Michael	2.25	3.50	4.00
☐ 978	3¢ Gettysburg Address	2.25	3.50	4.00
☐ 979	3¢ American Turners Society	2.25	3.50	4.00
☐ 980	3¢ Joel Chandler Harris	2.25	3.50	4.00
☐ 981	3¢ Minnesota Territory	1.90	3.50	4.00
☐ 982	3¢ Washington and Lee University	1.90	3.50	4.00
☐ 983	3¢ Puerto Rico Election	1.90	3.50	4.00
☐ 984	3¢ Annapolis, Md.	1.90	3.50	4.00
☐ 985	3¢ G.A.R.	1.90	3.50	4.00
☐ 986	3¢ Edgar Allan Poe	1.90	3.50	4.00
☐ 987	3¢ American Bankers Association	1.90	3.50	4.00
☐ 988	3¢ Samuel Gompers	1.90	3.50	4.00
☐ 990	3¢ Nat. Capital Sesqui. (Executive)	1.90	3.50	4.00
☐ 991	3¢ Nat. Capital Sesqui. (Judicial)	1.90	3.50	4.00
☐ 992	3¢ Nat. Capital Sesqui. (Legislative)	1.90	3.50	4.00
☐ 993	3¢ Railroad Engineers	1.90	3.50	4.00
☐ 994	3¢ Kansas City Centenary	1.90	3.00	4.00
☐ 995	3¢ Boy Scout	2.40	3.50	5.00
☐ 996	3¢ Indiana Ter. Sesquicentennial	1.90	3.00	4.00
☐ 997	3¢ California Statehood	1.90	3.00	4.00
☐ 998	3¢ United Confederate Veterans	1.90	3.00	4.00
☐ 999	3¢ Nevada Centennial	1.90	3.00	4.00
☐ 1000	3¢ Landing of Cadillac	1.90	3.00	4.00
☐ 1001	3¢ Colorado Statehood	1.90	3.00	4.00
☐ 1002	3¢ American Chemical Society	1.90	3.00	4.00
☐ 1003	3¢ Battle of Brooklyn	1.90	3.00	4.00

Scott No.		Single	Block	Plate Block
☐ 1004	3¢ Betsy Ross	2.40	3.35	4.50
☐ 1005	3¢ 4-H Clubs	1.90	3.50	4.00
☐ 1006	3¢ B & O Railroad	1.90	3.50	4.00
☐ 1007	3¢ American Automobile Assoc.	1.90	3.50	4.00
☐ 1008	3¢ NATO	1.90	3.50	4.00
☐ 1009	3¢ Grand Coulee Dam	1.90	3.50	4.00
☐ 1010	3¢ Lafayette	1.90	3.50	4.00
☐ 1011	3¢ Mt. Rushmore Memorial	1.90	3.50	4.00
☐ 1012	3¢ Civil Engineers	1.90	3.50	4.00
☐ 1013	3¢ Service Women	1.90	3.50	4.00
☐ 1014	3¢ Gutenberg Bible	1.90	3.50	4.00
☐ 1015	3¢ Newspaper boys	1.90	3.50	4.00
☐ 1016	3¢ Red Cross	1.90	3.50	4.00
☐ 1017	3¢ National Guard	1.90	3.50	4.00
☐ 1018	3¢ Ohio Sesquicentennial	1.90	3.50	4.00
☐ 1019	3¢ Washington Territory	1.90	3.50	4.00
☐ 1020	3¢ Louisiana Purchase	1.90	3.50	4.00
☐ 1021	5¢ Opening of Japan	1.90	3.50	4.00
☐ 1022	3¢ American Bar Association	1.90	3.50	4.00
☐ 1023	3¢ Sagamore Hill	1.90	3.50	4.00
☐ 1024	3¢ Future Farmers	1.90	3.50	4.00
☐ 1025	3¢ Trucking Industry	1.90	3.50	4.00
☐ 1026	3¢ Gen. G.S. Patton, Jr.	1.90	3.50	4.00
☐ 1027	3¢ New York City	1.90	3.50	4.00
☐ 1028	3¢ Gadsden Purchase	1.90	3.50	4.00
☐ 1029	3¢ Columbia University	1.90	3.50	4.00
☐ 1030	½¢ Franklin	1.90	3.50	4.00
☐ 1031	1¢ Washington	1.90	3.50	4.00
☐ 1031a	1¼¢ Palace	1.90	3.50	4.00
☐ 1032	1½¢ Mount Vernon	1.90	3.50	4.00
☐ 1033	2¢ Jefferson	1.90	3.50	4.00
☐ 1034	2½¢ Bunker Hill	1.90	3.50	4.00
☐ 1035	3¢ Statue of Liberty	1.90	3.50	4.00
☐ 1036	4¢ Lincoln	1.90	3.50	4.00
☐ 1037	4½¢ Hermitage	1.90	3.50	4.00
☐ 1038	5¢ Monroe	1.90	3.50	4.00
☐ 1039	6¢ Roosevelt	1.90	3.50	4.00
☐ 1040	7¢ Wilson	1.90	3.50	4.00
☐ 1041	8¢ Statue of Liberty	1.90	3.50	4.00
☐ 1042	8¢ Statue of Liberty	1.90	3.50	4.00
☐ 1042a	8¢ Pershing	2.25	3.50	4.00
☐ 1043	9¢ The Alamo	2.25	3.50	4.50
☐ 1044	10¢ Independence Hall	2.25	3.50	4.50
☐ 1045	12¢ Harrison	2.25	3.50	4.50
☐ 1046	15¢ John Jay	2.30	3.60	4.75
☐ 1046a	15¢ John Jay	2.30	3.60	4.75
☐ 1047	20¢ Monticello	2.30	3.60	4.75
☐ 1048	25¢ Paul Revere	2.30	3.60	4.75

Scott No.			Single	Block	Plate Block
☐ 1049	30¢	Robert Lee	2.50	3.50	5.00
☐ 1050	40¢	John Marshall	2.75	4.00	6.50
☐ 1051	50¢	Susan Anthony	3.50	6.00	8.00
☐ 1052	$1	Patrick Henry	7.00	10.00	15.00
☐ 1053	$5	Alexander Hamilton	46.00	75.00	100.00
☐ 1054	1¢	Washington	1.90	—	—
☐ 1055	2¢	Jefferson	1.90	—	—
☐ 1056	2½¢	Bunker Hill	1.90	—	—
☐ 1057	3¢	Statue of Liberty	1.90	—	—
☐ 1058	4¢	Lincoln	1.90	—	—
☐ 1059	4½¢	The Hermitage	1.90	—	—
☐ 1059A	25¢	Paul Revere	2.00	—	—
☐ 1059Ab	25¢	Tagged	16.00	—	—
☐ 1060	3¢	Nebraska Territory	1.90	3.00	4.00
☐ 1061	3¢	Kansas Territory	1.90	3.00	4.00
☐ 1062	3¢	George Eastman	1.90	3.00	4.00
☐ 1063	3¢	Lewis & Clark	1.90	3.00	4.00
☐ 1064	3¢	Pennsylvania Academy of the Fine Arts	1.90	3.00	4.00
☐ 1065	3¢	Land Grant Colleges	1.90	3.00	4.00
☐ 1066	8¢	Rotary International	1.90	3.00	4.00
☐ 1067	3¢	Armed Forces Reserve	1.90	3.00	4.00
☐ 1068	3¢	New Hampshire	1.90	3.00	4.00
☐ 1069	3¢	Soo Locks	1.90	3.00	4.00
☐ 1070	3¢	Atoms for Peace	1.90	3.00	4.00
☐ 1071	3¢	Fort Ticonderoga	1.90	3.00	4.00
☐ 1072	3¢	Andrew W. Mellon	1.90	3.00	4.00
☐ 1073	3¢	Benjamin Franklin	1.90	3.00	4.00
☐ 1074	3¢	Booker T. Washington	1.90	3.00	4.00
☐ 1075	3¢, 8¢	FIPEX Souvenir Sheet	1.90	3.00	4.00
☐ 1076	3¢	FIPEX	1.80	3.00	4.00
☐ 1077	3¢	Wildlife (Turkey)	1.80	3.00	4.00
☐ 1078	3¢	Wildlife (Antelope)	1.80	3.00	4.00
☐ 1079	3¢	Wildlife (Salmon)	1.80	3.00	4.00
☐ 1080	3¢	Pure Food and Drug Laws	1.80	3.00	4.00
☐ 1081	3¢	Wheatland	1.80	3.00	4.00
☐ 1082	3¢	Labor Day	1.80	3.00	4.00
☐ 1083	3¢	Nassau Hall	1.80	3.00	4.00
☐ 1084	3¢	Devils Tower	1.80	3.00	4.00
☐ 1085	3¢	Children	1.80	3.00	4.00
☐ 1086	3¢	Alexander Hamilton	1.80	3.00	4.00
☐ 1087	3¢	Polio	1.80	3.00	4.00
☐ 1088	3¢	Coast & Geodetic Survey	1.80	3.00	4.00
☐ 1089	3¢	Architects	1.80	3.00	4.00
☐ 1090	3¢	Steel Industry	1.80	3.00	4.00
☐ 1091	3¢	Naval Review	1.80	3.00	4.00
☐ 1092	3¢	Oklahoma Statehood	1.80	3.00	4.00
☐ 1093	3¢	School Teachers	1.80	3.00	4.00
☐ 1094	4¢	Flag	1.80	3.00	4.00

Scott No.		Single	Block	Plate Block
☐ 1095	3¢ Shipbuilding	1.80	2.90	4.00
☐ 1096	8¢ Ramon Magsaysay	1.80	2.90	4.00
☐ 1097	3¢ Lafayette Bicentenary	1.80	2.90	4.00
☐ 1098	3¢ Wildlife (Whooping Crane)	1.80	2.90	4.00
☐ 1099	3¢ Religious Freedom	1.80	2.90	4.00
☐ 1100	3¢ Gardening Horticulture	1.80	2.90	4.00
☐ 1104	3¢ Brussels Exhibition	1.80	2.90	4.00
☐ 1105	3¢ James Monroe	1.80	2.90	4.00
☐ 1106	3¢ Minnesota Statehood	1.80	2.90	4.00
☐ 1107	3¢ International Geophysical Year	1.80	2.90	4.00
☐ 1108	3¢ Gunston Hall	1.80	2.90	4.00
☐ 1109	3¢ Mackinac Bridge	1.80	2.90	4.00
☐ 1110	4¢ Simon Bolivar	1.80	2.90	4.00
☐ 1111	8¢ Simon Bolivar	1.80	2.90	4.00
☐ 1112	4¢ Atlantic Cable	1.80	2.90	4.00
☐ 1113	1¢ Lincoln Sesquicentennial	1.80	2.90	4.00
☐ 1114	3¢ Lincoln Sesquicentennial	1.80	2.90	4.00
☐ 1115	4¢ Lincoln-Douglas Debates	1.80	2.90	4.00
☐ 1116	4¢ Lincoln Sesquicentennial	1.80	2.90	4.00
☐ 1117	4¢ Lajos Kossuth	1.80	2.90	4.00
☐ 1118	8¢ Lajos Kossuth	1.80	2.90	4.00
☐ 1119	4¢ Freedom of Press	1.80	2.90	4.00
☐ 1120	4¢ Overland Mail	1.80	2.90	4.00
☐ 1121	4¢ Noah Webster	1.80	2.90	4.00
☐ 1122	4¢ Forest Conservation	1.80	2.90	4.00
☐ 1123	4¢ Fort Duquesne	1.80	2.90	4.00
☐ 1124	4¢ Oregon Statehood	1.80	2.90	4.00
☐ 1125	4¢ San Martin	1.80	2.90	4.00
☐ 1126	8¢ San Martin	1.80	2.90	4.00
☐ 1127	4¢ NATO	1.80	2.90	4.00
☐ 1128	4¢ Arctic Explorations	1.80	2.90	4.00
☐ 1129	8¢ World Trade	1.80	2.90	4.00
☐ 1130	4¢ Silver Centennial	1.80	2.90	4.00
☐ 1131	4¢ St. Lawrence Seaway	1.80	2.90	4.00
☐ 1132	4¢ Flag	1.80	2.75	4.00
☐ 1133	4¢ Soil Conservation	1.80	2.75	4.00
☐ 1134	4¢ Petroleum Industry	1.80	2.75	4.00
☐ 1135	4¢ Dental Health	1.80	2.75	4.00
☐ 1136	4¢ Reuter	1.80	2.75	4.00
☐ 1137	8¢ Reuter	1.80	2.75	4.00
☐ 1138	4¢ Dr. Ephraim McDowell	1.80	2.75	4.00
☐ 1139	4¢ Washington "Credo"	1.80	2.75	4.00
☐ 1140	4¢ Franklin "Credo"	1.80	2.75	4.00
☐ 1141	4¢ Jefferson "Credo"	1.80	2.75	4.00
☐ 1142	4¢ Frances Scott Key "Credo"	1.80	2.75	4.00
☐ 1143	4¢ Lincoln "Credo"	1.80	2.75	4.00
☐ 1144	4¢ Patrick Henry "Credo"	1.80	2.75	4.00
☐ 1145	4¢ Boy Scouts	1.80	2.75	4.00

Scott No.			Single	Block	Plate Block
☐ 1146	4¢	Olympic Winter Games	1.65	2.90	3.90
☐ 1147	4¢	Masaryk	1.65	2.90	3.90
☐ 1148	8¢	Masaryk	1.65	2.90	3.90
☐ 1149	4¢	World Refugee Year	1.65	2.90	3.90
☐ 1150	4¢	Water Conservation	1.65	2.90	3.90
☐ 1151	4¢	SEATO	1.65	2.90	3.90
☐ 1152	4¢	American Woman	1.65	2.90	3.90
☐ 1153	4¢	50-Star Flag	1.65	2.90	3.90
☐ 1154	4¢	Pony Express Centennial	1.65	2.90	3.90
☐ 1155	4¢	Employ the Handicapped	1.65	2.90	3.90
☐ 1156	4¢	World Forestry Congress	1.65	2.90	3.90
☐ 1157	4¢	Mexican Independence	1.65	2.90	3.90
☐ 1158	4¢	U.S. Japan Treaty	1.65	2.90	3.90
☐ 1159	4¢	Paderewski	1.65	2.90	3.90
☐ 1160	8¢	Paderewski	1.65	2.90	3.90
☐ 1161	4¢	Robert A. Taft	1.65	2.90	3.90
☐ 1162	4¢	Wheels of Freedom	1.65	2.90	3.90
☐ 1163	4¢	Boys' Clubs	1.65	2.90	3.90
☐ 1164	4¢	Automated P.O.	1.65	2.90	3.90
☐ 1165	4¢	Mannerheim	1.65	2.90	3.90
☐ 1166	8¢	Mannerheim	1.65	2.90	3.90
☐ 1167	4¢	Camp Fire Girls	1.65	2.90	3.90
☐ 1168	4¢	Garibaldi	1.65	2.90	3.90
☐ 1169	8¢	Garibaldi	1.65	2.90	3.90
☐ 1170	4¢	Senator George	1.65	2.90	3.90
☐ 1171	4¢	Andrew Carnegie	1.65	2.90	3.90
☐ 1172	4¢	John Foster Dulles	1.65	2.90	3.90
☐ 1173	4¢	Echo I	1.65	2.90	3.90
☐ 1174	4¢	Gandhi	1.65	2.90	3.90
☐ 1175	8¢	Gandhi	1.65	2.90	3.90
☐ 1176	4¢	Range Conservation	1.65	2.90	3.90
☐ 1177	4¢	Horace Greeley	1.65	2.90	3.90
☐ 1178	4¢	Fort Sumter	1.90	3.00	4.00
☐ 1179	4¢	Battle of Shiloh	1.90	3.00	4.00
☐ 1180	5¢	Battle of Gettysburg	1.90	3.00	4.00
☐ 1181	5¢	Battle of Wilderness	1.90	3.00	4.00
☐ 1182	5¢	Appomattox	1.90	3.00	4.00
☐ 1183	4¢	Kansas Statehood	1.90	3.00	4.00
☐ 1184	4¢	Senator Norris	1.65	3.00	4.00
☐ 1185	4¢	Naval Aviation	1.65	2.90	4.00
☐ 1186	4¢	Workmen's Compensation	1.65	2.90	4.00
☐ 1187	4¢	Frederic Remington	1.65	2.90	4.00
☐ 1188	4¢	China Republic	1.65	2.90	4.00
☐ 1189	4¢	Naismith	1.65	2.90	4.00
☐ 1190	4¢	Nursing	1.65	2.90	4.00
☐ 1191	4¢	New Mexico Statehood	1.65	2.90	4.00
☐ 1192	4¢	Arizona Statehood	1.65	2.90	4.00
☐ 1193	4¢	Project Mercury	2.10	3.00	4.00

Scott No.		Single	Block	Plate Block
☐ 1194	4¢ Malaria Eradication	1.65	2.90	3.90
☐ 1195	4¢ Charles Evans Hughes	1.65	2.90	3.90
☐ 1196	4¢ Seattle World's Fair	1.65	2.90	3.90
☐ 1197	4¢ Louisiana Statehood	1.65	2.90	3.90
☐ 1198	4¢ Homestead Act	1.65	2.90	3.90
☐ 1199	4¢ Girl Scouts	1.65	2.90	3.90
☐ 1200	4¢ Brien McMahon	1.65	2.90	3.90
☐ 1201	4¢ Apprenticeship	1.65	2.90	3.90
☐ 1202	4¢ Sam Rayburn	1.65	2.90	3.90
☐ 1203	4¢ Dag Hammarskjold	1.65	2.90	3.90
☐ 1204	4¢ Hammarskjold "Error"	4.50	8.50	12.00
☐ 1205	4¢ Christmas	1.65	3.25	3.90
☐ 1206	4¢ Higher Education	1.65	2.90	3.90
☐ 1207	4¢ Winslow Homer	1.65	2.90	3.90
☐ 1208	4¢ Flag	1.90	2.90	4.00
☐ 1209	4¢ Jackson	1.65	2.80	3.90
☐ 1213	5¢ Washington	1.65	2.80	3.90
☐ 1225	1¢ Jackson (coil)	1.65	2.50	2.90
☐ 1229	5¢ Washington (coil)	1.65	2.50	2.90
☐ 1230	5¢ Carolina Charter	1.65	2.75	3.90
☐ 1231	5¢ Food for Peace	1.65	2.75	3.90
☐ 1232	5¢ West Virginia Statehood	1.65	2.75	3.90
☐ 1233	5¢ Emancipation Proclamation	1.65	2.75	3.90
☐ 1234	5¢ Alliance for Progress	1.65	2.75	3.90
☐ 1235	5¢ Cordell Hull	1.65	2.75	3.90
☐ 1236	5¢ Eleanor Roosevelt	1.65	2.75	3.90
☐ 1237	5¢ Science	1.65	2.75	3.90
☐ 1238	5¢ City Mail Delivery	1.65	2.75	3.90
☐ 1239	5¢ Red Cross	1.65	2.75	3.90
☐ 1240	5¢ Christmas	1.65	2.75	3.90
☐ 1241	5¢ Audubon	1.65	2.75	3.90
☐ 1242	5¢ Sam Houston	1.65	2.75	3.90
☐ 1243	5¢ Charles Russell	1.65	2.75	3.90
☐ 1244	5¢ N.Y. World's Fair	1.65	2.75	3.90
☐ 1245	5¢ John Muir	1.65	2.75	3.90
☐ 1246	5¢ John F. Kennedy	1.65	2.75	3.90
☐ 1247	5¢ New Jersey Tercentenary	1.65	2.75	3.90
☐ 1248	5¢ Nevada Statehood	1.65	2.75	3.90
☐ 1249	5¢ Register & Vote	1.65	2.75	3.90
☐ 1250	5¢ Shakespeare	1.65	2.75	3.90
☐ 1251	5¢ Drs. Mayo	1.65	2.75	3.90
☐ 1252	5¢ American Music	1.65	2.75	3.90
☐ 1253	5¢ Homemakers	1.65	2.75	3.90
☐ 1254–57	5¢ Christmas	1.65	5.00	7.00
☐ 1258	5¢ Verrazano-Narrows Bridge	1.65	2.70	3.75
☐ 1259	5¢ Fine Arts	1.65	2.70	3.75
☐ 1260	5¢ Amateur Radio	1.65	2.70	3.75
☐ 1261	5¢ Battle of New Orleans	1.65	2.70	3.75

Scott No.			Single	Block	Plate Block
☐ 1262	5¢	Physical Fitness	1.60	2.60	3.60
☐ 1263	5¢	Cancer Crusade	1.60	2.60	3.60
☐ 1264	5¢	Churchill	1.60	2.60	3.60
☐ 1265	5¢	Magna Carta	1.60	2.60	3.60
☐ 1266	5¢	Intl. Cooperation Year	1.60	2.60	3.60
☐ 1267	5¢	Salvation Army	1.60	2.60	3.60
☐ 1268	5¢	Dante	1.60	2.60	3.60
☐ 1269	5¢	Herbert Hoover	1.60	2.60	3.60
☐ 1270	5¢	Robert Fulton	1.60	2.60	3.60
☐ 1271	5¢	Florida Settlement	1.60	2.60	3.60
☐ 1272	5¢	Traffic Safety	1.60	2.60	3.60
☐ 1273	5¢	Copley	1.60	2.60	3.60
☐ 1274	11¢	Intl. Telecommunication Union	1.60	2.60	3.60
☐ 1275	5¢	Adlai Stevenson	1.60	2.60	3.60
☐ 1276	5¢	Christmas	1.60	2.60	3.60
☐ 1278	1¢	Jefferson	1.60	2.60	3.60
☐ 1279	1¼¢	Gallatin	1.60	2.60	3.60
☐ 1280	2¢	Wright	1.60	2.60	3.60
☐ 1281	3¢	Parkman	1.60	2.60	3.60
☐ 1282	4¢	Lincoln	1.60	2.60	3.60
☐ 1283	5¢	Washington	1.60	2.60	3.60
☐ 1283B	5¢	Washington	1.60	2.60	3.60
☐ 1284	6¢	Roosevelt	1.60	2.60	3.60
☐ 1285	8¢	Einstein	1.90	2.65	3.75
☐ 1286	10¢	Jackson	1.90	2.65	3.75
☐ 1286a	12¢	Ford	1.90	2.65	3.75
☐ 1287	13¢	Kennedy	2.00	2.75	4.00
☐ 1288	15¢	Holmes	1.60	2.60	3.60
☐ 1289	20¢	Marshall	1.90	2.75	4.00
☐ 1290	25¢	Douglas	1.60	2.60	3.60
☐ 1291	30¢	Dewey	2.00	3.25	4.50
☐ 1292	40¢	Paine	2.00	3.00	4.50
☐ 1293	50¢	Stone	3.50	5.00	7.00
☐ 1294	$1	O'Neill	5.00	7.00	11.00
☐ 1295	$5	Moore	45.00	85.00	100.00
☐ 1304	5¢	Washington (coil)	—	pr. 1.50	lp. 3.00
☐ 1305	6¢	Roosevelt (coil)	—	pr. 1.50	lp. 3.00
☐ 1305C	$1	O'Neill (coil)	—	pr. 1.50	lp. 3.00
☐ 1306	5¢	Migratory Bird Treaty	1.60	2.50	3.60
☐ 1307	5¢	Humane Treatment of Animals	1.60	2.50	3.60
☐ 1308	5¢	Indiana Statehood	1.60	2.50	3.60
☐ 1309	5¢	Circus	1.60	2.50	3.60
☐ 1310	5¢	SIPEX	1.60	2.50	3.60
☐ 1311	5¢	SIPEX	1.60	2.50	3.60
☐ 1312	5¢	Bill of Rights	1.60	2.50	3.60
☐ 1313	5¢	Polish Millennium	1.60	2.50	3.60
☐ 1314	5¢	National Park Service	1.60	2.50	3.60
☐ 1315	5¢	Marine Corps Reserve	1.60	2.50	3.60

Scott No.		Single	Block	Plate Block
☐ 1316	5¢ Genl. Fed. of Women's Clubs	1.60	2.70	3.60
☐ 1317	5¢ Johnny Appleseed	1.60	2.70	3.60
☐ 1318	5¢ Beautification of America	1.60	2.70	3.60
☐ 1319	5¢ Great River Road	1.60	2.70	3.60
☐ 1320	5¢ Savings Bonds	1.60	2.70	3.60
☐ 1321	5¢ Christmas	1.60	2.70	3.60
☐ 1322	5¢ Mary Cassatt	1.60	2.70	3.60
☐ 1323	5¢ National Grange	1.60	2.70	3.60
☐ 1324	5¢ Canada Centenary	1.60	2.70	3.60
☐ 1325	5¢ Erie Canal	1.60	2.70	3.60
☐ 1326	5¢ Search for Peace	1.60	2.70	3.60
☐ 1327	5¢ Thoreau	1.60	2.70	3.60
☐ 1328	5¢ Nebraska Statehood	1.60	2.70	3.60
☐ 1329	5¢ Voice of America	1.60	2.70	3.60
☐ 1330	5¢ Davy Crockett	1.70	2.60	3.90
☐ 1331– 1332	5¢ Space Accomplishments	12.00 pr.	20.00	24.00
☐ 1333	5¢ Urban Planning	1.60	2.60	3.60
☐ 1334	5¢ Finland Independence	1.60	2.60	3.60
☐ 1335	5¢ Thomas Eakins	1.60	2.60	3.60
☐ 1336	5¢ Christmas	1.60	2.60	3.60
☐ 1337	5¢ Mississippi Statehood	1.60	2.60	3.60
☐ 1338	6¢ Flag	1.60	2.60	3.60
☐ 1339	6¢ Illinois Statehood	1.60	2.60	3.60
☐ 1340	6¢ Hemis Fair '68	1.60	2.60	3.60
☐ 1341	$1 Airlift	7.50	12.00	18.00
☐ 1342	6¢ Youth-Elks	1.60	2.60	3.60
☐ 1343	6¢ Law and Order	1.60	2.60	3.60
☐ 1344	6¢ Register and Vote	1.60	2.60	3.60
☐ 1345– 1354	6¢ Historic Flag series of 10, all on one cover	11.00	—	—
☐ 1355	6¢ Disney	5.00	4.60	10.00
☐ 1356	6¢ Marquette	1.60	2.60	3.50
☐ 1357	6¢ Daniel Boone	1.60	2.60	3.50
☐ 1358	6¢ Arkansas River	1.60	2.60	3.50
☐ 1359	6¢ Leif Erikson	1.60	2.60	3.50
☐ 1360	6¢ Cherokee Strip	1.60	2.60	3.50
☐ 1361	6¢ John Trumbull	1.60	2.60	3.50
☐ 1362	6¢ Waterfowl Conservation	1.60	2.60	3.50
☐ 1363	6¢ Christmas	1.60	2.60	3.50
☐ 1364	6¢ American Indian	1.60	2.60	3.50
☐ 1365– 1368	6¢ Beautification of America	5.00	7.00	9.00
☐ 1369	6¢ American Legion	1.60	2.70	3.50
☐ 1370	6¢ Grandma Moses	1.60	2.70	3.50
☐ 1371	6¢ Apollo 8	1.90	4.60	4.00

NOTE: From number 1372 to date, most First Day Covers have a value of $1.25 for single stamps, $2.25 for blocks of four and $3 for plate blocks of four.

MEMBERSHIP IN THE ANA COULD BE YOUR BEST INVESTMENT THIS YEAR.

As a rare coin collector or hobbyist, you continually deal with a variety of questions. How can you know that the coin you're about to purchase is not counterfeit? How can you find the detailed, current information you need to build your collection? There is no authority to help you solve all these problems. Unless you belong to the American Numismatic Association.

Coin Certification and Grading. ANA experts examine rare coins for authenticity to help safeguard against counterfeiting and misrepresentation. ANA now offers the ANACS Grading Service—third party expert opinions as to the condition of U.S. coins submitted for examination, and will issue certificates of authenticity.

Library Service. The largest circulating numismatic library in the world is maintained by the ANA. Its sole purpose is to provide you with free access to invaluable information that can't be found anywhere else.

The Numismatist. The Association's fully-illustrated magazine, considered *the* outstanding publication devoted exclusively to all phases of numismatics, is mailed free to all members.

And there are more benefits available through the ANA. Like coin insurance, special seminars, free booklets and photographic services. You can't find benefits like these anywhere else. Don't you owe it to yourself to join today?

I want some recognition!
Make me an ANA Member.

Check One:

☐ Regular $26 plus $6 first-year processing fee
☐ Junior $11 (age 17 or younger)
☐ Senior $22 plus $6 first-year processing fee (age 65 or older)
☐ 5-Year $120
☐ Life $750
☐ Foreign $28 plus $6 first-year processing fee

☐ Mr.   ☐ Mrs.   ☐ Ms.

Name _____
        Please Print

Street _____

City _____

State _____ Zip _____

Birthdate _____ / _____ / _____

I agree to abide by the American Numismatic Association's bylaws and Code of Ethics which require the publication of each applicant's name and state.

_____
Signature of Applicant

_____
Signature of Parent or Guardian
(required for Junior applicant)

☐ Check here if you DO NOT want your name and address forwarded to an ANA Club Representative in your area.

☐ Check here if you want your name provided to numismatic-related companies.

☐ Check   ☐ Money Order
☐ MasterCard   ☐ VISA
☐ AmExpress

_____
Credit Card Account No.
Expiration Date _____

_____
Signature of Cardholder (required)
SPONSOR _____ ANA No. _____
(optional)

Foreign applications must be accompanied by U.S. Funds drawn on a U.S. bank.

OR JOIN BY PHONE:
Use your VISA, MasterCard or American Express Card.
        Call 719-632-2646

Return application with payment to:
American Numismatic Association
818 N. Cascade Ave.
Colorado Springs, CO 80903-3279